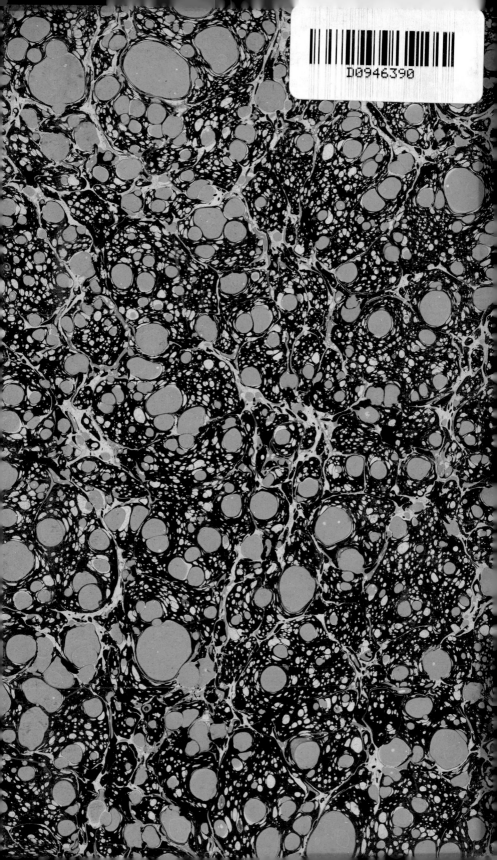

HISTORY

OF

THE REIGN OF

FERDINAND AND ISABELLA.

VOL. II

Ximeno & Camaron del.

G. F. Storm Sc.

Ferdinand the Catholic.

HISTORY

OF

THE REIGN OF

FERDINAND AND ISABELLA,

THE CATHOLIC.

By WILLIAM H. PRESCOTT.

Conjugio tali !

Quæ surgere regna

Virgil. Æneid. iv. 47.

Crevere vires, famaque et imperî
Porrecta majestas ab Euro
Solis ad Occiduum cubile.
Horat. Carm. iv. 15.

IN THREE VOLUMES.—VOL. II.

FIFTEENTH EDITION.

PHILADELPHIA:

J. B. LIPPINCOTT & CO.

1864.

CONTENTS

OF

VOLUME SECOND.

PART FIRST.

THE PERIOD, WHEN THE DIFFERENT KINGDOMS OF SPAIN
WERE FIRST UNITED UNDER ONE MONARCHY, AND A THOR
OUGH REFORM WAS INTRODUCED INTO THEIR INTERNAL
ADMINISTRATION; OR THE PERIOD EXHIBITING MOST FULLY
THE DOMESTIC POLICY OF FERDINAND AND ISABELLA.

(CONTINUED.)

CHAPTER XII.

CHAPTER XIII.

CHAPTER XIV.

WAR OF GRANADA. — CONQUEST OF BAZA. — SUBMISSION
OF EL ZAGAL 45

CHAPTER XV.

CHAPTER XVI.

CHAPTER XVII.

CHAPTER XVIII.

ATTEMPTED ASSASSINATION OF FERDINAND.—RETURN AND SECOND VOYAGE OF COLUMBUS

CHAPTER XIX.

CHAPTER XX.

PART SECOND

THE PERIOD WHEN, THE INTERIOR ORGANIZATION OF THE
MONARCHY HAVING BEEN COMPLETED, THE SPANISH NA-
TION ENTERED ON ITS SCHEMES OF DISCOVERY AND CON-
QUEST; OR THE PERIOD ILLUSTRATING MORE PARTICU-
LARLY THE FOREIGN POLICY OF FERDINAND AND ISABELLA.

CHAPTER I.

ITALIAN WARS. — GENERAL VIEW OF EUROPE. — INVASION
OF ITALY BY CHARLES VIII., OF FRANCE . . 253

CHAPTER II.

CHAPTER III.

ITALIAN WARS. — GONSALVO SUCCOURS THE POPE. — TREATY WITH FRANCE. — ORGANIZATION OF THE SPANISH MILITIA 330

CHAPTER IV.

CHAPTER V.

CHAPTER VI.

XIMENES IN GRANADA. — PERSECUTION, INSURRECTION, AND CONVERSION OF THE MOORS. 401

CONTENTS.

CHAPTER VII.

CHAPTER VIII.

CHAPTER IX.

VOL. II.

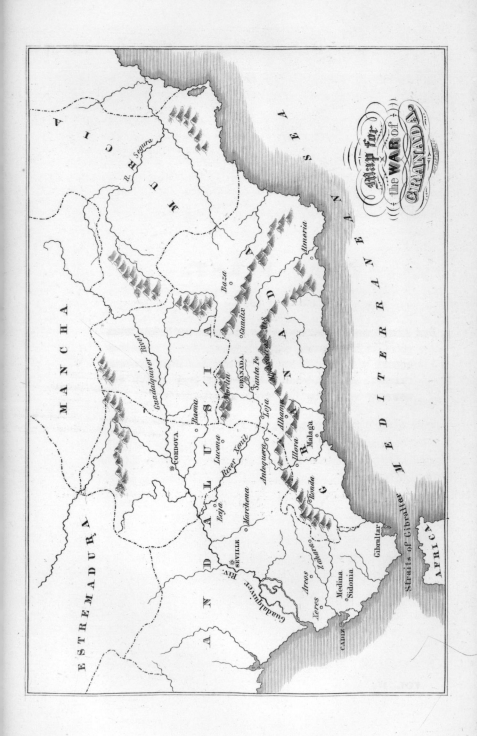

Map for the WAR of GRANADA

PART FIRST.

1406 — 1492.

The period, when the different kingdoms of Spain were first united under one monarchy, and a thorough reform was introduced into their internal administration; or the period exhibiting most fully the domestic policy of Ferdinand and Isabella.

(CONTINUED.)

PART FIRST.

CHAPTER XII

INTERNAL AFFAIRS OF THE KINGDOM. — INQUISITION IN
ARAGON.

1483 — 1487.

Isabella enforces the Laws. — Punishment of Ecclesiastics. — Inquisition in Aragon. — Remonstrances of the Cortes. — Conspiracy. — Assassination of the Inquisitor Arbues. — Cruel Persecutions. — Inquisition throughout Ferdinand's Dominions.

In such intervals of leisure as occurred amid their military operations, Ferdinand and Isabella were diligently occupied with the interior government of the kingdom, and especially with the rigid administration of justice, the most difficult of all duties in an imperfectly civilized state of society. The queen found especial demand for this in the northern provinces, whose rude inhabitants were little used to subordination. She compelled the great nobles to lay aside their arms, and refer their disputes to legal arbitration. She caused a number of the fortresses, which were still garrisoned by the baronial banditti, to be razed to the ground; and she enforced the utmost severity of the law against such inferior criminals as violated the public peace.[1]

[1] Lebrija, Rerum Gestarum Decades, iii. lib. 1, cap. 10. — Pulgar, Reyes Católicos, part. 3, cap. 27, 39, 67, et alibi. — L. Marineo, Cosas

Chastise-
ment of cer-
tain ecclesi-
astics.

Even ecclesiastical immunities, which proved so effectual a protection in most countries at tnis period, were not permitted to screen the offender. A remarkable instance of this occurred at the city of Truxillo, in 1486. An inhabitant of that place had been committed to prison for some offence by order of the civil magistrate. Certain priests, relations of the offender, alleged that his religious profession exempted him from all but ecclesiastical jurisdiction ; and, as the authorities refused to deliver him up, they inflamed the populace to such a degree, by their representations of the insult offered to the church, that they rose in a body, and, forcing the prison, set at liberty not only the malefactor in question, but all those confined there. The queen no sooner heard of this outrage on the royal authority, than she sent a detachment of her guard to Truxillo, which secured the persons of the principal rioters, some of whom were capitally punished, while the ecclesiastics, who had stirred up the sedition, were banished the realm. Isabella, while by her example, she inculcated the deepest reverence for the sacred profession, uniformly resisted every attempt from that quarter to encroach on the royal prerogative. The tendency of her administration was decidedly, as there will be occasion more particularly to notice, to abridge the authority, which that body had exercised in civil matters under preceding reigns. [2]

Memorables, fol. 175. — Zurita, Anales, tom. iv. fol. 348.

[2] Pulgar, Reyes Católicos, cap. 66. — A pertinent example of this occurred, December, 1485, at Alcalá de Henares, where the court

Nothing of interest occurred in the foreign relations of the kingdom, during the period embraced by the preceding chapter ; except perhaps the marriage of Catharine, the young queen of Navarre, with Jean d'Albret, a French nobleman, whose extensive hereditary domains, in the southwest corner of France, lay adjacent to her kingdom This connexion was extremely distasteful to the Spanish sovereigns, and indeed to many of the Navarrese, who were desirous of the alliance with Castile. This was ultimately defeated by the queen-mother, an artful woman, who, being of the blood royal of France, was naturally disposed to a union with that kingdom. Ferdinand did not neglect to maintain such an understanding with the malcontents of Navarre, as should enable him to counteract any undue advantage which the French monarch might derive from the possession of this key, as it were, to the Castilian territory.[3]

In Aragon, two circumstances took place in the period under review, deserving historical notice. The first relates to an order of the Catalan peasantry, denominated vassals *de remenza*. These per-

CHAPTER
XII

Marriage of
Catharine of
Navarre

1484.

Liberation
of Catalan
serfs.

---

was detained during the queen's illness, who there gave birth to her youngest child, Doña Catalina, afterwards so celebrated in English history as Catharine of Aragon. A collision took place in this city between the royal judges and those of the archbishop of Toledo, to whose diocese it belonged. The latter stoutly maintained the pretensions of the church. The queen with equal pertinacity asserted the supremacy of the royal jurisdiction over every other in the kingdom, secular or ecclesiastical. The affair was ultimately referred to the arbitration of certain learned men, named conjointly by the adverse parties. It was not then determined, however, and Pulgar has neglected to acquaint us with the award. Reyes Católicos, cap. 53. — Carbajal, Anales, MS., año 1485.

[3] Aleson, Annales de Navarra, tom. v. lib. 35, cap. 2.

PART
I.

1486.

Inqu'sition
in Aragon.

sons were subjected to a feudal bondage, which had its origin in very remote ages, but which had become in no degree mitigated, while the peasantry of every other part of Europe had been gradually rising to the rank of freemen. The grievous nature of the impositions had led to repeated rebellions in preceding reigns. At length, Ferdinand, after many fruitless attempts at a mediation between these unfortunate people and their arrogant masters, prevailed on the latter, rather by force of authority than argument, to relinquish the extraordinary seignorial rights, which they had hitherto enjoyed, in consideration of a stipulated annual payment from their vassals. [4]

The other circumstance worthy of record, but not in like manner creditable to the character of the sovereign, is the introduction of the modern Inquisition into Aragon. The ancient tribunal had existed there, as has been stated in a previous chapter, since the middle of the thirteenth century, but seems to have lost all its venom in the atmosphere of that free country; scarcely assuming a jurisdiction beyond that of an ordinary ecclesiastical court. No sooner, however, was the institution organized on its new basis in Castile, than Ferdinand resolved on its introduction, in a similar form, in his own dominions.

Measures were accordingly taken to that effect in a meeting of a privy council convened by the king at Taraçona, during the session of the cortes

[4] Zurita, Anales, tom. iv. cap. 52, 67. — Mariana, Hist. de España, lib. 25, cap. 8.

.n that place, in April, 1484; and a royal order was issued, requiring all the constituted authorities throughout the kingdom to support the new tribunal in the exercise of its functions. A Dominican monk, Fray Gaspard Juglar, and Pedro Arbues de Epila, a canon of the metropolitan church, were appointed by the general, Torquemada, inquisitors over the diocese of Saragossa; and, in the month of September following, the chief justiciary and the other great officers of the realm took the prescribed oaths. [5]

The new institution, opposed to the ideas of independence common to all the Aragonese, was particularly offensive to the higher orders, many of whose members, including persons filling the most considerable official stations, were of Jewish descent, and of course precisely the class exposed to the scrutiny of the Inquisition. Without difficulty, therefore, the cortes was persuaded in the following year to send a deputation to the court of Rome, and another to Ferdinand, representing the repugnance of the new tribunal to the liberties of the

Remonstrances of Cortes.

[5] Llorente, Hist. de l'Inquisition, tom. i. chap. 6, art. 2. — Zurita, Anales, lib. 20, cap. 65.

At this cortes, convened at Taraçona, Ferdinand and Isabella experienced an instance of the haughty spirit of their Catalan subjects, who refused to attend, alleging it to be a violation of their liberties to be summoned to a place without the limits of their principality. The Valencians also protested, that their attendance should not operate as a precedent to their prejudice. It was usual to convene a central or general cortes at Fraga, or Monzon, or some town, which the Catalans, who were peculiarly jealous of their privileges, claimed to be within their territory. It was still more usual, to hold separate cortes of the three kingdoms simultaneously in such contiguous places in each, as would permit the royal presence in all during their session. See Blancas, Modo de Proceder en Cortes de Aragon, (Zaragoza, 1641,) cap. 4.

nation, as well as to their settled opinions and habits
and praying that its operation might be suspended
for the present, so far at least as concerned the confiscation of property, which it rightly regarded as
the moving power of the whole terrible machinery.[6]

Both the pope and the king, as may be imagined, turned a deaf ear to these remonstrances. In
the mean while the Inquisition commenced operations, and autos da fe were celebrated at Saragossa, with all their usual horrors, in the months of
May and June, in 1485. The discontented Aragonese, despairing of redress in any regular way,
resolved to intimidate their oppressors by some appalling act of violence. They formed a conspiracy
for the assassination of Arbues, the most odious of
the inquisitors established over the diocese of Saragossa. The conspiracy, set on foot by some of the
principal nobility, was entered into by most of the
new Christians, or persons of Jewish extraction, in
the district. A sum of ten thousand reals was subscribed to defray the necessary expenses for the
execution of their project. This was not easy,
however, since Arbues, conscious of the popular
odium that he had incurred, protected his person

---

[6] By one of the articles in the
Privilegium Generale, the Magna
Charta of Aragon, it is declared,
" Que turment : ni inquisicion ; no
sian en Aragon como sian contra Fuero el qual dize que alguna
pesquisa no hauemos : et contra
el privilegio general, el qual vie-
da que inquisicion so sia feyta."
(Fueros y Observancias, fol. 11.)
The tenor of this clause (although
the term *inquisicion* must not be
confounded with the name of the
modern institution) was sufficiently
precise, one might have thought
to secure the Aragonese from the
fangs of this terrible tribunal

by wearing under his monastic robes a suit of mail, complete even to the helmet beneath his hood. With similar vigilance, he defended, also, every avenue to his sleeping apartment. [7]

At length, however, the conspirators found an opportunity of surprising him while at his devotions. Arbues was on his knees before the great altar of the cathedral, near midnight, when his enemies, who had entered the church in two separate bodies, suddenly surrounded him, and one of them wounded him in the arm with a dagger, while another dealt him a fatal blow in the back of his neck. The priests, who were preparing to celebrate matins in the choir of the church, hastened to the spot; but not before the assassins had effected their escape. They transported the bleeding body of the inquisitor to his apartment, where he survived only two days, blessing the Lord, that he had been permitted to seal so good a cause with his blood. The whole scene will readily remind the English reader of the assassination of Thomas a Becket. [8]

The event did not correspond with the expectations of the conspirators. Sectarian jealousy proved stronger than hatred of the Inquisition. The populace, ignorant of the extent or ultimate object of the conspiracy, were filled with vague apprehensions of an insurrection of the new Christians, who

7 Llorente, Hist. de l Inquisition, chap. 6, art. 2, 3.
8 Llorente, ubi supra.— Paramo, De Origine Inquisitionis, pp. 182. 183. — Ferreras, Hist. d'Espagne, tom. viii. pp. 37, 38.

had so often been the objects of outrage ; and they could only be appeased by the archbishop of Saragossa, riding through the streets, and proclaiming that no time should be lost in detecting and punishing the assassins.

Cruel persecutions.

This promise was abundantly fulfilled ; and wide was the ruin occasioned by the indefatigable zeal, with which the bloodhounds of the tribunal followed up the scent. In the course of this persecution, two hundred individuals perished at the stake, and a still greater number in the dungeons of the Inquisition ; and there was scarcely a noble family in Aragon but witnessed one or more of its members condemned to humiliating penance in the autos da fe. The immediate perpetrators of the murder were all hanged, after suffering the amputation of their right hands. One, who had appeared as evidence against the rest, under assurance of pardon, had his sentence so far commuted, that his hand was not cut off till after he had been hanged. It was thus that the Holy Office interpreted its promises of grace.[9]

Arbues received all the honors of a martyr. His ashes were interred on the spot where he had been assassinated.[10] A superb mausoleum was erected

[9] Llorente, Hist. de l'Inquisition, tom. i. chap. 6, art. 5. — Blancas, Aragonensium Rerum Commentarii, (Cæsaraugustæ, 1588,) p. 266. Among those, who after a tedious imprisonment were condemned to do penance in an auto da fe, was a nephew of king Ferdinand, Don James of Navarre. Mariana, willing to point the tale with a suitable moral, informs us, that, although none of the conspirators were ever brought to trial, they all perished miserably within a year, in different ways, by the judgment of God. (Hist. de España, tom. ii. p. 368.) Unfortunately for the effect of this moral, Llorente, who consulted the original processes, must be received as the better authority of the two.

[10] According to Paramo, when

over them, and, beneath his effigy, a bas-relief was sculptured representing his tragical death, with an inscription containing a suitable denunciation of the race of Israel. And at length, when the lapse of nearly two centuries had supplied the requisite amount of miracles, the Spanish Inquisition had the glory of adding a new saint to the calendar, by the canonization of the martyr under Pope Alexander the Seventh, in 1664. [11]

The failure of the attempt to shake off the tribunal, served only, as usual in such cases, to establish it more firmly than before. Efforts at resistance were subsequently, but ineffectually, made in other parts of Aragon, and in Valencia and Catalonia. It was not established in the latter province till 1487, and some years later in Sicily, Sardinia, and the Balearic Isles. Thus Ferdinand had the melancholy satisfaction of riveting the most galling yoke ever devised by fanaticism, round the necks of a people, who till that period had enjoyed probably the greatest degree of constitutional freedom which the world had witnessed.

the corpse of the inquisitor was brought to the place where he had been assassinated, the blood, which had been coagulated on the pavement, smoked up and boiled with most miraculous fervor! De Origine Inquisitionis, p. 382.

[11] Paramo, De Origine Inquitionis, p 183. — Llorente, Hist de l'Inquisition, chap. 6, art. 4. France and Italy also, according to Llorente, could each boast a saint inquisitor. Their renown, however, has been eclipsed by the superior splendors of their great master, St. Dominic ;

— "Fils inconnus d'un si glorieux père."

CHAPTER XIII.

1487.

Narrow Escape of Ferdinand before Velez. — Malaga invested by Sea
and Land. — Brilliant Spectacle. — The Queen visits the Camp. —
Attempt to assassinate the Sovereigns. — Distress and Resolution of
the besieged. — Enthusiasm of the Christians. — Outworks carried
by them. — Proposals for Surrender. — Haughty Demeanor of Ferdinand. — Malaga surrenders at Discretion. — Cruel Policy of the
Victors.

PART
I.

Position of
Velez Mala-
ga.

BEFORE commencing operations against Malaga,
it was thought expedient by the Spanish council of
war to obtain possession of Velez Malaga, situated
about five leagues distant from the former. This
strong town stood along the southern extremity of
a range of mountains that extend to Granada. Its
position afforded an easy communication with that
capital, and obvious means of annoyance to an enemy interposed between itself and the adjacent city
of Malaga. The reduction of this place, therefore,
became the first object of the campaign.

The forces assembled at Cordova, consisting of
the levies of the Andalusian cities principally, of
the retainers of the great nobility, and of the well-
appointed chivalry which thronged from all quarters
of the kingdom, amounted on this occasion, to

twelve thousand horse and forty thousand foot; a CHAPTER
XIII. number, which sufficiently attests the unslackened ardor of the nation in the prosecution of the war. On the 7th of April, King Ferdinand, putting himself at the head of this formidable host, quitted the fair city of Cordova amid the cheering acclamations of its inhabitants, although these were somewhat damped by the ominous occurrence of an earthquake, which demolished a part of the royal residence, among other edifices, during the preceding night. The route, after traversing the Yeguas and the old town of Antequera, struck into a wild, hilly country, that stretches towards Velez. The rivers were so much swollen by excessive rains, and the passes so rough and difficult, that the army in part of its march advanced only a league a day; and on one occasion, when no suitable place occurred for encampment for the space of five leagues, the men fainted with exhaustion, and the beasts dropped down dead in the harness. At length, on the 17th of April, the Spanish army sat down before Velez Malaga, where in a few days they were joined by the lighter pieces of their battering ordnance; the roads, notwithstanding the immense labor expended on them, being found impracticable for the heavier.[1]

The Moors were aware of the importance of Velez to the security of Malaga. The sensation

1487.

Army before
Velez.

Defeat of El
Zagal.

[1] Vedmar, Antiguedad y Grandezas de la Ciudad de Velez, (Granada, 1652,) fol. 148. — Mariana, Hist. de España, tom. ii. lib. 25, cap. 10. — Pulgar, Reyes Católicos, part. iii. cap. 70. — Carbajal, Anales, MS., año 1487. — Bleda, Corónica, lib. 5, cap. 14.

excited in Granada by the tidings of its danger
was so strong, that the old chief, El Zagal, found
it necessary to make an effort to relieve the beleaguered city, notwithstanding the critical posture
in which his absence would leave his affairs in
the capital. Dark clouds of the enemy were seen
throughout the day mustering along the heights,
which by night were illumined with a hundred
fires. Ferdinand's utmost vigilance was required
for the protection of his camp against the ambus-
cades and nocturnal sallies of his wily foe. At
length, however, El Zagal having been foiled in a
well-concerted attempt to surprise the Christian
quarters by night, was driven across the mountains
by the marquis of Cadiz, and compelled to retreat
on his capital, completely baffled in his enterprise.
There the tidings of his disaster had preceded him.
The fickle populace, with whom misfortune passes
for misconduct, unmindful of his former successes,
now hastened to transfer their allegiance to his
rival, Abdallah, and closed the gates against him ;
and the unfortunate chief withdrew to Guadix,
which, with Almeria, Baza, and some less considerable places, still remained faithful. [2]

Ferdinand conducted the siege all the while with
his usual vigor, and spared no exposure of his person to peril or fatigue. On one occasion, seeing
a party of Christians retreating in disorder before a
squadron of the enemy, who had surprised them

[2] Cardonne, Hist. d'Afrique et
d'Espagne, tom. iii. pp. 292–294.
—Pulgar, Reyes Católicos, ubi
supra.—Vedmar, Antiguedad de
Velez, fol. 151.

while fortifying an eminence near the city, the
king, who was at dinner in his tent, rushed out
with no other defensive armour than his cuirass,
and, leaping on his horse, charged briskly into the
midst of the enemy, and succeeded in rallying his
own men. In the midst of the rencontre, however, when he had discharged his lance, he found
himself unable to extricate his sword from the scab-
bard which hung from the saddle-bow. At this
moment he was assaulted by several Moors, and
must have been either slain or taken, but for the
timely rescue of the marquis of Cadiz, and a brave
cavalier, Garcilasso de la Vega, who galloping up
to the spot with their attendants, succeeded after a
sharp skirmish in beating off the enemy. Ferdinand's nobles remonstrated with him on this wanton exposure of his person, representing that he
could serve them more effectually with his head
than his hand. But he answered, that " he could
not stop to calculate chances, when his subjects
were perilling their lives for his sake;" a reply,
says Pulgar, which endeared him to the whole
army.[3]

At length, the inhabitants of Velez, seeing the
ruin impending from the bombardment of the Christians, whose rigorous blockade both by sea and
land excluded all hopes of relief from without,

CHAPTER
XIII.

Surrender of
Velez.

---

[3] L. Marineo, Cosas Memorables, fol. 175. — Vedmar, Antiguedad de Velez, fol. 150, 151. —
Marmol, Rebelion de Moriscos, lib.
l, cap. 14.
In commemoration of this event,
the city incorporated into its es-
cutcheon the figure of a king on
horseback, in the act of piercing a
Moor with his javelin. Vedmar
Antiguedad de Velez, fol. 12.

consented to capitulate on the usual conditions of security to persons, property, and religion. The capitulation of this place, April 27th, 1487, was followed by that of more than twenty places of inferior note lying between it and Malaga, so that the approaches to this latter city were now left open to the victorious Spaniards. [4]

Description of Malaga.

This ancient city, which, under the Spanish Arabs in the twelfth and thirteenth centuries, formed the capital of an independent principality, was second only to the metropolis itself, in the kingdom of Granada. Its fruitful environs furnished abundant articles of export, while its commodious port on the Mediterranean opened a traffic with the various countries washed by that inland sea, and with the remoter regions of India. Owing to these advantages, the inhabitants acquired unbounded opulence, which showed itself in the embellishments of their city, whose light forms of architecture, mingling after the eastern fashion with odoriferous gardens and fountains of sparkling water, presented an appearance most refreshing to the senses in this sultry climate. [5]

The city was encompassed by fortifications of great strength, and in perfect repair. It was commanded by a citadel, connected by a covered way

---

[4] Bernaldez, Reyes Católicos, MS., cap. 52. — Marmol, Rebelion de Moriscos, lib. 1, cap. 14.

[5] Conde doubts whether the name of Malaga is derived from the Greek μαλακὴ, signifying "agreeable," or the Arabic *malka*, meaning "royal." Either etymology is sufficiently pertinent. (See El Nubiense, Descripcion de España, p. 186, not.) For notices of sovereigns who swayed the sceptre of Malaga, see Casiri, Bibliotheca Escurialensis, tom. ii pp. 41, 56, 99, et alibi.

with a second fortress impregnable from its position, denominated Gebalfaro, which stood along the declivities of the bold sierra of the Axarquia, whose defiles had proved so disastrous to the Christians. The city lay between two spacious suburbs, the one on the land side being also encircled by a formidable wall; and the other declining towards the sea, showing an expanse of olive, orange, and pomegranate gardens, intermingled with the rich vineyards that furnished the celebrated staple for its export.

Malaga was well prepared for a siege by supplies of artillery and ammunition. Its ordinary garrison was reinforced by volunteers from the neighbouring towns, and by a corps of African mercenaries, Gomeres, as they were called, men of ferocious temper, but of tried valor and military discipline. The command of this important post had been intrusted by El Zagal to a noble Moor, named Hamet Zeli, whose renown in the present war had been established by his resolute defence of Ronda. [6]

Ferdinand, while lying before Velez, received intelligence that many of the wealthy burghers of Malaga were inclined to capitulate at once, rather than hazard the demolition of their city by an obstinate resistance. He instructed the marquis of Cadiz, therefore, to open a negotiation with Hamet Zeli, authorizing him to make the most liberal offers to the alcayde himself, as well as his garrison,

[6] Conde, Dominacion de los Arabes, tom. iii. p. 237. — Pulgar, Reyes Católicos, cap. 74.— El Nubiense, Descripcion de España, not., p. 144.

and the principal citizens of the place, on condition of immediate surrender. The sturdy chief, however, rejected the proposal with disdain, replying, that he had been commissioned by his master to defend the place to the last extremity, and that the Christian king could not offer a bribe large enough to make him betray his trust. Ferdinand, finding 'ittle prospect of operating on this Spartan temper, broke up his camp before Velez, on the 7th of May, and advanced with his whole army as far as Bezmillana, a place on the sea-board about two leagues distant from Malaga.[7]

The line of march now lay through a valley commanded at the extremity nearest the city by two eminences ; the one on the sea-coast, the other facing the fortress of the Gebalfaro, and forming part of the wild sierra which overshadowed Malaga on the north. The enemy occupied both these important positions. A corps of Galicians were sent forward to dislodge them from the eminence towards the sea. But it failed in the assault, and, notwithstanding it was led up a second time by the commander of Leon and the brave Garcilasso de la Vega,[8] was again repulsed by the intrepid foe.

[7] Bernaldez, Reyes Católicos, MS., cap. 82. — Vedmar, Antiguedad de Velez, fol. 154. — Pulgar, Reyes Católicos, cap. 74.

[8] This cavalier, who took a conspicuous part both in the military and civil transactions of this reign, was descended from one of the most ancient and honorable houses in Castile. Hyta, (Guerras Civiles de Granada, tom. i. p. 399.) with more effrontery than usual, has imputed to him a chivalrous rencontre with a Saracen, which is recorded of an ancestor, in the ancient Chronicle of Alonso XI.

" Garcilaso de la Vega
    desde alli se ha intitulado,
    porque en la Vega hiciera
    campo con aquel pagano."

Oviedo, however, with good reason, distrusts the etymology and the story, as he traces both the cognomen and the peculiar device

A similar fate attended the assault on the sierra,
which was conducted by the troops of the royal
household. They were driven back on the vanguard, which had halted in the valley under command of the grand master of St. James, prepared
to support the attack on either side. Being reinforced, the Spaniards returned to the charge with
the most determined resolution. They were encountered by the enemy with equal spirit. The latter, throwing away their lances, precipitated themselves on the ranks of the assailants, making use
only of their daggers, grappling closely man to
man, till both rolled promiscuously together down
the steep sides of the ravine. No mercy was asked, or shown. None thought of sparing or of spoil-
ing, for hatred, says the chronicler, was stronger
than avarice. The main body of the army, in the
mean while, pent up in the valley, were compelled
to witness the mortal conflict, and listen to the ex-
ulting cries of the enemy, which, after the Moorish
custom, rose high and shrill above the din of battle,
without being able to advance a step in support of
their companions, who were again forced to give
way before their impetuous adversaries, and fall
back on the vanguard under the grand master of
St. James. Here, however, they speedily rallied;
and, being reinforced, advanced to the charge a third
time, with such inflexible courage as bore down all
opposition, and compelled the enemy, exhausted, or
rather overpowered by superior numbers, to aban-

of the family to a much older date   Chronicle. Quincuagenas, MS.,
than the period assigned in the   bat. 1, quinc. 3, dial. 43.

don his position. At the same time the rising
ground on the seaside was carried by the Spaniards
under the commander of Leon and Garcilasso de la
Vega, who, dividing their forces, charged the Moors
so briskly in front and rear, that they were compelled to retreat on the neighbouring fortress of Gebalfaro.[9]

As it was evening before these advantages were
obtained, the army did not defile into the plains
around Malaga, before the following morning, when
dispositions were made for its encampment. The
eminence on the sierra, so bravely contested, was
assigned as the post of greatest danger to the marquis duke of Cadiz. It was protected by strong
works lined with artillery, and a corps of two
thousand five hundred horse and fourteen thousand
foot, was placed under the immediate command of
that nobleman. A line of defence was constructed
along the declivity from this redoubt to the sea-
shore. Similar works, consisting of a deep trench
and palisades, or, where the soil was too rocky to
admit of them, of an embankment or mound of
earth, were formed in front of the encampment,
which embraced the whole circuit of the city; and
the blockade was completed by a fleet of armed
vessels, galleys and caravels, which rode in the
harbour under the command of the Catalan admiral,
Requesens, and effectually cut off all communication
by water.[10]

[9] Pulgar, Reyes Católicos, cap.
75. — Salazar de Mendoza, Crón.
del Gran Cardenal, lib. 1, cap. 64.
[10] Bernaldez, Reyes Católicos,
MS., cap. 83. — Pulgar, Reyes Católicos, cap. 76. — Carbajal, Anales, MS., año 1487.

The old chronicler Bernaldez warms at the aspect of the fair city of Malaga, thus encompassed by Christian legions, whose deep lines, stretching far over hill and valley, reached quite round from one arm of the sea to the other. In the midst of this brilliant encampment was seen the royal pavilion, proudly displaying the united banners of Castile and Aragon, and forming so conspicuous a mark for the enemy's artillery, that Ferdinand, after imminent hazard, was at length compelled to shift his quarters. The Christians were not slow in erecting counter batteries ; but the work was obliged to be carried on at night, in order to screen them from the fire of the besieged. [11]

The first operations of the Spaniards were directed against the suburb, on the land side of the city. The attack was intrusted to the count of Cifuentes, the nobleman who had been made prisoner in the affair of the Axarquia, and subsequently ransomed. The Spanish ordnance was served with such effect, that a practicable breach was soon made in the wall. The combatants now poured their murderous volleys on each other through the opening, and at length met on the ruins of the breach. After a desperate struggle the Moors gave way. The Christians rushed into the enclosure, at the same time effecting a lodgment on the rampart ; and, although a part of it, undermined by the ene-

CHAPTER XIII.

Brilliant spectacle.

---

11 Pulgar, Reyes Católicos, ubi supra. — Bernaldez, Reyes Católicos MS., ubi supra.

my, gave way with a terrible crash, they still kept possession of the remainder, and at length drove their antagonists, who sullenly retreated step by step within the fortifications of the city. The lines were then drawn close around the place. Every avenue of communication was strictly guarded, and every preparation was made for reducing the town by regular blockade.[12]

Extensive
preparations.
In addition to the cannon brought round by water from Velez, the heavier lombards, which from the difficulty of transportation had been left during the late siege at Antequera, were now conducted across roads, levelled for the purpose, to the camp. Supplies of marble bullets were also brought from the ancient and depopulated city of Algezira, where they had lain ever since its capture in the preceding century by Alfonso the Eleventh. The camp was filled with operatives, employed in the manufacture of balls and powder, which were stored in subterranean magazines, and in the fabrication of those various kinds of battering enginery, which continued in use long after the introduction of gunpowder.[13]

During the early part of the siege, the camp experienced some temporary inconvenience from the occasional interruption of the supplies transported by water. Rumors of the appearance of the plague in some of the adjacent villages caused additional

[12] Peter Martyr, Opus Epist., lib. 1, epist. 63. — Pulgar, Reyes Católicos, cap. 76. — Bernaldez, Reyes Católicos, cap. 83. — Oviedo, Quincuagenas, MS., bat. 1, quinc. 1, dial. 36.
[13] Pulgar, Reyes Católicos, cap 76.

uneasiness; and deserters, who passed into Malaga, reported these particulars with the usual exaggeration, and encouraged the besieged to persevere, by the assurance that Ferdinand could not much longe keep the field, and that the queen had actually written to advise his breaking up the camp. Under these circumstances, Ferdinand saw at once the importance of the queen's presence in order to dispel the delusion of the enemy, and to give new heart to his soldiers. He accordingly sent a message to Cordova, where she was holding her court, requesting her appearance in the camp.

Isabella had proposed to join her husband before Velez, on receiving tidings of El Zagal's march from Granada, and had actually enforced levies of all persons capable of bearing arms, between twenty and seventy years of age, throughout Andalusia, but subsequently disbanded them, on learning the discomfiture of the Moorish army. Without hesitation, she now set forward, accompanied by the cardinal of Spain and other dignitaries of the church, together with the Infanta Isabella, and a courtly train of ladies and cavaliers in attendance on her person. She was received at a short distance from the camp by the marquis of Cadiz and the grandmaster of St. James, and escorted to her quarters amidst the enthusiastic greetings of the soldiery. Hope now brightened every countenance. A grace seemed to be shed over the rugged features of war; and the young gallants thronged from all quarters to the camp, eager to win the guerdon of

PART
I.

valor from the hands of those from whom it is most grateful to receive it. [14]

Ferdinand, who had hitherto brought into action only the lighter pieces of ordnance, from a willingness to spare the noble edifices of the city, now

Summons of
the town.

pointed his heaviest guns against its walls. Before opening his fire, however, he again summoned the place, offering the usual liberal terms in case of immediate compliance, and engaging otherwise, " with the blessing of God, to make them all slaves "! But the heart of the alcayde was hardened like that of Pharaoh, says the Andalusian chronicler, and the people were swelled with vain hopes, so that their ears were closed against the proposal ; orders were even issued to punish with death any attempt at a parley. On the contrary, they made answer by a more lively cannonade than before, along the whole line of ramparts and fortresses which overhung the city. Sallies were also made at almost every hour of the day and night on every assailable point of the Christian lines, so that the camp was kept in perpetual alarm. In one of the nocturnal sallies, a body of two thousand men from the castle of Gebalfaro succeeded

Danger of
the marquis
of Cadiz.

in surprising the quarters of the marquis of Cadiz, who, with his followers, was exhausted by fatigue and watching, during the two preceding nights. The Christians, bewildered with the sudden tumult which broke their slumber, were thrown into the

[14] Salazar de Mendoza, Crón. 70. — Bernaldez, Reyes Católicos. del Gran Cardenal, lib. 1, cap. 64. MS., cap. 83. — Zurita, Anales, tom. iv. cap.

greatest confusion ; and the marquis, who rushed half armed from his tent, found no little difficulty in bringing them to order, and beating off the assailants, after receiving a wound in the arm from an arrow ; while he had a still narrower escape from the ball of an arquebus, that penetrated his buckler and hit him below the cuirass, but fortunately so much spent as to do him no injury. [15]

Civil feuds
of the Moors.

The Moors were not unmindful of the importance of Malaga, or the gallantry with which it was defended. They made several attempts to relieve it, whose failure was less owing to the Christians than to treachery and their own miserable feuds. A body of cavalry, which El Zagal despatched from Guadix to throw succours into the beleaguered city, was encountered and cut to pieces by a superior force of the young king Abdallah, who consummated his baseness by sending an embassy to the Christian camp, charged with a present of Arabian horses sumptuously caparisoned to Ferdinand, and of costly silks and oriental perfumes to the queen ; at the same time complimenting them on their successes, and soliciting the continuance of their friendly dispositions towards himself. Ferdinand and Isabella requited this act of humiliation by securing to Abdallah's subjects the right of cultivating their fields in quiet, and of trafficking with the Spaniards in every commodity, save military stores. At this paltry price did the dastard

15 Bleda, Corónica, lib. 5, cap.   Reyes Católicos, MS., cap. 83.—
15 — Conde, Dominacion, tom.   Pulgar, Reyes Católicos, cap. 79.
iv. pp. 237, 238. — Bernaldez,

prince consent to stay his arm, at the only moment
when it could be used effectually for his country. [16]

More serious consequences were like to have resulted from an attempt made by another party of
Moors from Guadix to penetrate the Christian lines.
Part of them succeeded, and threw themselves
into the besieged city. The remainder were cut
in pieces. There was one, however, who making
no show of resistance, was made prisoner without
harm to his person. Being brought before the
marquis of Cadiz, he informed that nobleman, that
he could make some important disclosures to the
sovereigns. He was accordingly conducted to the
royal tent; but, as Ferdinand was taking his siesta,
in the sultry hour of the day, the queen, moved by
divine inspiration, according to the Castilian historian, deferred the audience till her husband should
awake, and commanded the prisoner to be detained
in the adjoining tent. This was occupied by Doña
Beatriz de Bobadilla, marchioness of Moya, Isabella's early friend, who happened to be at that time
engaged in discourse with a Portuguese nobleman,
Don Alvaro, son of the duke of Braganza. [17]

[16] Pulgar, Reyes Católicos, ubi
supra.
During the siege, ambassadors
arrived from an African potentate,
the king of Tremecen, bearing a
magnificent present to the Castilian sovereigns, interceding for the
Malagans, and at the same time
asking protection for his subjects
from the Spanish cruisers in the
Mediterranean. The sovereigns
graciously complied with the latter request, and complimented the
African monarch with a plate of
gold, on which the royal arms
were curiously embossed, says
Bernaldez, Reyes Católicos, cap.
84.

[17] This nobleman, Don Alvaro
de Portugal, had fled his native
country, and sought an asylum in
Castile from the vindictive enmity
of John II., who had put to death
the duke of Braganza, his elder
brother. He was kindly received
by Isabella, to whom he was near-

The Moor did not understand the Castilian language, and, deceived by the rich attire and courtly bearing of these personages, he mistook them for the king and queen. While in the act of refreshing himself with a glass of water, he suddenly drew a dagger from beneath the broad folds of his *albornoz*, or Moorish mantle, which he had been incautiously suffered to retain, and, darting on the Portuguese prince, gave him a deep wound on the head ; and then, turning like lightning on the marchioness, aimed a stroke at her, which fortunately glanced without injury, the point of the weapon being turned by the heavy embroidery of her robes. Before he could repeat his blow, the Moorish Scævola, with a fate very different from that of his Roman prototype, was pierced with a hundred wounds by the attendants, who rushed to the spot, alarmed by the cries of the marchioness, and his mangled remains were soon after discharged from a catapult into the city ; a foolish bravado, which the besieged requited by slaying a Galician gentleman, and sending his corpse astride upon a mule through the gates of the town into the Christian camp. [18]

This daring attempt on the lives of the king and queen spread general consternation throughout the army. Precautions were taken for the future, by

ly related, and subsequently preferred to several important offices of state. His son, the count of Gelves, married a granddaughter of Christopher Columbus. Oviedo, Quincuagenas, MS.

[18] Oviedo, Quincuagenas, MS., bat. 1, quinc. 1, dial. 23. — Peter Martyr, Opus Epist., lib. 1, epist. 63. — Bernaldez, Reyes Católicos, MS., cap. 84. — Bleda, Corónica de los Moros, lib. 5, cap. 15. — L. Marineo, Cosas Memorables, fol 175, 176.

ordinances prohibiting the introduction of any unknown person armed, or any Moor whatever, into
the royal quarters; and the body-guard was augmented by the addition of two hundred hidalgos of
Castile and Aragon who, with their retainers, were
to keep constant watch over the persons of the
sovereigns.

Distress and
resolution of
the besieged.
Meanwhile, the city of Malaga, whose natural
population was greatly swelled by the influx of its
foreign auxiliaries, began to be straitened for supplies, while its distress was aggravated by the spectacle of abundance which reigned throughout the
Spanish camp. Still, however, the people, overawed by the soldiery, did not break out into murmurs, nor did they relax in any degree the pertinacity of their resistance. Their drooping spirits
were cheered by the predictions of a fanatic, who
promised that they should eat the grain which they
saw in the Christian camp; a prediction, which
came to be verified, like most others that are verified at all, in a very different sense from that intended or understood.

The incessant cannonade kept up by the besieging army, in the mean time, so far exhausted their
ammunition, that they were constrained to seek
supplies from the most distant parts of the kingdom, and from foreign countries. The arrival of
two Flemish transports at this juncture, from the
emperor of Germany, whose interest had been
roused in the crusade, afforded a seasonable rein
forcement of military stores and munitions.

The obstinate defence of Malaga had given the

siege such celebrity, that volunteers, eager to share
in it, flocked from all parts of the Peninsula to the
royal standard. Among others, the duke of Medina
Sidonia, who had furnished his quota of troops at
the opening of the campaign, now arrived in person
with a reinforcement, together with a hundred galleys freighted with supplies, and a loan of twenty
thousand doblas of gold to the sovereigns for the
expenses of the war. Such was the deep interest
in it excited throughout the nation, and the alacrity which every order of men exhibited in supporting its enormous burdens.[19]

The Castilian army, swelled by these daily aug-
mentations, varied in its amount, according to different estimates, from sixty to ninety thousand men.
Throughout this immense host, the most perfect
discipline was maintained. Gaming was restrained
by ordinances interdicting the use of dice and
cards, of which the lower orders were passionately
fond. Blasphemy was severely punished. Prosti
tutes, the common pest of a camp, were excluded ;
and so entire was the subordination, that not a
knife was drawn, and scarcely a brawl occurred,
says the historian, among the motley multitude.
Besides the higher ecclesiastics who attended the
court, the camp was well supplied with holy men,
priests, friars, and the chaplains of the great nobility, who performed the exercises of religion in their
respective quarters with all the pomp and splendor

[19] Pulgar, Reyes Católicos, cap. 87 – 89. — Bernaldez, Reyes Católicos, MS., cap. 84.

of the Roman Catholic worship ; exalting the imaginations of the soldiers into the high devotional
feeling, which became those who were fighting the
battles of the Cross.[20]

Hitherto, Ferdinand relying on the blockade, and
yielding to the queen's desire to spare the lives of
her soldiers, had formed no regular plan of assault
upon the town. But, as the season rolled on without the least demonstration of submission on the
part of the besieged, he resolved to storm the
works, which, if attended by no other consequences, might at least serve to distress the enemy,
and hasten the hour of surrender. Large wooden
towers on rollers were accordingly constructed, and
provided with an apparatus of drawbridges and lad
ders, which, when brought near to the ramparts
would open a descent into the city. Galleries were
also wrought, some for the purpose of penetrating
into the place, and others to sap the foundations of
the walls. The whole of these operations was
placed under the direction of Francisco Ramirez,
the celebrated engineer of Madrid.

Feneral
ally.

But the Moors anticipated the completion of
these formidable preparations by a brisk, well concerted attack on all points of the Spanish lines
They countermined the assailants, and, encountering them in the subterraneous passages, drove them
back, and demolished the frame-work of the galleries. At the same time, a little squadron of armed
vessels, which had been riding in safety under the

[20] Bernaldez, Reyes Católicos, MS., cap. 87. — Pulgar, Reyes Católicos, cap. 71.

guns of the city, pushed out and engaged the Spanish fleet. Thus the battle raged with fire and sword, above and under ground, along the ramparts, the ocean, and the land, at the same time. Even Pulgar cannot withhold his tribute of admiration to this unconquerable spirit in an enemy, wasted by all the extremities of famine and fatigue. " Who does not marvel," he says, " at the bold heart of these infidels in battle, their prompt obedience to their chiefs, their dexterity in the wiles of war, their patience under privation, and undaunted perseverance in their purposes ? "[21]

Generosity of a Moorish knight.

A circumstance occurred in a sortie from the city, indicating a trait of character worth recording. A noble Moor, named Abrahen Zenete fell in with a number of Spanish children who had wandered from their quarters. Without injuring them, he touched them gently with the handle of his lance, saying, " Get ye gone, varlets; to your mothers." On being rebuked by his comrades, who inquired why he had let them escape so easily, he replied, " Because I saw no beard upon their chins." " An example of magnanimity," says the Curate of Los Palacios, " truly wonderful in a heathen, and which might have reflected credit on a Christian hidalgo."[22]

[21] Conde, Dominacion de los Arabes, tom. iii. pp. 237, 238. — Pulgar, Reyes Católicos, cap. 80. — Caro de Torres, Ordenes Militares, fol. 82, 83.

[22] Pulgar, Reyes Católicos, cap. 91. — Bernaldez, Reyes Católicos, MS., cap. 84.

The honest exclamation of the Curate brings to mind the similar encomium of the old Moorish ballad,

" Caballeros Granadinos,
    Aunque Moros, hijosdalgo."

Hyta, Guerras de Granada, tom. p. 257.

But no virtue nor valor could avail the unfortunate Malagans against the overwhelming force of their enemies, who, driving them back from every point, compelled them, after a desperate struggle of six hours, to shelter themselves within the defences of the town. The Christians followed up their success. A mine was sprung near a tower, connected by a bridge of four arches with the main works of the place. The Moors, scattered and intimidated by the explosion, retreated across the bridge, and the Spaniards, carrying the tower, whose guns completely enfiladed it, obtained possession of this important pass into the beleaguered city. For these and other signal services during the siege, Francisco Ramirez, the master of the ordnance, received the honors of knighthood from the hand of King Ferdinand. [23]

The citizens of Malaga, dismayed at beholding

[23] There is no older well-authenticated account of the employment of gunpowder in mining in European warfare, so far as I am aware, than this by Ramirez. Tiraboschi, indeed, refers, on the authority of another writer, to a work in the library of the Academy of Siena, composed by one Francesco Giorgio, architect of the duke of Urbino, about 1480, in which that person claims the merit of the invention. (Letteratura Italiana, tom. vi. p. 370.) The whole statement is obviously too loose to warrant any such conclusion. The Italian historians notice the use of gunpowder mines at the siege of the little town of Serezanello in Tuscany, by the Genoese, in 1487, precisely contemporaneous with the siege of Malaga. (Machiavelli, Istorie Fiorentine, lib. 8. — Guicciardini, Istoria d' Italia, (Milano, 1803,) tom. iii. lib. 6.) This singular coincidence, in nations having then but little intercourse, would seem to infer some common origin of greater antiquity. However this may be, the writers of both nations are agreed in ascribing the first successful use of such mines on any extended scale to the celebrated Spanish engineer, Pedro Navarro, when serving under Gonsalvo of Cordova, in his Italian campaigns at the beginning of the sixteenth century. Guicciardini, ubi supra. — Paolo Giovio, De Vitâ Magni Gonsalvi, (Vitæ Illustrium Virorum, Basiliæ, 1578,) lib. 2. — Aleson, Annales de Navarra, tom. v. lib. 35, cap. 12.

the enemy established in their defences, and fainting under exhaustion from a siege which had already lasted more than three months, now began
to murmur at the obstinacy of the garrison, and to
demand a capitulation. Their magazines of grain
were emptied, and for some weeks they had been
compelled to devour the flesh of horses, dogs, cats,
and even the boiled hides of these animals, or, in
default of other nutriment, vine leaves dressed with
oil, and leaves of the palm tree, pounded fine, and
baked into a sort of cake. In consequence of this
loathsome and unwholesome diet, diseases were
engendered. Multitudes were seen dying about
the streets. Many deserted to the Spanish camp,
eager to barter their liberty for bread; and the city
exhibited all the extremes of squalid and disgusting
wretchedness, bred by pestilence and famine among
an overcrowded population. The sufferings of the
citizens softened the stern heart of the alcayde.
Hamet Zeli, who at length yielded to their impor-
tunities, and, withdrawing his forces into the Gebalfaro, consented that the Malagans should make the
best terms they could with their conqueror.

A deputation of the principal inhabitants, with
an eminent merchant named Ali Dordux at their
head, was then despatched to the Christian quarters, with the offer of the city to capitulate, on the
same liberal conditions which had been uniformly
granted by the Spaniards. The king refused to
admit the embassy into his presence, and haughtily
answered through the commander of Leon, " that
these terms had been twice offered to the people

of Malaga, and rejected; that it was too late for them to stipulate conditions, and nothing now remained but to abide by those, which he, as their conqueror, should vouchsafe to them."[24]

Ferdinand's answer spread general consternation throughout Malaga. The inhabitants saw too plainly that nothing was to be hoped from an appeal to sentiments of humanity. After a tumultuous debate, the deputies were despatched a second time to the Christian camp, charged with propositions in which concession was mingled with menace. They represented that the severe response of King Ferdinand to the citizens had rendered them desperate. That, however, they were willing to resign to him their fortifications, their city, in short their property of every description, on his assurance of their personal security and freedom. If he refused this, they would take their Christian captives, amounting to five or six hundred, from the dungeons in which they lay, and hang them like dogs over the battlements; and then, placing their old men, women, and children in the fortress, they would set fire to the town, and cut a way for themselves through their enemies, or fall in the attempt. "So," they continued, "if you gain a victory, it shall be such a one as shall make the name of Malaga ring throughout the world, and to ages yet unborn!" Ferdinand, unmoved by these menaces.

24 Cardonne, Hist. d'Afrique et d'Espagne. tom. iii. p. 296. — L. Marineo, Cosas Memorables, fol. 175. — Rades y Andrada, Las Tres Ordenes, fol. 54. — Pulgar, Reyes Católicos, cap. 92. — Bernaldez Reyes Católicos, MS., cap. 85

coolly replied, that he saw no occasion to change
his former determination ; but they might rest
assured, if they harmed a single hair of a Christian,
he would put every soul in the place, man, woman,
and child, to the sword.

The anxious people, who thronged forth to meet
the embassy on its return to the city, were overwhelmed with the deepest gloom at its ominous
tidings. Their fate was now sealed. Every ave
nue to hope seemed closed by the stern response
of the victor. Yet hope will still linger ; and, although there were some frantic enough to urge the
execution of their desperate menaces, the greater
number of the inhabitants, and among them those
most considerable for wealth and influence, preferred the chance of Ferdinand's clemency to certain,
irretrievable ruin.

For the last time, therefore, the deputies issued
from the gates of the city, charged with an epistle
to the sovereigns from their unfortunate countrymen, in which, after deprecating their anger, and
lamenting their own blind obstinacy, they reminded
their highnesses of the liberal terms which their
ancestors had granted to Cordova, Antequera, and
other cities, after a defence as pertinacious as their
own. They expatiated on the fame which the
sovereigns had established by the generous policy
of their past conquests, and, appealing to their
magnanimity, concluded with submitting themselves, their families, and their fortunes to their
disposal. Twenty of the principal citizens were
then delivered up as hostages for the peaceable

demeanor of the city until its occupation by the Spaniards. " Thus," says the Curate of Los Palacios, " did the Almighty harden the hearts of these heathen, like to those of the Egyptians, in order that they might receive the full wages of the manifold oppressions which they had wrought on his people, from the days of King Roderic to the present time ! " [25]

On the appointed day, the commander of Leon rode through the gates of Malaga, at the head of his well-appointed chivalry, and took possession of the *alcazaba*, or lower citadel. The troops were then posted on their respective stations along the fortifications, and the banners of Christian Spain triumphantly unfurled from the towers of the city, where the crescent had been displayed for an uninterrupted period of nearly eight centuries.

Purification
of the city.

The first act was to purify the town from the numerous dead bodies, and other offensive matter, which had accumulated during this long siege, and lay festering in the streets, poisoning the atmosphere. The principal mosque was next consecrated with due solemnity to the service of Santa Maria de la Encarnacion. Crosses and bells, the

[25] Pulgar, Reyes Católicos, cap. 93. — Cardonne, Hist. d'Afrique et d'Espagne, tom. iii. p. 296.

The Arabic historians state, that Malaga was betrayed by Ali Dordux, who admitted the Spaniards into the castle, while the citizens were debating on Ferdinand's terms. (See Conde, Dominacion de los Arabes, tom. iii. cap. 39.) The letter of the inhabitants, quot-ed at length by Pulgar, would seem to be a refutation of this. And yet there are good grounds for suspecting false play on the part of the ambassador Dordux, since the Castilian writers admit, that he was exempted, with forty of his friends, from the doom of slavery and forfeiture of property, passed upon his fellow-citizens.

symbols of Christian worship, were distributed in CHAPTER
profusion among the sacred edifices; where, says XIII.
the Catholic chronicler last quoted, " the celestial
music of their chimes, sounding at every hour of
the day and night, caused perpetual torment to the
ears of the infidel." [26]

On the eighteenth day of August, being some- Entrance of
the sover-
what more than three months from the date of eigns.
opening trenches, Ferdinand and Isabella made
their entrance into the conquered city, attended by
the court, the clergy, and the whole of their mili
tary array. The procession moved in solemn state
up the principal streets, now deserted, and hushed
in ominous silence, to the new cathedral of St.
Mary, where mass was performed; and, as the glorious anthem of the Te Deum rose for the first time
within its ancient walls, the sovereigns, together
with the whole army, prostrated themselves in grateful adoration of the Lord of hosts, who had thus
reinstated them in the domains of their ancestors.

The most affecting incident was afforded by the Release of
Christian
multitude of Christian captives, who were rescued captives.
from the Moorish dungeons. They were brought
before the sovereigns, with their limbs heavily
manacled, their beards descending to their waists,
and their sallow visages emaciated by captivity and
famine. Every eye was suffused with tears at the
spectacle. Many recognised their ancient friends,
of whose fate they had long been ignorant. Some
had lingered in captivity ten or fifteen years; and

[26] Bernaldez, Reyes Católicos, MS., cap. 85.

among them were several belonging to the best families in Spain. On entering the presence, they would have testified their gratitude by throwing themselves at the feet of the sovereigns ; but the latter, raising them up and mingling their tears with those of the liberated captives, caused their fetters to be removed, and, after administering to their necessities, dismissed them with liberal presents. [27]

The fortress of Gebalfaro surrendered on the day after the occupation of Malaga by the Spaniards. The gallant Zegri chieftain, Hamet Zeli was loaded with chains ; and, being asked why he had persisted so obstinately in his *rebellion*, boldly answered, " Because I was commissioned to defend the place to the last extremity ; and, if I had been properly supported, I would have died sooner than surrender now ! "

The doom of the vanquished was now to be pronounced. On entering the city, orders had been issued to the Spanish soldiery, prohibiting them under the severest penalties from molesting either the persons or property of the inhabitants. These latter were directed to remain in their respective mansions with a guard set over them, while the cravings of appetite were supplied by a liberal distribution of food. At length, the whole population of the city, comprehending every age and

---

[27] Carbajal, whose meagre annals have scarcely any merit beyond that of a mere chronological table, postpones the surrender till September. Anales, año 1487. — Marmol, Rebelion de Moriscos, lib. 1, cap. 14.

sex, was commanded to repair to the great court-yard of the alcazaba, which was overlooked on all sides by lofty ramparts garrisoned by the Spanish soldiery. To this place, the scene of many a Moorish triumph, where the spoil of the border foray had been often displayed, and which still might be emblazoned with the trophy of many a Christian banner, the people of Malaga now direct-ed their steps. As the multitude swarmed through the streets, filled with boding apprehensions of their fate, they wrung their hands, and, raising their eyes to Heaven, uttered the most piteous lamentations. "Oh Malaga," they cried, "renowned and beau-tiful city, how are thy sons about to forsake thee! Could not thy soil on which they first drew breath, be suffered to cover them in death? Where is now the strength of thy towers, where the beauty of thy edifices? The strength of thy walls, alas, could not avail thy children, for they had sorely displeased their Creator. What shall become of thy old men and thy matrons, or of thy young maidens delicately nurtured within thy halls, when they shall feel the iron yoke of bondage? Can thy barbarous conquerors without remorse thus tear asunder the dearest ties of life?" Such are the melancholy strains, in which the Castilian chron-icler has given utterance to the sorrows of the captive city. [28]

[28] B_eda, Corónica, lib. 5, cap 15.

As a counterpart to the above scene, twelve Christian renegades, found in the city, were transfixed with canes, *acañavereados*, a barba-rous punishment derived from the Moors, which was inflicted by horsemen at full gallop, who dis-charged pointed reeds at the crim-

PART
L
———
Sentence
passed on
them.
The dreadful doom of slavery was denounced on the assembled multitude. One third was to be transported into Africa in exchange for an equal number of Christian captives detained there; and all, who had relatives or friends in this predicament, were required to furnish a specification of them. Another third was appropriated to reimburse the state for the expenses of the war. The remainder were to be distributed as presents at home and abroad. Thus, one hundred of the flower of the African warriors were sent to the pope, who incorporated them into his guard, and converted them all in the course of the year, says the Curate of Los Palacios, into very good Christians. Fifty of the most beautiful Moorish girls were presented by Isabella to the queen of Naples, thirty to the queen of Portugal, others to the ladies of her court ; and the residue of both sexes were apportioned among the nobles, cavaliers, and inferior members of the army, according to their respective rank and services.[29]

Wary de-
vice of Fer-
dinand
As it was apprehended that the Malagans, rendered desperate by the prospect of a hopeless, interminable captivity, might destroy or secrete their jewels, plate, and other precious effects, in which this wealthy city abounded, rather than suffer them to fall into the hands of their enemies, Ferdinand devised a politic expedient for preventing it. He

---

inal, until he expired under repeated wounds. A number of relapsed Jews were at the same time condemned to the flames. "These," says father Abarca, "were the *fêtes* and illuminations most grateful to the Catholic piety of our sovereigns"! Abarca, Reyes de Aragon, tom. ii. rey 30, cap. 3.

[29] Pulgar, Reyes Católicos, ubi supra. — Bernaldez, Reyes Católicos, MS., ubi supra. — Peter Martyr, Opus Epist., epist. 62.

proclaimed, that he would receive a certain sum, if paid within nine months, as the ransom of the whole population, and that their personal effects should be admitted in part payment. This sum averaged about thirty doblas a head, including in the estimate all those who might die before the determination of the period assigned. The ransom, thus stipulated, proved more than the unhappy people could raise, either by themselves, or agents employed to solicit contributions among their brethren of Granada and Africa; at the same time, it so far deluded their hopes, that they gave in a full inventory of their effects to the treasury. By this shrewd device, Ferdinand obtained complete possession both of the persons and property of his victims.[30]

Malaga was computed to contain from eleven to fifteen thousand inhabitants, exclusive of several thousand foreign auxiliaries, within its gates at the time of surrender. One cannot, at this day, read the melancholy details of its story, without feelings of horror and indignation. It is impossible to vindicate the dreadful sentence passed on this unfortunate people for a display of heroism, which should have excited admiration in every generous bosom. It was obviously most repugnant to Isabella's natural disposition, and must

[30] Bernaldez, Reyes Católicos, MS., cap. 87. — L. Marineo, Cosas Memorables, fol. 176. — Conde, Dominacion de los Arabes, tom. iii. p. 238. — Cardonne, Hist. d'Afrique et d'Espagne, tom. iii. p. 296. — Carbajal, Anales, MS., año 1487.

Not a word of comment escapes the Castilian historians on this merciless rigor of the conqueror towards the vanquished. It is evident that Ferdinand did no violence to the feelings of his orthodox subjects. *Tacendo clamant.*

be admitted to leave a stain on her memory, which no coloring of history can conceal. It may find some palliation, however, in the bigotry of the age, the more excusable in a woman, whom education, general example, and natural distrust of herself, accustomed to rely, in matters of conscience, on the spiritual guides, whose piety and professional learning seemed to qualify them for the trust. Even in this very transaction, she fell far short of the suggestions of some of her counsellors, who urged her to put every inhabitant without exception to the sword; which, they affirmed, would be a just requital of their obstinate *rebellion*, and would prove a wholesome warning to others! We are not told who the advisers of this precious measure were; but the whole experience of this reign shows, that we shall scarcely wrong the clergy much by imputing it to them. That their arguments could warp so enlightened a mind, as that of Isabella, from the natural principles of justice and humanity, furnishes a remarkable proof of the ascendency which the priesthood usurped over the most gifted intellects, and of their gross abuse of it, before the Reformation, by breaking the seals set on the sacred volume, opened to mankind the uncorrupted channel of divine truth.[31]

The fate of Malaga may be said to have decided that of Granada. The latter was now shut out

31 Bernaldez, Reyes Católicos, MS., cap. 87. — Bleda, Corónica, lib. 5, cap. 15.

About four hundred and fifty Moorish Jews were ransomed by a wealthy Israelite of Castile for 27,000 doblas of gold. A proof that the Jewish stock was one which thrived amidst persecution It is scarcely possible that the

from the most important ports along her coast ; and
she was environed on every point of her territory
by her warlike foe, so that she could hardly hope
more from subsequent efforts, however strenuous
and united, than to postpone the inevitable hour of
dissolution. The cruel treatment of Malaga was
the prelude to the long series of persecutions, which
awaited the wretched Moslems in the land of their
ancestors ; in that land, over which the " star of
Islamism," to borrow their own metaphor, had
shone in full brightness for nearly eight centuries,
but where it was now fast descending amid clouds
and tempests to the horizon.

The first care of the sovereigns was directed towards repeopling the depopulated city with their
own subjects. Houses and lands were freely granted to such as would settle there. Numerous towns
and villages with a wide circuit of territory were
placed under its civil jurisdiction, and it was made
the head of a diocese embracing most of the recent
conquests in the south and west of Granada. These
inducements, combined with the natural advantages
of position and climate, soon caused the tide of
Christian population to flow into the deserted city ;
but it was very long before it again reached the
degree of commercial consequence to which it had
been raised by the Moors. [32]

Measures for repeopling Malaga.

circumstantial Pulgar should have
omitted to notice so important a
fact as the scheme of the Moorish
ransom, had it occurred. It is still
more improbable, that the honest
Curate of Los Palacios should
have fabricated it. Any one who
attempts to reconcile the discrepancies of contemporary historians even, will have Lord Orford's
exclamation to his son Horace
brought to his mind ten times a
day ; "Oh ! read me not history,
for that I know to be false."

[32] Pulgar, Reyes Católicos, cap
94. — Col. de Céd. tom. vi. no. 321

After these salutary arrangements, the Spanish sovereigns led back their victorious legions in triumph to Cordova, whence dispersing to their various homes, they prepared, by a winter's repose, for new campaigns and more brilliant conquests.

CHAPTER XIV.

WAR OF GRANADA. — CONQUEST OF BAZA. — SUBMISSION OF EL
ZAGAL.

1487 — 1489.

The Sovereigns visit Aragon. — The King lays Siege to Baza. — Its
great Strength. — Gardens cleared of their Timber. — The Queen
raises the Spirits of her Troops. — Her patriotic Sacrifices. — Suspension of Arms. — Baza surrenders. — Treaty with Zagal. — Difficulties of the Campaign. — Isabella's Popularity and Influence.

In the autumn of 1487, Ferdinand and Isabella, CHAPTER
XIV.
accompanied by the younger branches of the royal
family, visited Aragon, to obtain the recognition
from the cortes, of Prince John's succession, now
in his tenth year, as well as to repress the disorders
into which the country had fallen during the long
absence of its sovereigns.　To this end, the principal cities and communities of Aragon had recently
adopted the institution of the hermandad, organized
on similar principles to that of Castile.　Ferdinand,
on his arrival at Saragossa in the month of November, gave his royal sanction to the association, extending the term of its duration to five years, a
measure extremely unpalatable to the great feudal
nobility, whose power, or rather abuse of power,

The sove-
reigns visits
Aragon.

was considerably abridged by this popular military force.[1]

The sovereigns, after accomplishing the objects of their visit, and obtaining an appropriation from the cortes for the Moorish war, passed into Valencia, where measures of like efficiency were adopted for restoring the authority of the law, which was exposed to such perpetual lapses in this turbulent age, even in the best constituted governments, as required for its protection the utmost vigilance, on the part of those intrusted with the supreme executive power. From Valencia the court proceeded to Murcia, where Ferdinand, in the month of June, 1488, assumed the command of an army amounting to less than twenty thousand men, a small force compared with those usually levied on these occasions ; it being thought advisable to suffer the nation to breathe a while, after the exhausting efforts in which it had been unintermittingly engaged for so many years.

Inroads into
Granada.

Ferdinand, crossing the eastern borders of Granada, at no great distance from Vera, which speedily opened its gates, kept along the southern slant of the coast as far as Almeria ; whence. after experiencing some rough treatment from a sortie of the garrison, he marched by a northerly circuit on Baza, for the purpose of reconnoitring its position, as his numbers were altogether inadequate to its siege. A division of the army under the marquis

---

[1] Zurita, Anales, tom. iv. fol. 351, 352, 356. — Mariana, Hist. de España, tcm. ii. lib. 25, cap. 12. — Pulgar, Reyes Católicos part. 3, cap. 95.

duke of Cadiz suffered itself to be drawn here into an ambuscade by the wily old monarch El Zagal, who lay in Baza with a strong force. After extricating his troops with some difficulty and loss from this perilous predicament, Ferdinand retreated on his own dominions by the way of Huescar, where he disbanded his army, and withdrew to offer up his devotions at the cross of Caravaca. The campaign, though signalized by no brilliant achievement, and indeed clouded with some slight reverses, secured the surrender of a considerable number of fortresses and towns of inferior note.[2]

The Moorish chief, El Zagal, elated by his recent success, made frequent forays into the Christian territories, sweeping off the flocks, herds, and growing crops of the husbandman; while the garrisons of Almeria and Salobrena, and the bold inhabitants of the valley of Purchena, poured a similar devastating warfare over the eastern borders of Granada into Murcia. To meet this pressure, the Spanish sovereigns reinforced the frontier with additional levies under Juan de Benavides and Garcilasso de la Vega; while Christian knights, whose prowess is attested in many a Moorish lay, flocked there from all quarters, as to the theatre of war.

During the following winter, of 1488, Ferdinand and Isabella occupied themselves with the interior government of Castile, and particularly the admin-

---

[2] Ferreras, Hist. d'Espagne, tom. viii. p. 76. — Pulgar, Reyes Católicos, cap. 98. — Zuñiga, Anales de Sevilla, p. 402. — Carbajal, Anales, MS., año 1488. donne, Hist. d'Afrique et d'Espagne, tom. iii. pp. 298, 299. —

istration of justice. A commission was specially appointed to supervise the conduct of the corregidors and subordinate magistrates, " so that every one," says Pulgar, " was most careful to discharge his duty faithfully, in order to escape the penalty, which was otherwise sure to overtake him." [3]

Embassy
from Maxi-
milian.
While at Valladolid, the sovereigns received an embassy from Maximilian, son of the emperor Frederic the Fourth, of Germany, soliciting their coöperation in his designs against France for the restitution of his late wife's rightful inheritance, the duchy of Burgundy, and engaging in turn to support them in their claims on Roussillon and Cerdagne. The Spanish monarchs had long entertained many causes of discontent with the French court, both with regard to the mortgaged territory of Roussillon, and the kingdom of Navarre ; and they watched with jealous eye the daily increasing authority of their formidable neighbour on their own frontier. They had been induced in the preceding summer, to equip an armament at Biscay

[3] Conde, Dominacion de los Arabes, tom. iii. pp. 239, 240. — Pulgar, Reyes Católicos, cap. 100, 101. — During the preceding year, while the court was at Murcia, we find one of the examples of prompt and severe exercise of justice, which sometimes occur in this reign. One of the royal collectors having been resisted and personally maltreated by the alcayde of Salvatierra, a place belonging to the crown, and by the alcalde of a territorial court of the duke of Alva, the queen caused one of the royal judges privately to enter into the place, and take cognizance of the affair. The latter, after a brief investigation, commanded the alcayde to be hung up over his fortress, and the alcalde to be delivered over to the court of chancery at Valladolid, who ordered his right hand to be amputated, and banished him the realm. This summary justice was perhaps necessary in a community, that might be said to be in transition from a state of barbarism to that of civilization, and had a salutary effect in proving to the people, that no rank was elevated enough to raise the offender above the law. Pulgar, cap. 99.

and Guipuscoa, to support the duke of Brittany in
his wars with the French regent, the celebrated
Anne de Beaujeu. This expedition, which proved
disastrous, was followed by another in the spring
of the succeeding year.[4] But, notwithstanding
these occasional episodes to the great work in
which they were engaged, they had little leisure
for extended operations; and, although they entered
into the proposed treaty of alliance with Maximilian, they do not seem to have contemplated any
movement of importance before the termination of
the Moorish war. The Flemish ambassadors, after
being entertained for forty days in a style suited to
impress them with high ideas of the magnificence
of the Spanish court, and of its friendly disposition
towards their master, were dismissed with costly
presents, and returned to their own country.[5]

These negotiations show the increasing intimacy
growing up between the European states, who, as
they settled their domestic feuds, had leisure to
turn their eyes abroad, and enter into the more extended field of international politics. The tenor
of this treaty indicates also the direction, which
affairs were to take, when the great powers should

---

[4] Ialigny, Hist. de Charles VIII.,
pp. 92, 94. — Sismondi, Hist. des
Français, tom. xv. p. 77. — Aleson, Annales de Navarra, tom. v.
p. 61. — Histoire du Royaume de
Navarre, pp. 578, 579. — Pulgar,
Reyes Católicos, cap. 102.

In the first of these expeditions,
more than a thousand Spaniards
were slain or taken at the disastrous oattle of St. Aubin, in 1488,
being the same in which lord Riv-

ers, the English noble, who made
such a gallant figure at the siege
of Loja, lost his life. In the spring
of 1489, the levies sent into France
amounted to two thousand in number. These efforts abroad, simultaneous with the great operations
of the Moorish war, show the resources as well as energy of the
sovereigns.

[5] Pulgar, Reyes Católicos, ubi
supra.

Preparations
for the siege
of Baza.

be brought into collision with each other on a common theatre of action.

All thoughts were now concentrated on the prosecution of the war with Granada, which, it was
determined, should be conducted on a more enlarged scale than it had yet been; notwithstanding the
fearful pest which had desolated the country during
the past year, and the extreme scarcity of grain,
owing to the inundations caused by excessive rains
in the fruitful provinces of the south. The great
object proposed in this campaign was the reduction
of Baza, the capital of that division of the empire,
which belonged to El Zagal. Besides this important city, that monarch's dominions embraced the
wealthy sea-port of Almeria, Guadix, and numerous
other towns and villages of less consequence, together with the mountain region of the Alpuxarras,
rich in mineral wealth; whose inhabitants, famous
for the perfection to which they had carried the
silk manufacture, were equally known for their
enterprise and courage in war, so that El Zagal's
division comprehended the most potent and opulent
portion of the empire. [6]

1489.

In the spring of 1489, the Castilian court passed to Jaen, at which place the queen was to estab

---

[6] Bernaldez, Reyes Católicos,
MS., cap. 91. — Zurita, Anales,
tom. iv. fol. 354. — Bleda, Corónica, fol. 607. — Abarca, Reyes
de Aragon, tom. ii. fol. 307.
Such was the scarcity of grain
that the prices in 1489, quoted by
Bernaldez, are double those of the
preceding year. — Both Abarca
and Zurita mention the report, that
four fifths of the whole population
were swept away by the pestilence of 1488. Zurita finds more
difficulty in swallowing this monstrous statement than father Abarca, whose appetite for the marvellous appears to have been fully
equal to that of most of his calling
in Spain.

lish her residence, as presenting the most favorable point of communication with the invading army. Ferdinand advanced as far as Sotogordo, where, on the 27th of May, he put himself at the head of a numerous force, amounting to about fifteen thousand horse and eighty thousand foot, including persons of every description; among whom was gathered, as usual, that chivalrous array of nobility and knighthood, who, with stately and well-appoint ed retinues, were accustomed to follow the royal standard in these crusades.[7]

[7] Peter Martyr, Opus Epist., lib. 2, epist. 70. — Pulgar, Reyes Católicos, cap. 104.

It may not be amiss to specify the names of the most distinguished cavaliers who usually attended the king in these Moorish wars: the heroic ancestors of many a noble house still extant in Spain.

Alonso de Cardenas, master of Saint Jago.

Juan de Zuñiga, master of Alcantara.

Juan Garcia de Padilla, master of Calatrava.

Rodrigo Ponce de Leon, marquis duke of Cadiz.

Enrique de Guzman, duke of Medina Sidonia.

Pedro Manrique, duke of Najera.

Juan Pacheco, duke of Escalona, marquis of Villena.

Juan Pimentel, count of Benavente.

Fadrique de Toledo, son of the duke of Alva.

Diego Fernandez de Cordova, count of Cabra.

Gomez Alvarez de Figueroa, count of Feria.

Alvaro Tellez Giron, count of Ureña.

Juan de Silva, count of Cifuentes.

Fadrique Enriquez, adelantado of Andalusia.

Alonso Fernandez de Cordova, lord of Aguilar.

Gonsalvo de Cordova, brother of the last, known afterwards as the Great Captain.

Luis Porto-Carrero, lord of Palma.

Gutierre de Cardenas, first commander of Leon.

Pedro Fernandez, de Velasco, count of Haro, constable of Castile.

Beltran de la Cueva, duke of Albuquerque.

Diego Fernandez de Cordova, alcayde of the royal pages, afterwards marquis of Comaras.

Alvaro de Zuñiga, duke of Bejar.

Iñigo Lopez de Mendoza, count of Tendilla, afterwards marquis of Mondejar.

Luis de Cerda, duke of Medina Celi.

Iñigo Lopez de Mendoza, marquis of Santillana, second duke of Infantado.

Garcilasso de la Vega, lord of Batras.

The first point, against which operations were directed, was the strong post of Cuxar, two leagues only from Baza, which surrendered after a brief but desperate resistance. The occupation of this place, and some adjacent fortresses, left the approaches open to El Zagal's capital. As the Spanish army toiled up the heights of the mountain barrier, which towers above Baza on the west, their advance was menaced by clouds of Moorish light troops, who poured down a tempest of musket-balls and arrows on their heads. These however were quickly dispersed by the advancing vanguard; and the Spaniards, as they gained the summits of the hills, beheld the lordly city of Baza, reposing in the shadows of the bold sierra that stretches towards the coast, and lying in the bosom of a fruitful valley, extending eight leagues in length, and three in breadth. Through this valley flowed the waters of the Guadalentin and the Guadalquiton, whose streams were conducted by a thousand canals over the surface of the vega. In the midst of the plain, adjoining the suburbs, might be descried the orchard or garden, as it was termed, of Baza, a league in length, covered with a thick growth of wood, and with numerous villas and pleasure-houses of the wealthy citizens, now converted into garrisoned fortresses. The suburbs were encompassed by a low mud wall; but the fortifications of the city were of uncommon strength. The place, in addition to ten thousand troops of its own, was garrisoned by an equal number from Almeria; picked men, under the command of the Moorish prince Cidi Yahye, a relative of E

Zagal, who lay at this time in Guadix, prepared to cover his own dominions against any hostile movement of his rival in Granada. These veterans were commissioned to defend the place to the last extremity; and, as due time had been given for preparation, the town was victualled with fifteen months' provisions, and even the crops growing in the vega had been garnered before their prime, to save them from the hands of the enemy.[8]

The first operation, after the Christian army had encamped before the walls of Baza, was to get possession of the garden, without which it would be impossible to enforce a thorough blockade, since its labyrinth of avenues afforded the inhabitants abundant facilities of communication with the surrounding country. The assault was intrusted to the grand master of St. James, supported by the principal cavaliers, and the king in person. Their reception by the enemy was such as gave them a foretaste of the perils and desperate daring they were to encounter in the present siege. The broken surface of the ground, bewildered with intricate passes, and thickly studded with trees and edifices, was peculiarly favorable to the desultory and illusory tactics of the Moors. The Spanish cavalry was brought at once to a stand; the ground proving impracticable for it, it was dismounted, and led to the charge by its officers on foot. The men, how-

CHAPTER XIV

Assault on the garden.

[8] Zurita, Anales, tom. iv. fol. 70. — Estrada, Poblacion de España, tom. ii. fol. 239. — Marmol, Rebelion de Moriscos, lib. 1, cap. 16. — Conde, Dominacion de los Arabes, tom. iii. p. 241. — Peter Martyr, Opus Epist., lib. 2, epist 16.

PART

ever, were soon scattered far asunder from their banners and their leaders. Ferdinand, who from a central position endeavoured to overlook the field, with the design of supporting the attack on the points most requiring it, soon lost sight of his columns amid the precipitous ravines, and the dense masses of foliage which everywhere intercepted the view. The combat was carried on, hand to hand, in the utmost confusion. Still the Spaniards pressed forward, and, after a desperate struggle for twelve hours, in which many of the bravest on both sides fell, and the Moslem chief Reduan Zafarga had four horses successively killed under him, the enemy were beaten back behind the intrenchments that covered the suburbs, and the Spaniards, hastily constructing a defence of palisades, pitched their tents on the field of battle.[9]

The following morning Ferdinand had the mortification to observe, that the ground was too much broken, and obstructed with wood, to afford a suitable place for a general encampment. To evacuate his position, however, in the face of the enemy, was a delicate manœuvre, and must necessarily expose him to severe loss. This he obviated, in a great measure, by a fortunate stratagem. He commanded the tents nearest the town to be left standing, and thus succeeded in drawing off the greater part

---

[9] Pulgar, Reyes Católicos, cap. 106, 107. — Conde, Dominacion de los Arabes, tom. iii. cap. 40. — Peter Martyr, Opus Epist., epist. 71. — Pulgar relates hese particulars with a perspicuity very different from his entangled narrative of some of the preceding operations in this war. Both he and Martyr were present during the whole siege of Baza.

of his forces, before the enemy was aware of his intention.

CHAPTER
XIV.

Desponden
cy of the
Spanish
chiefs.

After regaining his former position, a council of war was summoned to deliberate on the course next to be pursued. The chiefs were filled with despondency, as they revolved the difficulties of their situation. They almost despaired of enforcing the blockade of a place, whose peculiar situation gave it such advantages. Even could this be effected, the camp would be exposed, they argued, to the assaults of a desperate garrison on the one hand, and of the populous city of Guadix, hardly twenty miles distant, on the other; while the good faith of Granada could scarcely be expected to outlive a single reverse of fortune; so that, instead of besieging, they might be more properly regarded as themselves besieged. In addition to these evils, the winter frequently set in with much rigor in this quarter; and the torrents, descending from the mountains, and mingling with the waters of the valley, might overwhelm the camp with an inundation, which, if it did not sweep it away at once, would expose it to the perils of famine by cutting off all external communication. Under these gloomy impressions, many of the council urged Ferdinand to break up his position at once, and postpone all operations on Baza, until the reduction of the surrounding country should make it comparatively easy. Even the marquis of Cadiz gave in to this opinion; and Gutierre de Cardenas, commander of Leon, a cavalier deservedly high in the confidence of the king, was almost the only person of consideration

decidedly opposed to it. In this perplexity, Ferdinand, as usual in similar exigencies, resolved to
take counsel of the queen.[10]

Isabella received her husband's despatches a few
hours after they were written, by means of the
regular line of posts maintained between the camp
and her station at Jaen. She was filled with chagrin at their import, from which she plainly saw,
that all her mighty preparations were about to
vanish into air. Without assuming the responsibility of deciding the proposed question, however,
she besought her husband not to distrust the providence of God, which had conducted them through
so many perils towards the consummation of their
wishes. She reminded him, that the Moorish fortunes were never at so low an ebb as at present,
and that their own operations could probably never
be resumed on such a formidable scale or under so
favorable auspices as now, when their arms had

[10] Bernaldez, Reyes Católicos,
MS., cap. 92. — Cardonne, Hist.
d'Afrique et d'Espagne, tom. iii.
pp. 299, 300. — Bleda, Corónica,
p. 611. — Garibay, Compendio,
tom. ii. p. 664.

Don Gutierre de Cardenas, who
possessed so high a place in the
confidence of the sovereigns, occupied a station in the queen's
household, as we have seen, at the
time of her marriage with Ferdinand. His discretion and general
ability enabled him to retain the
influence which he had early acquired, as is shown by a popular
distich of that time.

"Cardenas, y el Cardenal, y Chacon, y
        Fray Mortero,
    Traen la Corte al retortero."

Fray Mortero was Don Alonso de

Burgos, bishop of Palencia, confessor of the sovereigns. Don Juan
Chacon was the son of Gonsalvo,
who had the care of Don Alfonso
and the queen during her minority,
when he was induced by the liberal largesses of John II., of Aragon, to promote her marriage with
his son Ferdinand. The elder
Chacon was treated by the sovereigns with the greatest deference
and respect, being usually called
by them "father." After his death,
they continued to manifest a similar regard towards Don Juan, his
eldest son, and heir of his ample
honors and estates. Salazar de
Mendoza, Dignidades, lib. 4, cap. 1.
— Oviedo, Quincuagenas, MS., bat.
1, quinc. 2, dial. 1, 2.

not been stained with a single important reverse.
She concluded with the assurance, that, if his soldiers would be true to their duty, they might rely
on her for the faithful discharge of hers in furnishing them with all the requisite supplies.

The exhilarating tone of this letter had an in-
stantaneous effect, silencing the scruples of the
most timid, and confirming the confidence of the
others.   The soldiers, in particular, who had received with dissatisfaction some intimation of what
was passing in the council, welcomed it with general enthusiasm ; and every heart seemed now intent
on furthering the wishes of their heroic queen by
prosecuting the siege with the utmost vigor.

The army was accordingly distributed into two
encampments ; one under the marquis duke of
Cadiz, supported by the artillery, the other under
king Ferdinand on the opposite side of the city.
Between the two, lay the garden or orchard before
mentioned, extending a league in length ; so that,
in order to connect the works of the two camps, it
became necessary to get possession of this contested ground, and to clear it of the heavy timber with
which it was covered.

This laborious operation was intrusted to the Gardens cleared of their timber.
commander of Leon, and the work was covered by
a detachment of seven thousand troops, posted in
such a manner as to check the sallies of the garrison.   Notwithstanding four thousand *taladores,*
or pioneers, were employed in the task, the forest
was so dense, and the sorties from the city so an-

noying, that the work of devastation did not advance more than ten paces a day, and was not completed before the expiration of seven weeks. When the ancient groves, so long the ornament and protection of the city, were levelled to the ground, preparations were made for connecting the two camps, by a deep trench, through which the mountain waters were made to flow; while the borders were fortified with palisades, constructed of the timber lately hewn, together with strong towers of mud or clay, arranged at regular intervals. In this manner, the investment of the city was complete on the side of the vega. [11]

City closely invested.

As means of communication still remained open, however, by the opposite sierra, defences of similar strength, consisting of two stone walls separated by a deep trench, were made to run along the rocky heights and ravines of the mountains until they touched the extremities of the fortifications on the plain; and thus Baza was encompassed by an unbroken line of circumvallation.

In the progress of the laborious work, which occupied ten thousand men, under the indefatigable commander of Leon, for the space of two months, it would have been easy for the people of Guadix, or of Granada, by coöperation with the sallies of the besieged, to place the Christian army in great peril. Some feeble demonstration of such a movement was made at Guadix, but it was easily dis-

[11] Cardonne, Hist. d'Afrique et d'Espagne, tom. iii. p. 304. — Pulgar, Reyes Católicos, cap. 109. — Peter Martyr, Opus Epist., lib. 2, epist. 73. Bernaldez, Reyes Católicos, MS., cap. 92.

concerted. Indeed, El Zagal was kept in check by the fear of leaving his own territory open to his rival, should he march against the Christians. Abdallah, in the mean while, lay inactive in Granada, incurring the odium and contempt of his people, who stigmatized him as a Christian in heart, and a pensioner of the Spanish sovereigns. Their discontent gradually swelled into a rebellion, which was suppressed by him with a severity, that at length induced a sullen acquiescence in a rule, which, however inglorious, was at least attended with temporary security. [12]

While the camp lay before Baza, a singular mission was received from the sultan of Egypt, who had been solicited by the Moors of Granada to interpose in their behalf with the Spanish sovereigns. Two Franciscan friars, members of a religious community in Palestine, were bearers of despatches; which, after remonstrating with the sovereigns on their persecution of the Moors, contrasted it with the protection uniformly extended by the sultan to the Christians in his dominions. The communication concluded with menacing a retaliation of similar severities on these latter, unless the sovereigns desisted from their hostilities towards Granada.

From the camp, the two ambassadors proceeded to Jaen, where they were received by the queen with all the deference due to their holy profession,

Mission from the Sultan of Egypt

---

12 Conde, Dominacion de los Arabes, tom. iii. cap. 40. — Mariana, Hist. de España, tom. ii. lib. 25, cap. 12. — Pulgar, Reyes Católicos, cap. 111.

which seemed to derive additional sanctity from the spot in which it was exercised. The menacing import of the sultan's communication, however, had no power to shake the purposes of Ferdinand and Isabella, who made answer, that they had uniformly observed the same policy in regard to their Mahometan, as to their Christian subjects; but that they could no longer submit to see their ancient and rightful inheritance in the hands of strangers; and that, if these latter would consent to live under their rule, as true and loyal subjects, they should experience the same paternal indulgence which had been shown to their brethren. With this answer the reverend emissaries returned to the Holy Land, accompanied by substantial marks of the royal favor, in a yearly pension of one thousand ducats, which the queen settled in perpetuity on their monastery, together with a richly embroidered veil, the work of her own fair hands, to be suspended over the Holy Sepulchre. The sovereigns subsequently despatched the learned Peter Martyr as their envoy to the Moslem court, in order to explain their proceedings more at length, and avert any disastrous consequences from the Christian residents. [13]

In the mean while, the siege went forward with spirit; skirmishes and single rencontres taking place every day between the high-mettled cavaliers on both sides. These chivalrous combats, however, were discouraged by Ferdinand, who would

[13] Pulgar, Reyes Católicos, cap. 112.—Ferreras, Hist. d'Espagne tom. viii. p. 86.

have confined his operations to strict blockade, and avoided the unnecessary effusion of blood ; especially as the advantage was most commonly on the side of the enemy, from the peculiar adaptation of their tactics to this desultory warfare. Although some months had elapsed, the besieged rejected with scorn every summons to surrender ; relying on their own resources, and still more on the tempestuous season of autumn, now fast advancing, which, if it did not break up the encampment at once, would at least, by demolishing the roads, cut off all external communication.

In order to guard against these impending evils, Ferdinand caused more than a thousand houses, or rather huts, to be erected, with walls of earth or clay, and roofs made of timber and tiles ; while the common soldiers constructed cabins by means of palisades loosely thatched with the branches of trees. The whole work was accomplished in four days ; and the inhabitants of Baza beheld with amazement a city of solid edifices, with all its streets and squares in regular order, springing as it were by magic out of the ground, which had before been covered with the light and airy pavilions of the camp. The new city was well supplied, owing to the providence of the queen, not merely with the necessaries, but the luxuries of life. Traders flocked there as to a fair, from Aragon, Valencia, Catalonia, and even Sicily, freighted with costly merchandise, and with jewelry and other articles of luxury ; such as, in the indignant lament of an old chronicler, " too often corrupt the

Its strict
discipline.

souls of the soldiery, and bring waste and dissi
pation into a camp."

That this was not the result, however, in the
present instance, is attested by more than one historian. Among others, Peter Martyr, the Italian
scholar before mentioned, who was present at this
siege, dwells with astonishment on the severe decorum and military discipline, which everywhere
obtained among this motley congregation of soldiers.
" Who would have believed," says he, " that the
Galician, the fierce Asturian, and the rude inhabitant
of the Pyrenees, men accustomed to deeds of atrocious violence, and to brawl and battle on the
lightest occasions at home, should mingle amicably,
not only with one another, but with the Toledans,
La-Manchans, and the wily and jealous Andalusian ;
all living together in harmonious subordination to
authority, like members of one family, speaking one
tongue, and nurtured under a common discipline ,
so that the camp seemed like a community modelled
on the principles of Plato's republic ! " In another
part of this letter, which was addressed to a Milanese prelate, he panegyrizes the camp hospital of
the queen, then a novelty in war ; which, he says,
" is so profusely supplied with medical attendants,
apparatus, and whatever may contribute to the restoration or solace of the sick, that it is scarcely
surpassed in these respects by the magnificent
establishments of Milan." [14]

[14] Bernaldez, Reyes Católicos,   lib. 2, epist. 73, 80.—Pulgar, Reyes
MS.—Peter Martyr, Opus Epis*.,   Católicos, cap. 113, 114 117.—

During the five months which the siege had now lasted, the weather had proved uncommonly propitious to the Spaniards, being for the most part of a bland and equal temperature, while the sultry heats of midsummer were mitigated by cool and moderate showers. As the autumnal season advanced, however, the clouds began to settle heavily around the mountains; and at length one of those storms, predicted by the people of Baza, burst forth with incredible fury, pouring a volume of waters down the rocky sides of the sierra, which, mingling with those of the vega, inundated the camp of the besiegers, and swept away most of the frail edifices constructed for the use of the common soldiery. A still greater calamity befell them in the dilapidation of the roads, which, broken up or worn into deep gullies by the force of the waters, were rendered perfectly impassable. All communication was of course suspended with Jaen, and a temporary interruption of the convoys filled the camp with consternation. This disaster, however, was speedily repaired by the queen, who, with an energy always equal to the occasion, caused six thousand pioneers to be at once employed in reconstructing the roads; the rivers were bridged over, causeways new laid, and two separate passes opened through the mountains,

---

Garibay, Compendio, tom. ii. p. 667. — Bleda, Corónica, p. 64.

The plague, which fell heavily this year on some parts of Andalusia, does not appear to have attacked the camp, which Bleda imputes to the healing influence of the Spanish sovereigns, " whose good faith, religion, and virtue, banished the contagion from their army, where it must otherwise have prevailed." Personal comforts and cleanliness of the soldiers, though not quite so miraculous a cause, may be considered perhaps full as efficacious.

by which the convoys might visit the camp, and return without interrupting each other. At the same time, the queen bought up immense quantities of grain from all parts of Andalusia, which she caused to be ground in her own mills; and when the roads, which extended more than seven leagues in length, were completed, fourteen thousand mules might be seen daily traversing the sierra, laden with supplies, which from that time forward were poured abundantly, and with the most perfect regularity, into the camp.[15]

Isabella's energy.

Isabella's next care was to assemble new levies of troops, to relieve or reinforce those now in the camp; and the alacrity with which all orders of men from every quarter of the kingdom answered her summons is worthy of remark. But her chief solicitude was to devise expedients for meeting the enormous expenditures incurred by the protracted operations of the year. For this purpose, she had recourse to loans from individuals and religious corporations, which were obtained without much difficulty, from the general confidence in her good faith. As the sum thus raised, although exceedingly large for that period, proved inadequate to the expenses, further supplies were obtained from wealthy individuals, whose loans were secured by mortgage of the royal demesne; and, as a deficiency still remained in the treasury, the queen, as a last resource, pawned the crown jewels and her own personal ornaments to the merchants of Barcelona

Her patriotic sacrifices

---

[15] Peter Martyr, Opus Epist., lib. 2, epist. 73. — Pulgar, Reyes Católicos, cap. 116.

and Valencia, for such sums as they were willing
to advance on them. [16] Such were the efforts made
by this high-spirited woman, for the furtherance of
her patriotic enterprise. The extraordinary results,
which she was enabled to effect, are less to be ascribed to the authority of her station, than to that
perfect confidence in her wisdom and virtue, with
which she had inspired the whole nation, and which
secured their earnest coöperation in all her undertakings. The empire, which she thus exercised,
indeed, was far more extended than any station
however exalted, or any authority however des-
potic, can confer ; for it was over the hearts of her
people.

Notwithstanding the vigor with which the siege
was pressed, Baza made no demonstration of submission. The garrison was indeed greatly reduced
in number ; the ammunition was nearly expended ;
yet there still remained abundant supplies of provisions in the town, and no signs of despondency
appeared among the people. Even the women of
the place, with a spirit emulating that of the dames
of ancient Carthage, freely gave up their jewels,
bracelets, necklaces, and other personal ornaments,

Resolution
of the be-
sieged.

[16] Pulgar, Reyes Católicos, cap.
118. — Archivo de Simancas, in
Mem. de la Acad. de Hist., tom.
vi. p. 311.

The city of Valencia lent 35,000
florins on the crown and 20,000
on a collar of rubies. They
were not wholly redeemed till
1495. Señor Clemencin has given
a catalogue of the royal jewels,
(see Mem. de la Acad. de Hist.,

tom. vi. Ilustracion 6,) which appear to have been extremely rich
and numerous, for a period anterior to the discovery of those
countries, whose mines have since
furnished Europe with its *bijou-
terie.* Isabella, however, set so little value on them, that she divested herself of most of them in
favor of her daughters.

of which the Moorish ladies were exceedingly fond, in order to defray the charges of the mercenaries.

The camp of the besiegers, in the mean while, was also greatly wasted both by sickness and the sword. Many, desponding under perils and fatigues, which seemed to have no end, would even at this late hour have abandoned the siege; and they earnestly solicited the queen's appearance in the camp, in the hope that she would herself countenance this measure, on witnessing their sufferings. Others, and by far the larger part, anxiously desired the queen's visit, as likely to quicken the operations of the siege, and bring it to a favorable issue. There seemed to be a virtue in her presence, which, on some account or other, made it earnestly desired by all.

Isabella yielded to the general wish, and on the 7th of November arrived before the camp, attended by the infanta Isabella, the cardinal of Spain, her friend the marchioness of Moya, and other ladies of the royal household. The inhabitants of Baza, says Bernaldez, lined the battlements and housetops, to gaze at the glittering cavalcade as it emerged from the depths of the mountains, amidst flaunting banners and strains of martial music, while the Spanish cavaliers thronged forth in a body from the camp to receive their beloved mistress, and gave her the most animated welcome. "She came," says Martyr, "surrounded by a choir of nymphs, as if to celebrate the nuptials of her child; and her presence seemed at once to gladden and reanimate our spirits, drooping under long vigils, dangers, and fatigue." Another writer, also present, remarks, that, from the moment of her appearance, a change seemed to come over the scene. No more of the cruel skirmishes, which had before occurred every day; no report of artillery, or clashing of arms, or any of the rude sounds of war, was to be heard, but all seemed disposed to reconcilia tion and peace.[17]

The Moors probably interpreted Isabella's visit into an assurance, that the Christian army would never rise from before the place until its surrender. Whatever hopes they had once entertained of wearying out the besiegers, were therefore now dispelled. Accordingly, a few days after the queen's arrival, we find them proposing a parley for arranging terms of capitulation.

On the third day after her arrival, Isabella reviewed her army, stretched out in order of battle along the slope of the western hills; after which, she proceeded to reconnoitre the beleaguered city, accompanied by the king and the cardinal of Spain, together with a brilliant escort of the Spanish chivalry. On the same day, a conference was opened with the enemy through the *comendador* of Leon; and an armistice arranged, to continue until the old monarch, El Zagal, who then lay at Guadix, could be informed of the real condition of the besieged,

Suspension of arms.

17 Bernaldez, Reyes Católicos, MS., cap. 92. — Pulgar, Reyes Católicos, cap 120, 121. — Ferre- ras, Hist. d'Espagne, tom. viii. p. 93. — Peter Martyr, Opus Epist., lib. 3, epist. 80.

PART
I.
_____

Baza surren-
ders.

and his instructions be received, determining the
course to be adopted.

The alcayde of Baza represented to his master
the low state to which the garrison was reduced by
the loss of lives and the failure of ammunition.
Still, he expressed such confidence in the spirit of his
people, that he undertook to make good his defence
some time longer, provided any reasonable expectation of succour could be afforded ; otherwise, it
would be a mere waste of life, and must deprive
him of such vantage ground as he now possessed,
for enforcing an honorable capitulation. The Moslem prince acquiesced in the reasonableness of
these representations. He paid a just tribute to
his brave kinsman Cidi Yahye's loyalty, and the
gallantry of his defence ; but, confessing at the
same time his own inability to relieve him, authorized him to negotiate the best terms of surrender
which he could, for himself and garrison. [18]

Conditions.

A mutual desire of terminating the protracted
hostilities infused a spirit of moderation into both
parties, which greatly facilitated the adjustment of
the articles. Ferdinand showed none of the arrogant bearing, which marked his conduct towards
the unfortunate people of Malaga, whether from a
conviction of its impolicy, or, as is more probable,
because the city of Baza was itself in a condition
to assume a more imposing attitude. The principal

_____

[18] Peter Martyr, Opus Epist.,   — Carbajal, Anales, MS , año
lib. 3, epist. 80. — Conde, Domina-   1489. — Cardonne, Hist. d'Afriqua
cion de los Arabes, tom. iii. p. 242. et d'Espagne, tom. iii. p. 305.

stipulations of the treaty were, that the foreign
mercenaries employed in the defence of the place
should be allowed to march out with the honors of
war; that the city should be delivered up to the
Christians; but that the natives might have the
choice of retiring with their personal effects where
they listed; or of occupying the suburbs, as subjects of the Castilian crown, liable only to the same
tribute which they paid to their Moslem rulers, and
secured in the enjoyment of their property, religion,
laws, and usages. [19]

On the fourth day of December, 1489, Ferdinand and Isabella took possession of Baza, at the
head of their legions, amid the ringing of bells, the
peals of artillery, and all the other usual accompaniments of this triumphant ceremony; while the standard of the Cross, floating from the ancient battlements of the city, proclaimed the triumph of the
Christian arms. The brave alcayde, Cidi Yahye,
experienced a reception from the sovereigns very
different from that of the bold defender of Malaga.
He was loaded with civilities and presents; and
these acts of courtesy so won upon his heart, that he
expressed a willingness to enter into their service.
" Isabella's compliments," says the Arabian historian, drily, " were repaid in more substantial coin."

Cidi Yahye was soon prevailed on to visit his
royal kinsman El Zagal, at Guadix, for the purpose
of urging his submission to the Christian sovereigns.
In his interview with that prince, he represented

Marginal notes:
CHAPTER XIV.

Occupation of the city.

Treaty of surrender with El Zagal.

---

[19] Pulgar, Reyes Católicos, cap. 124. — Marmol, Rebelion de Moris-
tos, lib. 1, cap. 16.

the fruitlessness of any attempt to withstand the accumulated forces of the Spanish monarchies; that he would only see town after town pared away from his territory, until no ground was left for him to stand on, and make terms with the victor. He reminded him, that the baleful horoscope of Abdallah had predicted the downfall of Granada, and that experience had abundantly shown how vain it was to struggle against the tide of destiny. The unfortunate monarch listened, says the Arabian annalist, without so much as moving an eyelid; and, after a long and deep meditation, replied with the resignation characteristic of the Moslems, " What Allah wills, he brings to pass in his own way. Had he not decreed the fall of Granada, this good sword might have saved it; but his will be done!" It was then arranged, that the principal cities of Almeria, Guadix, and their dependencies, constituting the domain of El Zagal, should be formally surrendered by that prince to Ferdinand and Isabella, who should instantly proceed at the head of their army to take possession of them. [20]

Painful march of the Spanish army.

On the seventh day of December, therefore, the Spanish sovereigns, without allowing themselves or their jaded troops any time for repose, marched out of the gates of Baza, king Ferdinand occupying the centre, and the queen the rear of the army. Their route lay across the most savage district of the long sierra, which stretches towards Almeria; leading

[20] Conde, Dominacion de los Arabes, tom iii. cap. 40. — Bleda, Corónica, p. 612. — Bernaldez, Reyes Católicos, MS., cap. 92. — Marmol, Rebelion de Moriscos, lib 1, cap. 16.

through many a narrow pass, which a handful of resolute Moors, says an eyewitness, might have made good against the whole Christian army, over mountains whose peaks were lost in clouds, and valleys whose depths were never warmed by a sun. The winds were exceedingly bleak, and the weather inclement, so that men, as well as horses, exhausted by the fatigues of previous service, were benumbed by the intense cold, and many of them frozen to death. Many more, losing their way in the intricacies of the sierra, would have experienced the same miserable fate, had it not been for the marquis of Cadiz, whose tent was pitched on one of the loftiest hills, and who caused beacon fires to be lighted around it, in order to guide the stragglers back to their quarters.

At no great distance from Almeria, Ferdinand Interview between Ferdinand and El Zagal. was met, conformably to the previous arrangement, by El Zagal, escorted by a numerous body of Moslem cavaliers. Ferdinand commanded his nobles to ride forward and receive the Moorish prince. " His appearance," says Martyr, who was in the royal retinue, " touched my soul with compassion ; for, although a lawless barbarian, he was a king, and had given signal proofs of heroism." El Zagal, without waiting to receive the courtesies of the Spanish nobles, threw himself from his horse, and advanced towards Ferdinand with the design of kissing his hand ; but the latter, rebuking his followers for their " rusticity," in allowing such an act of humiliation in the unfortunate monarch, prevailed on him to remount, and then rode by his side towards Almeria. [21]

This city was one of the most precious jewels in the diadem of Granada. It had amassed great wealth by its extensive commerce with Syria, Egypt, and Africa; and its corsairs had for ages been the terror of the Catalan and Pisan marine It might have stood a siege as long as that of Baza, but it was now surrendered without a blow, on conditions similar to those granted to the former city. After allowing some days for the refreshment of their wearied forces in this pleasant region, which, sheltered from the bleak winds of the north by the sierra they had lately traversed, and fanned by the gentle breezes of the Mediterranean, is compared by Martyr to the gardens of the Hesperides, the sovereigns established a strong garrison there, under the commander of Leon, and then, striking again into the recesses of the mountains, marched on Guadix, which, after some opposition on the part of the populace, threw open its gates to them. The surrender of these principal cities was followed by that of all the subordinate dependencies belonging to El Zagal's territory, comprehending a multitude of hamlets scattered along the green sides of the mountain chain that stretched from Granada to the coast. To all these places the same liberal terms, in regard to personal rights and property, were secured, as to Baza.

[21] Peter Martyr, Opus Epist., lib. 3, epist. 81. — Cardonne, Hist. d'Afrique et d'Espagne, tom. iii. p. 340. — Pulgar, Reyes Católicos, loc. cit. — Conde, Dominacion de los Arabes, tom. iii. cap. 40

As an equivalent for these broad domains, the **CHAPTER XIV.**
Moorish chief was placed in possession of the *taha*,
or district, of Andaraz, the vale of Alhaurin, and
half the salt-pits of Maleha, together with a considerable revenue in money. He was, moreover, to
receive the title of King of Andaraz, and to render
homage for his estates to the crown of Castile.

Equivalent assigned to him.

This shadow of royalty could not long amuse the
mind of the unfortunate prince. He pined away
amid the scenes of his ancient empire ; and, after
experiencing some insubordination on the part of
his new vassals, he determined to relinquish his
petty principality, and withdraw for ever from his
native land. Having received a large sum of
money, as an indemnification for the entire cession
of his territorial rights and possessions to the Castilian crown, he passed over to Africa, where, it is
reported, he was plundered of his property by the
barbarians, and condemned to starve out the remainder of his days in miserable indigence.[22]

The suspicious circumstances attending this
prince's accession to the throne, throw a dark
cloud over his fame, which would otherwise seem,
at least as far as his public life is concerned, to be
unstained by any opprobrious act. He possessed
such energy, talent, and military science, as, had
he been fortunate enough to unite the Moorish
nation under him by an undisputed title, might

[22] El Nubiense, Descripcion de España, p. 160, not. — Carbajal, Anales, MS., año 1488. — Cardonne, Hist. d'Afrique et d'Espagne, tom. iii. p. 304. -- Peter Martyr, Opus Epist., lib. 3, epist. 81. — Conde, Dominacion de los Arabes, tom. iii. pp. 245, 246. — Bernaldez, Reyes Católicos, MS., cap. 93.

have postponed the fall of Granada for many years.
As it was, these very talents, by dividing the state
in his favor, served only to precipitate its ruin.

1490.   The Spanish sovereigns, having accomplished
the object of the campaign, after stationing part of
their forces on such points as would secure the permanence of their conquests, returned with the remainder to Jaen, where they disbanded the army
on the 4th of January, 1490.   The losses sustained
by the troops, during the whole period of their
prolonged service, greatly exceeded those of any
former year, amounting to not less than twenty
thousand men, by far the larger portion of whom
are said to have fallen victims to diseases incident
to severe and long-continued hardships and exposure.[23]

Difficulties
of this cam-
paign.

Thus terminated the eighth year of the war of
Granada ; a year more glorious to the Christian
arms, and more important in its results, than any
of the preceding.   During this period, an army of
eighty thousand men had kept the field, amid all
the inclemencies of winter, for more than seven
months ; an effort scarcely paralleled in these times,
when both the amount of levies, and period of service, were on the limited scale adapted to the exigencies of feudal warfare.[24]   Supplies for this im-

---

[23] Zurita, Anales, tom. *i*. fol.
360. — Abarca, Reyes de Aragon,
tom. ii. fol. 308.

[24] The city of Seville alone
maintained 600 horse and 8,000

foot under the count of Cifuentes,
for the space of eight months during this siege.   See Zuñiga, Annales de Sevilla, p. 404.

Notice of
Pater Mar-
tyr.

Pietro Martire, or, as he is called in English, Peter Martyr, so

often quoted in the present chapter, and who will constitute one

mense host, notwithstanding the severe famine of
the preceding year, were punctually furnished, in
spite of every embarrassment presented by the want
of navigable rivers, and the interposition of a pre
cipitous and pathless sierra.

The history of this campaign is, indeed, most
honorable to the courage, constancy, and thorough
discipline of the Spanish soldier, and to the patriotism and general resources of the nation ; but most
of all to Isabella. She it was, who fortified the

of our best authorities during the remainder of the history, was a native of Arona (not of Anghiera, as commonly supposed), a place situated on the borders of Lake Maggiore in Italy. (Mazzuchel-.i, Scrittori d' Italia, (Brescia, 1753 –63,) tom. ii. *voce* Anghiera.) He was of noble Milanese extraction. In 1477, at twenty-two years of age, he was sent to complete his education at Rome, where he continued ten years, and formed an intimacy with the most distinguished literary characters of that cultivated capital. In 1487, he was persuaded by the Castilian ambassador, the count of Tendilla, to accompany him to Spain, where he was received with marked distinction by the queen, who would have at once engaged him in the tuition of the young nobility of the court, but, Martyr having expressed a preference of a military life, she, with her usual delicacy, declined to press him on the point. He was present, as we have seen, at the siege of Baza, and continued with the army during the subsequent campaigns of the Moorish war. Many passages of his correspondence, at this period, show a whimsical mixture of self-complacency with a consciousness of the ludicrous figure which he made in " exchanging the Muses for Mars."

At the close of the war, he entered the ecclesiastical profession, for which he had been originally destined, and was persuaded to resume his literary vocation. He opened his school at Valladolid, Saragossa, Barcelona, Alcalá de Henares, and other places ; and it was thronged with the principal young nobility from all parts of Spain, who, as he boasts in one of his letters, drew their literary nourishment from him. " Suxerunt mea literalia ubera Castellæ principes fere omnes." His important services were fully estimated by the queen, and, after her death, by Ferdinand and Charles V., and he was recompensed with high ecclesiastical preferment as well as civil dignities. He died about the year 1525, at the age of seventy, and his remains were interred beneath a monument in the cathedral church of Granada, of which he was prior.

Among Martyr's principal works is a treatise " De Legatione Babylonicà," being an account of a visit to the sultan of Egypt, in 1501, for the purpose of deprecating the retaliation with which he had menaced the Christian residents in Palestine, for the injuries inflicted on the Spanish Moslems. Peter Martyr conducted his negotiation with such address, that he not only

timid councils of the leaders, after the disasters of the garden, and encouraged them to persevere in the siege. She procured all the supplies, constructed the roads, took charge of the sick, and furnished, at no little personal sacrifice, the immense sums demanded for carrying on the war; and, when at last the hearts of the soldiers were fainting under long-protracted sufferings, she appeared among them, like some celestial visitant, to cheer their faltering spirits, and inspire them with her own energy.

appeased the sultan's resentment, but obtained several important immunities for his Christian subjects, in addition to those previously enjoyed by them.

He also wrote an account of the discoveries of the new world, entitled "De Rebus Oceanicis et Novo Orbe," (Coloniæ, 1574,) a book largely consulted and commended by subsequent historians. But the work of principal value in our researches is his "Opus Epistolarum," being a collection of his multifarious correspondence with the most considerable persons of his time, whether in political or literary life. The letters are in Latin, and extend from the year 1488 to the time of his death. Although not conspicuous for elegance of diction, they are most valuable to the historian, from the fidelity and general accuracy of the details, as well as for the intelligent criticism in which they abound, for all which, uncommon facilities were afforded by the writer's intimacy with the leading actors, and the most recondite sources of information of the period.

This high character is fully authorized by the judgments of those best qualified to pronounce on their merits, — Martyr's own contemporaries. Among these, Dr. Galindez de Carbajal, a counsellor of King Ferdinand and constantly employed in the highest concerns of state, commends these epistles as "the work of a learned and upright man, well calculated to throw light on the transactions of the period." (Anales, MS., prólogo.) Alvaro Gomez, another contemporary who survived Martyr, in the Life of Ximenes, which he was selected to write by the University of Alcalá, declares, that "Martyr's Letters abundantly compensate by their fidelity for the unpolished style in which they are written." (De Rebus Gestis, fol. 6.) And John de Vergara, a name of the highest celebrity in the literary annals of the period, expresses himself in the following emphatic terms. "I know no record of the time more accurate and valuable. I myself have often witnessed the promptness with which he put down things the moment they occurred. I have sometimes seen him write one or two letters, while they were setting the table. For, as he did not pay much attention to style and mere finish of expression, his composition required but little time, and experienced no interruption from his ordinary avocations." (See his letter to Florian de Ocampo, apud Quintanilla y Mendoza, Archetypo de Virtudes, Espejo de Prelados, el Venerable

The attachment to Isabella seemed to be a per- vading principle, which animated the whole nation by one common impulse, impressing a unity of design on all its movements. This attachment was imputable to her sex as well as character. The sympathy and tender care, with which she regarded her people, naturally raised a reciprocal sentiment in their bosoms. But, when they beheld her directing their counsels, sharing their fatigues and dangers, and displaying all the comprehensive intellectual powers of the other sex, they looked up to her as to some superior being, with feelings far

Padre y Siervo de Dios, F. Francisco Ximenez de Cisneros, (Paermo, 1653,) Archivo, p. 4.) This account of the precipitate manner in which the epistles were composed, may help to explain the cause of the occasional inconsistencies and anachronisms, that are to be found in them; and which their author, had he been more patient of the labor of revision, would doubtless have corrected. But he seems to have had little relish for this, even in his more elaborate works, composed with a view to publication. (See his own honest confessions in his book "De Rebus Oceanicis," dec. 8, cap. 8, 9.) After all, the errors, such as they are, in his Epistles, may probably be chiefly charged on the publisher. The first edition appeared at Alcalá de Henares, in 1530, about four years after the author's death. It has now become exceedingly rare. The second and last, being the one used in the present History, came out in a more beautiful form from the Elzevir press, Amsterdam, in 1670, folio. Of this also but a small number of copies were struck off. The learned editor takes much credit to himself

for having purified the work from many errors, which had flowed from the heedlessness of his predecessor. It will not be difficult to detect several yet remaining. Such, for example, as a memorable letter on the *lues venerea* (No. 68.) obviously misplaced, even according to its own date; and that numbered 168, in which two letters are evidently blended into one. But it is unnecessary to multiply examples. — It is very desirable, that an edition of this valuable correspondence should be published, under the care of some one qualified to illustrate it by his intimacy with the history of the period, as well as to correct the various inaccuracies which have crept into it, whether through the carelessness of the author or of his editors.

I have been led into this length of remark by some strictures which met my eye in the recent work of Mr. Hallam; who intimates his belief, that the Epistles of Martyr, instead of being written at their respective dates, were produced by him at some later period; (Introduction to the Literature of Europe, (London, 1837,) vol. i. pp. 439 – 441;) a conclusion which I

more exalted than those of mere loyalty. The
chivalrous heart of the Spaniard did homage to her,
as to his tutelar saint; and she held a control over
her people, such as no man could have acquired in
any age, — and probably no woman, in an age and
country less romantic.

suspect this acute and candid critic
would have been slow to adopt,
had he perused the correspondence
in connexion with the history of
the times, or weighed the unqualified testimony borne by contempo
raries to its minute accuracy.

CHAPTER XV.

WAR OF GRANADA. — SIEGE AND SURRENDER OF THE CITY
OF GRANADA.

1490 — 1492.

The Infanta Isabella affianced to the Prince of Portugal. — Isabella deposes Judges at Valladolid. — Encampment before Granada. — The Queen surveys the City. — Moslem and Christian Chivalry. — Conflagration of the Christian Camp. — Erection of Santa Fe. — Capitulation of Granada. — Results of the War. — Its moral Influence. — Its military Influence. — Fate of the Moors. — Death and Character of the Marquis of Cadiz.

IN the spring of 1490, ambassadors arrived from Lisbon for the purpose of carrying into effect the treaty of marriage, which had been arranged between Alonso, heir of the Portuguese monarchy, and Isabella, infanta of Castile. An alliance with this kingdom, which from its contiguity possessed such ready means of annoyance to Castile, and which had shown such willingness to employ them in enforcing the pretensions of Joanna Beltraneja, was an object of importance to Ferdinand and Isabella. No inferior consideration could have reconciled the queen to a separation from this beloved daughter, her eldest child, whose gentle and uncommonly amiable disposition seems to have endeared her beyond their other children to her parents.

The ceremony of the affiancing took place at Se·
ville, in the month of April, Don Fernando de Sil-
veira appearing as the representative of the prince
of Portugal; and it was followed by a succession
of splendid *fêtes* and tourneys. Lists were en-
closed, at some distance from the city on the shores
of the Guadalquivir, and surrounded with galleries
hung with silk and cloth of gold, and protected
from the noontide heat by canopies or awnings,
richly embroidered with the armorial bearings of
the ancient houses of Castile. The spectacle was
graced by all the rank and beauty of the court,
with the infanta Isabella in the midst, attended by
seventy noble ladies, and a hundred pages of the
royal household. The cavaliers of Spain, young
and old, thronged to the tournament, as eager to
win laurels on the mimic theatre of war, in the
presence of so brilliant an assemblage, as they had
shown themselves in the sterner contests with the
Moors. King Ferdinand, who broke several lances
on the occasion, was among the most distinguished
of the combatants for personal dexterity and horse-
manship. The martial exercises of the day were
relieved by the more effeminate recreations of dancing and music in the evening; and every one
seemed willing to welcome the season of hilarity,
after the long-protracted fatigues of war.[1]

In the following autumn, the infanta was escort-

[1] Carbajal, Anales, MS., año
1490. — Bernaldez, Reyes Católicos, MS., cap. 95. — Zuñiga, Annales de Sevilla, pp. 404, 405. —
Pulgar, Reyes Católicos, part. 3,
cap. 127. — La Clède, Hist. de
Portugal, tom. iv. p. 19. — Faria
y Sousa, Europa Portuguesa, tom.
ii. p. 452.

ed into Portugal by the cardinal of Spain, the CHAPTER
XV.
grand master of St. James, and a numerous and
magnificent retinue. Her dowry exceeded that
usually assigned to the infantas of Castile, by five
hundred marks of gold and a thousand of silver;
and her wardrobe was estimated at one hundred
and twenty thousand gold florins. The contemporary chroniclers dwell with much complacency on
these evidences of the stateliness and splendor of
the Castilian court. Unfortunately, these fair auspices were destined to be clouded too soon by the
death of the prince, her husband.[2]

No sooner had the campaign of the preceding Granada
summoned
in vain.
year been brought to a close, than Ferdinand and
Isabella sent an embassy to the king of Granada,
requiring a surrender of his capital, conformably to
his stipulations at Loja, which guarantied this, on
the capitulation of Baza, Almeria, and Guadix.
That time had now arrived; King Abdallah, however, excused himself from obeying the summons
of the Spanish sovereigns, replying that he was no
longer his own master, and that, although he had
all the inclination to keep his engagements, he
was prevented by the inhabitants of the city, now
swollen much beyond its natural population, who
resolutely insisted on its defence.[3]

[2] Faria y Sousa, Europa Portu-
gesa, tom. ii. p. 452–456. — Florez, Reynas Cathólicas, p. 845. —
Pulgar, Reyes Católicos, cap. 129.
— Oviedo, Quincuagenas, MS., bat.
1, quinc. 2, dial. 3.
[3] Conde, Dominacion de los Arabes, tom. iii. cap. 41. — Bernal-

dez, Reyes Católicos, MS., cap.
90.
    Neither the Arabic nor Castilian
authorities impeach the justice of
the summons made by the Spanish
sovereigns. I do not, however,
find any other foundation for the
obligation imputed to Abdallah in

It is not probable that the Moorish king did any great violence to his feelings, in this evasion of a promise extorted from him in captivity. At least, it would seem so from the hostile movements which immediately succeeded. The people of Granada resumed all at once their ancient activity, foraying into the Christian territories, surprising Alhendin and some other places of less importance, and stirring up the spirit of revolt in Guadix and other conquered cities. Granada, which had slept through the heat of the struggle, seemed to revive at the very moment when exertion became hopeless.

Ferdinand was not slow in retaliating these acts of aggression. In the spring of 1490, he marched with a strong force into the cultivated plain of Granada, sweeping off, as usual, the crops and cattle, and rolling the tide of devastation up to the very

Knighthood
of Don Juan.

walls of the city. In this campaign he conferred the honor of knighthood on his son, prince John, then only twelve years of age, whom he had brought with him, after the ancient usage of the Castilian nobles, of training up their children from very tender years in the Moorish wars. The ceremony was performed on the banks of the grand canal under the battlements almost of the beleaguered city. The dukes of Cadiz and Medina Sidonia were prince John's sponsors; and, after the

them, than that monarch's agreement during his captivity at Loja, in 1486, to surrender his capital in exchange for Guadix, provided the latter should be conquered within six months. Pulgar, Reyes Católicos, p. 275. — Garibay, Compendio, tom. iv. p. 418.

completion of the ceremony, the new knight conferred the honors of chivalry in like manner on
several of his young companions in arms. [4]

In the following autumn, Ferdinand repeated his
ravages in the vega, and, at the same time appearing before the disaffected city of Guadix with a
force large enough to awe it into submission, proposed an immediate investigation of the conspiracy
He promised to inflict summary justice on all who
had been in any degree concerned in it ; at the
same time offering permission to the inhabitants, in
the abundance of his clemency, to depart with all
their personal effects wherever they would, provid
ed they should prefer this to a judicial investigation of their conduct. This politic proffer had its
effect. There were few, if any of the citizens,
who had not been either directly concerned in the
conspiracy, or privy to it. With one accord, therefore, they preferred exile to trusting to the tender
mercies of their judges. In this way, says the
Curate of Los Palacios, by the mystery of our
Lord, was the ancient city of Guadix brought again
within the Christian fold ; the mosques converted
into Christian temples, filled with the harmonies of
Catholic worship, and the pleasant places, which
for nearly eight centuries had been trampled under
the foot of the infidel, were once more restored to
the followers of the Cross.

A similar policy produced similar results in the

---

[4] L. Marineo, Cosas Memorables, fol. 176. — Pulgar, Reyes
Católicos, cap. 130. — Zurita, Anales, tom. iv. cap. 85. — Cardonne,
Hist. d'Afrique et d'Espagne, tom.
iii. p. 309.

cities of Almeria and Baza, whose inhabitants, evacuating their ancient homes, transported themselves,
with such personal effects as they could carry, to
the city of Granada, or the coast of Africa. The
space thus opened by the fugitive population was
quickly filled by the rushing tide of Spaniards. [5]

It is impossible at this day, to contemplate these
events with the triumphant swell of exultation,
with which they are recorded by contemporary
chroniclers. That the Moors were guilty (though
not so generally as pretended) of the alleged conspiracy, is not in itself improbable, and is corroborated indeed by the Arabic statements. But the
punishment was altogether disproportionate to the
offence. Justice might surely have been satisfied
by a selection of the authors and principal agents
of the meditated insurrection ; — for no overt act
appears to have occurred. But avarice was too
strong for justice ; and this act, which is in perfect
conformity to the policy systematically pursued by
the Spanish crown for more than a century afterwards, may be considered as one of the first links
in the long chain of persecution, which terminated
in the expulsion of the Moriscoes.

Isabella
deposes the
judges of
chancery.

During the following year, 1491, a circumstance
occurred illustrative of the policy of the present
government in reference to ecclesiastical matters.
The chancery of Valladolid having appealed to the

---

[5] Pulgar, Reyes Católicos, cap.
131, 132. — Bernaldez, Reyes Católicos, MS., cap. 97. — Conde,
Dominacion de los Arabes, tom.
iii. cap. 41.—Peter Martyr, Opus
Epist., lib. 3, epist. 84. — Garibay
Compendio, tom. iv. p. 424. — Cardonne, Hist. d'Afrique et d'Espagne, tom. iii. pp. 309, 310.

pope in a case coming within its own exclusive
jurisdiction, the queen commanded Alonso de Val-
divieso, bishop of Leon, the president of the court,
together with all the auditors, to be removed from
their respective offices, which she delivered to a
new board, having the bishop of Oviedo at its head.
This is one among many examples of the constancy with which Isabella, notwithstanding her
reverence for religion, and respect for its ministers,
refused to compromise the national independence
by recognising in any degree the usurpations of
Rome. From this dignified attitude, so often abandoned by her successors, she never swerved for a
moment during the course of her long reign.[6]

The winter of 1490 was busily occupied with
preparations for the closing campaign against Granada. Ferdinand took command of the army in the
month of April, 1491, with the purpose of sitting
down before the Moorish capital, not to rise until
its final surrender. The troops, which mustered in
the Val de Velillos, are computed by most historians at fifty thousand horse and foot, although
Martyr, who served as a volunteer, swells the number to eighty thousand. They were drawn from
the different cities, chiefly, as usual, from Andalusia,
which had been stimulated to truly gigantic efforts
throughout this protracted war,[7] and from the nobility of every quarter, many of whom, wearied out

---

6 Carbajal, Anales, MS., año   horse, who were recruited by fresh
1491.   reinforcements no less than five
  7 According to Zuñiga, the quota   times during the campaign. An-
furnished by Seville this season   nales de Sevilla, p. 406.—See also
amounted to 6,000 foot and 500   Col. de Cédulas, tom. iii. no. 3.

with the contest, contented themselves with sending their quotas, while many others, as the mar
quises of Cadiz, Villena, the counts of Tendilla
Cabra, Ureña, and Alonso de Aguilar, appeared ir
person, eager, as they had borne the brunt of so
many hard campaigns, to share in the closing scene
of triumph.

On the 26th of the month, the army encamped
near the fountain of Ojos de Huescar, in the vega,
about two leagues distant from Granada. Ferdinand's first movement was to detach a considerable
force, under the marquis of Villena, which he subsequently supported in person with the remainder
of the army, for the purpose of scouring the fruitful regions of the Alpuxarras, which served as the
granary of the capital. This service was performed
with such unsparing rigor, that no less than twenty-
four towns and hamlets in the mountains were
ransacked, and razed to the ground. After this,
Ferdinand returned loaded with spoil to his former
position on the banks of the Xenil, in full view of
the Moorish metropolis, which seemed to stand
alone, like some sturdy oak, the last of the forest,
bidding defiance to the storm which had prostrated
all its brethren.

Notwithstanding the failure of all external resources, Granada was still formidable from its local
position and its defences. On the east it was
fenced in by a wild mountain barrier, the *Sierra
Nevada*, whose snow-clad summits diffused a grateful coolness over the city through the sultry heats
of summer. The side towards the vega, facing the

Christian encampment, was encircled by walls and towers of massive strength and solidity. The population, swelled to two hundred thousand by the immigration from the surrounding country, was likely, indeed, to be a burden in a protracted siege ; but among them were twenty thousand, the flower of the Moslem chivalry, who had escaped the edge of the Christian sword. In front of the city, for an extent of nearly ten leagues, lay unrolled, the magnificent vega,

> " Fresca y regalada vega,
> Dulce recreacion de damas
> Y de hombres gloria immensa ; "

whose prolific beauties could scarcely be exaggerated in the most florid strains of the Arabian minstrel, and which still bloomed luxuriant, notwithstanding the repeated ravages of the preceding season. [8]

The inhabitants of Granada were filled with indignation at the sight of their enemy, thus encamped under the shadow, as it were, of their battlements. They sallied forth in small bodies, or singly, challenging the Spaniards to equal en-

Moslem and Christian chivalry.

---

[8] Conde, Dominacion de los Arabes, tom. iii. cap. 42. — Bernaldez, Reyes Católicos, MS., cap. 100. — Peter Martyr, Opus Epist., lib. 3, epist. 89. — Marmol, Rebelion de Moriscos, lib. 1, cap. 18. — L. Marineo, Cosas Memorables, fol. 177.

Martyr remarks, that the Genoese merchants, " voyagers to every clime, declare this to be the largest fortified city in the world." Casiri has collected a body of interesting particulars respecting the wealth, population, and social habits of Granada, from various Arabic authorities. Bibliotheca Escurialensis, tom. ii. pp. 247 - 260.

The French work of Laborde, Voyage Pittoresque, (Paris, 1807,) and the English one of Murphy, Engravings of Arabian Antiquities of Spain, (London, 1816,) do ample justice in their finished designs to the general topography and architectural magnificence of Granada.

counter. Numerous were the combats which took place between the high-mettled cavaliers on both sides, who met on the level arena, as on a tilting-ground, where they might display their prowess in the presence of the assembled beauty and chivalry of their respective nations ; for the Spanish camp was graced, as usual, by the presence of queen Isabella and the infantas, with the courtly train of ladies, who had accompanied their royal mistress from Alcalá la Real. The Spanish ballads glow with picturesque details of these knightly tourneys, forming the most attractive portion of this romantic minstrelsy, which, celebrating the prowess of Moslem, as well as Christian warriors, sheds a dying glory round the last hours of Granada. [9]

The festivity, which reigned throughout the camp on the arrival of Isabella, did not divert her attention from the stern business of war. She superintended the military preparations, and personally inspected every part of the encampment. She appeared on the field superbly mounted, and dressed in complete armour ; and, as she visited the different quarters and reviewed her troops, she adminis-

[9] On one occasion, a Christian knight having discomfited with a handful of men a much superior body of Moslem chivalry, King Abdallah testified his admiration of his prowess by sending him on the following day a magnificent present, together with his own sword superbly mounted. (Mem. de la Acad. de Hist., tom. vi. p. 178.) The Moorish ballad beginning

"Al Rey Chico de Granada,"

describes the panic occasioned in the city by the Christian encampment on the Xenil.

" Por ese fresco Genil
  un campo viene marchando,
  todo de lucida gente,
  las armas van relumbrando.
  " Las vanderas traen tendidas,
  y un estandarte dorado ;
  el General de esta gente
  es el invicto Fernando.
  Y tambien viene la Reyna,
  Muger del Rey don Fernando,
  la qual tiene tanto esfuerzo
  que anima a qualquier soldado "

tered words of commendation or sympathy, suited CHAPTER XV.
to the condition of the soldier. [10]

On one occasion, she expressed a desire to take The queen surveys the city.
a nearer survey of the city. For this purpose, a
house was selected, affording the best point of
view, in the little village of Zubia, at no great distance from Granada. The king and queen stationed themselves before a window, which commanded
an unbroken prospect of the Alhambra, and the
most beautiful quarter of the town. In the mean
while, a considerable force, under the marquis duke
of Cadiz, had been ordered, for the protection of
the royal persons, to take up a position between
the village and the city of Granada, with strict in-
junctions on no account to engage the enemy, as
Isabella was unwilling to stain the pleasures of the
day with unnecessary effusion of blood.

The people of Granada, however, were too im- Skirmish with the enemy
patient long to endure the presence, and as they
deemed it, the bravado of their enemy. They
burst forth from the gates of the capital, dragging
along with them several pieces of ordnance, and
commenced a brisk assault on the Spanish lines.
The latter sustained the shock with firmness, till
the marquis of Cadiz, seeing them thrown into
some disorder, found it necessary to assume the offensive, and, mustering his followers around him,
made one of those desperate charges, which had so
often broken the enemy. The Moorish cavalry fal-
tered ; but might have disputed the ground, had it

10 Bernaldez, Reyes Católicos, MS., cap. 101.

not been for the infantry, which, composed of the rabble population of the city, was easily thrown into confusion, and hurried the horse along with it. The rout now became general. The Spanish cavaliers, whose blood was up, pursued to the very gates of Granada, "and not a lance," says Bernaldez, "that day, but was dyed in the blood of the infidel." Two thousand of the enemy were slain and taken in the engagement, which lasted only a short time; and the slaughter was stopped only by the escape of the fugitives within the walls of the city. [11]

Conflagration of the Christian camp.

About the middle of July, an accident occurred in the camp, which had like to have been attended with fatal consequences. The queen was lodged in a superb pavilion, belonging to the marquis of Cadiz, and always used by him in the Moorish war. By the carelessness of one of her attendants, a lamp was placed in such a situation, that during the night, perhaps owing to a gust of wind, it set fire to the drapery or loose hangings of the pavilion, which was instantly in a blaze. The flame communicated with fearful rapidity to the neighbouring tents, made of light, combustible materials, and the camp was menaced with general conflagration. This occurred at the dead of night, when all but

[11] Bernaldez, Reyes Católicos, MS., cap. 101. — Conde, Dominacion de los Arabes, tom. iii. cap. 42. — Peter Martyr, Opus Epist., lib. 4, epist. 90. — Pulgar, Reyes Católicos, cap. 133. — Zurita, Anales, tom. iv. cap. 88.

Isabella afterwards caused a Franciscan monastery to be built in commemoration of this event at Zubia, where, according to Mr. Irving, the house from which she witnessed the action is to be seen at the present day. See Conquest of Granada, chap. 90, note.

the sentinels were buried in sleep. The queen, and her children, whose apartments were near hers, were in great peril, and escaped with difficulty, though fortunately without injury. The alarm soon spread. The trumpets sounded to arms, for it was supposed to be some night attack of the enemy. Ferdinand snatching up his arms hastily, put himself at the head of his troops ; but, soon ascertaining the nature of the disaster, contented himself with posting the marquis of Cadiz, with a strong body of horse, over against the city, in order to repel any sally from that quarter. None, however, was attempted, and the fire was at length extinguished without personal injury, though not without loss of much valuable property, in jewels, plate, brocade, and other costly decorations of the tents of the nobility. [12]

In order to guard against a similar disaster, as well as to provide comfortable winter quarters for the army, should the siege be so long protracted as to require it, it was resolved to build a town of substantial edifices on the place of the present encampment. The plan was immediately put in execution. The work was distributed in due proportions among the troops of the several cities and of the great nobility ; the soldier was on a sudden converted into an artisan, and, instead of war, the camp echoed with the sounds of peaceful labor.

[12] Peter Martyr, Opus Epist., lib. 1, epist. 91. — Bernaldez, Reyes Católicos, MS., cap. 101. — Garibay, Compendio, tom. ii. p. 673. — Bleda, Corónica, p. 619. — Marmol, Rebelion de Moriscos, lib. 1, cap. 18.

In less than three months, this stupendous task
was accomplished. The spot so recently occupied
by light, fluttering pavilions, was thickly covered
with solid structures of stone and mortar, comprehending, besides dwellinghouses, stables for a
thousand horses. The town was thrown into a
quadrangular form, traversed by two spacious avenues, intersecting each other at right angles in the
centre, in the form of a cross, with stately portals
at each of the four extremities. Inscriptions on
blocks of marble in the various quarters, recorded
the respective shares of the several cities in the
execution of the work. When it was completed,
the whole army was desirous that the new city
should bear the name of their illustrious queen;
but Isabella modestly declined this tribute, and
bestowed on the place the title of *Santa Fe*, in
token of the unshaken trust, manifested by her
people throughout this war, in Divine Providence.
With this name it still stands as it was erected in
1491, a monument of the constancy and enduring
patience of the Spaniards, " the only city in
Spain," in the words of a Castilian writer, " that
has never been contaminated by the Moslem heresy. " [13]

The erection of Santa Fe by the Spaniards struck

[13] Estrada, Poblacion de España,
tom. ii. pp. 344, 348. — Peter Martyr, Opus Epist., lib. 4, epist. 91.
— Marmol, Rebelion de Moriscos,
lib. 1, cap. 18.

Hyta, who embellishes his florid
prose with occasional extracts from
the beautiful ballad poetry of Spain,

gives one commemorating the erection of Santa Fe.

" Cercada esta Santa Fe
con mucho lienzo encerado
al rededor muchas tiendas
de seda, oro, y brocado.
" Donde estan Duques, y Condes,
Señores de gran estado," &c.
            Guerras de Granada. p. 515.

a greater damp into the people of Granada, than the most successful military achievement could have done. They beheld the enemy setting foot on their soil, with a resolution never more to resign it. They already began to suffer from the rigorous blockade, which effectually excluded supplies from their own territories, while all communication with Africa was jealously intercepted. Symptoms of insubordination had begun to show themselves among the overgrown population of the city, as it felt more and more the pressure of famine. In this crisis, the unfortunate Abdallah and his principal counsellors became convinced, that the place could not be maintained much longer ; and at length, in the month of October, propositions were made through the vizier Abul Cazim Abdelmalic, to open a negotiation for the surrender of the place. The affair was to be conducted with the utmost caution ; since the people of Granada, notwithstanding their precarious condition, and their disquietude, were buoyed up by indefinite expectations of relief from Africa, or some other quarter.

The Spanish sovereigns intrusted the negotiation to their secretary Fernando de Zafra, and to Gonsalvo de Cordova, the latter of whom was selected for this delicate business, from his uncommon address, and his familiarity with the Moorish habits and language. Thus the capitulation of Granada was referred to the man, who acquired in her long wars the military science, which enabled him, at a later period, to foil the most distinguished generals of Europe.

PART
I.

  The conferences were conducted by night with
the utmost secrecy, sometimes within the walls of
Granada, and at others, in the little hamlet of Chur
riana, about a league distant from it. At length,
after large discussion on both sides, the terms of
capitulation were definitively settled, and ratified
by the respective monarchs on the 25th of Novem
ber, 1491.[14]

Capitulation
of Granada.

  The conditions were of similar, though somewhat
more liberal import, than those granted to Baza.
The inhabitants of Granada were to retain possession of their mosques, with the free exercise of
their religion, with all its peculiar rites and ceremonies ; they were to be judged by their own laws,
under their own cadis or magistrates, subject to
the general control of the Castilian governor , they
were to be unmolested in their ancient usages,
manners, language, and dress; to be protected in
the full enjoyment of their property, with the right
of disposing of it on their own account, and of
migrating when and where they would ; and to be
furnished with vessels for the conveyance of such
as chose within three years to pass into Africa.
No heavier taxes were to be imposed than those
customarily paid to their Arabian sovereigns, and

[14] Pedraza, Antiguedad de Granada, fol. 74. — Giovio, De Vitâ
Gonsalvi, apud Vitæ Illust. Virorum, pp. 211, 212. — Salazar de
Mendoza, Crón. del Gran Cardenal,
p. 236. — Cardonne, Hist. d'Afrique et d'Espagne, tom. iii. pp.
316, 317. — Conde, Dominacion de
los Arabes, tom. iii. cap. 42. — L.
Marineo, Cosas Memorables, fol.
178. — Marmol, however, assigns
the date in the text to a separate
capitulation respecting Abdallah,
dating that made in behalf of the
city three days later. (Rebelion de
Moriscos, lib. 1, cap. 19.) This
author has given the articles of the
treaty with greater fulness and
precision than any other Spanish
historian.

none whatever before the expiration of three years. CHAPTER
King Abdallah was to reign over a specified ter-   XV.
ritory in the Alpuxarras, for which he was to do
homage to the Castilian crown. The artillery and
the fortifications were to be delivered into the
hands of the Christians, and the city was to be surrendered in sixty days from the date of the capitulation. Such were the principal terms of the surrender of Granada, as authenticated by the most
accredited Castilian and Arabian authorities; which
I have stated the more precisely, as affording the
best data for estimating the extent of Spanish perfidy in later times.[15]

The conferences could not be conducted so Commotions
secretly, but that some report of them got air   in Granada
among the populace of the city, who now regarded
Abdallah with an evil eye for his connexion with
the Christians. When the fact of the capitulation
became known, the agitation speedily mounted into
an open insurrection, which menaced the safety of
the city, as well as of Abdallah's person. In this
alarming state of things, it was thought best by
that monarch's counsellors, to anticipate the ap-

[15] Marmol, Rebelion de Moriscos, lib. 1, cap. 19. — Conde, Dominacion de los Arabes, tom. iii.
cap. 42. — Zurita, Anales, tom. ii.
cap. 90. — Cardonne, Hist. d'Afrique et d'Espagne, tom. iii. pp.
317, 318. — Oviedo, Quincuagenas,
MS., bat. 1, quinc. 1, dial. 28.
Martyr adds, that the principal
Moorish nobility were to remove
,rom the city. (Opus Epist., lib. 4,
epist. 92.) Pedraza, who has devoted a volume to the history of

Granada, does not seem to think
the capitulations worth specifying.
Most of the modern Castilians pass
very lightly over them. They furnish too bitter a comment on the
conduct of subsequent Spanish
monarchs. Marmol and the judicious Zurita agree in every substantial particular with Conde, and this
coincidence may be considered as
establishing the actual terms of the
treaty.

Preparations
for occupy-
ing the city.

1 4 9 2.
Jan. 2.

pointed day of surrender ; and the 2d of January 1492, was accordingly fixed on for that purpose.

Every preparation was made by the Spaniards for performing this last act of the drama with suitable pomp and effect. The mourning which the court had put on for the death of Prince Alonso of Portugal, occasioned by a fall from his horse a few months after his marriage with the infanta Isabella, was exchanged for gay and magnificent apparel. On the morning of the 2d, the whole Christian camp exhibited a scene of the most animating bustle. The grand cardinal Mendoza was sent forward at the head of a large detachment, comprehending his household troops, and the veteran infantry grown grey in the Moorish wars, to occupy the Alhambra preparatory to the entrance of the sovereigns. [16]   Ferdinand stationed himself at some distance in the rear, near an Arabian mosque, since consecrated as the hermitage of St. Sebastian. He was surrounded by his courtiers, with their stately retinues, glittering in gorgeous panoply, and proudly displaying the armorial bearings of their ancient houses.   The queen halted still farther in the rear, at the village of Armilla. [17]

[16] Oviedo, whose narrative exhibits many discrepancies with those of other contemporaries, assigns this part to the count of Tendilla, the first captain-general of Granada. (Quincuagenas, MS., bat. 1, quinc. 1, dial. 28.) But, as this writer, though an eyewitness, was but thirteen or fourteen years of age at the time of the capture, and wrote some sixty years later from his early recollections, his authority cannot be considered of equal weight with that of persons, who, like Martyr, described events as they were passing before them.

[17] Pedraza, Antiguedad de Granada, fol. 75. — Salazar de Mendoza, Crón. del Gran Cardenal, p. 238. — Zurita, Anales, tom. iv. cap. 90. — Peter Martyr, Opus Epist., lib. 4, epist. 92. — Abarca, Reyes de Aragon, tom. ii fol. 309. — Marmol, Rebelion de Moriscos, lib. 1, cap. 20.

As the column under the grand cardinal advanced CHAPTER
XV
up the Hill of Martyrs, over which a road had been
constructed for the passage of the artillery, he was
met by the Moorish prince Abdallah, attended by
fifty cavaliers, who descending the hill rode up to
the position occupied by Ferdinand on the banks
of the Xenil. As the Moor approached the Spanish king, he would have thrown himself from his
norse, and saluted his hand in token of homage,
but Ferdinand hastily prevented him, embracing
him with every mark of sympathy and regard.
Abdallah then delivered up the keys of the Alhambra to his conqueror saying, " They are thine, O
king, since Allah so decrees it ; use thy success
with clemency and moderation." Ferdinand would
have uttered some words of consolation to the unfortunate prince, but he moved forward with de-
jected air to the spot occupied by Isabella, and,
after similar acts of obeisance, passed on to join his
family, who had preceded him with his most valuable effects on the route to the Alpuxarras. [18]

The sovereigns during this time waited with im- The cross
raised on
the Alham-
bra.
patience the signal of the occupation of the city by
the cardinal's troops, which, winding slowly along
the outer circuit of the walls, as previously arranged,
in order to spare the feelings of the citizens as far
as possible, entered by what is now called the gate
of Los Molinos. In a short time, the large silver

---

[18] Marmol, Rebelion de Moriscos, ubi supra. — Conde, Dominacion de los Arabes, tom. iii. cap.
43. — Pedraza, Antiguedad de
Granada, fol. 76. — Bernaldez,
Reyes Católicos, MS., cap. 102.
— Zurita, Anales, tom. iv. cap.
90. — Oviedo, Quincuagenas, MS.,
bat. 1, quinc. 1, dial. 28.

cross, borne by Ferdinand throughout the crusade, was seen sparkling in the sun-beams, while the standards of Castile and St. Jago waved triumphantly from the red towers of the Alhambra. At this glorious spectacle, the choir of the royal chapel broke forth into the solemn anthem of the Te Deum, and the whole army, penetrated with deep emotion, prostrated themselves on their knees in adoration of the Lord of hosts, who had at length granted the consummation of their wishes, in this last and glorious triumph of the Cross.[19] The grandees who surrounded Ferdinand then advanced towards the queen, and kneeling down saluted her hand in token of homage to her as sovereign of Granada. The procession took up its march towards the city, ' the king and queen moving in the midst," says an historian, " emblazoned with royal magnificence ; and, as they were in the prime of life, and had now achieved the completion of this glorious conquest, they seemed to represent even more than their wonted majesty. Equal with each other, they were raised far above the rest of the world. They appeared, indeed, more than mortal, and as if sent by Heaven for the salvation of Spain."[20]

[19] Oviedo, Quincuagenas, MS., ubi supra.—One is reminded of Tasso's description of the somewhat similar feelings exhibited by the crusaders on their entrance into Jerusalem.

" Ecco apparir Gerusalem si vede,
Ecco additar Gerusalem si scorge ;
Ecco da mille voci unitamente
Gerusalemme salutar si sente.
*   *   *   *   *
" Al gran piacer che quella prima vista
Dolcemente pirò nell' altrui petto,

Alta contrizion successe, mista
Di timoroso e riverente affetto.
Osano appena d' innalzar la vista
Ver la città."

Gerusalemme Liberata,
Cant. iii. st. 3. 5.

[20] Mariana, Hist. de España tom. ii. p. 597.—Pedraza, Antiguedad de Granada, fol. 76.—Carbajal, Anales, MS., año 1492.—Conde, Dominacion de los Arabes, tom. iii. cap. 43.—Bleda, Coróni

In the mean while the Moorish king, traversing the route of the Alpuxarras, reached a rocky eminence which commanded a last view of Granada. He checked his horse, and, as his eye for the last time wandered over the scenes of his departed greatness, his heart swelled, and he burst into tears. " You do well," said his more masculine mother, " to weep like a woman, for what you could not defend like a man!" "Alas!" exclaimed the unhappy exile, " when were woes ever equal to mine!" The scene of this event is still pointed out to the traveller by the people of the district; and the rocky height, from which the Moorish chief took his sad farewell of the princely abodes of his youth, is commemorated by the poetical title of *El Ultimo Sospiro del Moro*, " The Last Sigh of the Moor."

CHAPTER
XV.

The sequel of Abdallah's history is soon told. Like his uncle, El Zagal, he pined away in his barren domain of the Alpuxarras, under the shadow, as it were, of his ancient palaces. In the following year, he passed over to Fez with his family, having

Fate of
Abdallah.

---

ca, pp. 621, 622.—Zurita, Anales, tom. iv. cap. 90.—Marmol, Rebelion de Moriscos, lib. 1, cap. 20. —L. Marineo, and indeed most of the Spanish authorities, represent the sovereigns as having postponed their entrance into the city until the 5th or 6th of January. A letter transcribed by Pedraza, addressed by the queen to the prior of Guadalupe, one of her council, dated from the city of Granada on the 2d of January, 1492, shows the inaccuracy of this statement. See folio 76.

In Mr Lockhart's picturesque version of the Moorish ballads, the reader may find an animated description of the triumphant entry of the Christian army into Granada.

" There was crying in Granada when the
  sun was going down,
Some calling on the Trinity, some calling
  on Mahoun;
Here passed away the Koran, there in the
  cross was borne,
And here was heard the Christian bell, and
  there the Moorish horn;
Te Deum laudamus was up the Alcala sung,
Down from the Alhambra's minarets were
  all the crescents flung;
The arms thereon of Aragon and Castile
  they display;
One king comes in in triumph, one weeping goes away."

commuted his petty sovereignty for a considerable sum of money paid him by Ferdinand and Isabella, and soon after fell in battle in the service of an African prince, his kinsman. "Wretched man," exclaims a caustic chronicler of his nation, "who could lose his life in another's cause, though he did not dare to die in his own. Such," continues the Arabian, with characteristic resignation, "was the immutable decree of destiny. Blessed be Allah, who exalteth and debaseth the kings of the earth, according to his divine will, in whose fulfilment consists that eternal justice, which regulates all human affairs." The portal, through which King Abdallah for the last time issued from his capital, was at his request walled up, that none other might again pass through it. In this condition it remains to this day, a memorial of the sad destiny of the last of the kings of Granada.[21]

The fall of Granada excited general sensation throughout Christendom, where it was received as counterbalancing, in a manner, the loss of Constan-

---

[21] Conde, Dominacion de los Arabes, tom. iii. cap. 90. — Cardonne, Hist. d'Afrique et d'Espagne, tom. iii. pp. 319, 320. — Garibay, Compendio, tom. iv. lib. 40, cap. 42. — Marmol, Rebelion de Moriscos, lib. 1, cap. 20.

Mr. Irving, in his beautiful Spanish Sketch-book, "The Alhambra," devotes a chapter to mementos of Boabdil, in which he traces minutely the route of the deposed monarch after quitting the gates of his capital. The same author, in the Appendix to his Chronicle of Granada, concludes a notice of Abdallah's fate with the following description of his person. "A portrait of Boabdil el Chico is to be seen in the picture gallery of the Generalife. He is represented with a mild, handsome face, a fair complexion, and yellow hair. His dress is of yellow brocade, relieved with black velvet; and he has a black velvet cap, surmounted with a crown. In the armory of Madrid are two suits of armour said to have belonged to him, one of solid steel, with very little ornament; the morion closed. From the proportions of these suits of armour, he must have been of full stature and vigorous form." Note, p. 398.

tinople, nearly half a century before. At Rome, the event was commemorated by a solemn procession of the pope and cardinals to St. Peter's, where high mass was celebrated, and the public rejoicing continued for several days. [22] The intelligence was welcomed with no less satisfaction in England, where Henry the Seventh was seated on the throne. The circumstances attending it, as related by Lord Bacon, will not be devoid of interest for the reader. [23]

[22] Senarega, Commentarii de Rebus Genuensibus, apud Muratori, Rerum Italicarum Scriptores, (Mediolani, 1723 – 51,) tom. xxiv. p. 531.—It formed the subject of a theatrical representation before the court at Naples, in the same year. This drama, or *Farsa*, as it is called by its distinguished author, Sannazaro, is an allegorical medley, in which Faith, Joy, and the false prophet Mahomet play the principal parts. The difficulty of a precise classification of this piece, has given rise to warmer discussion among Italian critics, than the subject may be thought to warrant. See Signorelli, Vicende della Coltura nelle due Sicilie, (Napoli, 1810,) tom. iii. pp. 543 et seq.

[23] "Somewhat about this time, came letters from Ferdinando and Isabella, king and queen of Spain; signifying the final conquest of Granada from the Moors; which action, in itself so worthy, King Ferdinando, whose manner was, never to lose any virtue for the showing, had expressed and displayed in his letters, at large, with all the particularities and religious punctos and ceremonies, that were observed in the reception of that city and kingdom; showing amongst other things, that the king would not by any means in person enter the city until he had first aloof seen the Cross set up upon the greater tower of Granada, whereby it became Christian ground. That likewise, before he would enter, he did homage to God above, pronouncing by an herald from the height of that tower, that he did acknowledge to have recovered that kingdom by the help of God Almighty, and the glorious Virgin, and the virtuous apostle St. James, and the holy father Innocent VIII., together with the aids and services of his prelates, nobles, and commons. That yet he stirred not from his camp, till he had seen a little army of martyrs, to the number of seven hundred and more Christians, that had lived in bonds and servitude, as slaves to the Moors, pass before his eyes, singing a psalm for their redemption; and that he had given tribute unto God, by alms and relief extended to them all, for his admission into the city. These things were in the letters, with many more ceremonies of a kind of holy ostentation.

"The king, ever willing to put himself into the consort or quire of all religious actions, and naturally affecting much the king of Spain, as far as one king can affect another, partly for his virtues, and partly for a counterpoise to France;

Thus ended the war of Granada, which is often
compared by the Castilian chroniclers to that of
Troy in its duration, and which certainly fully
equalled the latter in variety of picturesque and
romantic incidents, and in circumstances of poetical
interest. With the surrender of its capital, terminated the Arabian empire in the Peninsula, after an
existence of seven hundred and forty-one years
from the date of the original conquest. The consequences of this closing war were of the highest
moment to Spain. The most obvious, was the recovery of an extensive territory, hitherto held by a
people, whose difference of religion, language, and
general habits, made them not only incapable of

upon the receipt of these letters,
sent all his nobles and prelates
that were about the court, together
with the mayor and aldermen of
London, in great solemnity to the
church of Paul ; there to hear a
declaration from the lord chancellor, now cardinal. When they
were assembled, the cardinal, standing upon the uppermost step, or
halfpace, before the quire, and all
the nobles, prelates, and governors
of the city at the foot of the stairs,
made a speech to them ; letting
them know that they were assembled in that consecrated place to
sing unto God a new song. For
that, said he, these many years
the Christians have not gained
new ground or territory upon the
infidels, nor enlarged and set farther the bounds of the Christian
world. But this is now done by
the prowess and devotion of Ferdinando and Isabella, kings of Spain ;
who have, to their immortal honor,
recovered the great and rich kingdom of Granada, and the populous
and mighty city of the same name

from the Moors, having been in
possession thereof by the space of
seven hundred years, and more ; for
which this assembly and all Christians are to render laud and thanks
to God, and to celebrate this noble
act of the king of Spain ; who in
this is not only victorious but
apostolical, in the gaining of new
provinces to the Christian faith.
And the rather for that this victory and conquest is obtained without much effusion of blood. Whereby it is to be hoped, that there
shall be gained not only new territory, but infinite souls to the
Church of Christ, whom the Almighty, as it seems, would have
live to be converted. Herewithal
he did relate some of the most
memorable particulars of the war
and victory. And, after his speech
ended, the whole assembly went
solemnly in procession, and Te
Deum was sung." Lord Bacon,
History of the Reign of King Henry VII., in his Works, (ed. London,
1819,) vol. v. pp. 85, 86. — See
also Hall, Chronicle, p. 453.

assimilating with their Christian neighbours, but almost their natural enemies; while their local position was a matter of just concern, as interposed between the great divisions of the Spanish monarchy, and opening an obvious avenue to invasion from Africa. By the new conquest, moreover, the Spaniards gained a large extent of country, possessing the highest capacities for production, in its natural fruitfulness of soil, temperature of climate, and in the state of cultivation to which it had been brought by its ancient occupants; while its shores were lined with commodious havens, that afforded every facility for commerce. The scattered fragments of the ancient Visigothic empire were now again, with the exception of the little state of Navarre, combined into one great monarchy, as originally destined by nature; and Christian Spain gradually rose by means of her new acquisitions from a subordinate situation, to the level of a first-rate European power.

The moral influence of the Moorish war, its influence on the Spanish character, was highly important. The inhabitants of the great divisions of the country, as in most countries during the feudal ages, had been brought too frequently into collision with each other to allow the existence of a pervading national feeling. This was particularly the case in Spain, where independent states insensibly grew out of the detached fragments of territory recovered at different times from the Moorish monarchy. The war of Granada subjected all the various sections of the country to one common action,

PART
I.

Its military
influence.

under the influence of common motives of the most
exciting interest; while it brought them in conflict
with a race, the extreme repugnance of whose institutions and character to their own, served greatly
to nourish the nationality of sentiment. In this
way, the spark of patriotism was kindled throughout the whole nation, and the most distant provinces of the Peninsula were knit together by a bond
of union, which has remained indissoluble.

The consequences of these wars in a military aspect are also worthy of notice. Up to this period,
war had been carried on by irregular levies, extremely limited in numerical amount and in period
of service; under little subordination, except to
their own immediate chiefs, and wholly unprovided
with the apparatus required for extended operations. The Spaniards were even lower than most
of the European nations in military science, as is
apparent from the infinite pains of Isabella to avail
herself of all foreign resources for their improvement.
In the war of Granada, masses of men were brought
together, far greater than had hitherto been known
in modern warfare. They were kept in the field
not only through long campaigns, but far into the
winter; a thing altogether unprecedented. They
were made to act in concert, and the numerous
petty chiefs brought in complete subjection to one
common head, whose personal character enforced
the authority of station. Lastly, they were supplied with all the requisite munitions, through the
providence of Isabella, who introduced into the
service the most skilful engineers from other coun-

tries, and kept in pay bodies of mercenaries, as the CHAPTER XV.
Swiss for example, reputed the best disciplined
troops of that day. In this admirable school, the
Spanish soldier was gradually trained to patient
endurance, fortitude, and thorough subordination ;
and those celebrated captains were formed, with
that invincible infantry, which in the beginning of
the sixteenth century spread the military fame. of
their country over all Christendom.

But, with all our sympathy for the conquerors, it Destiny of the Moors
is impossible, without a deep feeling of regret, to
contemplate the decay and final extinction of a
race, who had made such high advances in civilization as the Spanish Arabs ; to see them driven from
the stately palaces reared by their own hands, wan-
dering as exiles over the lands, which still blos-
somed with the fruits of their industry, and wasting
away under persecution, until their very name as a
nation was blotted out from the map of history.[24]
It must be admitted, however, that they had long
since reached their utmost limit of advancement as
a people. The light shed over their history shines
from distant ages ; for, during the later period of
their existence, they appear to have reposed in a
state of torpid, luxurious indulgence, which would
seem to argue, that, when causes of external excitement were withdrawn, the inherent vices of

[24] The African descendants of the Spanish Moors, unable wholly to relinquish the hope of restoration to the delicious abodes of their ancestors, continued for many gen- erations, and perhaps still continue, to put up a petition to that ef- fect in their mosques every Friday. Pedraza, Antiguedad de Granada, fol. 7.

their social institutions had incapacitated them for the further production of excellence. In this impotent condition, it was wisely ordered, that their territory should be occupied by a people, whose religion and more liberal form of government, however frequently misunderstood or perverted, qualified them for advancing still higher the interests of humanity.

Death and
character of
the marquis
of Cadiz.
It will not be amiss to terminate the narrative of the war of Granada, with some notice of the fate of Rodrigo Ponce de Leon, marquis duke of Cadiz; for he may be regarded in a peculiar manner as the hero of it, having struck the first stroke by the surprise of Alhama, and witnessed every campaign till the surrender of Granada. A circumstantial account of his last moments is afforded by the pen of his worthy countryman, the Andalusian Curate of Los Palacios. The gallant marquis survived the close of the war only a short time, terminating his days at his mansion in Seville, on the 28th of August, 1492, with a disorder brought on by fatigue and incessant exposure. He had reached the forty-ninth year of his age, and, although twice married, left no legitimate issue. In his person, he was of about the middle stature, of a compact, symmetrical frame, a fair complexion, with light hair inclining to red. He was an excellent horseman, and well skilled indeed in most of the exercises of chivalry. He had the rare merit of combining sagacity with intrepidity in action. Though somewhat impatient, and slow to forgive, he was frank

and generous, a warm friend, and a kind master to
his vassals. [25]

He was strict in his observance of the Catholic
worship, punctilious in keeping all the church festivals and in enforcing their observance throughout his domains ; and, in war, he was a most
devout champion of the Virgin. He was ambitious
of acquisitions, but lavish of expenditure, especially in the embellishment and fortification of his
towns and castles ; spending on Alcalá de Guada-
ira, Xerez, and Alanis, the enormous sum of seventeen million maravedies. To the ladies he was
courteous as became a true knight. At his death,
the king and queen with the whole court went into
mourning ; " for he was a much-loved cavalier,"
says the Curate, " and was esteemed, like the Cid,
both by friend and foe ; and no Moor durst abide
in that quarter of the field where his banner was
displayed."

His body, after lying in state for several days in
his palace at Seville, with his trusty sword by his
side, with which he had fought all his battles,
was borne in solemn procession by night through
the streets of the city, which was everywhere filled
with the deepest lamentation ; and was finally deposited in the great chapel of the Augustine church,
in the tomb of his ancestors. Ten Moorish ban
ners, which he had taken in battle with the infidel,

[25] Carbajal, Anales, MS., año
1492.

Don Henrique de Guzman, duke
of Medina Sidonia, the ancient
enemy, and, since the commencement of the Moorish war, the firm
friend of the marquis of Cadiz,
died the 28th of August, on the
same day with the latter.

before the war of Granada, were borne along at his funeral, "and still wave over his sepulchre," says Bernaldez, "keeping alive the memory of his exploits, as undying as his soul." The banners have long since mouldered into dust; the very tomb which contained his ashes has been sacrilegiously demolished; but the fame of the hero will survive as long as any thing like respect for valor, courtesy, unblemished honor, or any other attribute of chivalry, shall be found in Spain. [26]

[26] Zuñiga, Annales de Sevilla, p. 411. — Bernaldez, Reyes Católicos, MS., cap. 104.

The marquis left three illegitimate daughters by a noble Spanish lady, who all formed high connexions. He was succeeded in his titles and estates, by the permission of Ferdinand and Isabella, by Don Rodrigo Ponce de Leon, the son of his eldest daughter, who had married with one of her kinsmen. Cadiz was subsequently annexed by the Spanish sovereigns to the crown, from which it had been detached in Henry IV.'s time, and considerable estates were given as an equivalent, together with the title of Duke of Arcos, to the family of Ponce de Leon.

Notice of Bernaldez, Curate of Los Palacios.

One of the chief authorities on which the account of the Moorish war rests, is Andres Bernaldez, Curate of Los Palacios. He was a native of Fuente in Leon, and appears to have received his early education under the care of his grandfather, a notary of that place, whose commendations of a juvenile essay in historical writing led him later in life, according to his own account, to record the events of his time in the extended and regular form of a chronicle. After admission to orders, he was made chaplain to Deza, archbishop of Seville, and curate of Los Palacios, an Andalusian town not far from Seville, where he discharged his ecclesiastical functions with credit, from 1488 to 1513, at which time, as we find no later mention of him, he probably closed his life with his labors.

Bernaldez had ample opportunities for accurate information relative to the Moorish war, since he lived, as it were, in the theatre of action, and was personally intimate with the most considerable men of Andalusia, especially the marquis of Cadiz, whom he has made the Achilles of his epic, assigning him a much more important part in the principal transactions, than is always warranted by other authorities. His Chronicle is just such as might have been anticipated from a person of lively imagination, and competent scholarship for the time, deeply dyed with the bigotry and superstition of the Spanish clergy in that century. There is no great discrimination apparent in the work of the worthy curate, who dwells with goggle-eyed credulity on the most absurd marvels, and expends more pages on an empty court show, than on the most important schemes of policy. But if he is no philosopher, he has, perhaps for that very reason, succeeded in making us completely master of the popular feelings and prejudices of the time ; while he gives a most vivid portraiture of the principal scenes and actors in this stirring war, with all their chivalrous exploit, and rich theatrical accompaniment. His credulity and fanaticism, moreover, are well compensated by a simplicity and loyalty of purpose, which secure much more credit to his narrative than attaches to those of more ambitious writers, whose judgment is perpetually swayed by personal or party interests. The chronicle descends as late as 1513, although, as might be expected from the author's character, it is entitled to much less confidence in the discussion of events which fell without the scope of his personal observation. Notwithstanding its historical value is fully recognised by the Castilian critics, it has never been admitted to the press, but still remains ingulfed in the ocean of manuscripts, with which the Spanish libraries are deluged.

It is remarkable that the war of Granada, which is so admirably suited in all its circumstances to poetical purposes, should not have been more frequently commemorated by the epic muse. The only successful attempt in this way, with which I am acquainted, is the "Conquisto di Granata," by the Florentine Girolamo Gratiani, Modena, 1650. The author has taken the license, independently of his machinery, of deviating very freely from the historic track ; among other things, introducing Columbus and the Great Captain as principal actors in the drama, in which they played at most but a very subordinate part. The poem, which swells into twenty-six cantos, is in such repute with the Italian critics, that Quadrio does not hesitate to rank it " among the best epical productions of the age." A translation of this work has recently appeared at Nuremberg, from the pen of C. M. Winterling, which is much commended by the German critics.

Mr. Irving's late publication, the " Chronicle of the Conquest of Granada," has superseded all further necessity for poetry, and unfortunately for me, for history. He has fully availed himself of all the picturesque and animating movements of this romantic era ; and the reader, who will take the trouble to compare his Chronicle with the present more prosaic and literal narrative, will see how little he has been seduced from historic accuracy by the poetical aspect of his subject. The fictitious and romantic dress of his work has enabled him to make it the medium for reflecting more vividly the floating opinions and chimerical fancies of the age, while he has illuminated the picture with the dramatic brilliancy of coloring denied to sober history.

CHAPTER XV.

Irving's Chronicl Granada

CHAPTER XVI.

APPLICATION OF CHRISTOPHER COLUMBUS AT THE SPANISH COURT.

1492.

Early Discoveries of the Portuguese. — Of the Spaniards. — Columbus. — His Application at the Castilian Court. — Rejected. — Negotiations resumed. — Favorable Disposition of the Queen. — Arrangement with Columbus. — He sails on his first Voyage. — Indifference to the Enterprise. — Acknowledgments due to Isabella.

CHAPTER
XVI.

WHILE Ferdinand and Isabella were at Santa Fe, the capitulation was signed, that opened the way to an extent of empire, compared with which their recent conquests, and indeed all their present dominions, were insignificant. The extraordinary intellectual activity of the Europeans in the fifteenth century, after the torpor of ages, carried them forward to high advancement in almost every department of science, but especially nautical, whose surprising results have acquired for the age, the glory of being designated as peculiarly that of maritime discovery. This was eminently favored by the political condition of modern Europe. Under the Roman empire, the traffic with the east naturally centred in Rome, the commercial capital of the west. After the dismemberment of the empire, it continued to be conducted principally through the channel of the Italian ports, whence it was diffused over the remoter regions of Christendom. But these countries, which had now risen from the rank of subordinate provinces to that of separate, independent states, viewed with jealousy this monopoly of the Italian cities, by means of which these latter were rapidly advancing beyond them in power and opulence. This was especially the case with Portugal and Castile,[1] which, placed on the remote frontiers of the European continent, were far removed from the great routes of Asiatic intercourse; while this disadvantage was not compensated by such an extent of territory, as secured consideration to some other of the European states, equally unfavorably situated for commercial purposes with themselves. Thus circumstanced, the two nations of Castile and Portugal were naturally led to turn their eyes on the great ocean which washed their western borders, and to seek in its hitherto unexplored recesses for new domains, and if possible strike out some undiscovered track towards the opulent regions of the east.

The spirit of maritime enterprise was fomented, and greatly facilitated in its operation, by the invention of the astrolabe, and the important discovery of the polarity of the magnet, whose first application to the purposes of navigation on an extended

Aragon, or rather Catalonia, maintained an extensive commerce with the Levant, and the remote regions of the east, during the middle ages, through the flourishing port of Barcelona. See Capmany y Montpalau, Memorias Históricas sobre la Marina, Comercio y Artes de Barcelona, (Madrid, 1779 – 92,) passim.

scale, may be referred to the fifteenth century.[2] The Portuguese were the first to enter on the brilliant path of nautical discovery, which they pursued under the infant Don Henry with such activity, that, before the middle of the fifteenth century, they had penetrated as far as Cape de Verd, doubling many a fearful headland, which had shut in the timid navigator of former days ; until at length, in 1486, they descried the lofty promontory which terminates Africa on the south, and which, hailed by King John the Second, under whom it was discovered, as the harbinger of the long sought passage to the east, received the cheering appellation of the Cape of Good Hope.

The Spaniards, in the mean while, did not languish in the career of maritime enterprise. Certain adventurers from the northern provinces of Biscay and Guipuscoa, in 1393, had made themselves

---

[2] A council of mathematicians in the court of John II., of Portugal, first devised the application of the ancient astrolabe to navigation, thus affording to the mariner the essential advantages appertaining to the modern quadrant. The discovery of the polarity of the needle, which vulgar tradition assigned to the Amalfite Flavio Gioja, and which Robertson has sanctioned without scruple, is clearly proved to have occurred more than a century earlier. Tiraboschi, who investigates the matter with his usual erudition, passing by the doubtful reference of Guiot de Provins, whose age and personal identity even are contested, traces the familiar use of the magnetic needle as far back as the first half of the thirteenth century, by a pertinent passage from Cardinal Vitri, who died 1244 ; and sus-

tains this by several similar references to other authors of the same century. Capmany finds no notice of its use by the Castilian navigators earlier than 1403. It was not until considerably later in the fifteenth century, that the Portuguese voyagers, trusting to its guidance, ventured to quit the Mediterranean and African coasts, and extend their navigation to Madeira and the Azores. See Navarrete, Coleccion de los Viages y Descubrimientos que hicieron por Mar los Españoles, (Madrid, 1825 – 29,) tom. i. Int. sec. 33. — Tiraboschi, Letteratura Italiana, tom. iv. pp. 173, 174. — Capmany, Mem. de Barcelona, tom. iii. part. 1, cap. 4. — Koch, Tableau des Révolutions de l'Europe, (Paris, 1814,) tom. i. pp 358 – 360.

masters of one of the smallest of the group of islands, supposed to be the Fortunate Isles of the ancients, since known as the Canaries. Other private adventurers from Seville extended their conquests over these islands in the beginning of the following century. These were completed in behalf of the crown under Ferdinand and Isabella, who equipped several fleets for their reduction, which at length terminated in 1495 with that of Teneriffe.[3] From the commencement of their reign, Ferdinand and Isabella had shown an earnest solicitude for the encouragement of commerce and nautical science, as is evinced by a variety of regulations which, however imperfect, from the misconception of the true principles of trade in that day, are sufficiently indicative of the dispositions of the government.[4] Under them, and indeed under their predecessors as far back as Henry the Third, a considerable

[3] Four of the islands were conquered on behalf of private adventurers chiefly from Andalusia, before the accession of Ferdinand and Isabella, and under their reign were held as the property of a noble Castilian family, named Peraza. The sovereigns sent a considerable armament from Seville in 1480, which subdued the great island of Canary on behalf of the crown, and another in 1493, which effected the reduction of Palma and Teneriffe after a sturdy resistance from the natives. Bernaldez postpones the last conquest to 1495. Salazar de Mendoza, Monarquia, tom. i. p. 347 – 349. — Pulgar, Reyes Católicos, pp. 136, 203. — Bernaldez, Reyes Católicos, MS., cap. 64, 65, 66, 133. — Navarrete, Coleccion de Viages, tom. i. introd., sec. 28.

[4] Among the provisions of the sovereigns enacted previous to the present date, may be noted those for regulating the coin and weights; for opening a free trade between Castile and Aragon; for security to Genoese and Venetian trading vessels; for safe conduct to mariners and fishermen; for privileges to the seamen of Palos; for prohibiting the plunder of vessels wrecked on the coast; and an ordinance of the very last year, requiring foreigners to take their return cargoes in the products of the country. See these laws as extracted from the Ordenancas Reales and the various public archives, in Mem. de la Acad. de Hist., tom. vi. Ilust. 11.

traffic had been carried on with the western coast of Africa, from which gold dust and slaves were imported into the city of Seville. The annalist of that city notices the repeated interference of Isabella in behalf of these unfortunate beings, by ordinances tending to secure them a more equal protection of the laws, or opening such social indulgences as might mitigate the hardships of their condition. A misunderstanding gradually arose between the subjects of Castile and Portugal, in relation to their respective rights of discovery and commerce on the African coast, which promised a fruitful source of collision between the two crowns; but which was happily adjusted by an article in the treaty of 1479, that terminated the war of the succession. By this it was settled, that the right of traffic and of discovery on the western coast of Africa should be exclusively reserved to the Portuguese, who in their turn should resign all claims on the Canaries to the crown of Castile. The Spaniards, thus excluded from further progress to the south, seemed to have no other opening left for naval adventure than the hitherto untravelled regions of the great western ocean. Fortunately, at this juncture, an individual appeared among them, in the person of Christopher Columbus, endowed with capacity for stimulating them to this heroic enterprise, and conducting it to a glorious issue.[5]

[5] Zuñiga, Annales de Sevilla, pp. 373, 374, 398. — Zurita, Anales, tom. iv. lib. 20, cap. 30, 34. — Navarrete, Coleccion de Viages, tom. i. introd., sec. 21, 24. — Ferreras, Hist. d'Espagne, tom. vii. p. 548.

This extraordinary man was a native of Genoa, of humble parentage, though perhaps honorable descent.[6] He was instructed in his early youth at Pavia, where he acquired a strong relish for the mathematical sciences, in which he subsequently excelled. At the age of fourteen, he engaged in a seafaring life, which he followed with little intermission till 1470; when, probably little more than thirty years of age,[7] he landed in Portugal, the country to which adventurous spirits from all parts

CHAPTER XVI.

Early history of Columbus.

[6] Spotorno, Memorials of Columbus, (London, 1823,) p. 14. — Senarega, apud Muratori, Rerum Ital. Script., tom. xxiv. p. 535. — Antonio Gallo, De Navigatione Columbi, apud Muratori, Rerum Ital. Script., tom. xxiii. p. 202.

It is very generally agreed that the father of Columbus exercised the craft of a wool-carder, or weaver. The admiral's son, Ferdinand, after some speculation on the genealogy of his illustrious parent, concludes with remarking, that, after all, a noble descent would confer less lustre on him than to have sprung from such a father; a philosophical sentiment, indicating pretty strongly that he had no great ancestry to boast of. Ferdinand finds something extremely mysterious and typical in his father's name of *Columbus*, signifying *a dove*, in token of his being ordained to "carry the olive-branch and oil of baptism over the ocean, like Noah's dove, to denote the peace and union of the heathen people with the church, after they had been shut up in the ark of darkness and confusion." Fernando Colon, Historia del Almirante, cap. 1, 2, apud Barcia, Historiadores Primitivos de las Indias Occidentales, (Madrid, 1749,) tom. i.

[7] Bernaldez, Reyes Católicos,

MS., cap. 131. — Muñoz, Historia del Nuevo-Mundo, (Madrid, 1793,) lib. 2, sec. 13.

There are no sufficient data for determining the period of Columbus's birth. The learned Muñoz places it in 1446. (Hist. del Nuevo-Mundo, lib. 2, sec. 12.) Navarrete, who has weighed the various authorities with caution, seems inclined to remove it back eight or ten years further, resting chiefly on a remark of Bernaldez, that he died in 1506, "in a good old age, at the age of seventy, a little more or less." (Cap. 131.) The expression is somewhat vague. In order to reconcile the facts with this hypothesis, Navarrete is compelled to reject, as a chirographical blunder, a passage in a letter of the admiral, placing his birth in 1456, and to distort another passage in his book of "Prophecies," which, if literally taken, would seem to establish his birth near the time assigned by Muñoz. Incidental allusions in some other authorities, speaking of Columbus's old age at or near the time of his death, strongly corroborate Navarrete's inference. (See Coleccion de Viages, tom. i. introd., sec. 54.) — Mr. Irving seems willing to rely exclusively on the authority of Bernaldez.

of the world then resorted, as the great theatre of maritime enterprise. After his arrival, he continued to make voyages to the then known parts of the world, and, when on shore, occupied himself with the construction and sale of charts and maps ; while his geographical researches were considerably aided by the possession of papers belonging to an eminent Portuguese navigator, a deceased relative of his wife. Thus stored with all that nautical science in that day could supply, and fortified by large practical experience, the reflecting mind of Columbus was naturally led to speculate on the existence of some other land beyond the western waters ; and he conceived the possibility of reaching the eastern shores of Asia, whose provinces of Zipango and Cathay were emblazoned in such gorgeous colors in the narratives of Mandeville and the Poli, by a more direct and commodious route than that which traversed the eastern continent.[8]

The existence of land beyond the Atlantic, which was not discredited by some of the most enlightened ancients,[9] had become matter of common

[8] Antonio de Herrera, Historia General de las Indias Occidentales, (Amberes, 1728,) tom. i. dec. 1, lib. 1. cap. 7. — Gomara, Historia de las Indias, cap. 14, apud Barcia, Hist. Primitivos, tom. ii. — Bernaldez, Reyes Católicos, MS., cap. 118. — Navarrete, Coleccion de Viages, tom. i. introd., sec. 30. Ferdinand Columbus enumerates three grounds on which his father's conviction of land in the west was founded. First, natural reason, — or conclusions drawn from science ; secondly, authority of writers, — amounting to little more than vague speculations of the ancients ; thirdly, testimony of sailors, comprehending, in addition to popular rumors of land described in western voyages, such relics as appeared to have floated to the European shores from the other side of the Atlantic. Hist. del Almirante, cap. 6 – 8.

[9] None of the intimations are so precise as that contained in the well-known lines of Seneca's Medea,

    " Venient annis sæcula," &c.,

although, when regarded as a mere poetical vagary, it has not the

speculation at the close of the fifteenth century; when maritime adventure was daily disclosing the mysteries of the deep, and bringing to light new regions, that had hitherto existed only in fancy. A proof of this popular belief occurs in a curious passage of the "Morgante Maggiore" of the Florentine poet Pulci, a man of letters, but not distinguished for scientific attainments beyond his day.[10] The passage is remarkable, independently of the cosmographical knowledge it implies, for its allusion to phenomena in physical science, not established till more than a century later. The Devil, alluding to the vulgar superstition respecting the Pillars of Hercules, thus addresses his companion Rinaldo

> "Know that this theory is false; his bark
> The daring mariner shall urge far o'er
> The western wave, a smooth and level plain,
> Albeit the earth is fashioned like a wheel.
> Man was in ancient days of grosser mould,
> And Hercules might blush to learn how far
> Beyond the limits he had vainly set,
> The dullest sea-boat soon shall wing her way.
> Men shall descry another hemisphere,

weight which belongs to more serious suggestions, of similar import, in the writings of Aristotle and Strabo. The various allusions in the ancient classic writers to an undiscovered world form the subject of an elaborate essay in the Memorias da Acad. Real das Sciencias de Lisboa, (tom. v. pp. 101 – 112,) and are embodied, in much greater detail, in the first section of Humboldt's "Histoire de la Géographie du Nouveau Continent"; a work in which the author, with his usual acuteness, has successfully applied the vast stores of his erudition and experience to the illustration of many interesting points connected with the discovery of the New World, and the personal history of Columbus.

[10] It is probably the knowledge of this which has led some writers to impute part of his work to the learned Marsilio Ficino, and others, with still less charity and probability, to refer the authorship of the whole to Politian. Comp. Tasso, Opere, (Venezia, 1735 – 42,) tom. x. p. 129, — and Crescimbeni, Istoria della Volgar Poesia, (Venezia, 1731,) tom. iii. pp. 273, 274.

Since to one common centre all things tend ;
So earth, by curious mystery divine
Well balanced, hangs amid the starry spheres.
At our Antipodes are cities, states,
And thronged empires, ne'er divined of yore.
But see, the Sun speeds on his western path
To glad the nations with expected light." [11]

Columbus's hypothesis rested on much higher ground than mere popular belief. What indeed was credulity with the vulgar, and speculation with the learned, amounted in his mind to a settled practical conviction, that made him ready to peril life and fortune on the result of the experiment. He was fortified still further in his conclusions by a correspondence with the learned Italian Toscanelli, who furnished him with a map of his own projection, in which the eastern coast of Asia was delineated opposite to the western frontier of Europe. [12]

[11] Pulci, Morgante Maggiore, canto 25, st. 229, 230. — I have used blank verse, as affording facility for a more literal version than the corresponding *ottava rima* of the original. This passage of Pulci, which has not fallen under the notice of Humboldt, or any other writer on the same subject whom I have consulted, affords, probably, the most circumstantial prediction that is to be found of the existence of a western world. Dante, two centuries before, had intimated more vaguely his belief in an undiscovered quarter of the globe.

" De' vostri sensi, ch' è del rimanente,
Non vogliate negar l'esperienza,
Diretro al sol, del mondo senza gente."
          Inferno, cant. 26, v. 115.

[12] Navarrete, Coleccion de Viages, tom. ii., Col Dipl., no. 1. —

Muñoz, Hist. del Nuevo-Mundo, lib. 2, sec. 17. — It is singular that Columbus, in his visit to Iceland, in 1477, (see Fernando Colon, Hist. del Almirante, cap. 4.) should have learned nothing of the Scandinavian voyages to the northern shores of America in the tenth and following centuries; yet if he was acquainted with them, it appears equally surprising that he should not have adduced the fact in support of his own hypothesis of the existence of land in the west; and that he should have taken a route so different from that of his predecessors in the path of discovery. It may be, however, as M. de Humboldt has well remarked, that the information he obtained in Iceland was too vague to suggest the idea that the lands thus discovered by

Filled with lofty anticipations of achieving a discovery, which would settle a question of such moment, so long involved in obscurity. Columbus submitted the theory on which he had founded his belief in the existence of a western route to King John the Second, of Portugal. Here he was doomed to encounter for the first time the embarrassments and mortifications, which so often obstruct the conceptions of genius, too sublime for the age in which they are formed. After a long and fruitless negotiation, and a dishonorable attempt on the part of the Portuguese to avail themselves clandestinely of his information, he quitted Lisbon in disgust, determined to submit his proposals to the Spanish sovereigns, relying on their reputed character for wisdom and enterprise.[13]

The period of his arrival in Spain, being the latter part of 1484, would seem to have been the most unpropitious possible to his design. The nation was then in the heat of the Moorish war, and the sovereigns were unintermittingly engaged, as we have seen, in prosecuting their campaigns, or in active preparation for them. The large expenditure, incident to this, exhausted all their resources ;

CHAPTER
XVI.

Columbus
applies to
Portugal

To the court
of Castile

---

the Northmen had any connexion with the Indies, of which he was in pursuit. In Columbus's day, indeed, so little was understood of the true position of these countries, that Greenland is laid down on the maps in the European seas, and as a peninsular prolongation of Scandinavia. See Humboldt, Géographie du Nouveau Continent, tom. ii. pp 118, 125.

[13] Herrera, Indias Occidentales, tom. i. dec. 1, lib. 1, cap. 7. — Muñoz, Hist. del Nuevo-Mundo, lib. 2, sec. 19. — Gomara, Hist. de las Indias, cap. 15. — Benzoni, Novi Orbis Historia, lib. 1, cap. 6. — Fernando Colon, Hist. del Almirante, cap. 10. — Faria y Sousa, Europa Portuguesa, tom. ii. part. 3, cap. 4.

and indeed the engrossing character of this domes
tic conquest left them little leisure for indulging in
dreams of distant and doubtful discovery. Columbus, moreover, was unfortunate in his first channel
of communication with the court. He was furnished by Fray Juan Perez de Marchena, guardian of
the convent of La Rabida in Andalusia, who had
early taken a deep interest in his plans, with an introduction to Fernando de Talavera, prior of Prado,
and confessor of the queen, a person high in the
royal confidence, and gradually raised through a
succession of ecclesiastical dignities to the archiepiscopal see of Granada. He was a man of ir-.
reproachable morals, and of comprehensive bene
volence for that day, as is shown in his subsequent
treatment of the unfortunate Moriscoes.[14] He was
also learned ; although his learning was that of the
cloister, deeply tinctured with pedantry and superstition, and debased by such servile deference even
to the errors of antiquity, as at once led him to
discountenance every thing like innovation or enterprise.[15]

Referred to a
council.
With these timid and exclusive views, Talavera
was so far from comprehending the vast conceptions of Columbus, that he seems to have regarded
him as a mere visionary, and his hypothesis as in-

[14] Oviedo, Quincuagenas, MS.,
dial. de Talavera.
[15] Salazar de Mendoza, Crón.
del Gran Cardenal, p. 214. — Herrera, Indias Occidentales, tom. i.
dec. 1, lib. 1, cap. 8. — Fernando
Colon, Hist. del Almirante, cap.
11.

Muñoz postpones his advent to
Spain to 1485, on the supposition
that he offered his services to Genoa immediately after this rupture
with Portugal. Hist. del Nuevo-
Mundo, lib. 2, sec. 21.

volving principles not altogether orthodox. Ferdinand and Isabella, desirous of obtaining the opinion of the most competent judges on the merits of Columbus's theory, referred him to a council selected by Talavera from the most eminent scholars of the kingdom, chiefly ecclesiastics, whose profession embodied most of the science of that day. Such was the apathy exhibited by this learned conclave, and so numerous the impediments suggested by dulness, prejudice, or skepticism, that years glided away before it came to a decision. During this time, Columbus appears to have remained in attendance on the court, bearing arms occasionally in the campaigns, and experiencing from the sovereigns an unusual degree of deference and personal attention; an evidence of which is afforded in the disbursements repeatedly made by the royal order for his private expenses, and in the instructions, issued to the municipalities of the different towns in Andalusia, to supply him gratuitously with lodging and other personal accommodations. [16]

At length, however, Columbus, wearied out by this painful procrastination, pressed the court for a definite answer to his propositions; when he was informed, that the council of Salamanca pronounced his scheme to be " vain, impracticable, and resting on grounds too weak to merit the support of the government." Many in the council, however, were too enlightened to acquiesce in this sentence

[16] Herrera, Indias Occidentales, dec. 1, lib. 1, cap. 8. — Zuñiga, Annales de Sevilla, p. 104. — Navarrete, Coleccion de Viages, tom. i. sec. 60, 61, tom. ii., Col. Dipl. nos 2, 4.

of the majority. Some of the most considerable persons of the court, indeed, moved by the cogency of Columbus's arguments, and affected by the elevation and grandeur of his views, not only cordially embraced his scheme, but extended their personal intimacy and friendship to him. Such, among others, were the grand cardinal Mendoza, a man whose enlarged capacity, and acquaintance with affairs, raised him above many of the narrow prejudices of his order, and Deza, archbishop of Seville, a Dominican friar, whose commanding talents were afterwards unhappily perverted in the service of the Holy Office, over which he presided as successor to Torquemada. [17] The authority of these individuals had undoubtedly great weight with the sovereigns, who softened the verdict of the junto, by an assurance to Columbus, that, " although they were too much occupied at present to embark in his undertaking, yet, at the conclusion of the war, they should find both time and inclination to treat with him." Such was the ineffectual result of Columbus's long and painful solicitation ; and far from receiving the qualified assurance of the sovereigns in mitigation of their refusal, he seems to have considered it as peremptory and final. In

[17] This prelate, Diego de Deza, was born of poor, but respectable parents, at Toro. He early entered the Dominican order, where his learning and exemplary life recommended him to the notice of the sovereigns, who called him to court to take charge of Prince John's education. He was afterwards raised, through the usual course of episcopal preferment, to the metropolitan see of Seville. His situation, as confessor of Ferdinand, gave him great influence over that monarch, with whom he appears to have maintained an intimate correspondence, to the day of his death. Oviedo, Quincuagenas, MS., dial. de Deza.

great dejection of mind, therefore, but without
further delay, he quitted the court, and bent his
way to the south, with the apparently almost desperate intent of seeking out some other patron to
his undertaking. [18]

Columbus had already visited his native city of
Genoa, for the purpose of interesting it in his scheme
of discovery ; but the attempt proved unsuccessful.
He now made application, it would seem, to the
dukes of Medina Sidonia and Medina Celi, successively, from the latter of whom he experienced much
kindness and hospitality; but neither of these nobles, whose large estates lying along the sea-shore
had often invited them to maritime adventure, was
disposed to assume one which seemed too hazard-
ous for the resources of the crown. Without wasting time in further solicitation, Columbus prepared
with a heavy heart to bid adieu to Spain, and carry
his proposals to the king of France, from whom he
had received a letter of encouragement while detained in Andalusia. [19]

CHAPTER
XVI.

He prepares
to leave
Spain

1491

[18] Fernando Colon, Hist. del
Almirante, cap. 11. — Salazar de
Mendoza, Crón. del Gran Cardenal,
p. 215. — Muñoz, Hist. del Nuevo-
Mundo, lib. 2, sec. 25, 29. — Navarrete, Coleccion de Viages, tom.
i., introd., sec. 60.

[19] Herrera, Indias Occidentales,
dec. 1, lib. 1, cap. 8. — Muñoz,
Hist. del Nuevo-Mundo, lib. 2,
sec. 27. — Spotorno, Memorials of
Columbus, pp. 31 – 33. — The last
dates the application to Genoa prior
to that to Portugal.

A letter from the duke of Medina Celi to the cardinal of Spain,
dated 19th March, 1493, refers to

his entertaining Columbus as his
guest for two years. It is very
difficult to determine the date of
these two years. If Herrera is
correct in the statement, that, after
a five years' residence at court,
whose commencement he had previously referred to 1484, he carried his proposals to the duke of
Medina Celi, (see cap. 7, 8,) the
two years may have intervened
between 1489 – 1491. Navarrete
places them between the departure
from Portugal, and the first application to the court of Castile, in
1486. Some other writers, and
among them Muñoz and Irving,

His progress, however, was arrested at the con-vent of La Rabida, which he visited previous to his departure, by his friend the guardian, who prevailed on him to postpone his journey till another effort had been made to move the Spanish court in his favor. For this purpose the worthy ecclesiastic undertook an expedition in person to the newly erected city of Santa Fe, where the sovereigns lay encamped before Granada. Juan Perez had formerly been confessor of Isabella, and was held in great consideration by her for his excellent qualities. On arriving at the camp, he was readily admitted to an audience, when he pressed the suit of Columbus with all the earnestness and reasoning of which he was capable. The friar's eloquence was supported by that of several eminent persons, whom Columbus during his long residence in the country had interested in his project, and who viewed with sincere regret the prospect of its abandonment. Among these individuals, are particularly mentioned Alonso de Quintanilla, comptroller general of Castile, Louis de St. Angel, a fiscal officer of the crown of Aragon, and the marchioness of Moya, the personal friend of Isabella, all of whom exercised considerable influence

referring his application to Genoa to 1485, and his first appearance in Spain to a subsequent period, make no provision for the residence with the duke of Medina Celi. Mr. Irving indeed is betrayed into a chronological inaccuracy, in speaking of a seven years' residence at the court in 1491, which he had previously noticed as having before begun in 1486. (Life of Columbus, (London, 1828,) comp. vol. i. pp. 109, 141.) In fact, the discrepancies among the earliest authorities are such as to render hopeless any attempt to settle with precision the chronology of Columbus's movements previous to his first voyage.

over her counsels. Their representations, combined with the opportune season of the application,
occurring at the moment when the approaching
termination of the Moorish war allowed room for
interest in other objects, wrought so favorable a
change in the dispositions of the sovereigns, that
they consented to resume the negotiation with Columbus. An invitation was accordingly sent to
him to repair to Santa Fe, and a considerable sum
provided for his suitable equipment, and his expenses on the road. [20]

Columbus, who lost no time in availing himself   Columbus at
Santa Fe
of this welcome intelligence, arrived at the camp
in season to witness the surrender of Granada,
when every heart, swelling with exultation at the
triumphant termination of the war, was naturally
disposed to enter with greater confidence on a new
career of adventure. At his interview with the
king and queen, he once more exhibited the arguments on which his hypothesis was founded. He
then endeavoured to stimulate the cupidity of his
audience, by picturing the realms of Mangi and
Cathay, which he confidently expected to reach by
this western route, in all the barbaric splendors
which had been shed over them by the lively fancy
of Marco Polo and other travellers of the middle
ages; and he concluded with appealing to a higher
principle, by holding out the prospect of extending

[20] Ferreras, Hist. d'Espagne, tom. viii. pp. 129, 130. — Muñoz, Hist. del Nuevo-Mundo, lib. 2, sec. 31. — Herrera, Indias Occi- dentales, dec. 1, lib. 1, cap. 8. — Navarrete, Coleccion de Viages, tom. i., introd., sec. 60.

the empire of the Cross over nations of benighted heathen, while he proposed to devote the profits of his enterprise to the recovery of the Holy Sepulchre. This last ebullition, which might well have passed for fanaticism in a later day, and given a visionary tinge to his whole project, was not quite so preposterous in an age, in which the spirit of the crusades might be said still to linger, and the romance of religion had not yet been dispelled by sober reason. The more temperate suggestion of the diffusion of the gospel was well suited to affect Isabella, in whose heart the principle of devotion was deeply seated, and who, in all her undertakings, seems to have been far less sensible to the vulgar impulses of avarice or ambition, than to any argument connected, however remotely, with the interests of religion. [21]

Amidst all these propitious demonstrations towards Columbus, an obstacle unexpectedly arose in the nature of his demands, which stipulated for himself and heirs the title and authority of Admiral and Viceroy over all lands discovered by him, with one tenth of the profits. This was deemed wholly inadmissible. Ferdinand, who had looked with cold distrust on the expedition from the first, was supported by the remonstrances of Talavera, the new archbishop of Granada; who declared, that " such demands savoured of the highest degree of arrogance, and would be unbecoming in their High-

---

[21] Herrera, Indias Occidentales, dec. 1, lib. 1, cap. 8. — Primer Viage de Colon, apud Navarrete, Coleccion de Viages, tom. i. pp. 2 117. — Fernando Colon, Hist. de. Almirante, cap. 13

nesses to grant to a needy foreign adventurer." CHAPTER
XVI.
Columbus, however, steadily resisted every attempt
to induce him to modify his propositions. On this
ground, the conferences were abruptly broken off,
and he once more turned his back upon the Spanish
court, resolved rather to forego his splendid anticipations of discovery, at the very moment when the
career so long sought was thrown open to him,
than surrender one of the honorable distinctions
due to his services. This last act is perhaps the
most remarkable exhibition in his whole life, of
that proud, unyielding spirit, which sustained him
through so many years of trial, and enabled him at
length to achieve his great enterprise, in the face
of every obstacle which man and nature had opposed to it.[22]

The misunderstanding was not suffered to be of The queen
favorable
disposition.
long duration. Columbus's friends, and especially
Louis de St. Angel, remonstrated with the queen
on these proceedings in the most earnest manner.
He frankly told her, that Columbus's demands, if
high, were at least contingent on success, when
they would be well deserved; that, if he failed, he
required nothing. He expatiated on his qualifications for the undertaking, so signal as to insure in
all probability the patronage of some other monarch,
who would reap the fruits of his discoveries; and
he ventured to remind the queen, that her present
policy was not in accordance with the magnanimous
spirit, which had hitherto made her the ready patron

<hr>

[22] Muñoz, Hist. del Neuvo-Mun- Colon, Hist. del Almirante, ubi
do, lib. 2, sec. 28, 29. —Fernando supra.

of great and heroic enterprise. Far from being displeased, Isabella was moved by his honest eloquence. She contemplated the proposals of Columbus in their true light; and, refusing to hearken any longer to the suggestions of cold and timid counsellors, she gave way to the natural impulses of her own noble and generous heart; " I will assume the undertaking," said she, " for my own crown of Castile, and am ready to pawn my jewels to defray the expenses of it, if the funds in the treasury shall be found inadequate." The treasury had been reduced to the lowest ebb by the late war; but the receiver, St. Angel, advanced the sums required, from the Aragonese revenues deposited in his hands. Aragon however was not considered as adventuring in the expedition, the charges and emoluments of which were reserved exclusively for Castile. [23]

Final arrangement with Columbus.
Columbus, who was overtaken by the royal messenger at a few leagues' distance only from Granada, experienced the most courteous reception on his return to Santa Fe, where a definitive arrange ment was concluded with the Spanish sovereigns, April 17th, 1492. By the terms of the capitulation, Ferdinand and Isabella, as lords of the ocean-seas, constituted Christopher Columbus their admiral, viceroy, and governor-general of all such islands and continents as he should discover in the western ocean, with the privilege of nominating three can-

[23] Herrera, Indias Occidentales, dec. 1, lib. 1, cap. 8. — Muñoz, Hist. del Nuevo-Mundo, lib. 2, sec. 32, 33. — Fernando Colon, Hist. del Almirante, cap. 14. — Gomara, Hist. de las Indias, cap. 15.

didates, for the selection of one by the crown, for the government of each of these territories. He was to be vested with exclusive right of jurisdiction over all commercial transactions within his admiralty. He was to be entitled to one tenth of all the products and profits within the limits of his discoveries, and an additional eighth, provided he should contribute one eighth part of the expense. By a subsequent ordinance, the official dignities above enumerated were settled on him and his heirs for ever, with the privilege of prefixing the title of Don to their names, which had not then degenerated into an appellation of mere courtesy.[24]

No sooner were the arrangements completed, than Isabella prepared with her characteristic promptness to forward the expedition by the most efficient measures. Orders were sent to Seville and the other ports of Andalusia, to furnish stores and other articles requisite for the voyage, free of duty, and at as low rates as possible. The fleet, consisting of three vessels, was to sail from the little port of Palos in Andalusia, which had been condemned for some delinquency to maintain two caravels for a twelvemonth for the public service. The third vessel was furnished by the admiral, aided, as it would seem, in defraying the charges, by his friend the guardian of La Rabida, and the Pinzons, a family in Palos long distinguished for its enterprise among the mariners of that active community.

He sails on his first voyage

---

[24] Navarrete, Coleccion de Viages, tom. ii., Col. Diplomat., nos. 5, 6.—Zuñiga, Annales de Sevilla, p. 412.—Mariana, Hist de España, tom. ii. p. 605.

With their assistance, Columbus was enabled to surmount the disinclination, and indeed open opposition, manifested by the Andalusian mariners to his perilous voyage; so that in less than three months his little squadron was equipped for sea. A sufficient evidence of the extreme unpopularity of the expedition is afforded by a royal ordinance of the 30th of April, promising protection to all persons. who should embark in it, from criminal prosecution of whatever kind, until two months after their return. The armament consisted of two caravels, or light vessels without decks, and a third of larger burden. The total number of persons who embarked amounted to one hundred and twenty; and the whole charges of the crown for the expedition did not exceed seventeen thousand florins. The fleet was instructed to keep clear of the African coast, and other maritime possessions of Portugal At length, all things being in readiness, Columbus and his whole crew partook of the sacrament, and confessed themselves, after the devout manner of the ancient Spanish voyagers, when engaged in any important enterprise; and on the morning of the 3d of August, 1492, the intrepid navigator, bidding adieu to the old world, launched forth on that unfathomed waste of waters where no sail had been ever spread before.[25]

---

[25] Peter Martyr, De Rebus Oceanicis et Novo Orbe, (Coloniæ, 1574,) dec. 1, lib. 1. — Navarrete, Coleccion de Viages, tom. ii., Co. Diplomat., nos. 7, 8, 9, 10, 12. — Herrera, Indias Occidentales, dec. 1, lib. 1, cap. 9. — Fernando Colon, Hist. del Almirante, cap. 14. — Muñoz, Hist. del Nuevo-Mundo, lib. 2, sec. 33. — Benzoni, Novi Orbis Hist., lib. 1, cap. 6. — Gomara, Hist. de las Indias, cap. 15. The expression in the text will not seem too strong, even admitting

CHAPTER
XVI.

Indifference
to his enter-
prise.

It is impossible to peruse the story of Columbus without assigning to him almost exclusively the glory of his great discovery; for, from the first moment of its conception to that of its final execution, he was encountered by every species of mortification and embarrassment, with scarcely a heart to cheer, or a hand to help him.[26] Those more enlightened persons, whom, during his long residence in Spain, he succeeded in interesting in his expedition, looked to it probably as the means of solving a dubious problem, with the same sort of vague and skeptical curiosity as to its successful result, with which we contemplate, in our day, an attempt to arrive at the Northwest passage. How feeble was the interest excited, even among those, who from their science and situation would seem to have their attention most naturally drawn towards it, may be inferred from the infrequency of allusion to

the previous discoveries of the Northmen, which were made in so much higher latitudes. Humboldt has well shown the probability, a priori, of such discoveries, made in a narrow part of the Atlantic, where the Orcades, the Feroe Islands, Iceland, and Greenland afforded the voyager so many intermediate stations, at moderate distances from each other. (Géographie du Nouveau Continent, tom. ii. pp. 183 et seq.) The publication of the original Scandinavian MSS., (of which imperfect notices and selections, only, have hitherto found their way into the world,) by the Royal Society of Northern Antiquaries, at Copenhagen, is a matter of the deepest interest; and it is fortunate, that it is to be conducted under auspices, which must insure its execution in the most

faithful and able manner. It may be doubted, however, whether the declaration of the Prospectus, that " it was the knowledge of the Scandinavian voyages, in all probability, which prompted the expedition of Columbus," can ever be established. His personal history furnishes strong internal evidence to the contrary.

26 How strikingly are the forlorn condition and indomitable energy of Columbus depicted in the following noble verses of Chiabrera;

" Certo da cor, ch' alto destin non scelse,
Son l' imprese magnanime neglette;
Ma le bell' alme alle bell' opre elette
Sanno gioir nelle fatiche eccelse;
Nè biasmo popolar, frale catena,
Spirto d' onore, il suo cammin reffrena.
Così lunga stagion per modi indegni
Europa disprezzò l' inclita speme,
Schernendo il vulgo, e seco i Regi insieme,
Nudo nocchier, promettitor di Regni."
Rime, parte 1, canzone 12.

it in the correspondence and other writings of that time, previous to the actual discovery. Peter Martyr, one of the most accomplished scholars of the period, whose residence at the Castilian court must have fully instructed him in the designs of Columbus, and whose inquisitive mind led him subsequently to take the deepest interest in the results of his discoveries, does not, so far as I am aware, allude to him in any part of his voluminous correspondence with the learned men of his time, previous to the first expedition. The common people regarded, not merely with apathy, but with terror, the prospect of a voyage, that was to take the mariner from the safe and pleasant seas which he was accustomed to navigate, and send him roving on the boundless wilderness of waters, which tradition and superstitious fancy had peopled with innumerable forms of horror.

It is true that Columbus experienced a most honorable reception at the Castilian court; such as naturally flowed from the benevolent spirit of Isabella, and her just appreciation of his pure and elevated character. But the queen was too little of a proficient in science to be able to estimate the merits of his hypothesis; and, as many of those, on whose judgment she leaned, deemed it chimerical, it is probable that she never entertained a deep conviction of its truth; at least not enough to warrant the liberal expenditure, which she never refused to schemes of real importance. This is certainly inferred by the paltry amount actually expended on the armament, far inferior to that

appropriated to the equipment of two several fleets
in the course of the late war for a foreign expedition, as well as to that, with which in the ensuing
year she followed up Columbus's discoveries.

But while, on a review of the circumstances, we
are led more and more to admire the constancy
and unconquerable spirit, which carried Columbus
victorious through all the difficulties of his under
taking, we must remember, in justice to Isabella,
that, although tardily, she did in fact furnish the
resources essential to its execution ; that she undertook the enterprise when it had been explicitly declined by other powers, and when probably none
other of that age would have been found to countenance it ; and that, after once plighting her faith
to Columbus, she became his steady friend, shielding him against the calumnies of his enemies, reposing in him the most generous confidence, and
serving him in the most acceptable manner, by
supplying ample resources for the prosecution of his
glorious discoveries.[27]

[27] Columbus, in a letter written on his third voyage, pays an honest, heartfelt tribute to the effectual patronage which he experienced from the queen. " In the midst of the general incredulity," says he, " the Almighty infused into the queen, my lady, the spirit of intelligence and energy ; and, whilst every one else, in his ignorance, was expatiating only on the inconvenience and cost, her Highness approved it, on the contrary, and gave it all the support in her power." See Carta al Ama del Principe D. Juan, apud Navarrete, Coleccion de Viages, tom. i. p. 266.

It is now more than thirty years since the Spanish government intrusted Don Martin Fernandez de Navarrete, one of the most eminent scholars of the country, with the care of exploring the public archives, for the purpose of collecting information relative to the voyages and discoveries of the early Spanish navigators.   In 1825, Señor Navarrete gave to the world the first fruits of his indefatigable researches, in two volumes, the commencement of a series, comprehending letters, private journals, royal ordinances, and other original documents, illustrative of the discovery of America. These two volumes are devoted exclusively to the adventures and personal history of Columbus, and must be regarded as the only authentic basis, on which any notice of the great navigator can hereafter rest. Fortunately, Mr. Irving's visit to Spain, at this period, enabled the world to derive the full benefit of Señor Navarrete's researches, by presenting their results in connexion with whatever had been before

known of Columbus, in the lucid and attractive form, which engages the interest of every reader. I would seem highly proper, that the fortunes of the discoverer of America should engage the pen of an inhabitant of her most favored and enlightened region ; and it is un necessary to add, that the task has been executed in a manner which must secure to the historian a share in the imperishable renown of his subject. The adventures of Columbus, which form so splendid an episode to the reign of Ferdinand and Isabella, cannot properly come within the scope of its historian, except so far as relates to his personal intercourse with the government, or to their results on the fortunes of the Spanish monarchy

CHAPTER XVII.

EXPULSION OF THE JEWS FROM SPAIN.

1492.

Excitement against the Jews. — Edict of Expulsion. — Dreadful Sufferings of the Emigrants. — Whole number of Exiles. — Disastrous Results. — True Motives of the Edict. — Contemporary Judgments.

WHILE the Spanish sovereigns were detained before Granada, they published their memorable and most disastrous edict against the Jews ; inscribing it, as it were, with the same pen which drew up the glorious capitulation of Granada and the treaty with Columbus. The reader has been made acquainted in a preceding chapter with the prosperous condition of the Jews in the Peninsula, and the preëminent consideration, which they attained there beyond any other part of Christendom. The envy raised by their prosperity, combined with the high religious excitement kindled in the long war with the infidel, directed the terrible arm of the Inquisition, as has been already stated, against this unfortunate people ; but the result showed the failure of the experiment, since comparatively few conversions, and those frequently of a suspicious character, were effected, while the great mass still

PART
————

Fomented
by the
clergy.

maintained a pertinacious attachment to ancient errors.[1]

Under these circumstances, the popular odium, inflamed by the discontent of the clergy at the resistance which they encountered in the work of proselytism, gradually grew stronger and stronger against the unhappy Israelites. Old traditions, as old indeed as the thirteenth and fourteenth centuries, were revived, and charged on the present generation, with all the details of place and action. Christian children were said to be kidnapped, in order to be crucified in derision of the Saviour; the host, it was rumored, was exposed to the grossest indignities; and physicians and apothecaries, whose science was particularly cultivated by the Jews in the middle ages, were accused of poisoning their Christian patients. No rumor was too absurd for the easy credulity of the people. The Israelites were charged with the more probable offence of attempting to convert to their own faith the *ancient Christians*, as well as to reclaim such of their own race as had recently embraced Christianity. A great scandal was occasioned also by the intermarriages, which still occasionally took place between Jews and Christians; the latter condescending to repair their dilapidated fortunes by these wealthy

---

[1] It is a proof of the high consideration in which such Israelites as were willing to embrace Christianity were held, that three of that number, Alvarez, Avila, and Pulgar were private secretaries of the queen. (Mem. de la Acad. de Hist., tom. vi. Ilust. 18.)

An incidental expression of Martyr's, among many similar ones by contemporaries, affords the true key to the popular odium against the Jews. " Cum namque viderent, Judæorum tabido commercio, qui hac horâ sunt in Hispaniâ *innumeri Christianis ditiores*, plurimorum animos corrumpi ac seduci,' etc. Opus Epist., epist. 92.

CHAPTER
XVII.

alliances, though at the expense of their vaunted purity of blood.[2]

These various offences were urged against the Jews with great pertinacity by their enemies, and the sovereigns were importuned to adopt a more rigorous policy. The inquisitors, in particular, to whom the work of conversion had been specially intrusted, represented the incompetence of all lenient measures to the end proposed. They asserted, that the only mode left for the extirpation of the Jewish heresy, was to eradicate the seed; and they boldly demanded the immediate and total banishment of every unbaptized Israelite from the land.[3]

The Jews, who had obtained an intimation of these proceedings, resorted to their usual crafty policy for propitiating the sovereigns. They commissioned one of their body to tender a donative of thirty thousand ducats towards defraying the expenses of the Moorish war. The negotiation however was suddenly interrupted by the inquisitor general, Torquemada, who burst into the apartment of the palace, where the sovereigns were giving audience to the Jewish deputy, and, drawing forth a crucifix from beneath his mantle, held it up, exclaiming, "Judas Iscariot sold his master for thirty

Violent con
duct of Tor
quemada.

[2] Paramo, De Origine Inquisitionis, p. 164. — Llorente, Hist. de l'Inquisition, tom. i. cap. 7, sec. 3. — Peter Martyr, Opus Epist., epist. 94. — Ferreras, Hist. d'Espagne, tom. viii. p. 128.

[3] Paramo, De Origine Inquisitionis, p. 163.
Salazar de Mendoza refers the

sovereign's consent to the banishment of the Jews, in a great measure, to the urgent remonstrances of the cardinal of Spain. The bigotry of the biographer makes him claim the credit of every fanatical act for his illustrious hero. See Crón. del Gran Cardenal, p. 250.

pieces of silver. Your Highnesses would sell him anew for thirty thousand; here he is, take him, and barter him away." So saying, the frantic priest threw the crucifix on the table, and left the apartment. The sovereigns, instead of chastising this presumption, or despising it as a mere freak of insanity, were overawed by it. Neither Ferdinand nor Isabella, had they been left to the unbiassed dictates of their own reason, could have sanctioned for a moment so impolitic a measure, which involved the loss of the most industrious and skilful portion of their subjects. Its extreme injustice and cruelty rendered it especially repugnant to the naturally humane disposition of the queen.[4] But she had been early schooled to distrust her own reason, and indeed the natural suggestions of humanity, in cases of conscience. Among the reverend counsellors, on whom she most relied in these matters, was the Dominican Torquemada. The situation which this man enjoyed as the queen's confessor, during the tender years of her youth, gave him an ascendency over her mind, which must have been denied to a person of his savage, fanatical temper, even with the advantages of this spiritual connexion, had it been formed at a riper period of her life. Without opposing further resistance to the representations, so emphatically expressed,

---

[4] Llorente, Hist. de l'Inquisition, tom. i. chap. 7, sect. 5.

Pulgar, in a letter to the cardinal of Spain, animadverting with much severity on the tenor of certain municipal ordinances against the Jews in Guipuscoa and Toledo, in 1482, plainly intimates, that they were not at all to the taste of the queen. See Letras, (Amstelodami, 1670,) let. 31.

of the holy persons in whom she most confided, CHAPTER
Isabella, at length, silenced her own scruples, and _{XVII.}
consented to the fatal measure of proscription.

The edict for the expulsion of the Jews was Edict of ex-
signed by the Spanish sovereigns at Granada, pulsion.
March 30th, 1492. The preamble alleges, in vindication of the measure, the danger of allowing
further intercourse between the Jews and their
Christian subjects, in consequence of the incorri-
gible obstinacy, with which the former persisted in
their attempts to make converts of the latter to
their own faith, and to instruct them in their heret-
ical rites, in open defiance of every legal prohibi-
tion and penalty. When a college or corporation of
any kind, — the instrument goes on to state, — is
convicted of any great or detestable crime, it is
right that it should be disfranchised, the less suffering with the greater, the innocent with the guilty.
If this be the case in temporal concerns, it is much
more so in those, which affect the eternal welfare
of the soul. It finally decrees, that all unbaptized
Jews, of whatever sex, age, or condition, should
depart from the realm by the end of July next
ensuing; prohibiting them from revisiting it, on any
pretext whatever, under penalty of death and confiscation of property. It was, moreover, interdicted to every subject, to harbour, succour, or minister
to the necessities of any Jew, after the expiration
of the term limited for his departure. The persons
and property of the Jews, in the mean time, were
taken under the royal protection. They were allowed to dispose of their effects of every kind on

their own account, and to carry the proceeds along with them, in bills of exchange, or merchandise not prohibited, but neither in gold nor silver. [5]

The doom of exile fell like a thunderbolt on the heads of the Israelites. A large proportion of them had hitherto succeeded in shielding themselves from the searching eye of the Inquisition, by an affectation of reverence for the forms of Catholic worship, and a discreet forbearance of whatever might offend the prejudices of their Christian brethren. They had even hoped, that their steady loyalty, and a quiet and orderly discharge of their social duties, would in time secure them higher immunities. Many had risen to a degree of opulence, by means of the thrift and dexterity peculiar to the race, which gave them a still deeper interest in the land of their residence. [6] Their families were reared in all the elegant refinements of life; and their wealth and education often disposed them to turn their attention to liberal pursuits, which ennobled the character, indeed, but rendered them personally more sensible to physical annoyance, and less fitted to encounter the perils and privations of their dreary pilgrimage. Even the mass of the common people, possessed a dexterity in various handicrafts, which afforded a comfortable livelihood,

---

[5] Carbajal, Anales, MS., año. 1492. — Recop. de las Leyes, lib. 8, tit. 2, ley 2. — Pragmáticas del Reyno, ed. 1520, fol. 3.

[6] The Curate of Los Palacios speaks of several Israelites worth one or two millions of maravedies, and another even as having amassed ten. He mentions one, in particular, by the name of Abraham, as renting the *greater part of Castile!* It will hardly do to take the good Curate's statement *à la lettre.* See Reyes Católicos, MS., cap. 112.

raising them far above similar classes in most other nations, who might readily be detached from the soil on which they happened to be cast, with comparatively little sacrifice of local interests.[7] These ties were now severed at a blow. They were to go forth as exiles from the land of their birth; the land where all, whom they ever loved, had lived or died; the land, not so much of their adoption, as of inheritance; which had been the home of their ancestors for centuries, and with whose prosperity and glory they were of course as intimately associated, as was any ancient Spaniard. They were to be cast out helpless and defenceless, with a brand of infamy set on them, among nations who had always held them in derision and hatred.

Those provisions of the edict, which affected a show of kindness to the Jews, were contrived so artfully, as to be nearly nugatory. As they were excluded from the use of gold and silver, the only medium for representing their property was bills of exchange. But commerce was too limited and imperfect to allow of these being promptly obtained to any very considerable, much less to the enormous amount required in the present instance. It was impossible, moreover, to negotiate a sale of their effects under existing circumstances, since the market was soon glutted with commodities; and few would be found willing to give any thing like an equivalent for what, if not disposed of within the prescribed term, the proprietors must relinquish at

[7] Bernaldez, Reyes Católicos, ubi supra.

any rate. So deplorable, indeed, was the sacrifice of property, that a chronicler of the day mentions, that he had seen a house exchanged for an ass, and a vineyard for a suit of clothes! In Aragon, matters were still worse. The government there discovered, that the Jews were largely indebted to individuals and to certain corporations. It accordingly caused their property to be sequestrated for the benefit of their creditors, until their debts should be liquidated. Strange indeed, that the balance should be found against a people, who have been everywhere conspicuous for their commercial sagacity and resources, and who, as factors of the great nobility and farmers of the revenue, enjoyed at least equal advantages in Spain with those possessed in other countries, for the accumulation of wealth.[8]

Constancy
of the Jews.

While the gloomy aspect of their fortunes pressed heavily on the hearts of the Israelites, the Spanish clergy were indefatigable in the work of conversion. They lectured in the synagogues and public squares, expounding the doctrines of Christianity, and thundering forth both argument and invective against the Hebrew heresy. But their laudable endeavours were in a great measure counteracted by the more authoritative rhetoric of the Jewish Rabbins, who compared the persecutions of their brethren, to those which their ancestors had suffered under Pharaoh. They encouraged them to

---

[8] Bernaldez, Reyes Católicos, MS., cap. 10. — Zurita, Anales, tom. v. fol. 9.

Capmany notices the number of synagogues existing in Aragon, in 1428, as amounting to nineteen. In Galicia at the same time there were but three, and in Catalonia but one. See Mem. de Barcelona, tom. iv. Apend. num. 11.

persevere, representing that the present afflictions were intended as a trial of their faith by the Almighty, who designed in this way to guide them to the promised land, by opening a path through the waters, as he had done to their fathers of old. The more wealthy Israelites enforced their exhortations by liberal contributions for the relief of their indigent brethren. Thus strengthened, there were found but very few, when the day of departure arrived, who were not prepared to abandon their country rather than their religion. This extraordinary act of self-devotion by a whole people for conscience' sake may be thought, in the nineteenth century, to merit other epithets than those of " perfidy, incredulity, and stiff-necked obstinacy," with which the worthy Curate of Los Palacios, in the charitable feeling of that day, has seen fit to stigmatize it.[9]

CHAPTER XVII.

When the period of departure arrived, all the principal routes through the country might be seen swarming with emigrants, old and young, the sick and the helpless, men, women, and children, mingled promiscuously together, some mounted on horses or mules, but far the greater part undertaking their painful pilgrimage on foot. The sight of so much misery touched even the Spaniards with pity, though none might succour them ; for the grand inquisitor, Torquemada, enforced the ordinance to that effect, by denouncing heavy ecclesiastical cen-

Routes of the emigrants.

[9] Bernaldez, Reyes Católicos, MS., cap. 10. 113. — Ferreras, Hist. d' Espagne, tom. viii. p. 131.

sures on all who should presume to violate it. The fugitives were distributed along various routes, being determined in their destination by accidental circumstances, much more than any knowledge of the respective countries to which they were bound. Much the largest division, amounting according to some estimates to eighty thousand souls, passed into Portugal; whose monarch, John the Second, dispensed with his scruples of conscience so far, as to give them a free passage through his dominions on their way to Africa, in consideration of a tax of a *cruzado* a head. He is even said to have silenced his scruples so far, as to allow certain ingenious artisans to establish themselves permanently in the kingdom.[10]

Their sufferings in Africa.

A considerable number found their way to the ports of Santa Maria and Cadiz, where, after lingering some time in the vain hope of seeing the waters open for their egress, according to the promises of the Rabbins, they embarked on board a Spanish fleet for the Barbary coast. Having crossed over to Ercilla, a Christian settlement in Africa, whence they proceeded by land towards Fez, where a considerable body of their countrymen resided, they were assaulted on their route by the roving tribes of the desert, in quest of plunder. Notwithstanding the interdict, the Jews had contrived to secrete small sums of money, sewed up in their

---

[10] Zurita, Anales, tom. v. fol. 9. — Ferreras, Hist. d'Espagne, tom. viii. p. 133.— Bernaldez, Reyes Católicos, ubi supra.— La Clède, Hist. de Portugal, tom. iv. p. 95. — Mariana, Hist. de España, tom ii. p. 602.

garments or the linings of their saddles. These
did not escape the avaricious eyes of their spoilers,
who are even said to have ripped open the bodies
of their victims, in search of gold, which they were
supposed to have swallowed. The lawless barbarians, mingling lust with avarice, abandoned themselves to still more frightful excesses, violating the
wives and daughters of the unresisting Jews, or
massacring in cold blood such as offered resistance.
But without pursuing these loathsome details further, it need only be added, that the miserable exiles endured such extremity of famine, that they
were glad to force a nourishment from the grass
which grew scantily among the sands of the desert;
until at length great numbers of them, wasted by
disease, and broken in spirit, retraced their steps to
Ercilla, and consented to be baptized, in the hope
of being permitted to revisit their native land.
The number, indeed, was so considerable, that the
priest who officiated was obliged to make use of
the mop, or hyssop, with which the Roman catholic
missionaries were wont to scatter the holy drops,
whose mystic virtue could cleanse the soul in a moment from the foulest stains of infidelity. " Thus,"
says a Castilian historian, " the calamities of these
poor blind creatures proved in the end an excellent
remedy, that God made use of to unseal their eyes,
which they now opened to the vain promises of the
Rabbins; so that, renouncing their ancient heresies,
they became faithful followers of the Cross!" [11]

11 Ferreras, Hist. d'Espagne, tom. viii. p. 133. — Bernaldez, Reyes
Católicos, MS., cap. 113.

Many of the emigrants took the direction of Italy. Those who landed at Naples brought with them an infectious disorder, contracted by long confinement in small, crowded, and ill-provided vessels. The disorder was so malignant, and spread with such frightful celerity, as to sweep off more than twenty thousand inhabitants of the city, in the course of the year, whence it extended its devastation over the whole Italian peninsula.

A graphic picture of these horrors is thus given by a Genoese historian, an eyewitness of the scenes he describes. "No one," he says, "could behold the sufferings of the Jewish exiles unmoved. A great many perished of hunger, especially those of tender years. Mothers, with scarcely strength to support themselves, carried their famished infants in their arms, and died with them. Many fell victims to the cold, others to intense thirst, while the unaccustomed distresses incident to a sea voyage aggravated their maladies. I will not enlarge on the cruelty and the avarice which they frequently experienced from the masters of the ships, which transported them from Spain. Some were murdered to gratify their cupidity, others forced to sell their children for the expenses of the passage. They arrived in Genoa in crowds, but were not suffered to tarry there long, by reason of the ancient law which interdicted the Jewish traveller from a longer residence than three days. They were allowed, however, to refit their vessels, and to recruit themselves for some days from the fatigues of their voyage. One might have taken them for spectres, so emaciated were they, so cadaverous in their aspect, and with eyes so sunken; they differed in nothing from the dead, except in the power of motion, which indeed they scarcely retained. Many fainted and expired on the mole, which being completely surrounded by the sea, was the only quarter vouchsafed to the wretched emigrants. The infection bred by such a swarm of dead and dying persons was not at once perceived; but, when the winter broke up, ulcers began to make their appearance, and the malady, which lurked for a long time in the city, broke out into the plague in the following year." [12]

Many of the exiles passed into Turkey, and to different parts of the Levant, where their descendants continued to speak the Castilian language far into the following century. Others found their way to France, and even England. Part of their religious services is recited to this day in Spanish, in one or more of the London synagogues; and the modern Jew still reverts with fond partiality to Spain, as the cherished land of his fathers, illustrated by the most glorious recollections in their eventful history. [13]

---

[12] Senarega, apud Muratori, Rerum Ital. Script., tom. xxiv. pp. 531, 532.

[13] See a sensible notice of Hebrew literature in Spain, in the Retrospective Review, vol. iii. p. 209. — Mariana, Hist. de España, tom. ii. lib. 26, cap. 1. — Zurita, Anales, tom. v. fol. 9.

Not a few of the learned exiles attained to eminence in those countries of Europe where they transferred their residence. One is mentioned by Castro as a leading practitioner of medicine in Genoa; another, as filling the posts of astronomer and chronicler, under king Emanuel of Portugal. Many of them published works in various departments of science, which were translated into the Spanish and other European languages. Biblioteca Española tom. i. pp. 359 – 372.

The whole number of Jews expelled from Spain by Ferdinand and Isabella, is variously computed from one hundred and sixty thousand to eight hundred thousand souls ; a discrepancy sufficiently indicating the paucity of authentic data. Most modern writers, with the usual predilection for startling results, have assumed the latter estimate ; and Llorente has made it the basis of some important calculations, in his History of the Inquisition. A view of all the circumstances will lead us without much hesitation to adopt the more moderate computation. [14] This, moreover, is placed beyond reasonable doubt by the direct testimony of the Curate of Los Palacios. He reports, that a Jewish Rabbin, one of the exiles, subsequently returned to Spain, where he was baptized by him. This person, whom Bernaldez commends for his intelligence, estimated the whole number of his unbaptized countrymen in the dominions of Ferdinand

[14] From a curious document in the *Archives of Simancas*, consisting of a report made to the Spanish sovereigns by their accountant general, Quintanilla, in 1492, it would appear, that the population of the kingdom of Castile, exclusive of Granada, was then estimated at 1,500,000 *vecinos*, or householders. (See Mem. de la Acad. de Hist., Apend. no. 12.) This, allowing four and a half to a family, would make the whole population 6,750,000. It appears from the statement of Bernaldez, that the kingdom of Castile contained five sixths of the whole amount of Jews in the Spanish monarchy. This proportion, if 800,000 be received as the total, would amount in round numbers to 670,000 or ten per cent. of the whole population of the kingdom. Now it is manifestly improbable, that so large a portion of the whole nation, conspicuous moreover for wealth and intelligence, could have been held so light in a political aspect, as the Jews certainly were, or have tamely submitted for so many years to the most wanton indignities without resistance ; or finally, that the Spanish government would have ventured on so bold a measure as the banishment of so numerous and powerful a class, and that too with as few precautions apparently, as would be required for driving ou of the country a roving gang of gipsies.

and Isabella, at the publication of the edict, at thirty-six thousand families. Another Jewish authority, quoted by the Curate, reckoned them at thirty-five thousand. This, assuming an average of four and a half to a family, gives the sum total of about one hundred and sixty thousand individuals, agreeably to the computation of Bernaldez. There is little reason for supposing, that the actual amount would suffer diminution in the hands of either the Jewish or Castilian authority; since the one might naturally be led to exaggerate, in order to heighten sympathy with the calamities of his nation, and the other, to magnify as far as possible the glorious triumphs of the Cross. [15]

The detriment incurred by the state, however, is not founded so much on any numerical estimate, as on the subtraction of the mechanical skill, intelligence, and general resources of an orderly, industrious population. In this view, the mischief was incalculably greater than that inferred by the mere number of the exiled ; and, although even this might have been gradually repaired in a country allowed the free and healthful developement of its energies, yet in Spain this was so effectually counteracted by the Inquisition, and other causes in the following century, that the loss may be deemed irretrievable.

Disastrous results.

The expulsion of so numerous a class of subjects by an independent act of the sovereign, might well

[15] Bernaldez, Reyes Católicos, MS., cap. 110. — Llorente, Hist. de l'Inquisition, tom. i. chap. 7, sect. 7. — Mariana, Hist. de España, tom. ii. lib. 26. — Zurita, Anales, tom. v. fol. 9.

be regarded as an enormous stretch of prerogative, altogether incompatible with any thing like a free government. But to judge the matter rightly, we must take into view the actual position of the Jews at that time. Far from forming an integral part of the commonwealth, they were regarded as alien to it, as a mere excrescence, which, so far from contributing to the healthful action of the body politic, was nourished by its vicious humors, and might be lopped off at any time, when the health of the system demanded it. Far from being protected by the laws, the only aim of the laws, in reference to them, was to define more precisely their civil incapacities, and to draw the line of division more broadly between them and the Christians. Even this humiliation by no means satisfied the national prejudices, as is evinced by the great number of tumults and massacres of which they were the victims. In these circumstances, it seemed to be no great assumption of authority, to pronounce sentence of exile against those, whom public opinion had so long proscribed as enemies to the state. It was only carrying into effect that opinion, expressed as it had been in a great variety of ways; and, as far as the rights of the nation were concerned, the banishment of a single Spaniard would have been held a grosser violation of them, than that of the whole race of Israelites.

True motives of the edict.

It has been common with modern historians to detect a principal motive for the expulsion of the Jews, in the avarice of the government. It is only necessary, however, to transport ourselves back to

those times, to find it in perfect accordance with CHAPTER
their spirit, at least in Spain. It is indeed incredible, that persons possessing the political sagacity of
Ferdinand and Isabella could indulge a temporary
cupidity, at the sacrifice of the most important and
permanent interests, converting their wealthiest
districts into a wilderness, and dispeopling them of a
class of citizens, who contributed beyond all others,
not only to the general resources, but the direct
revenues of the crown ; a measure so manifestly
uns)und, as to lead even a barbarian monarch of
that day to exclaim, " Do they call this Ferdinand
a politic prince, who can thus impoverish his own
kingdom and enrich ours ! " [16] It would seem, indeed, when the measure had been determined on,
that the Aragonese monarch was willing, by his
expedient of sequestration, to control its operation in such a manner as to secure to his own
subjects the full pecuniary benefit of it. [17] No imputation of this kind attaches to Castile. The
clause of the ordinance, which might imply such a
design, by interdicting the exportation of gold and
silver, was only enforcing a law, which had been
already twice enacted by cortes in the present
reign, and which was deemed of such moment, that
the offence was made capital. [18]

We need look no further for the principle of

Contempo-
rary judg-
ments.

[16] Bajazet. See Abarca, Reyes
de Aragon, tom. ii. p. 310. — Paramo, De Origine Inquisitionis, p.
168.

[17] " In truth," father Abarca somewhat innocently remarks,
' King Ferdinand was a politic

Christian, making the interests of
church and state mutually subservient to each other " ! Reyes de
Aragon, tom. ii. fol. 310.

[18] Once at Toledo, 1480, and at
Murcia, 1488. See Recop. de las
Leyes, lib. 6, tit. 18, ley 1.

action, in this case, than the spirit of religious bigotry, which led to a similar expulsion of the Jews from England, France, and other parts of Europe, as well as from Portugal, under circumstances of peculiar atrocity, a few years later.[19] Indeed, the spirit of persecution did not expire with the fifteenth century, but extended far into the more luminous periods of the seventeenth and eighteenth; and that, too, under a ruler of the enlarged capacity of Frederic the Great, whose intolerance could not plead in excuse the blindness of fanaticism.[20] How far the banishment of the Jews was conformable to the opinions of the most enlightened contemporaries, may be gathered from the encomiums lavished on its authors from more than one quarter. Spanish writers, without exception, celebrate it as a sublime sacrifice of all temporal interests to religious principle. The best instructed foreigners, in like manner, however they may condemn the details of its execution, or commiserate the sufferings of the Jews, commend the

[19] The Portuguese government caused all children of fourteen years of age, or under, to be taken from their parents and retained in the country, as fit subjects for a Christian education. The distress occasioned by this cruel provision may be well imagined. Many of the unhappy parents murdered their children to defeat the ordinance; and many laid violent hands on themselves. Faria y Sousa coolly remarks, that "It was a great mistake in King Emanuel to think of converting any Jew to Christianity, old enough to pronounce the name of Moses!" He fixes three years of age as the utmost limit. (Eu-

ropa Portuguesa, tom. ii. p. 496.)

Mr. Turner has condensed, with his usual industry, the most essential chronological facts relative to modern Jewish history, into a note contained in the second volume of his History of England, pp. 114 – 120.

[20] They were also ejected from Vienna, in 1669. The illiberal, and indeed most cruel legislation of Frederic II., in reference to his Jewish subjects, transports us back to the darkest periods of the Visigothic monarchy. The reader will find a summary of these enactments in the third volume of Milman' agreeable History of the Jews

act, as evincing the most lively and laudable zeal for the true faith. [21]

It cannot be denied, that Spain at this period surpassed most of the nations of Christendom in religious enthusiasm, or, to speak more correctly, in bigotry. This is doubtless imputable to the long war with the Moslems, and its recent glorious issue, which swelled every heart with exultation, disposing it to consummate the triumphs of the Cross, by purging the land from a heresy, which, strange as it may seem, was scarcely less detested than that of Mahomet. Both the sovereigns partook largely of these feelings. With regard to Isabella, moreover, it must be borne constantly in mind, as has been repeatedly remarked in the course of this History, that she had been used to surrender her own judgment, in matters of conscience, to those spiritual guardians, who were supposed in that age to be its rightful depositaries, and the only casuists who could safely determine the doubtful line of duty. Isabella's pious disposition, and her trembling solicitude to discharge her duty, at whatever cost of personal inclination, greatly enforced the precepts of education. In this way, her very virtues

---

[21] The accomplished and amiable Florentine, Pico di Mirandola, in his treatise on Judicial Astrology, remarks that, "the sufferings of the Jews, *in which the glory of divine justice delighted*, were so extreme as to fill us Christians with commiseration." The Genoese historian, Senarega, indeed admits, that the measure savoured *of some slight degree of cruelty.* " Res hæc primo conspectu laudabilis visa est, quia decus nostræ Religionis respiceret, sed aliquantulum in se crudelitatis continere, si eos non belluas, sed homines a Deo creatos, consideravimus." De Rebus Genuensibus, apud Muratori, Rerum Ital. Script., tom. xxiv. — Illescas, Hist. Pontif., apud Paramo, De Origine Inquisitionis, p. 167.

became the source of her errors. Unfortunately, she lived in an age and station, which attached to these errors the most momentous consequences.[22] — But we gladly turn from these dark prospects to a brighter page of her history.

[22] Llorente sums up his account of the expulsion, by assigning the following motives to the principal agents in the business. "The measure," he says, "may be referred to the fanaticism of Torquemada, to the avarice and superstition of Ferdinand, to the false ideas and inconsiderate zeal with which they had inspired Isabella, to whom history cannot refuse the praise of great sweetness of disposition, and an enlightened mind." Hist. de l'Inquisition, tom. i. ch. 7, sec. 10.

CHAPTER XVIII.

ATTEMPTED ASSASSINATION OF FERDINAND. — RETURN AND
SECOND VOYAGE OF COLUMBUS.

1492 — 1493.

Attempt on Ferdinand's Life. — Consternation and Loyalty of the People. — Return of Columbus. — His Progress to Barcelona. — Interviews with the Sovereigns. — Sensations caused by the Discovery. — Regulations of Trade. — Conversion of the Natives. — Famous Bulls of Alexander VI. — Jealousy of Portugal. — Second Voyage of Columbus. — Treaty of Tordesillas.

TOWARDS the latter end of May, 1492, the Spanish sovereigns quitted Granada, between which and Santa Fe they had divided their time since the surrender of the Moorish metropolis. They were occupied during the two following months with the affairs of Castile. In August they visited Aragon, proposing to establish their winter residence there in order to provide for its internal administration, and conclude the negotiations for the final surrender of Roussillon and Cerdagne by France, to which these provinces had been mortgaged by Ferdinand's father, John the Second; proving ever since a fruitful source of diplomacy, which threatened more than once to terminate in open rupture. Ferdinand and Isabella arrived in Aragon on the 8th of August, accompanied by Prince John and the infantas, and a brilliant train of Castilian nobles. In their progress through the country they were everywhere received with the most lively enthusiasm. The whole nation seemed to abandon itself to jubilee, at the approach of its illustrious sovereigns, whose heroic constancy had rescued Spain from the detested empire of the Saracens. After devoting some months to the internal police of the kingdom, the court transferred its residence to Catalonia, whose capital it reached about the middle of October. During its detention in this place, Ferdinand's career was wellnigh brought to an untimely close.[1]

It was a good old custom of Catalonia, long since fallen into desuetude, for the monarch to preside in the tribunals of justice, at least once a week, for the purpose of determining the suits of the poorer classes especially, who could not afford the more expensive forms of litigation. King Ferdinand, in conformity with this usage, held a court in the house of deputation, on the 7th of December, being the vigil of the conception of the Virgin. At noon, as he was preparing to quit the palace, after the conclusion of business, he lingered in the rear of his retinue, conversing with some of the officers of the court. As the party was issuing from a little chapel contiguous to the royal saloon, and just as the king was descending a flight of stairs, a ruffian darted from an obscure recess in which he had

---

[1] Zurita, Anales, tom. v. fol. 13. — Oviedo, Quincuagenas, MS, bat. 1, quinc. 1, dial. 28

concealed himself early in the morning, and aimed a blow with a short sword, or knife, at the back of Ferdinand's neck. Fortunately the edge of the weapon was turned by a gold chain or collar which he was in the habit of wearing. It inflicted, however, a deep wound between the shoulders. Ferdinand instantly cried out, " St. Mary preserve us! treason, treason! " and his attendants, rushing on the assassin, stabbed him in three places with their poniards, and would have despatched him on the spot, had not the king, with his usual presence of mind, commanded them to desist, and take the man alive, that they might ascertain the real authors of the conspiracy. This was done accordingly, and Ferdinand, fainting with loss of blood, was carefully removed to his apartments in the royal palace.[2]

The report of the catastrophe spread like wild- General con-
fire through the city. All classes were thrown into sternation. consternation by so foul an act, which seemed to cast a stain on the honor and good faith of the Catalans. Some suspected it to be the work of a vindictive Moor, others of a disappointed courtier. The queen, who had swooned on first receiving intelligence of the event, suspected the ancient enmity of the Catalans, who had shown such determined opposition to her husband in his early youth. She gave instant orders to hold in readiness one of

2 Zurita, Anales, tom. v. fol. 15. — Bernaldez, Reyes Católicos, MS., cap. 116. — Garibay, Compendio, tom. ii. pp. 678, 679. — Abarca, Reyes de Aragon, tom. ii. fol. 315. — Carbajal, Anales, MS., año 1492. — Oviedo, Quincuagenas MS., bat. 1, quinc 4, dial. 9.

the galleys lying in the port, in order to transport her children from the place, as she feared the conspiracy might be designed to embrace other victims.[3]

Loyalty of the people.

The populace, in the mean while, assembled in great numbers round the palace where the king lay. All feelings of hostility had long since given way to devoted loyalty towards a government, which had uniformly respected the liberties of its subjects, and whose paternal sway had secured similar blessings to Barcelona with the rest of the empire. They thronged round the building, crying out that the king was slain, and demanding that his murderers should be delivered up to them. Ferdinand exhausted as he was, would have presented himself at the window of his apartment, but was prevented from making the effort by his physicians. It was with great difficulty, that the people were at length satisfied that he was still living, and that they finally consented to disperse, on the assurance, that the assassin should be brought to condign punishment.

Slow recovery of the king.

The king's wound, which did not appear dangerous at first, gradually exhibited more alarming symptoms. One of the bones was found to be fractured, and a part of it was removed by the surgeons. On the seventh day his situation was con-

[3] Peter Martyr, Opus Epist., epist. 125. — Bernaldez, Reyes Católicos, MS., cap. 116. — Abarca, Reyes de Aragon, ubi supra.

The great bell of Velilla, whose miraculous tolling always announced some disaster to the monarchy, was heard to strike at the time of this assault on Ferdinand, being the fifth time since the subversion of the kingdom by the Moors. The fourth was on the assassination of the inquisitor Arbues. All which is established by a score of good orthodox witnesses, as reported by Dr. Diego Dormer, in his Discursos Varios, pp. 206, 207.

sidered extremely critical. During this time, the queen was constantly by his side, watching with him day and night, and administering all his medicines with her own hand. At length, the unfavorable symptoms yielded; and his excellent constitution enabled him so far to recover, that in less than three weeks he was able to show himself to the eyes of his anxious subjects, who gave themselves up to a delirium of joy, offering thanksgivings and grateful oblations in the churches; while many a pilgrimage, which had been vowed for his restoration to health, was performed by the good people of Barcelona, with naked feet, and even on their knees, among the wild sierras that surround the city.

Punishment
of the assas-
sin.

The author of the crime proved to be a peasant, about sixty years of age, of that humble class, *de remenza*, as it was termed, which Ferdinand had been so instrumental some few years since in releasing from the baser and more grinding pains of servitude. The man appeared to be insane; alleging in vindication of his conduct, that he was the rightful proprietor of the crown, which he expected to obtain by Ferdinand's death. He declared himself willing, however, to give up his pretensions, on condition of being set at liberty. The king, convinced of his alienation of mind, would have discharged him; but the Catalans, indignant at the reproach which such a crime seemed to attach to their own honor, and perhaps distrusting the plea of insanity, thought it necessary to expiate it by the blood of the offender, and condemned the

PART
I.

unhappy wretch to the dreadful doom of a traitor, the preliminary barbarities of the sentence, however, were remitted, at the intercession of the queen. [4]

Return of
Columbus.

In the spring of 1493, while the court was still at Barcelona, letters were received from Christopher Columbus, announcing his return to Spain, and the successful achievement of his great enterprise, by the discovery of land beyond the western ocean. The delight and astonishment, raised by this intelligence, were proportioned to the skepticism, with which his project had been originally viewed. The sovereigns were now filled with a natural impatience to ascertain the extent and other particulars of the important discovery; and they transmitted instant instructions to the admiral to repair to Barcelona, as soon as he should have made the preliminary arrangements for the further prosecution of his enterprise. [5]

[4] L. Marineo, Cosas Memorables, fol. 186. — Peter Martyr, Opus Epist., epist. 125, 127, 131. — Zurita, Anales, tom. v. fol. 16. — Bernaldez, Reyes Católicos, MS., loc. cit. — Garibay, after harrowing the reader's feelings with half a column of inhuman cruelties inflicted on the miserable man, concludes with the comfortable assurance, " Pero ahogaronle primero por clemencia y misericordia de la Reyna." (Compendio, tom. ii. lib. 19, cap. 1.)

A letter written by Isabella to her confessor, Fernando de Talavera, during her husband's illness, shows the deep anxiety of her own mind, as well as that of the citizens of Barcelona, at his critical situation, furnishing abundant evidence, if it were needed, of her tenderness of heart, and the warmth of her conjugal attachment. See Correspondencia Epistolar, apud Mem. de la Acad. de Hist., tom. vi. Ilust. 13.

[5] Herrera, Indias Occidentales, dec. 1, lib. 2, cap. 3. — Muñoz, Hist. del Nuevo-Mundo, lib. 4, sect. 13, 14.

Columbus concludes a letter addressed, on his arrival at Lisbon, to the treasurer Sanchez, in the following glowing terms ; " Let processions be made, festivals held, temples be filled with branches and flowers, for Christ rejoices on earth as in Heaven, seeing the future redemption of souls. Let us rejoice, also, for the temporal benefit likely to result, not merely to Spain, but

The great navigator had succeeded, as is well
known, after a voyage the natural difficulties of
which had been much augmented by the distrust
and mutinous spirit of his followers, in descrying
land on Friday, the 12th of October, 1492. After
some months spent in exploring the delightful regions, now for the first time thrown open to the
eyes of a European, he embarked in the month of
January, 1493, for Spain. One of his vessels had
previously foundered, and another had deserted
him; so that he was left alone to retrace his course
across the Atlantic. After a most tempestuous
voyage, he was compelled to take shelter in the
Tagus, sorely against his inclination.[6] He experienced, however, the most honorable reception from
the Portuguese monarch, John the Second, who did
ample justice to the great qualities of Columbus,
although he had failed to profit by them.[7] After a

CHAPTER
XVIII.

Discovery o
the West
Indies.

1492.
Oct. 12.

to all Christendom." See Primer
Viage de Colon, apud Navarrete,
Coleccion de Viages, tom. i.

[6] Herrera, Indias Occidentales,
tom. i. dec. 1, lib. 2, cap. 2.—
Primer Viage de Colon, apud Navarrete, Coleccion de Viages, tom.
i. — Fernando Colon, Hist. del
Almirante, cap. 39.

The Portuguese historian, Faria
y Sousa, appears to be nettled at
the prosperous issue of the voyage; for he testily remarks, that
' the admiral entered Lisbon with
a vainglorious exultation, in order
to make Portugal feel, by displaying the tokens of his discovery,
how much she had erred in not
acceding to his propositions." Europa Portuguesa, tom. ii. pp. 462,
463.

[7] My learned friend, Mr. John

Pickering, has pointed out to me a
passage in a Portuguese author,
giving some particulars of Columbus's visit to Portugal. The passage, which I have not seen noticed
by any writer, is extremely interesting, coming, as it does, from a
person high in the royal confidence,
and an eyewitness of what he relates. "In the year 1493, on the
sixth day of March, arrived in
Lisbon Christopher Columbus, an
Italian, who came from the discovery, made under the authority of
the sovereigns of Castile, of the
islands of Cipango and Antilia;
from which countries he brought
with him the first specimens of the
people, as well as of the gold and
other things to be found there; and
he was entitled admiral of them
The king, being forthwith inform-

brief delay, the admiral resumed his voyage, and crossing the bar of Saltes entered the harbour of Palos about noon, on the 15th of March, 1493, being exactly seven months and eleven days since his departure from that port.[8]

Great was the agitation in the little community of Palos, as they beheld the well-known vessel of the admiral reëntering their harbour. Their desponding imaginations had long since consigned him to a watery grave; for, in addition to the preternatural horrors which hung over the voyage, they had experienced the most stormy and disastrous winter within the recollection of the oldest

ed of this, commanded him into his presence; and appeared to be annoyed and vexed, as well from the belief that the said discovery was made within the seas and boundaries of his seigniory of Guinea, — which might give rise to disputes, — as because the said admiral, having become somewhat haughty by his situation, and in the relation of his adventures always exceeding the bounds of truth, made this affair, as to gold, silver, and riches, much greater than it was. Especially did the king accuse himself of negligence, in having declined this enterprise, when Columbus first came to ask his assistance, from want of credit and confidence in it. And, notwithstanding the king was importuned to kill him on the spot; since with his death the prosecution of the undertaking, so far as the sovereigns of Castile were concerned, would cease, from want of a suitable person to take charge of it; and notwithstanding this might be done without suspicion of the king's being privy to it, — for inasmuch as the admiral was

overbearing and puffed up by his success, they could easily bring it about, that his own indiscretion should appear the occasion of his death, — yet the king, as he was a prince greatly fearing God, not only forbade this, but even showed the admiral honor and much favor, and therewith dismissed him." Ruy de Pina, Chronica d'el Rei Dom Joaõ II., cap. 66, apud Collecçaõ de Livros Ineditos de Historia Portugueza, (Lisboa, .1790 – 93,) tom. ii.

8 Fernando Colon, Hist. del Almirante, cap. 40, 41. — Charlevoix, Histoire de S. Domingue, (Paris, 1730,) tom. i. pp. 84 – 90. — Primer Viage de Colon, apud Navarrete, Coleccion de Viages, tom. i. — La Clède, Hist. de Portugal, tom. iv. pp. 53 – 58.

Columbus sailed from Spain on Friday, discovered land on Friday, and reëntered the port of Palos on Friday. These curious coincidences should have sufficed, one might think, to dispel, especially with American mariners, the superstitious dread, still so prevalent

mariners. [9] Most of them had relatives or friends
on board. They thronged immediately to the
shore, to assure themselves with their own eyes of
the truth of their return. When they beheld their
faces once more, and saw them accompanied by
the numerous evidences which they brought back
of the success of the expedition, they burst forth in
acclamations of joy and gratulation. They awaited the landing of Columbus, when the whole population of the place accompanied him and his crew
to the principal church, where solemn thanksgivings
were offered up for their return; while every bell in
he village sent forth a joyous peal in honor of the
glorious event. The admiral was too desirous of
presenting himself before the sovereigns, to pro-
tract his stay long at Palos. He took with him on
his journey specimens of the multifarious products of the newly discovered regions. He was
accompanied by several of the native islanders,
arrayed in their simple barbaric costume, and decorated, as he passed through the principal cities,
with collars, bracelets, and other ornaments of gold,
rudely fashioned ; he exhibited also considerable
quantities of the same metal in dust, or in crude
masses, [10] numerous vegetable exotics, possessed of
aromatic or medicinal virtue, and several kinds of

of commencing a voyage on that
ominous day.

[9] Primer Viage de Colon, Let. 2.

[10] Muñoz, Hist. del Nuevo-Mundo, lib. 4, sec. 14. — Fernando
Colon, Hist. del Almirante, cap.
41.

Among other specimens, was a

lump of gold, of sufficient magnitude to be fashioned into a vessel
for containing the host; "thus,"
says Salazar de Mendoza, "converting the first fruits of the new
dominions to pious uses" Monarquía, pp. 351, 352.

quadrupeds unknown in Europe, and birds, whose varieties of gaudy plumage gave a brilliant effect to the pageant. The admiral's progress through the country was everywhere impeded by the multitudes thronging forth to gaze at the extraordinary spectacle, and the more extraordinary man, who, in the emphatic language of that time, which has now lost its force from its familiarity, first revealed the existence of a "New World." As he passed through the busy, populous city of Seville, every window, balcony, and housetop, which could afford a glimpse of him, is described to have been crowded with spectators. It was the middle of April before Columbus reached Barcelona. The nobility and cavaliers in attendance on the court, together with the authorities of the city, came to the gates to receive him, and escorted him to the royal presence. Ferdinand and Isabella were seated, with their son, Prince John, under a superb canopy of state, awaiting his arrival. On his approach, they rose from their seats, and extending their hands to him to salute, caused him to be seated before them. These were unprecedented marks of condescension to a person of Columbus's rank, in the haughty and ceremonious court of Castile. It was, indeed, the proudest moment in the life of Columbus. He had fully established the truth of his long-contested theory, in the face of argument, sophistry, sneer, skepticism, and contempt. He had achieved this, not by chance, but by calculation, supported through the most adverse circumstances by consummate conduct. The honors paid him, which had hitherto been reserved only for rank, or fortune, or military success, purchased by the blood and tears of thousands, were, in his case, a homage to intellectual power, successfully exerted in behalf of the noblest interests of humanity. [11]

After a brief interval, the sovereigns requested from Columbus a recital of his adventures. His manner was sedate and dignified, but warmed by the glow of natural enthusiasm. He enumerated the several islands which he had visited, expatiated on the temperate character of the climate, and the capacity of the soil for every variety of agricultural production, appealing to the samples imported by him, as evidence of their natural fruitfulness. He dwelt more at large on the precious metals to be found in these islands, which he inferred, less from the specimens actually obtained, than from the uniform testimony of the natives to their abundance in the unexplored regions of the interior. Lastly, he pointed out the wide scope afforded to Christian zeal, in the illumination of a race of men, whose minds, far from being wedded to any system of idolatry, were prepared by their extreme simplicity for the reception of pure and uncorrupted doctrine. The last consideration touched Isabella's heart most sensibly; and the whole audience, kindled with various emotions by the speaker's eloquence, filled

[11] Peter Martyr, Opus Epist., epist. 133, 134, 140. — Bernaldez, Reyes Católicos, MS., cap. 118. — Ferreras, Hist. d'Espagne, tom. viii. pp. 141, 142. — Fernando Colon, Hist. del Almirante, ubi supra. — Zuñiga, Annales de Sevilla, p. 413. — Gomara, Hist. de las Indias, cap. 17. — Benzoni, Novi Orbis Hist., lib. 1, cap. 8, 9. — Gallo, apud Muratori Rerum Ital. Script., tom. xxiii. p. 203

up the perspective with the gorgeous coloring of their own fancies, as ambition, or avarice, or devotional feeling predominated in their bosoms. When Columbus ceased, the king and queen, togethei with all present, prostrated themselves on their knees in grateful thanksgivings, while the solemn strains of the Te Deum were poured forth by the choir of the royal chapel, as in commemoration of some glorious victory.[12]

Sensations
caused by
the discov-
ery.

The discoveries of Columbus excited a sensation, particularly among men of science, in the most distant parts of Europe, strongly contrasting with the apathy which had preceded them. They congratulated one another on being reserved for an age, which had witnessed the consummation of so grand an event. The learned Martyr, who, in his multifarious correspondence, had not even deigned to notice the preparations for the voyage of discovery, now lavished the most unbounded panegyric on its results ; which he contemplated with the eye of a philosopher, having far less reference to considerations of profit or policy, than to the prospect which they unfolded of enlarging the boundaries of knowledge.[13] Most of the scholars of the day, however,

[12] Herrera, Indias Occidental., tom. i. dec. 1, lib. 2, cap. 3. — Muñoz, Hist. del Nuevo-Mundo, lib. 4, sec. 15, 16, 17. — Fernando Colon, Hist. del Almirante, ubi supra.

[13] In a letter, written soon after the admiral's return, Martyr announces the discovery to his correspondent, cardinal Sforza, in the following manner. " Mira res ex eo terrarum orbe, quem sol horarum quatuor et viginti spatio circuit, ad nostra usque tempora, quod minime te latet, trita cognitaque dimidia tantum pars, ab Aurea utpote Chersoneso, ad Gades nostras Hispanas, reliqua vero a cosmographis pro incognità relicta est. Et si quæ mentio facta, ea tenuis et incerta. Nunc autem, o beatum facinus ! meorum regum auspiciis, quod latuit hactenus a rerum primordio, intelligi cœptum est." In a subsequent epistle to the learned

adopted the erroneous hypothesis of Columbus, who
considered the lands he had discovered, as bordering
on the eastern shores of Asia, and lying adjacent
to the vast and opulent regions depicted in such
golden colors by Mandeville and the Poli. This
conjecture, which was conformable to the admiral's
opinions before undertaking the voyage, was corroborated by the apparent similarity between various natural productions of these islands, and of the
east. From this misapprehension, the new dominions soon came to be distinguished as the West
Indies, an appellation by which they are still recognised in the titles of the Spanish crown. [14]

Columbus, during his residence at Barcelona,
continued to receive from the Spanish sovereigns
the most honorable distinctions which royal bounty
could confer. When Ferdinand rode abroad, he
was accompanied by the admiral at his side. The

Pomponio Leto, he breaks out in
a strain of warm and generous sentiment. " Præ lætitiâ prosiliisse
te, vixque a lachrymis præ gaudio
temperasse, quando literas adspex-
isti meas, quibus de Antipodum
Orbe latenti hactenus, te certiorem
feci, mi suavissime Pomponi, in-
sinuasti. Ex tuis ipse literis col-
ligo, quæ senseris. Sensisti autem,
tantique rem fecisti, quanti virum
summâ doctrinâ insignitum decuit.
Quis namque cibus sublimibus præ-
stari potest ingeniis isto suavior?
quod condimentum gravius? a me
facio conjecturam. Beari sentio
spiritus meos, quando accitos allo-
quor prudentes aliquos ex his quæ
ab eâ redeunt provinciâ. Implicent
animos pecuniarum tumulis augen-
dis miseri avari, libidinibus obscœni;
nostras nos mentes postquam Deo
pleni aliquandiu fuerimus, contem-

plando, hujuscemodi rerum notitiâ
demulceamus." Opus Epist., epist.
124, 152.

[14] Bernaldez, Reyes Católicos,
MS., cap. 118. — Gallo, apud Muratori, Rerum Ital. Script., tom.
xxiii. p. 203. — Gomara, Hist. de
las Indias, cap. 18.

Peter Martyr seems to have received the popular inference, respecting the identity of the new
discoveries with the East Indies,
with some distrust. " Insulas re-
perit plures; has esse, de quibus fit
apud cosmographos mentio extra
Oceanum Orientalem, adjacentes
Indiæ arbitrantur. Nec inficior ego
penitus, quamvis sphæræ magnitu-
do aliter sentire videatur; neque
enim desunt qui parvo tractu a fini-
bus Hispanis distare littus Indicum,
putent." Opus Epist., epist. 135.

PART
I.

courtiers, in emulation of their master, made frequent entertainments, at which he was treated with
the punctilious deference paid to a noble of the
highest class.[15] But the attentions most grateful
to his lofty spirit were the preparations of the
Spanish court for prosecuting his discoveries, on

Board for Indian affairs. a scale commensurate with their importance. A
board was established for the direction of Indian
affairs, consisting of a superintendent and two subordinate functionaries. The first of these officers
was Juan de Fonseca, archdeacon of Seville, an
active, ambitious prelate, subsequently raised to
high episcopal preferment, whose shrewdness, and
capacity for business, enabled him to maintain the
control of the Indian department during the whole
of the present reign. An office for the transaction
of business was instituted at Seville, and a custom-
house placed under its direction at Cadiz. This
was the origin of the important establishment of the
Casa de la Contratacion de las Indias, or India
House.[16]

Regulations of trade. The commercial regulations adopted exhibit a
narrow policy in some of their features, for which a

[15] Herrera, Indias Occidentales,
dec. 1, lib. 2, cap. 3. — Benzoni,
Novi Orbis Hist., lib. 1, cap. 8. —
Gomara, Hist. de las Indias, cap.
17. — Zuñiga, Annales de Sevilla,
p. 413. — Fernando Colon, Hist.
del Almirante, ubi supra.

He was permitted to quarter the
royal arms with his own, which
consisted of a group of golden islands amid azure billows. To these
were afterwards added five an-
chors, with the celebrated motto,
well known as being carved on his

sepulchre. (See Part II. Chap. 18.)
He received besides, soon after his
return, the substantial gratuity of
a thousand doblas of gold, from the
royal treasury, and the premium
of 10,000 maravedies, promised to
the person who first descried land
See Navarrete, Coleccion de Viages, Col. Diplom., nos. 20, 32, 38.
[16] Navarrete, Coleccion de Viages, tom. ii. Col. Diplom., no. 45.
— Muñoz, Hist. del Nuevo-Mundo,
lib. 4, sec. 21.

justification may be found in the spirit of the age,
and in the practice of the Portuguese particularly,
but which entered still more largely into the colonial legislation of Spain under later princes. The
new territories, far from being permitted free intercourse with foreign nations, were opened only under
strict limitations to Spanish subjects, and were reserved, as forming, in some sort, part of the exclusive revenue of the crown. All persons of whatever
description were interdicted, under the severest
penalties, from trading with, or even visiting the
Indies, without license from the constituted author
ities. It was impossible to evade this, as a minute
specification of the ships, cargoes, crews, with the
property appertaining to each individual, was required to be taken at the office in Cadiz, and a
corresponding registration in a similar office established at Hispaniola. A more sagacious spirit was
manifested in the ample provision made of whatever could contribute to the support or permanent
prosperity of the infant colony. Grain, plants, the
seeds of numerous vegetable products, which in the
genial climate of the Indies might be made valuable
articles for domestic consumption or export, were
•liberally furnished. Commodities of every description for the supply of the fleet were exempted from
duty. The owners of all vessels throughout the
ports of Andalusia were required, by an ordinance
somewhat arbitrary, to hold them in readiness for
the expedition. Still further authority was given
to impress both officers and men, if necessary, into
the service. Artisans of every sort, provided with

Preparations
for a second
voyage

the implements of their various crafts, including a great number of miners for exploring the subterraneous treasures of the new regions, were enrolled in the expedition ; in order to defray the heavy charges of which, the government, in addition to the regular resources, had recourse to a loan, and to the sequestrated property of the exiled Jews. [17]

Conversion
of the na-
tives.

Amid their own temporal concerns, the Spanish sovereigns did not forget the spiritual interests of their new subjects. The Indians, who accompanied Columbus to Barcelona, had been all of them baptized, being offered up, in the language of a Castilian writer, as the first-fruits of the gentiles. King Ferdinand, and his son, Prince John, stood as sponsors to two of them, who were permitted to take their names. One of the Indians remained attached to the prince's establishment ; the residue were sent to Seville, whence, after suitable religious instruction, they were to be returned as missionaries for the propagation of the faith among their own countrymen. Twelve Spanish ecclesiastics were also destined to this service ; among whom was the celebrated Las Casas, so conspicuous afterwards for his benevolent exertions in behalf of the unfortunate natives. The most explicit directions were given to the admiral, to use every effort for the illumination of the poor heathen, which was set forth as the primary object of the expedition. He was particularly enjoined " to abstain from all means of annoyance, and to treat them well and

[17] Navarrete, Coleccion de Viages, Col. Diplom., nos. 33, 35, 45. — Herrera, Indias Occidentales, dec. 1, lib. 2, cap. 4. — Muñoz Hist. del Nuevo-Mundo, lib. 4 sec. 21.

lovingly, maintaining a familiar intercourse with them, rendering them all the kind offices in his power, distributing presents of the merchandise and various commodities, which their Highnesses had caused to be embarked on board the fleet for that purpose; and finally, to chastise, in the most exemplary manner, all who should offer the natives the slightest molestation." Such were the instructions emphatically urged on Columbus for the regulation of his intercourse with the savages; and their indulgent tenor sufficiently attests the benevolent and rational views of Isabella, in religious matters, when not warped by any foreign influence.[18]

New powers granted to Columbus

Towards the last of May, Columbus quitted Barcelona for the purpose of superintending and expediting the preparations for departure on his second voyage. He was accompanied to the gates of the city by all the nobility and cavaliers of the court. Orders were issued to the different towns, to provide him and his suite with lodgings free of expense. His former commission was not only confirmed in its full extent, but considerably enlarged. For the sake of despatch, he was authorized to

[18] See the original instructions, apud Navarrete, Coleccion de Viages, Col. Diplom., no. 45.—Muñoz, Hist. del Nuevo-Mundo, lib. 4, sec. 22.—Zuñiga, Annales de Sevilla, p. 413.

L. Marineo eagerly claims the conversion of the natives, as the prime object of the expedition with the sovereigns, far outweighing all temporal considerations. The passage is worth quoting, if only to show what egregious blunders a contemporary may make in the relation of events passing, as it were, under his own eyes. "The Catholic sovereigns having subjugated the Canaries, and established Christian worship there, sent *Peter Colon*, with *thirty-five* ships, called caravels, and *a great number of men* to other much larger islands abounding in mines of gold, not so much, however, for the sake of the gold, as for the salvation of the poor heathen natives." *Cosas Memorables*, fol. 161.

nominate to all offices, without application to government; and ordinances and letters patent, bearing the royal seal, were to be issued by him, subscribed by himself or his deputy. He was intrusted, in fine, with such unlimited jurisdiction, as showed, that, however tardy the sovereigns may have been in granting him their confidence, they were not disposed to stint the measure of it, when his deserts were once established.[19]

Application
o Rome.

Soon after Columbus's return to Spain, Ferdinand and Isabella applied to the court of Rome, to confirm them in the possession of their recent discoveries, and invest them with similar extent of jurisdiction with that formerly conferred on the kings of Portugal. It was an opinion, as ancient perhaps as the crusades, that the pope, as vicar of Christ, had competent authority to dispose of all countries inhabited by heathen nations, in favor of Christian potentates. Although Ferdinand and Isabella do not seem to have been fully satisfied of this right, yet they were willing to acquiesce in its assumption in the present instance, from the conviction that the papal sanction would most effectually exclude the pretensions of all others, and especially their Portuguese rivals. In their application to the Holy See, they were careful to represent their own discoveries as in no way interfering with the rights formerly conceded by it to their neighbours. They enlarged on their services in the propagation of the faith, which they affirmed to

[19] See copies of the original documents, apud Navarrete, Coleccion de Viages, tom. ii , Col. Diplom. nos. 39, 41, 42, 43.

be a principal motive of their present operations. They intimated, finally, that, although many competent persons deemed their application to the court of Rome, for a title to territories already in their possession, to be unnecessary, yet, as pious princes, and dutiful children of the church, they were unwilling to proceed further without the sanction of him, to whose keeping its highest interests were intrusted.[20]

The pontifical throne was at that time filled by Alexander the Sixth; a man who, although degraded by unrestrained indulgence of the most sordid appetites, was endowed by nature with singular acuteness, as well as energy of character. He lent a willing ear to the application of the Spanish government, and made no hesitation in granting what cost him nothing, while it recognised the assumption of powers, which had already begun to totter in the opinion of mankind.

On the 3d of May, 1493, he published a bull, in which, taking into consideration the eminent services of the Spanish monarchs in the cause of the church, especially in the subversion of the Mahometan empire in Spain, and willing to afford still wider scope for the prosecution of their pious labors, he, " out of his pure liberality, infallible knowledge, and plenitude of apostolic power," confirmed them in the possession of all lands discovered, or hereafter to be discovered by them in the western ocean, comprehending the same extensive rights of

Famous bulls of Alexander VI

[20] Herrera, Indias Occidentales, Hist. del Nuevo-Mundo, lib. 4, dec. 1, lib. 2, cap. 4. — Muñoz, sec. 18.

jurisdiction with those formerly conceded to the kings of Portugal.

This bull he supported by another, dated on the following day, in which the pope, in order to obviate any misunderstanding with the Portuguese, and acting no doubt on the suggestion of the Spanish sovereigns, defined with greater precision the intention of his original grant to the latter, by bestowing on them all such lands as they should discover to the west and south of an imaginary line, to be drawn from pole to pole, at the distance of one hundred leagues to the west of the Azores and Cape de Verd Islands.[21] It seems to have escaped his Holiness, that the Spaniards, by pursuing a western route, might in time reach the eastern limits of countries previously granted to the Portuguese. At least this would appear from the import of a third bull, issued September 25th of the same year, which invested the sovereigns with plenary authority over all countries discovered by them, whether in the east, or within the boundaries of India, all previous concessions to the contrary notwithstanding. With the title derived from actual possession, thus fortified by the highest ecclesiastical sanction, the Spaniards might have promised themselves an uninterrupted career of discovery, but for the jealousy of their rivals, the Portuguese.[22]

[21] A point south of the meridian is something new in geometry; yet so says the bull of his Holiness. "Omnes insulas et terras firmas inventas et inveniendas, detectas et detegendas, versus Occidentem et meridiem, fabricando et constituendo unam lineam a Polo Arctico scilicet septentrione, ad Polum Antarcticum, scilicet meridiem."

[22] See the original papal grants, transcribed by Navarrete, Coleccion de Viages, tom. ii., Col. Diplom., nos. 17, 18. Appendice al Col. Diplom., no. 11.

The court of Lisbon viewed with secret disquietude the increasing maritime enterprise of its
neighbours. While the Portuguese were timidly
creeping along the barren shores of Africa, the
Spaniards had boldly launched into the deep, and
rescued unknown realms from its embraces, which
teemed in their fancies with treasures of inestimable
wealth. Their mortification was greatly enhanced
by the reflection, that all this might have been
achieved for themselves, had they but known how
to profit by the proposals of Columbus.[23] From
the first moment in which the success of the admiral's enterprise was established, John the Second,
a politic and ambitious prince, had sought some
pretence to check the career of discovery, or at
least to share in the spoils of it.[24]

In his interview with Columbus, at Lisbon, he
suggested, that the discoveries of the Spaniards
might interfere with the rights secured to the Portuguese by repeated papal sanctions since the beginning of the present century, and guarantied by
the treaty with Spain, in 1479. Columbus, without
entering into the discussion, contented himself with
declaring, that he had been instructed by his own
government to steer clear of all Portuguese settlements on the African coast, and that his course
indeed had led him in an entirely different direc-

[23] Padre Abarca considers "that
the discovery of a new world, first
offered to the kings of Portugal and
England, was reserved by Heaven
for Spain, being *forced*, in a manner, on Ferdinand, in recompense
for the subjugation of the Moors,
and the expulsion of the Jews!"
Reyes de Aragon, fol. 310, 311.

[24] La Clède, Hist. de Portugal,
tom. iv. pp. 53 – 58.

tion   Although John professed himself satisfied
with the explanation, he soon after despatched an
ambassador to Barcelona, who, after dwelling on
some irrelevant topics, touched, as it were, incidentally on the real object of his mission, the late
voyage of discovery.   He congratulated the Spanish
sovereigns on its success; expatiated on the civilities shown by the court of Lisbon to Columbus, on
his late arrival there; and acknowledged the satisfaction felt by his master at the orders given to the
admiral, to hold a western course from the Canaries,
expressing a hope that the same course would be
pursued in future, without interfering with the
rights of Portugal by deviation to the south.   This
was the first occasion, on which the existence of
such claims had been intimated by the Portuguese.

Wary diplo-
macy.

In the mean while, Ferdinand and Isabella received intelligence that King John was equipping a
considerable armament in order to anticipate or defeat their discoveries in the west.   They instantly
sent one of their household, Don Lope de Herrera,
as ambassador to Lisbon, with instructions to make
their acknowledgments to the king for his hospitable reception of Columbus, accompanied with a request that he would prohibit his subjects from interference with the discoveries of the Spaniards in
the west, in the same manner as these latter had
been excluded from the Portuguese possessions in
Africa.   The ambassador was furnished with orders
of a different import, provided he should find the
reports correct, respecting the equipment and proba-
able destination of a Portuguese armada.   Instead

of a conciliatory deportment, he was, in that case, to assume a tone of remonstrance, and to demand a full explanation from king John, of his designs. The cautious prince, who had received, through his secret agents in Castile, intelligence of these latter instructions, managed matters so discreetly as to give no occasion for their exercise. He abandoned, or at least postponed his meditated expedition, in the hope of adjusting the dispute by negotiation, in which he excelled. In order to quiet the apprehensions of the Spanish court, he engaged to fit out no fleet from his dominions within sixty days; at the same time he sent a fresh mission to Barcelona, with directions to propose an amicable adjustment of the conflicting claims of the two nations, by making the parallel of the Canaries a line of partition between them; the right of discovery to the north being reserved to the Spaniards, and that to the south to the Portuguese. [25]

While this game of diplomacy was going on, the Castilian court availed itself of the interval afforded by its rival, to expedite preparations for the second voyage of discovery; which, through the personal activity of the admiral, and the facilities everywhere afforded him, were fully completed before the close of September. Instead of the reluctance, and indeed avowed disgust, which had been manifested by all classes to his former voyage, the only

Second voyage of Columbus.

[25] Faria y Sousa, Europa Portuguesa, tom. ii. p. 463. — Herrera, Indias Occidentales, loc. cit.— Muñoz, Hist. del Nuevo-Mundo lib. 4, sec. 27, 28. — Mariana, Hist. de España, tom. ii. pp. 606, 607. — La Clède, Hist. de Portugal, tom. iv. pp. 53 – 58.

embarrassment now arose from the difficulty of selection among the multitude of competitors, who pressed to be enrolled in the present expedition. The reports and sanguine speculations of the first adventurers had inflamed the cupidity of many, which was still further heightened by the exhibition of the rich and curious products which Columbus had brought back with him, and by the popular belief that the new discoveries formed part of that gorgeous east,

> " whose caverns teem
> With diamond flaming, and with seeds of gold,"

and which tradition and romance had alike invested with the supernatural splendors of enchantment. Many others were stimulated by the wild love of adventure, kindled in the long Moorish war, but which, now excluded from that career, sought other objects in the vast, untravelled regions of the New World. The complement of the fleet was originally fixed at twelve hundred souls, which, through importunity or various pretences of the applicants, was eventually swelled to fifteen hundred. Among these were many who enlisted without compensation, including several persons of rank, hidalgos, and members of the royal household. The whole squadron amounted to seventeen vessels, three of them of one hundred tons' burden each. With this gallant navy, Columbus, dropping down the Guadalquivir, took his departure from the bay of Cadiz, on the 25th of September, 1493 ; presenting a striking contrast to the melancholy plight, in which, but the year previous, he sallied forth like some

forlorn knight-errant, on a desperate and chimerical
enterprise. [26]

No sooner had the fleet weighed anchor, than
Ferdinand and Isabella despatched an embassy in
solemn state to advise the king of Portugal of it.
This embassy was composed of two persons of
distinguished rank, Don Pedro de Ayala, and Don
Garci Lopez de Carbajal. Agreeably to their instructions, they represented to the Portuguese monarch the inadmissibility of his propositions respecting
the boundary line of navigation : they argued that
the grants of the Holy See, and the treaty with
Spain in 1479, had reference merely to the actual
possessions of Portugal, and the right of discovery
by an eastern route along the coasts of Africa to
the Indies ; that these rights had been invariably
respected by Spain ; that the late voyage of Columbus struck into a directly opposite track ; and that
the several bulls of Pope Alexander the Sixth,
prescribing the line of partition, not from east to
west, but from the north to the south pole, were
intended to secure to the Spaniards the exclusive
right of discovery in the western ocean. The ambassadors concluded with offering, in the name of
their sovereigns, to refer the whole matter in dispute to the arbitration of the court of Rome, or of
any common umpire.

[26] Zuñiga, Annales de Sevilla, p. 113. — Fernando Colon, Hist. del Almirante, cap. 44. — Bernaldez, Reyes Católicos, MS., cap. 118. — Peter Martyr, De Rebus Oceanicis dec. 1, lib. 1. — Benzoni, Novi Orbis Historia, lib. 1, cap. 9. — Gomara, Hist. de las Indias, cap. 20.

King John was deeply chagrined at learning the departure of the Spanish expedition. He saw that his rivals had been acting, while he had been amused with negotiation. He at first threw out hints of an immediate rupture; and endeavoured, it is said to intimidate the Castilian ambassadors, by bringing them accidentally, as it were, in presence of a splendid array of cavalry, mounted and ready for immediate service. He vented his spleen on the embassy, by declaring, that " it was a mere abortion; having neither head nor feet; " alluding to the personal infirmity of Ayala, who was lame, and to the light, frivolous character, of the other envoy. [27]

These symptoms of discontent were duly notified to the Spanish government; who commanded the superintendent, Fonseca, to keep a vigilant eye on the movements of the Portuguese, and, in case any hostile armament should quit their ports, to be in readiness to act against it with one double its force. King John, however, was too shrewd a prince to be drawn into so impolitic a measure as war with a powerful adversary, quite as likely to baffle him in the field, as in the council. Neither did he relish the suggestion of deciding the dispute by arbitration; since he well knew, that his claim rested on too unsound a basis, to authorize the expectation of a favorable award from any impartial umpire. He had already failed in an application

<hr>

[27] La Clède, Hist. de Portugal, tom iv pp. 53–58. — Muñoz, Hist. del Nuevo-Mundo, lib. 4 sec. 27, 28.

for redress to the court of Rome, which answered
him by reference to its bulls, recently published. In
this emergency, he came to the resolution at last,
which should have been first adopted, of deciding
the matter by a fair and open conference. It was
not until the following year, however, that his discontent so far subsided as to allow his acquiescence
in this measure.

At length, commissioners named by the two
crowns convened at Tordesillas, and on the 7th of
June, 1494, subscribed articles of agreement, which
were ratified, in the course of the same year, by the
respective powers. In this treaty, the Spaniards
were secured in the exclusive right of navigation
and discovery in the western ocean. At the urgent
remonstrance of the Portuguese, however, who
complained that the papal line of demarcation cooped up their enterprises within too narrow limits,
they consented, that instead of one hundred, it
should be removed three hundred and seventy
leagues west of the Cape de Verd islands, beyond
which all discoveries should appertain to the Spanish nation. It was agreed that one or two caravels
should be provided by each nation, to meet at the
Grand Canary, and proceed due west, the appointed distance, with a number of scientific men on
board, for the purpose of accurately determining
the longitude; and if any lands should fall under
the meridian, the direction of the line should be
ascertained by the erection of beacons at suitable
distances. The proposed meeting never took place.
But the removal of the partition line was followed

PART
I.

by important consequences to the Portuguese, who derived from it their pretensions to the noble empire of Brazil. [28]

Thus this singular misunderstanding, which menaced an open rupture at one time, was happily adjusted. Fortunately, the accomplishment of the passage round the Cape of Good Hope, which occurred soon afterwards, led the Portuguese in an opposite direction to their Spanish rivals, their Brazilian possessions having too little attractions, at first, to turn them from the splendid path of discovery thrown open in the east. It was not many years, however, before the two nations, by pursuing opposite routes of circumnavigation, were brought into collision on the other side of the globe ; a circumstance never contemplated, apparently, by the treaty of Tordesillas. Their mutual pretensions were founded, however, on the provisions of that treaty, which, as the reader is aware, was itself only supplementary to the original bull of demarcation of Alexander the Sixth. [29] Thus this bold stretch of papal authority, so often ridiculed as chimerical and absurd, was in a measure

---

[28] Navarrete, Coleccion de Viages, Doc. Diplom., no. 75. — Faria y Sousa, Europa Portuguesa, tom. ii. p. 463. — Herrera, Indias Occidentales, dec. 1, lib. 2. cap. 8, 10. — Mariana, Hist. de España, tom. ii. pp. 606, 607. — La Clède, Hist. de Portugal, tom. iv. pp. 60 – 62, Zurita, Anales, tom. v. fol. 31.

[29] The contested territory was the Molucca islands, which each party claimed for itself, by virtue of the treaty of Tordesillas. After more than one congress, in which all the cosmographical science of the day was put in requisition, the affair was terminated à l'amiable by the Spanish government's relinquishing its pretensions, in consideration of 350,000 ducats, paid by the court of Lisbon. See La Clède, Hist. de Portugal, tom. iv. pp. 309, 401, 402, 480. —Mariana, Hist. de España, tom. ii. pp. 607, 875. — Salazar de Mendoza, Monarquía, tom. ii. pp. 205, 206.

justified by the event, since it did, in fact, determine the principles on which the vast extent of unappropriated empire in the eastern and western hemispheres was ultimately divided between two petty states of Europe.

CHAPTER XIX.

PART
I.

WE have now arrived at the period, when the
history of Spain becomes incorporated with that of
the other states of Europe. Before embarking on
the wide sea of European politics, however, and
bidding adieu, for a season, to the shores of Spain,
it will be necessary, in order to complete the view
of the internal administration of Ferdinand and
Isabella, to show its operation on the intellectual
culture of the nation. This, as it constitutes, when
taken in its broadest sense, a principal end of all
government, should never be altogether divorced
from any history. It is particularly deserving of
note in the present reign, which stimulated the active developement of the national energies in every
department of science, and which forms a leading
epoch in the ornamental literature of the country.
The present and the following chapter will embrace
the mental progress of the kingdom, not merely

down to the period at which we have arrived, but through the whole of Isabella's reign, in order to exhibit as far as possible its entire results, at a single glance, to the eye of the reader.

We have beheld, in a preceding chapter, the auspicious literary promise afforded by the reign of Isabella's father, John the Second, of Castile. Under the anarchical sway of his son, Henry the Fourth, the court, as we have seen, was abandoned to unbounded license, and the whole nation sunk into a mental torpor, from which it was roused only by the tumults of civil war. In this deplorable state of things, the few blossoms of literature, which had begun to open under the benign influence of the preceding reign, were speedily trampled under foot, and every vestige of civilization seemed in a fair way to be effaced from the land.

The first years of Ferdinand and Isabella's government were too much clouded by civil dissensions, to afford a much more cheering prospect. Ferdinand's early education, moreover, had been greatly neglected. Before the age of ten, he was called to take part in the Catalan wars. His boyhood was spent among soldiers, in camps instead of schools, and the wisdom which he so eminently displayed in later life, was drawn far more from his own resources, than from books.[1]

Ferdinand's education neglected.

Isabella was reared under more favorable auspices; at least more favorable to mental culture. She was allowed to pass her youth in retirement,

Instruction of Isabella.

[1] L. Marineo, Cosas Memorables, fol. 153.

PART

and indeed oblivion, as far as the world was concerned, under her mother's care, at Arevalo. In this modest seclusion, free from the engrossing vanities and vexations of court life, she had full leisure to indulge the habits of study and reflection, to which her temper naturally disposed her. She was acquainted with several modern languages, and both wrote and discoursed in her own with great precision and elegance. No great expense or solicitude, however, appears to have been lavished on her education. She was uninstructed in the Latin, which in that day was of greater importance than at present; since it was not only the common medium of communication between learned men, and the language in which the most familiar treatises were often composed, but was frequently used by well-educated foreigners at court, and especially employed in diplomatic intercourse and negotiation.[2]

Isabella resolved to repair the defects of education, by devoting herself to the acquisition of the Latin tongue, so soon as the distracting wars with Portugal, which attended her accession, were terminated. We have a letter from Pulgar, addressed to the queen soon after that event, in which he inquires concerning her progress, intimating his surprise, that she can find time for study amidst her multitude of engrossing occupations, and expressing his confidence that she will acquire the Latin with the same facility with which she had already mas-

---

[2] L. Marineo, Cosas Memorables, fol. 154, 182.

tered other languages. The result justified his prediction; for "in less than a year," observes another
contemporary, " her admirable genius enabled her
to obtain a good knowledge of the Latin language,
so that she could understand without much difficulty whatever was written or spoken in it." [3]

Isabella inherited the taste of her father, John
the Second, for the collecting of books. She endowed the convent of San Juan de los Reyes at
Toledo, at the time of its foundation, 1477, with a
library consisting principally of manuscripts. [4] The
archives of Simancas contain catalogues of part of
two separate collections, belonging to her, whose
broken remains have contributed to swell the mag-

Her collec-
tion of
books

---

[3] Carro de las Doñas, lib. 2,
cap. 62 et seq., apud Mem. de la
Acad. de Hist., tom. vi. Ilust. 21.
— Pulgar, Letras, (Amstelodami,
1670,) let. 11. — L. Marineo, Cosas Memorables, fol. 182. — It is
sufficient evidence of her familiarity with the Latin, that the letters
addressed to her by her confessor
seem to have been written in that
language and the Castilian indifferently, exhibiting occasionally a
curious patchwork in the alternate
use of each in the same epistle. See Correspondencia Epistolar, apud Mem. de la Acad. de
Hist., tom. vi. Ilust. 13.

[4] Previous to the introduction of
printing, collections of books were
necessarily very small and thinly
scattered, owing to the extreme
cost of manuscripts. The learned
Saez has collected some curious
particulars relative to this matter.
The most copious library which
he could find any account of, in the
middle of the fifteenth century,
was owned by the counts of Benavente, and contained not more than

one hundred and twenty volumes
Many of these were duplicates;
of Livy alone there were eight
copies. The cathedral churches
in Spain rented their books every
year by auction to the highest bid-
ders, whence they derived a considerable revenue.

It would appear from a copy of
Gratian's Canons, preserved in the
Celestine monastery in Paris, that
the copyist was engaged twenty-
one months in transcribing that
manuscript. At this rate, the production of four thousand copies by
one hand would require nearly
eight thousand years, a work now
easily performed in less than four
months. Such was the tardiness
in multiplying copies before the invention of printing. Two thousand volumes may be procured
now at a price, which in those days
would hardly have sufficed to purchase fifty. See Tratado de Mo-
nedas de Enrique III., apud Moratin, Obras, ed. de la Acad., (Madrid, 1830,) tom. i. pp. 91, 92. Moratin argues from extreme cases.

nificent library of the Escurial. Most of them are in manuscript; the richly colored and highly decorated binding of these volumes (an art which the Spaniards derived from the Arabs) show how highly they were prized, and the worn and battered condition of some of them prove that they were not kept merely for show. [5]

Tuition of
the infantas.

The queen manifested the most earnest solicitude for the instruction of her own children. Her daughters were endowed by nature with amiable dispositions, that seconded her maternal efforts. The most competent masters, native and foreign, especially from Italy, then so active in the revival of ancient learning, were employed in their tuition. This was particularly intrusted to two brothers, Antonio and Alessandro Geraldino, natives of that country. Both were conspicuous for their abilities and classical erudition, and the latter, who survived his brother Antonio, was subsequently raised to high ecclesiastical preferments. [6] Under these mas-

[5] Navagiero, Viaggio fatto in Spagna et in Francia, (Vinegia, 1563,) fol. 23. — Mem. de la Acad. de Hist., tom. vi. Ilust. 17.

The largest collection comprised about two hundred and one articles, or distinct works. Of these, about a third is taken up with theology, comprehending bibles, psalters, missals, lives of saints, and works of the fathers; one fifth, civil law and the municipal code of Spain; one fourth, ancient classics, modern literature, and romances of chivalry; one tenth, history; the residue is devoted to ethics, medicine, grammar, astrology, &c. The only Italian author, besides Leonardo Bruno d' Arezzo, is Boc-

caccio. The works of the latter writer consisted of the "Fiammetta," the treatises "De Casibus Illustrium Virorum," and "De Claris Mulieribus," and probably the "Decameron"; the first in the Italian, and the three last translated into the Spanish. It is singular, that neither of Boccaccio's great contemporaries, Dante and Petrarch, the former of whom had been translated by Villena, and imitated by Juan de Mena, half a century before, should have found a place in the collection.

[6] Antonio, the eldest, died in 1488. Part of his Latin poetical works, entitled, "Sacred Bucolics," was printed in 1505, at Sala-

ters, the infantas made attainments rarely permitted
to the sex, and acquired such familiarity with the
Latin tongue especially, as excited lively admiration among those over whom they were called to
preside in riper years. [7]

A still deeper anxiety was shown in the education of her only son, Prince John, heir of the united
Spanish monarchies. Every precaution was taken
to train him up in a manner that might tend to the
formation of the character suited to his exalted station. He was placed in a class consisting of ten
youths, selected from the sons of the principal nobility. Five of them were of his own age, and five
of riper years, and they were all brought to reside

---

manca. The younger brother, Alessandro, after bearing arms in the
Portuguese war, was subsequently
employed in the instruction of the
infantas, finally embraced the ecclesiastical state, and died bishop of
St. Domingo, in 1525. Mem. de
la Acad. de Hist., tom. vi. Ilust.
16. — Tiraboschi, Letteratura Italiana, tom. vi. part. 2, p. 285.

[7] The learned Valencian, Luis
Vives, in his treatise " De Christianâ Feminâ," remarks, " Ætas noster quatuor illas Isabellæ reginæ
filias, quas paullo ante memoravi,
eruditas vidit. Non sine laudibus
et admiratione refertur mihi passim
in hac terrâ Joannam, Philippi con-
jugem, Caroli hujus matrem, ex
tempore latinis orationibus, quæ
de more apud novos principes op-
pidatim habentur, latine respondis-
se. Idem de reginâ suâ, Joannæ
sorore, Britanni prædicant; idem
omnes de duabus aliis, quæ in Lu-
sitaniâ fato concessere." (De
Christianâ Feminâ, cap. 4, apud
Mem. de la Acad. de Hist., tom. vi.
Ilust. 16.) — It appears, however,

that Isabella was not inattentive to
the more humble accomplishments,
in the education of her daughters.
" Regina," says the same author,
" nere, suere, acu pingere quatuor
filias suas doctas esse voluit."
Another contemporary, the author
of the Carro de las Doñas, (lib. 2,
cap. 62, apud Mem. de la Acad.
de Hist., Ilust. 21.) says, " she
educated her son and daughters,
giving them masters of life and
letters, and surrounding them with
such persons as tended to make
them vessels of election, and kings
in Heaven."

Erasmus notices the literary attainments of the youngest daughter
of the sovereigns, the unfortunate
Catharine of Aragon, with unqualified admiration. In one of his
letters, he styles her " egregie doc-
tam "; and in another he remarks,
" Regina non tantum in sexus mi-
raculum literata est; nec minus
pietate suspicienda, quam eruditi-
one." Epistolæ, (Londini, 1642,)
lib. 19, epist. 31 ; lib. 2, epist. 24

with him in the palace. By this means, it was hoped to combine the advantages of public, with those of private education; which last, from its solitary character, necessarily excludes the subject of it from the wholesome influence exerted by bringing the powers into daily collision with antag onists of a similar age. [8]

A mimic council was also formed on the model of a council of state, composed of suitable persons of more advanced standing, whose province it was to deliberate on, and to discuss, topics connected with government and public policy. Over this body the prince presided, and here he was initiated into a practical acquaintance with the important duties, which were to devolve on him at a future period of life. The pages, in attendance on his person, were also selected with great care from the cavaliers and young nobility of the court, many of whom afterwards filled with credit the most considerable posts in the state. The severer discipline of the prince was relieved by attention to more light and elegant accomplishments. He devoted many of his leisure hours to music, for which he had a fine natural taste, and in which he attained sufficient proficiency to perform with skill on a variety of instruments. In short, his education was happily designed to produce that combination of mental and moral excellence, which should fit him for reigning over his subjects with benevolence and wisdom. How well the scheme succeeded is abun-

[8] Oviedo, Quincuagenas, MS., dial. de Deza. — Mem. de la Acad. de Hist.. tom. vi. Ilust. 14.

dantly attested by the commendations of contemporary writers, both at home and abroad, who enlarge on his fondness for letters, and for the society of learned men. on his various attainments, and more especially his Latin scholarship, and above all on his disposition, so amiable, as to give promise of the highest excellence in maturer life, — a promise alas! most unfortunately for his own nation, destined never to be realized.[9]

Next to her family, there was no object which the queen had so much at heart, as the improvement of the young nobility. During the troubled reign of her predecessor, they had abandoned themselves to frivolous pleasure, or to a sullen apathy, from which nothing was potent enough to arouse them, but the voice of war.[10] She was obliged to relinquish her plans of amelioration, during the all-engrossing struggle with Granada, when it would have been esteemed a reproach for a Spanish knight to have exchanged the post of danger in the field for the effeminate pursuit of letters. But, no sooner was the war brought to a close, than Isabella resumed her purpose. She requested the learned

The queen's care for the education of her nobles

---

[9] Mem. de la Acad. de Hist., tom. vi. Ilust. 14.

Juan de la Encina, in the dedication to the prince, of his translation of Virgil's Bucolics, pays the following compliment to the enlightened and liberal taste of Prince John. " Favoresceis tanto la sciencia andando acompañado de tantos e tan doctísimos varones, que lo menos dejareis perdurable memoria de haber alargado e estendido los límites e términos de la sciencia que los del imperio." The extra-

ordinary promise of this young prince, made his name known in distant parts of Europe, and his untimely death, which occurred in the twentieth year of his age, was commemorated by an epitaph of the learned Greek exile, Constantine Lascaris.

[10] " Aficionados á la guerra," says Oviedo, speaking of some young nobles of his time, *" por su Española y natural inclinacion."* Quincuagenas, MS., bat. 1, quinc. 1, dial. 36.

Peter Martyr, who had come into Spain with the
count of Tendilla, a few years previous, to repair to
the court, and open a school there for the instruction of the young nobility. [11] In an epistle addressed by Martyr to Cardinal Mendoza, dated at
Granada, April, 1492, he alludes to the promise of
a liberal recompense from the queen, if he would
assist in reclaiming the young cavaliers of the court
from the idle and unprofitable pursuits, in which, to
her great mortification, they consumed their hours.
The prejudices to be encountered seem to have
filled him with natural distrust of his success; for
he remarks, " Like their ancestors, they hold the
pursuit of letters in light estimation, considering
them an obstacle to success in the profession of
arms, which alone they esteem worthy of honor "
He however expresses his confidence, that the generous nature of the Spaniards will make it easy to
infuse into them a more liberal taste ; and, in a
subsequent letter, he enlarges on the " good effects
likely to result from the literary ambition exhibited
by the heir apparent, on whom the eyes of the
nation were naturally turned." [12]

Martyr, in obedience to the royal summons, in-

[11] For some account of this eminent Italian scholar, see the postscript to Part I. Chap. 14, of this
History.

[12] Peter Martyr, Opus Epist.,
epist. 102, 103.

Lucio Marineo, in a discourse
addressed to Charles V., thus notices the queen's solicitude for the
instruction of her young nobility
" Isabella præsertim Regina mag-
nanima, virtutum omnium maxima

cultrix.   Quæ quidem multis et
magnis occupata negotiis, ut aliis
exemplum præberet, a primis gram-
maticæ rudimentis studere cœpit,
et omnes suæ domûs adolescentes
utriusque sexûs nobilium liberos,
præceptoribus liberaliter et honori-
fice conductis erudiendos commen-
dabat." Mem. de la Acad. de
Hist., tom. vi. Apend. 16. — See
also Oviedo, Quincuagenas, MS..
bat. 1, quinc. 1, dial. 36.

stantly repaired to court, and in the month of September following, we have a letter dated from Saragossa, in which he thus speaks of his success. " My house, all day long, swarms with noble youths, who, reclaimed from ignoble pursuits to those of letters, are now convinced that these, so far from being a hindrance, are rather a help in the profession of arms   I earnestly inculcate on them, that consummate excellence in any department, whether of war or peace, is unattainable without science. It has pleased our royal mistress, the pattern of every exalted virtue, that her own near kinsman, the duke of Guimaraens, as well as the young duke of Villahermosa, the king's nephew, should remain under my roof during the whole day; an example which has been imitated by the principal cavaliers of the court, who, after attending my lectures in company with their private tutors, retire at evening to review them with these latter in their own quarters " [13]

Another Italian scholar, often cited as authority in the preceding portion of this work, Lucio Marineo Siculo, coöperated with Martyr in the introduction of a more liberal scholarship among the Castilian nobles. He was born at Bedino in Sicily, and, after completing his studies at Rome under the celebrated Pomponio Leto, opened a school in his native island, where he continued to teach for five years. He was then induced to visit Spain, in 1486, with the admiral Henriquez, and soon took

---

[13] Peter Martyr, Opus Epist., epist. 115

his place among the professors of Salamanca, where he filled the chairs of poetry and grammar with great applause for twelve years. He was subsequently transferred to the court, which he helped to illumine, by his exposition of the ancient classics, particularly the Latin.[14] Under the auspices of these and other eminent scholars, both native and foreign, the young nobility of Castile shook off the indolence in which they had so long rusted, and applied with generous ardor to the cultivation of science ; so that, in the language of a contemporary, " while it was a most rare occurrence, to meet with a person of illustrious birth, before the present reign, who had even studied Latin in his youth, there were now to be seen numbers every day, who sought to shed the lustre of letters over the martial glory inherited from their ancestors."[15]

[14] A particular account of Marineo's writings may be found in Nic. Antonio. (Bibliotheca Nova, tom. ii. Apend. p. 369.) The most important of these, is his work "De Rebus Hispaniæ Memorabilibus," often cited, in the Castilian, in this History. It is a rich repository of details respecting the geography, statistics, and manners of the Peninsula, with a copious historical notice of events in Ferdinand and Isabella's reign. The author's insatiable curiosity, during a long residence in the country, enabled him to collect many facts, of a kind that do not fall within the ordinary compass of history ; while his extensive learning, and his familiarity with foreign models, peculiarly qualified him for estimating the institutions he describes. It must be confessed he is sufficiently partial to the land of his adoption. The edition, referred to in this work, is in black letter, printed before, or soon after, the author's death (the date of which is uncertain), in 1539, at Alcalá de Henares, by Juan Brocar, one of a family long celebrated in the annals of Castilian printing. Marineo's prologue concludes with the following noble tribute to letters. " Porque todos los otros bienes son subjectos a la fortuna y mudables y en poco tiempo mudan muchos dueños passando de unos señores en otros, mas los dones de letras y hystorias que se ofrescen para perpetuidad de memoria y fama son immortales y prorogan y guardan para siempre la memoria assi de los que los reciben, como de los que los ofrescen."

[15] Sepulveda, Democrites, apud Mem. de la Acad. de Hist., tom. vi. Ilust. 16. — Signorelli, Coltura nelle Sicilie, tom. iv. p. 318. —

The extent of this generous emulation may be gathered from the large correspondence both of Martyr and Marineo with their disciples, including the most considerable persons of the Castilian court; it may be still further inferred from the numerous dedications to these persons, of contemporary publications, attesting their munificent patronage of literary enterprise;[16] and, still more unequivocally, from the zeal with which many of the highest rank entered on such severe literary labor as few, from the mere love of letters, are found willing to encounter. Don Gutierre de Toledo, son of the duke of Alva, and a cousin of the king, taught in the university of Salamanca. At the same place, Don Pedro Fernandez de Velasco, son of the count of Haro, who subsequently succeeded his father in the hereditary dignity of grand constable of Castile, read lectures on Pliny and Ovid. Don Alfonso de Manrique, son of the count of Paredes, was professor of Greek in the university of Alcalá. All ages seemed to catch the generous enthusiasm; and the marquis of Denia, although

Tiraboschi, Letteratura Italiana, tom. vii. part. 3, lib. 3, cap. 4. — Comp. Lampillas, Saggio Storico-Apologetico de la Letteratura Spagnuola, (Genova, 1778,) tom. ii. dis. 2, sect. 5. — The patriotic Abate is greatly scandalized by the degree of influence, which Tiraboschi and other Italian critics ascribe to their own language over the Castilian, especially at this period. The seven volumes, in which he has discharged his bile on the heads of the offenders, afford valuable materials for the historian of Spanish literature. Tiraboschi must be admitted to have the better of his antagonist in temper, if not in argument.

16 Among these we find copious translations from the ancient classics, as Cæsar, Appian, Plutarch, Plautus, Sallust, Æsop, Justin, Boëthius, Apulius, Herodian, affording strong evidence of the activity of the Castilian scholars in this department. Mem. de la Acad. de Hist., tom. vi. pp. 406, 407. — Mendez, Typographia Española, pp. 133, 139.

PART
I.

turned of sixty, made amends for the sins of his youth, by learning the elements of the Latin tongue at this late period. In short, as Giovio remarks in his eulogium on Lebrija, "No Spaniard was accounted noble who held science in indifference." From a very early period, a courtly stamp was impressed on the poetic literature of Spain. A similar character was now imparted to its erudition ; and men of the most illustrious birth seemed eager to lead the way in the difficult career of science, which was thrown open to the nation. [17]

Accomplished women.

In this brilliant exhibition, those of the other sex must not be omitted, who contributed by their intellectual endowments to the general illumination of the period. Among them, the writers of that day lavish their panegyrics on the marchioness of Monteagudo, and Doña Maria Pacheco, of the ancient house of Mendoza, sisters of the historian, Don Diego Hurtado, [18] and daughters of the accomplished count of Tendilla, [19] who, while ambas-

[17] Salazar de Mendoza, Dignidades, cap. 21.

Lucio Marineo Siculo, in his discourse above alluded to, in which he exhibits the condition of letters under the reign of Ferdinand and Isabella, enumerates the names of the nobility most conspicuous for their scholarship. This valuable document was to be found only in the edition of Marineo's work, " De Rebus Hispaniæ Memorabilibus," printed at Alcalá, in 1630, whence it has been transferred by Clemencin to the sixth volume of the Memoirs of the Royal Academy of History.

[18] His work " Guerra de Granada," was first published at Madrid,

in 1610, and "may be compared," says Nic. Antonio, in a judgment which has been ratified by the general consent of his countrymen, " with the compositions of Sallust, or any other ancient historian." His poetry and his celebrated *picaresco* novel "Lazarillo de Tormes," have made an epoch in the ornamental literature of Spain.

[19] Oviedo has devoted one of his dialogues to this nobleman, equally distinguished by his successes in arms, letters, and love ; the last of which, according to that writer, he had not entirely resigned at the age of seventy. — Quincuagenas, MS., bat. 1, quinc. 1, dial 28

sador at Rome, induced Martyr to visit Spain, and who was grandson of the famous marquis of Santillana, and nephew of the grand cardinal. [20] This illustrious family, rendered yet more illustrious by its merits than its birth, is worthy of specification, as affording altogether the most remarkable combination of literary talent in the enlightened court of Castile. The queen's instructer in the Latin language was a lady named Doña Beatriz de Galindo, called from her peculiar attainments *la Latina*. Another lady, Doña Lucia de Medrano, publicly lectured on the Latin classics in the university of Salamanca. And another, Doña Francisca de Lebrija, daughter of the historian of that name, filled the chair of rhetoric with applause at Alcalá. But our limits will not allow a further enumeration of names, which should never be permitted to sink into oblivion, were it only for the rare scholarship, peculiarly rare in the female sex, which they displayed, in an age comparatively unenlightened. [21] Female education in that day embraced a wider

[20] For an account of Santillana, see the First Chapter of this History. The cardinal, in early life, is said to have translated for his father the Æneid, the Odyssey, Ovid, Valerius Maximus, and Sallust. (Mem. de la Acad. de Hist., tom. vi. Ilust. 16.) This Herculean feat would put modern school-boys to shame, and we may suppose that partial versions only of these authors are intended.

[21] Mem. de la Acad. de Hist., tom. vi. Ilust. 16. — Oviedo, Quincuagenas, MS., dial. de Grizio. Señor Clemencin has examined with much care the intellectual culture of the nation under Isabella, in the sixteenth *Ilustracion* of his work. He has touched lightly on its poetical character, considering, no doubt, that this had been sufficiently developed by other critics. His essay, however, is rich in information in regard to the scholarship and severer studies of the period. The reader, who would pursue the inquiry still further, may find abundant materials in Nic. Antonio, Bibliotheca Vetus, tom. ii. lib. 10, cap. 13 et seq. — Idem, Bibliotheca Hispana Nova, (Matriti, 1783-8,) — tom i. ii. passim.

compass of erudition, in reference to the ancient
languages, than is common at present; a circumstance attributable, probably, to the poverty of
modern literature at that time, and the new and
general appetite excited by the revival of classical
learning in Italy. I am not aware, however, that
it was usual for learned ladies, in any other country
than Spain, to take part in the public exercises of
the gymnasium, and deliver lectures from the chairs
of the universities. This peculiarity, which may
be referred in part to the queen's influence, who
encouraged the love of study by her own example,
as well as by personal attendance on the academic
examinations, may have been also suggested by a
similar usage, already noticed, among the Spanish
Arabs. [22]

*Classical
learning.*

While the study of the ancient tongues came
thus into fashion with persons of both sexes, and
of the highest rank, it was widely and most thoroughly cultivated by professed scholars. Men of
letters, some of whom have been already noticed,
were invited into Spain from Italy, the theatre at
that time, on which, from obvious local advantages,
classical discovery was pursued with greatest ardor
and success. To this country it was usual also for
Spanish students to repair, in order to complete
their discipline in classical literature, especially the
Greek, as first taught on sound principles of criticism, by the learned exiles from Constantinople.

Lebrija

The most remarkable of the Spanish scholars, who

[22] See Part I. Chap. 8, of this History.

made this literary pilgrimage to Italy, was Antonio de Lebrija, or Nebrissensis, as he is more frequently called from his Latin name. [23] After ten years passed at Bologna and other seminaries of repute, with particular attention to their interior discipline, he returned, in 1473, to his native land, richly laden with the stores of various erudition. He was invited to fill the Latin chair at Seville, whence he was successively transferred to Salamanca and Alcalá, both of which places he long continued to enlighten by his oral instruction and publications. The earliest of these was his *Introducciones Latinas*, the third edition of which was printed in 1485, being four years only from the date of the first; a remarkable evidence of the growing taste for classical learning. A translation in the vernacular accompanied the last edition, arranged, at the queen's suggestion, in columns parallel with those of the original text; a form which, since become common, was then a novelty. [24] The publication of his Castilian grammar, " *Grammatica Castillana*," followed in 1492; a treatise designed particularly for the instruction of the ladies of the court. The other productions of this indefatigable scholar, embrace a large circle of topics, independently of his various treatises on philology and criticism Some were translated into French and Italian, and their republication has been continued to the last

[23] For a notice of his scholar, see the postscript to Part I. Chap. 11, of this History.

[24] Mendez, Typographia Española, pp. 271, 272.

In the second edition, published 1482, the author states, that no work of the time had a greater circulation, more than a thousand copies of it, at a high price, having been disposed of in the preceding year. Ibid., p. 237.

century. No man of his own, or of later times, contributed more essentially than Lebrija to the introduction of a pure and healthful erudition into Spain. It is not too much to say, that there was scarcely an eminent Spanish scholar in the beginning of the sixteenth century, who had not formed himself on the instructions of this master.[25]

Arias Bar-
bosa.

Another name worthy of commemoration, is that of Arias Barbosa, a learned Portuguese, who, after passing some years, like Lebrija, in the schools of Italy, where he studied the ancient tongues under the guidance of Politiano, was induced to establish his residence in Spain. In 1489 we find him at Salamanca, where he continued for twenty, or, according to some accounts, forty years, teaching in the departments of Greek and rhetoric. At the close of that period he returned to Portugal, where he superintended the education of some of the members of the royal family, and survived to a good old age. Barbosa was esteemed inferior to Lebrija in extent of various erudition, but to

---

[25] Nic. Antonio, Bibliotheca Nova, tom. i. pp. 132–139. — Lampillas, Letteratura Spagnuola, tom. ii. dis. 2, sec. 3. — Dialogo de las Lenguas, apud Mayans y Siscar, Orígenes, (Madrid, 1737,) tom. ii. pp. 46, 47.

Lucio Marineo pays the following elegant compliment to this learned Spaniard, in his discourse before quoted. "Amisit nuper Hispania maximum sui cultorem in re litterariâ, Antonium Nebrissensem, qui primus ex Italiâ in Hispaniam Musas adduxit, quibuscum barbariem ex suâ patriâ fugavit, et Hispaniam totam linguæ Latinæ lectionibus illustravit." "Meruerat id," says Gomez de Castro of Lebrija, "et multo majora hominis eruditio, cui Hispania debet, quicquid habet bonarum literarum."

The acute author of the "Dialogo de las Lenguas," while he renders ample homage to Lebrija's Latin erudition, disputes his critical acquaintance with his own language, from his being a native of Andalusia, where the Castilian was not spoken with purity. "Hablaba y escrivia como en el Andalucia y no como en la Castilla." p. 92 See also pp. 9, 10, 46, 53.

CHAPTER
XIX.

have surpassed him in an accurate knowledge of the Greek, and poetical criticism. In the former, indeed, he seems to have obtained a greater repute than any Spanish scholar of the time. He composed some valuable works, especially on ancient prosody. The unwearied assiduity and complete success of his academic labors have secured to him a high reputation among the restorers of ancient learning, and especially that of reviving a livelier relish for the study of the Greek, by conducting it on principles of pure criticism, in the same manner as Lebrija did with the Latin.[26]

The scope of the present work precludes the possibility of a copious enumeration of the pioneers of ancient learning, to whom Spain owes so large a debt of gratitude.[27] The Castilian scholars of the close of the fifteenth, and the beginning of the

Merits of the
Spanish
scholars

[26] Barbosa, Bibliotheca Lusitana, (Lisboa Occidental, 1741,) tom. i. pp. 76 – 78. — Signorelli, Coltura nelle Sicilie, tom. iv. pp. 315 – 321. — Mayans y Siscar, Origenes, tom. i. p. 173. — Lampillas, Letteratura Spagnuola, tom. ii. dis. 2, sect. 5. — Nic. Antonio, Bibliotheca Nova, tom. i. pp. 170, 171.

[27] Among these are particularly deserving of attention the brothers John and Francis Vergara, professors at Alcalá, the latter of whom was esteemed one of the most accomplished scholars of the age ; Nuñez de Guzman, of the ancient house of that name, professor for many years at Salamanca and Alcalá, and the author of the Latin version in the famous Polyglot of Cardinal Ximenes ; he left behind him numerous works, especially commentaries on the classics ; Olivario, whose curious erudition was abundantly exhibited in his illustra-

tions of Cicero and other Latin authors ; and lastly Vives, whose fame rather belongs to Europe than his own country, who, when only twenty-six years old, drew from Erasmus the encomium, that "there was scarcely any one of the age whom he could venture to compare with him in philosophy, eloquence, and liberal learning." But the most unequivocal testimony to the deep and various scholarship of the period is afforded by that stupendous literary work of Cardinal Ximenes, the Polyglot Bible, whose versions in the Greek, Latin, and oriental tongues were collated, with a single exception, by Spanish scholars. Erasmus, Epistolæ, lib. 19, epist. 101. — Lampillas, Letteratura Spagnuola, tom. ii. pp. 382 – 384, 495, 792 – 794 ; tom. ii. p. 208 et seq. — Gomez, De Rebus Gestis, fol. 37.

sixteenth century, may take rank with their illustrious contemporaries of Italy. They could not
indeed achieve such brilliant results in the discovery
of the remains of antiquity, for such remains had
been long scattered and lost amid the centuries of
exile and disastrous warfare consequent on the
Saracen invasion. But they were unwearied in
their illustrations, both oral and written, of the
ancient authors ; and their numerous commentaries,
translations, dictionaries, grammars, and various
works of criticism, many of which, though now ob-
solete, passed into repeated editions in their own
day, bear ample testimony to the generous zeal,
with which they conspired to raise their contemporaries to a proper level for contemplating the
works of the great masters of antiquity ; and well
entitled them to the high eulogium of Erasmus,
that " liberal studies were brought, in the course
of a few years, in Spain to so flourishing a condition, as might not only excite the admiration, but
serve as a model to the most cultivated nations of
Europe." [28]

Universities.

The Spanish universities were the theatre, on
which this classical erudition was more especially
displayed. Previous to Isabella's reign, there were
but few schools in the kingdom ; not one indeed
of any note, except in Salamanca ; and this did
not escape the blight which fell on every generous
study. But under the cheering patronage of the
present government, they were soon filled, and

[28] Erasmus, Epistolæ, p. 977.

widely multiplied. Academies of repute were to
be found in Seville, Toledo, Salamanca, Granada,
and Alcalá ; and learned teachers were drawn from
abroad by the most liberal emoluments. At the
head of these establishments stood "the illustrious
city of Salamanca," as Marineo fondly terms it,
"mother of all liberal arts and virtues, alike renowned for noble cavaliers and learned men." [29]
Such was its reputation, that foreigners as well
as natives were attracted to its schools, and at
one time, according to the authority of the same
professor, seven thousand students were assembled
within its walls. A letter of Peter Martyr, to his
patron the count of Tendilla, gives a whimsical picture of the literary enthusiasm of this place. The
throng was so great to hear his introductory lecture
on one of the Satires of Juvenal, that every avenue
to the hall was blockaded, and the professor was
borne in on the shoulders of the students. Pro-
fessorships in every department of science then
studied, as well as of polite letters, were established
at the university, the "new Athens," as Martyr
somewhere styles it. Before the close of Isabella's
reign, however, its glories were rivalled, if not
eclipsed, by those of Alcalá ;[30] which combined

[29] "La muy esclarecida ciudad
de Salamanca, madre de las artes
liberales, y todas virtudes, y ansi
de cavalleros como de letrados varones, muy ilustre." Cosas Memorables, fol. 11. — Chacon, Hist.
de la Universidad de Salamanca,
apud Semanario Erudito, tom. xviii.
pp. 1 – 61.

[30] "Academia Complutensis,"

says Erasmus of this university,
"non aliunde celebritatem nominis
auspicata est quàm a complectendo
linguas ac bonas literas. Cujus
præcipuum ornamentum est egre-
gius ille senex, planéque dignus
qui multos vincat Nestoras, Antonius Nebrissensis." Epist. ad Lu-
dovicum Vivem, 1521. Epistolæ,
p. 755.

higher advantages for ecclesiastical with civil education, and which, under the splendid patronage of
Cardinal Ximenes, executed the famous Polyglot
version of the Scriptures, the most stupendous lite--
rary enterprise of that age.[31]

**Sacred
studies**

This active cultivation was not confined to the
dead languages, but spread more or less over every
department of knowledge. Theological science, in
particular, received a large share of attention. It
had always formed a principal object of academic
instruction, though suffered to languish under the
universal corruption of the preceding reign. It
was so common for the clergy to be ignorant of the
most elementary knowledge, that the council of
Aranda found it necessary to pass an ordinance,
the year before Isabella's accession, that no person
should be admitted to orders who was ignorant of
Latin. The queen took the most effectual means
for correcting this abuse, by raising only competent
persons to ecclesiastical dignities. The highest
stations in the church were reserved for those, who
combined the highest intellectual endowments with
unblemished piety. Cardinal Mendoza, whose acute
and comprehensive mind entered with interest into
every scheme for the promotion of science, was

---

[31] Cosas Memorables, ubi supra.
— Peter Martyr, Opus Epist., epist.
57. — Gomez, De Rebus Gestis, lib.
4. — Chacon, Universidad de Salamanca, ubi supra.

It appears that the practice of
scraping with the feet as an expression of disapprobation, familiar in
our universities, is of venerable antiquity; for Martyr mentions, that

he was saluted with it before finishing his discourse by one or two
idle youths, dissatisfied with its
length. The lecturer, however,
seems to have given general satisfaction, for he was escorted back in
triumph to his lodgings, to use his
own language, " like a victor in the
Olympic games," after the conclu
sion of the exercise.

archbishop of Toledo; Talavera, whose hospitable mansion was itself an academy for men of letters, and whose princely revenues were liberally dispensed for their support, was raised to the see of Granada; and Ximenes, whose splendid literary projects will require more particular notice hereafter, succeeded Mendoza in the primacy of Spain. Under the protection of these enlightened patrons, theological studies were pursued with ardor, the Scriptures copiously illustrated, and sacred eloquence cultivated with success.

A similar impulse was felt in the other walks of science. Jurisprudence assumed a new aspect, under the learned labors of Montalvo.[32] The mathematics formed a principal branch of education, and were successfully applied to astronomy and geography. Valuable treatises were produced on medicine, and on the more familiar practical arts, as husbandry, for example.[33] History, which since the time of Alfonso the Tenth, had been held in higher honor and more widely cultivated in Castile than in any other European state, began to lay aside the garb of chronicle, and to be studied on more scientific principles. Charters and diplomas were consulted, manuscripts collated, coins and lapidary inscriptions deciphered, and collections made of these materials, the true basis of authentic

Other sciences

---

[32] For some remarks on the labors of this distinguished jurisconsult, see Part I. Chap. 6, and Part II. Chap. 26. of the present work.

[33] The most remarkable of these latter is Herrera's treatise on Agriculture, which, since its publication in Toledo, in 1520, has passed through a variety of editions at home, and translations abroad. Nic. Antonio, Bibliotheca Nova. tom. i. p. 503.

history; and an office of public archives, like that now existing at Simancas, was established at Burgos, and placed under the care of Alonso de Mota, as keeper, with a liberal salary.[34]

Nothing could have been more opportune for the enlightened purposes of Isabella, than the introduction of the art of printing into Spain, at the commencement, indeed in the very first year, of her reign. She saw, from the first moment, all the advantages which it promised for diffusing and perpetuating the discoveries of science. She encouraged its establishment, by large privileges to those who exercised it, whether natives or foreigners, and by causing many of the works, composed by her subjects, to be printed at her own charge.[35]

Among the earlier printers we frequently find the names of Germans; a people, who to the original merits of the discovery may justly add that of its propagation among every nation of Europe. We meet with a *pragmática*, or royal ordinance, dated in 1477, exempting a German, named Theodoric from taxation, on the ground of being "one of the principal persons in the discovery and practice of the art of printing books, which he had brought with him into Spain at great risk and expense, with the design of ennobling the libraries of the king-

---

[34] This collection, with the ill luck which has too often befallen such repositories in Spain, was burnt in the war of the Communities, in the time of Charles V. Mem. de la Acad. de Hist., tom. vi. Ilust. 16 — Morales, Obras, tom. vii. p. 18. — Informe de Riol, who particularly notices the solicitude of Ferdinand and Isabella for preserving the public documents.

[35] Mendez, Typographia Española, p. 51.

dom." [36] Monopolies for printing and selling books for a limited period, answering to the modern copyright, were granted to certain persons, in consideration of their doing so at a reasonable rate. [37] It seems to have been usual for the printers to be also the publishers and venders of books. These exclusive privileges, however, do not appear to have been carried to a mischievous extent. Foreign books, of every description, by a law of 1480, were allowed to be imported into the kingdom, free of all duty whatever; an enlightened provision, which might furnish a useful hint to legislators of the nineteenth century. [38]

The first press appears to have been erected at Valencia, in 1474; although the glory of precedence is stoutly contested by several places, and especially by Barcelona. [39] The first work printed was a collection of songs, composed for a poetical contest in honor of the Virgin, for the most part in

Its rapid diffusion

[36] Archivo de Murcia, apud Mem. de la Acad. de Hist., tom. vi. p. 244.

[37] Mendez, Typographia Española, pp. 52, 332.

[38] Ordenanças Reales, lib. 4, tit. 4, ley 22. — The preamble of this statute is expressed in the following enlightened terms; "Considerando los Reyes de gloriosa memoria quanto era provechoso y honroso, que a estos sus reynos se truxessen libros de otras partes para que con ellos se hiziessen los hombres letrados, quisieron y ordenaron, que de los libros no se pagasse el alcavala. . . . . . Lo qual parece que redunda en provecho universal de todos, y en enno-

blecimiento de nuestros Reynos."

[39] Capmany, Mem. de Barcelona, tom. i. part. 2, lib. 2, cap. 6. — Mendez, Typographia Española, pp. 55, 93.

Bouterwek intimates, that the art of printing was first practised in Spain by German printers at Seville, *in the beginning of the sixteenth century.* (Bouterwek, Geschichte der Poesie und Beredsamkeit, (Göttingen, 1801 – 17.) band iii, p. 98.) — He appears to have been misled by a solitary example quoted from Mayans y Siscar. The want of materials has more than once led this eminent critic to build sweeping conclusions on slender premises.

the Limousin or Valencian dialect.[40] In the follow
ing year the first ancient classic, being the works
of Sallust, was printed; and in 1478 there appeared from the same press a translation of the Scriptures, in the Limousin, by father Boniface Ferrer,
brother of the famous Dominican, St. Vincent
Ferrer.[41] Through the liberal patronage of the
government, the art was widely diffused; and, before the end of the fifteenth century, presses were
established and in active operation in the principal
cities of the united kingdom; in Toledo, Seville,
Ciudad Real, Granada, Valladolid, Burgos, Salamanca, Zamora, Saragossa, Valencia, Barcelona,
Monte Rey, Lerida, Murcia, Tolosa, Tarragona,
Alcalá de Henares, and Madrid.

It is painful to notice amidst the judicious provisions for the encouragement of science, one so entirely repugnant to their spirit as the establishment
of the censorship. By an ordinance, dated at Toledo, July 8th, 1502, it was decreed, that, " as many
of the books sold in the kingdom were defective, or
false, or apocryphal, or pregnant with vain and superstitious novelties, it was therefore ordered that
no book should hereafter be printed without special
license from the king, or some person regularly commissioned by him for the purpose." The
names of the commissioners then follow, consisting
mostly of ecclesiastics, archbishops and bishops,

---

[40] The title of the book is " Certamen poetich en lohor de la Con-
cecio," Valencia, 1474, 4to. The
name of the printer is wanting.

Mendez, Typographia Española
p. 56.
[41] Ibid., pp. 61 – 63.

with authority respectively over their several dioceses.[42] This authority was devolved in later times, under Charles the Fifth and his successors. on the Council of the Supreme, over which the inquisitor general presided *ex officio*. The immediate agents employed in the examination were also drawn from the Inquisition, who exercised this important trust, as is well known, in a manner most fatal to the interests of letters and humanity. Thus a provision, destined in its origin for the advancement of science, by purifying it from the crudities and corruptions which naturally infect it in a primitive age, contributed more effectually to its discouragement, than any other which could have been devised, by interdicting the freedom of expression, so indispensable to freedom of inquiry.[43]

While endeavouring to do justice to the progress of civilization in this reign, I should regret to present to the reader an over-colored picture of its results. Indeed, less emphasis should be laid on any actual results, than on the spirit of improvement, which they imply in the nation, and the liberal dispositions of the government. The fifteenth

Actual progress of science.

[42] Mendez, Typographia Española, pp. 52, 53. — Pragmáticas del Reyno, fol. 138, 139.

[43] Llorente, Hist. de l'Inquisition, tom. i. chap. 13, art. 1.

"Adempto per *inquisitiones*," says Tacitus of the gloomy times of Domitian, "et loquendi audiendique commercio." (Vita Agricolæ, sec. 2.) Beaumarchais, in a merrier vein, indeed, makes the same bitter reflections. " Il s'est établi dans Madrid un système de liberté sur la vente des productions, qui s'étend même à celles de la presse ; et que, pourvu que je ne parle en mes écrits ni de l'autorité, ni de culte, ni de la politique, ni de la morale, ni des gens en place, ni des corps en crédit, ni de l'Opéra, ni des autres spectacles, ni de personne qui tienne à quelque chose, je puis tout imprimer librement, sous l'inspection de deux ou trois censeurs." Mariage de Figaro, acte 5, sc. 3.

century was distinguished by a zeal for research and laborious acquisition, especially in ancient literature, throughout Europe, which showed itself in Italy in the beginning of the age, and in Spain, and some other countries, towards the close. It was natural that men should explore the long-buried treasures descended from their ancestors, before venturing on any thing of their own creation. Their efforts were eminently successful; and, by opening an acquaintance with the immortal productions of ancient literature, they laid the best foundation for the cultivation of the modern.

In the sciences, their success was more equivocal. A blind reverence for authority, a habit of speculation, instead of experiment, so pernicious in physics, in short an ignorance of the true principles of philosophy, often led the scholars of that day in a wrong direction. Even when they took a right one, their attainments, under all these impediments, were necessarily so small, as to be scarcely perceptible, when viewed from the brilliant heights to which science has arrived in our own age. Unfortunately for Spain, its subsequent advancement has been so retarded, that a comparison of the fifteenth century with those which succeeded it, is by no means so humiliating to the former as in some other countries of Europe; and it is certain, that in general intellectual fermentation, no period has surpassed, if it can be said to have rivalled, the age of Isabella.

CHAPTER XX.

CASTILIAN LITERATURE. — ROMANCES OF CHIVALRY. — LYRI
CAL POETRY. — THE DRAMA.

This Reign an Epoch in Polite Letters. — Romances of Chivalry. –
Ballads or *Romances*. — Moorish Minstrelsy. — "Cancionero General."
— Its Literary Value. — Rise of the Spanish Drama. — Criticism on
"Celestina." — Encina. — Naharro. — Low Condition of the Stage.
— National Spirit of the Literature of this Epoch.

CHAPTER
XX.

This reign
an epoch in
polite let-
ters

ORNAMENTAL or polite literature, which, emanat-
ing from the taste and sensibility of a nation,
readily exhibits its various fluctuations of fashion
and feeling, was stamped in Spain with the distinguishing characteristics of this revolutionary age.
The Provençal, which reached such high perfection in Catalonia, and subsequently in Aragon, as
noticed in an introductory chapter,[1] expired with
the union of this monarchy with Castile, and the
dialect ceased to be applied to literary purposes
altogether, after the Castilian became the language
of the court in the united kingdoms. The poetry
of Castile, which throughout the present reign continued to breathe the same patriotic spirit, and to
exhibit the same national peculiarities that had dis-

---

[1] Eichhorn, Geschichte der Kul-
ur und Litteratur der Neueren
Europa, (Göttingen, 1796 – 1811,)
pp. 129, 130. — See also the conclusion of the Introduction, Sec. 2,
of this History.

tinguished it from the time of the Cid, submitted
soon after Ferdinand's death to the influence of the
more polished Tuscan, and henceforth, losing somewhat of its distinctive physiognomy, assumed many
of the prevalent features of continental literature.
Thus the reign of Ferdinand and Isabella becomes
an epoch as memorable in literary, as in civil history.

The most copious vein of fancy, in that day, was
turned in the direction of the prose romance of
chivalry ; now seldom disturbed, even in its own
country, except by the antiquary.   The circumstances of the age naturally led to its production.
The romantic Moorish wars, teeming with adventurous exploit and picturesque incident, carried on
with the natural enemies of the Christian knight,
and opening moreover all the legendary stores of
oriental fable, — the stirring adventures by sea as
well as land, — above all, the discovery of a world
beyond the waters, whose unknown regions gave
full scope to the play of the imagination, all contributed to stimulate the appetite for the incredible
chimeras, the *magnanime menzogne*, of chivalry.
The publication of " Amadis de Gaula " gave a
decided impulse to this popular feeling.   This romance, which seems now well ascertained to be the
production of a Portuguese in the latter half of the
fourteenth century, [2] was first printed in a Spanish

[2] Nic. Antonio seems unwilling
to relinquish the pretensions of his
own nation to the authorship of this
romance. (See Bibliotheca Nova,
tom. ii. p. 394.)   Later critics. and
among them Lampillas, (Ensayc
Historico-Apologético de la Literatura Española,(Madrid,1789,) tom.
v. p. 168,) who resigns no more
than he is compelled to do, are less

version, probably not far from 1490.[3] Its editor, Garci Ordoñez de Montalvo, states, in his prologue, that " he corrected it from the ancient originals, pruning it of all superfluous phrases, and substituting others of a more polished and elegant style."[4] How far its character was benefited by this work of purification may be doubted ; although it is probable it did not suffer so much by such a

disposed to contest the claims of the Portuguese. Mr. Southey has cited two documents, one historical, the other poetical, which seem to place its composition by Lobeira in the latter part of the fourteenth century beyond any reasonable doubt. (See Amadis of Gaul, pref., — also Sarmiento, Memorias para la Historia de la Poesía y Poetas Españoles, Obras Posthumas, (Madrid, 1775,) tom. i. p. 239.) Bouterwek, and after him Sismondi, without adducing any authority, have fixed the era of Lobeira's death at 1325. Dante, who died but four years previous to that date, furnishes a negative argument, at least, against this, since in his notice of some doughty names of chivalry then popular, he makes no allusion to Amadis, the best of all. Inferno, cantos v., xxxi.

[3] The excellent old romance " Tirante the White," *Tirant lo Blanch*, was printed at Valencia in 1490. (See Mendez, Typographia Española, tom. i. pp. 72 – 75.) If, as Cervantes asserts, the " Amadis " was the first book of chivalry printed in Spain, it must have been anterior to this date. This is rendered probable by Montalvo's prologue to his edition at Saragossa, in 1521, still preserved in the royal library at Madrid, where he alludes to his former publication of it in the time of Ferdinand and Isabella. (Cervantes, Don Quixote, ed. Pelicer, Discurso Prelim.)

Mr. Dunlop, who has analyzed these romances with a patience that more will be disposed to commend than imitate, has been led into the error of supposing that the first edition of the " Amadis " was printed at Seville, in 1526, from detached fragments appearing in the time of Ferdinand and Isabella, and subsequently by Montalvo, at Salamanca, in 1547. See History of Prose Fiction, vol. ii. chap. 10.

[4] The following is Montalvo's brief prologue to the introduction of the first book. " Aqvi comiença el primero libro del esforçado et virtuoso cauallero Amadis hijo del rey Perion de Gaula : y dela reyna Elisena : el qual fue coregido y emendado por el honrado y virtuoso cauallero Garciordoñes de Montalvo, regidor dela noble uilla de Medina del campo ; et corregiole delos antiguos originales que estauan corruptos, et compuestos en antiguo estilo : por falta delos diferentes escriptores. Quitando muchas palabras superfluas : et poniendo otras de mas polido y elegante estilo : tocantes ala caualleria et actos della, animando los coraçones gentiles de manzebos belicosos que con grandissimo affetto abrazan el arte dela milicia corporal animando la immortal memoria del arte de caualleria no menos honestissimo que glorioso." Amadis de Gaula, (Venecia, 1533,) fol. 1.

process as it would have done in a later and more cultivated period. The simple beauties of this fine old romance, its bustling incidents, relieved by the delicate play of oriental machinery, its general truth of portraiture, above all, the knightly character of the hero, who graced the prowess of chivalry with a courtesy, modesty, and fidelity, unrivalled in the creations of romance, soon recommended it to popular favor and imitation. A continuation, bearing the title of " Las Sergas de Esplandian," was given to the world by Montalvo himself, and grafted on the original stock, as the fifth book of the Amadis, before 1510. A sixth, containing the adventures of his nephew, was printed at Salamanca in the course of the last-mentioned year ; and thus the idle writers of the day continued to propagate dulness through a series of heavy tomes, amounting in all to four and twenty books, until the much abused public would no longer suffer the name of Amadis to cloak the manifold sins of his posterity.[5] Other knights-errant were sent roving about the world at the same time, whose exploits would fill a library ; but fortunately they have been permitted to pass

[5] Nic. Antonio enumerates the editions of thirteen of this doughty family of knights-errant. (Bibliotheca Nova, tom. ii. pp. 394, 395.) He dismisses his notice with the reflection, somewhat more charitable than that of Don Quixote's curate, that " he had felt little interest in investigating these fables, yet was willing to admit with others, that their reading was not wholly useless."

Moratin has collected an appalling catalogue of *part* of the books of chivalry published in Spain at the close of the fifteenth and the following century. The first on the list is the *Carcel de Amor*, por Diego Hernandez de San Pedro, en Burgos, año de 1496. Obras, tom. i. pp. 93 – 98.

into oblivion, from which a few of their names only have been rescued by the caustic criticism of the curate in Don Quixote; who, it will be remembered, after declaring that the virtues of the parent shall not avail his posterity, condemns them and their companions, with one or two exceptions only, to the fatal funeral pile.[6]

Their perni cious effects

These romances of chivalry must have undoubtedly contributed to nourish those exaggerated sentiments, which from a very early period entered into the Spanish character. Their evil influence, in a literary view, resulted less from their improbabilities of situation, which they possessed in common with the inimitable Italian epics, than from the false pictures which they presented of human character, familiarizing the eye of the reader with such models as debauched the taste, and rendered him incapable of relishing the chaste and sober productions of art. It is remarkable that the chivalrous romance, which was so copiously cultivated through the greater part of the sixteenth century, should not have assumed the poetic form, as in Italy, and indeed among our Norman ancestors; and that, in its prose dress, no name of note appears to raise it

---

[6] Cervantes, Don Quixote, tom. ι. part. 1, cap. 6.
The curate's wrath is very emphatically expressed. "Pues vayan todos al corral, dixo el Cura, que a trueco de quemar a la reyna Pintiquiniestra, y al pastor Darinel y a sus eglogas, y a las endiabladas y revueltas razones de su autor, quemara con ellos al padre que me engendro si andubiera en figura de caballero andante." The author of the "Dialogo de las Lenguas" chimes in with the same tone of criticism. "Los quales," he says, speaking of books of chivalry, "de mas de ser mentirossissimos, son tal mal compuestos, assi por dezir las mentiras tan desvergonçadas, como por tener el estilo desbaraçado, que no ay buen estomago que lo pueda leer." Apud Mayans y Siscar, Orígenes, tom. ii. p. 158.

PART
I.
to a high degree of literary merit. Perhaps such a result might have been achieved, but for the sublime parody of Cervantes, which cut short the whole race of knights-errant, and by the fine irony, which it threw around the mock heroes of chivalry, extinguished them for ever. [7]

Ballads or romances.

The most popular poetry of this period, that springing from the body of the people, and most intimately addressed to it, is the ballads, or *romances*, as they are termed in Spain. These indeed were familiar to the Peninsula as far back as the twelfth and thirteenth centuries; but in the present reign they received a fresh impulse from the war with Granada, and composed, under the name of the Moorish ballads, what may perhaps be regarded, without too high praise, as the most exquisite popular minstrelsy of any age or country.

Early cultivation in Spain.

The humble narrative lyrics making up the mass of ballad poetry, and forming the natural expression of a simple state of society, would seem to be most abundant in nations endowed with keen sensibilities, and placed in situations of excitement and powerful interest, fitted to develope them. The light and lively French have little to boast of

[7] The labors of Bowles, Rios, Arrieta, Pellicer, and Navarrete, would seem to have left little to desire in regard to the illustration of Cervantes. But the commentaries of Clemencin, published since this chapter was written, in 1833, show how much yet remained to be supplied. They afford the most copious illustrations, both literary and historical of his author, and exhibit that nice taste in verbal criticism, which is not always joined with such extensive erudition. Unfortunately, the premature death of Clemencin has left the work unfinished; but the fragment completed, which reaches to the close of the First Part, is of sufficient value permanently to associate the name of its author with that of the greatest genius of his country.

in this way.[8] The Italians, with a deeper poetic feeling, were too early absorbed in the gross business habits of trade, and their literature received too high a direction from its master spirits, at its very commencement, to allow any considerable deviation in this track. The countries where it has most thriven, are probably Great Britain and Spain. The English and the Scotch, whose constitutionally pensive and even melancholy temperament has been deepened by the sober complexion of the climate, were led to the cultivation of this poetry still further by the stirring scenes of feudal warfare in which they were engaged, especially along the borders. The Spaniards, to similar sources of excitement, added that of high religious feeling in their struggles with the Saracens, which gave a somewhat loftier character to their effusions. Fortunately for them, their early annals gave birth, in the Cid, to a hero, whose personal renown was identified with that of his country, round whose name might be concentrated all the scattered lights of song, thus enabling the nation to build up its poetry on the proudest historic recollections.[9] The feats of many other heroes, fabulous as well as real, were

[8] The fabliaux cannot fairly be considered as an exception to this. These graceful little performances, the work of professed bards, who had nothing further in view than the amusement of a listless audience, have little claim to be considered as the expression of national feeling or sentiment. The poetry of the south of France, more impassioned and lyrical in its character, wears the stamp, not merely of patrician elegance, but refined artifice, which must not be confounded with the natural flow of popular minstrelsy.

[9] How far the achievements claimed for the Campeador are strictly true, is little to the purpose. It is enough that they were received as true, throughout the Peninsula, as far back as the twelfth, or at latest, the thirteenth century.

permitted to swell the stream of traditionary verse ;
and thus a body of poetical annals, springing up as
it were from the depths of the people, was be-
queathed from sire to son, contributing, perhaps,
more powerfully than any real history could have
done, to infuse a common principle of patriotism
into the scattered members of the nation.

Resem-
blance to the
English.
There is considerable resemblance between the
early Spanish ballad and the British. The latter
affords more situations of pathos and deep tenderness, particularly those of suffering, uncomplaining
love, a favorite theme with old English poets of
every description. [10] We do not find, either, in the
ballads of the Peninsula, the wild, romantic adventures of the roving outlaw, of the Robin Hood
genus, which enter so largely into English minstrelsy. The former are in general of a more sustained
and chivalrous character, less gloomy, and although
fierce not so ferocious, nor so decidedly tragical in
their aspect, as the latter. The ballads of the Cid,
however, have many points in common with the
border poetry ; the same free and cordial manner,
the same love of military exploit, relieved by a
certain tone of generous gallantry, and accompanied by a strong expression of national feeling.

Moorish
minstrelsy
The resemblance between the minstrelsy of the

[10] One exception, among others, readily occurs in the pathetic
old ballad of the Conde Alarcos,
whose woful catastrophe, with the
unresisting suffering of the count-
ess, suggests many points of coincidence with the English minstrelsy. The English reader will
find a version of it in the " Ancient Poetry and Romances of
Spain " from the pen of Mr. Bow-
ring, to whom the literary world
is so largely indebted for an acquaintance with the popular minstrelsy of Europe.

two countries vanishes, however, as we approach the Moorish ballads. The Moorish wars had always afforded abundant themes of interest for the Castilian muse; but it was not till the fall of the capital, that the very fountains of song were broken up, and those beautiful ballads were produced, which seem like the echoes of departed glory, lingering round the ruins of Granada. Incompetent as these pieces may be as historical records, they are doubtless sufficiently true to manners. [11] They present a most remarkable combination, of not merely the exterior form, but the noble spirit of European chivalry, with the gorgeousness and effeminate luxury of the east. They are brief, seizing single situations of the highest poetic interest, and striking the eye of the reader with a brilliancy of execution, so artless in appearance withal as to seem rather the effect of accident than study. We are transported to the gay seat of Moorish power, and witness the animating bustle, its pomp

[11] I have already noticed the insufficiency of the *romances* to authentic history, Part. I. Chap. 8, Note 30. My conclusions there have been confirmed by Mr. Irving, (whose researches have led him in a similar direction,) in his "Alhambra," published nearly a year after the above note was written.

The great source of the popular misconceptions respecting the domestic history of Granada, is Gines Perez de Hyta, whose work, under the title of "Historia de los Vandos de los Zegries y Abencerrages, Cavalleros Moros de Granada, y las Guerras Civiles que huvo en ella," was published at Alcalá in 1601. This romance, written in prose, embodied many of the old Moorish ballads in it, whose singular beauty, combined with the romantic and picturesque character of the work itself, soon made it extremely popular, until at length it seems to have acquired a degree of the historical credit claimed for it by its author as a translation from an Arabian chronicle; a credit which has stood it in good stead with the tribe of travel-mongers and *raconteurs*, persons always of easy faith, who have propagated its fables far and wide. Their credulity, however, may be pardoned in what has imposed on the perspicacity of so cautious an historian as Müller. Allgemeine Geschichte, (1817,) band ii. p. 504.

and its revelry, prolonged to the last hour of its existence. The bull-fight of the Vivarrambla, the graceful tilt of reeds, the amorous knights with their quaint significant devices, the dark Zegris, or Gomeres, and the royal, self-devoted Abencerrages, the Moorish maiden radiant at the tourney, the moonlight serenade, the stolen interview, where the lover gives vent to all the intoxication of passion in the burning language of Arabian metaphor and hyperbole, [12] — these, and a thousand similar scenes are brought before the eye, by a succession of rapid and animated touches, like the lights and shadows of a landscape. The light trochaic structure of the *redondilla*, [13] as the Spanish ballad

[12] Thus, in one of their *romances*, we have a Moorish lady " shedding drops of liquid silver, and scattering her hair of Arabian gold " over the corpse of her murdered husband!

" Sobre el cuerpo de Albencayde
Destila liquida plata,
Y convertida en cabellos
Esparce el oro de Arabia."

Can any thing be more oriental than this imagery? In another we have " an hour of years of impatient hopes " ; a passionate sally, that can scarcely be outmatched by Scriblerus. This taint of exaggeration, however, so far from being peculiar to the popular minstrelsy, has found its way, probably through this channel in part, into most of the poetry of the Peninsula.

[13] The *redondilla* may be considered as the basis of Spanish versification. It is of great antiquity, and compositions in it are still extant, as old as the time of the infante Don Manuel, at the close of

the thirteenth century. (See Cancionero General, fol. 207.) The *redondilla* admits of great variety; but in the *romances* it is most frequently found to consist of eight syllables, the last foot, and some or all of the preceding, as the case may be, being trochees. (Rengifo, Arte Poética Española, (Barcelona, 1727,) cap. 9, 44.) Critics have derived this delightful measure from various sources. Sarmiento traces it to the hexameter of the ancient Romans, which may be bisected into something analogous to the redondillas. (Memorias, pp. 168 – 171.) Bouterwek thinks it may have been suggested by the songs of the Roman soldiery. (Geschichte der Poesie und Beredsamkeit, band iii. Einleitung, p. 20.) — Velazquez borrows it from the rhyming hexameters of the Spanish Latin poets, of which he gives specimens of the beginning of the fourteenth century. (Poesía Castellana, pp. 77, 78.) Later critics refer its derivation to

measure is called, rolling on its graceful, negligent *asonante*, [14] whose continued repetition seems by its monotonous melody to prolong the note of feeling originally struck, is admirably suited by its flexibility to the most varied and opposite expression; a circumstance which has recommended it as the ordinary measure of dramatic dialogue.

Nothing can be more agreeable than the general effect of the Moorish ballads, which combine the elegance of a riper period of literature, with the natural sweetness and simplicity, savouring

the Arabic. Conde has given a translation of certain Spanish-Arabian poems, in the measure of the original, from which it is evident, that the hemistich of an Arabian verse corresponds perfectly with the redondilla. (See his Dominacion de los Arabes, passim.) The same author, in a treatise, which he never published, on the " poesia oriental," shows more precisely the intimate affinity subsisting between the metrical form of the Arabian and the old Castilian verse. The reader will find an analysis of his manuscript in Part. I. Chap. 8, Note 49, of this History.

This theory is rendered the more plausible, by the influence which the Arabic has exercised on Castilian versification in other respects, as in the prolonged repetition of the rhyme, for example, which is wholly borrowed from the Spanish Arabs; whose superior cultivation naturally affected the unformed literature of their neighbours, and through no channel more obviously than its popular minstrelsy.

[14] The *asonante* is a rhyme made by uniformity of the vowels, without reference to the consonants; the regular rhyme, which obtains in other European literatures, is distinguished in Spain by the term *consonante*. Thus the four following words, taken at random from a Spanish ballad, are consecutive *asonantes*; *regozyo*, *pellico*, *luzido*, *amarillo*. In this example, the two last syllables have the assonance; although this is not invariable, it sometimes falling on the antepenultima and the final syllable. (See Rengifo, Arte Poética Española, pp. 214, 215, 218.) There is a wild, artless melody in the *asonante*, and a graceful movement coming somewhere, as it does, betwixt regular rhyme and blank verse, which would make its introduction very desirable, but not very feasible, in our own language. An attempt of the kind has been made by a clever writer, in the Retrospective Review. (Vol. iv. art. 2.) If it has failed, it is from the impediments presented by the language, which has not nearly the same amount of vowel terminations, nor of simple uniform vowel sounds, as the Spanish; the double termination, however full of grace and beauty in the Castilian, assumes, perhaps from the effect of association, rather a doggrel air in the English.

sometimes even of the rudeness, of a primitive age. Their merits have raised them to a sort of classical dignity in Spain, and have led to their cultivation by a higher order of writers, and down to a far later period, than in any other country in Europe. The most successful specimens of this imitation may be assigned to the early part of the seventeenth century; but the age was too late to enable the artist, with all his skill, to seize the true coloring of the antique. It is impossible, at this period, to ascertain the authors of these venerable lyrics, nor can the exact time of their production be now determined; although, as their subjects are chiefly taken from the last days of the Spanish Arabian empire, the larger part of them was probably posterior, and, as they were printed in collections at the beginning of the sixteenth century, could not have been long posterior, to the capture of Granada. How far they may be referred to the conquered Moors, is uncertain. Many of these wrote and spoke the Castilian with elegance, and there is nothing improbable in the supposition, that they should seek some solace under present evils in the splendid visions of the past. The bulk of this poetry, however, was in all probability the creation of the Spaniards themselves, naturally attracted by the picturesque circumstances in the character and condition of the conquered nation to invest them with poetic interest.

Its high re-
pute.

The Moorish *romances* fortunately appeared after the introduction of printing into the Peninsula, so that they were secured a permanent existence, in-

stead of perishing with the breath that made them,
like so many of their predecessors. This misfortune, which attaches to so much of popular poetry in all nations, is not imputable to any insensibility in the Spaniards to the excellence of their own Men of more erudition than taste may have held them light, in comparison with more ostentatious and learned productions. This fate has befallen them in other countries than Spain. [15] But persons of finer poetic feeling, and more enlarged spirit of criticism, have estimated them as a most essential and characteristic portion of Castilian literature. Such was the judgment of the great Lope de Vega, who, after expatiating on the extraordinary compass and sweetness of the *romance*, and its adaptation to the highest subjects, commends it as worthy of all estimation for its peculiar national character. [16] The modern Spanish writers have adopted a

---

[15] This may be still further inferred from the tenor of a humorous, satirical old *romance*, in which the writer implores the justice of Apollo on the heads of the swarm of traitor poets, who have deserted the ancient themes of song, the Cids, the Laras, the Gonzalez, to celebrate the Ganzuls and Abderrahmans and the fantastical fables of the Moors.

" Tanta Zayda y Adalifa,
  tanta Draguta y Daraxa,
  tanto Azarque y tanto Adulce,
  tanto Gazul, y Abenamar,
  tanto alquizer y marlota,
  tanto almayzar, y almalafa,
  tantas emprisas y plumas,
  tantas cifras y medallas,
  tanta roperia Mora.
  Y en vanderillas y adargas,
  tanto mote, y tantas motas
  muera yo sino me cansan."
    *   *   *   *   *
" Los Alfonsos, los Henricos,
  los Sanchos, y los de Lara,

que es dellos, y que es del Cid?
tanto olvido en glorias tantas?
ninguna pluma las buela,
ninguna Musa las canta?
Justicia, Apollo, justicia,
vengadores rayos lança
contra Poetas Moriscos."

Dr. Johnson's opinions are well known, in regard to this department of English literature, which, by his ridiculous parodies, he succeeded for a time in throwing into the shade, or, in the language of his admiring biographer, made "perfectly contemptible."

Petrarch, with like pedantry, rested his hopes of fame on his Latin epic, and gave away his lyrics, as alms to ballad-singers. Posterity, deciding on surer principles of taste, has reversed both these decisions.

[16] " Algunos quieren que sean la cartilla de los Poetas; yo no lo

similar tone of criticism, insisting on its study, as essential to a correct appreciation and comprehension of the genius of the language. [17]

The Castilian ballads were first printed in the "Cancionero General" of Fernando del Castillo, in 1511. They were first incorporated into a separate work, by Sepulveda, under the name of "Romances sacados de Historias Antiguas," printed at Antwerp, in 1551. [18] Since that period, they have passed into repeated editions, at home and abroad, especially in Germany, where they have been illustrated by able critics. [19] Ignorance of their authors, and of the era of their production, has prevented any attempt at exact chronological arrangement; a circumstance rendered, moreover, nearly impossible, by the perpetual modification which the original style of the more ancient ballads has experienced, in their transition through successive generations; so that, with one or two exceptions, no earlier date

siento assi; antes bien los hallo capaces, no solo de exprimir y declarar qualquier concepto con facil dulzura, pero de prosequir toda grave accion de numeroso Poema. Y soy tan de veras Español, que por ser en nuestro idioma natural este genero, no me puedo persuadir que no sea digno de toda estimacion." (Coleccion de Obras Sueltas, (Madrid, 1776–9,) tom. iv. p. 176, Prólogo.) In another place, he finely styles them "Iliads without a Homer."

[17] See, among others, the encomiastic and animated criticism of Fernandez and Quintana. Fernandez, Poesías Escogidas, de Nuestros Cancioneros y Romanceros Antiguos, (Madrid, 1796,) tom. xvi.,

Prólogo.—Quintana, Poesías Selectas Castellanas, Introd. art. 4.

[18] Nic. Antonio, Bibliotheca Nova, tom. ii. p. 10.—The Spanish translators of Bouterwek, have noticed the principal "collections and earliest editions" of the *Romances*. This original edition of Sepulveda has escaped their notice. See Literatura Española, pp. 217, 218.

[19] See Grimm, Depping, Herder, &c. This last poet has embraced a selection of the Cid ballads, chronologically arranged, and translated with eminent simplicity and spirit, if not with the scrupulous fidelity usually aimed at by the Germans. See his Sämmtliche Werke, (Wien, 1813,) band iii.

should probably be assigned to the oldest of them, in their present form, than the fifteenth century.[20] Another system of classification has been adopted, of distributing them according to their subjects; and independent collections also of the separate departments, as ballads of the Cid, of the Twelve Peers, the Morisco ballads, and the like, have been repeatedly published, both at home and abroad.[21]

The higher, and educated classes of the nation, were not insensible to the poetic spirit, which drew forth such excellent minstrelsy from the body of the people. Indeed Castilian poetry bore the same patrician stamp through the whole of the present reign, which had been impressed on it in its infancy.

CHAPTER XX.

Lyric poetry.

[20] Sarmiento, Memorias, pp. 242, 243. — Moratin considers that none have come down to us, in their original costume, of an earlier date than John II.'s reign, the first half of the fifteenth century. (Obras, tom. i. p. 84.) The Spanish translators of Bouterwek transcribe a *romance*, relating to the Cid, from the fathers Berganza and Merino, purporting to exhibit the primitive, uncorrupted diction of the thirteenth century. Native critics are of course the only ones competent to questions of this sort; but, to the less experienced eye of a foreigner, the style of this ballad would seem to resemble much less that genuine specimen of the versification of the preceding age, the poem of the Cid, than the compositions of the fifteenth and sixteenth centuries.

[21] The principle of philosophical arrangement, if it may so be called, is pursued still further in the latest Spanish publications of the *romances*, where the Moorish minstrelsy is embodied in a separate volume, and distributed with reference to its topics. This system is the more practicable with this class of ballads, since it far exceeds in number any other. See Duran, Romancero de Romances Moriscos.

The Romancero I have used is the ancient edition of Medina del Campo, 1602. It is divided into nine parts, though it is not easy to see on what principle, since the productions of most opposite date and tenor are brought into juxtaposition. The collection contains nearly a thousand ballads, which, however, fall far short of the entire number preserved, as may easily be seen by reference to other compilations. When to this is added the consideration of the large number which insensibly glided into oblivion without ever coming to the press, one may form a notion of the immense mass of these humble lyrics, which floated among the common people of Spain; and we shall be the less disposed to wonder at the proud and chivalrous bearing that marks even the peasantry of a nation, which seems to breathe the very air of romantic song.

Fortunately the new art of printing was employed here, as in the case of the *romances*, to arrest those fugitive sallies of imagination, which in other countries were permitted, from want of this care, to pass into oblivion; and *cancioneros*, or collections of lyrics, were published, embodying the productions of this reign and that of John the Second, thus bringing under one view the poetic culture of the fifteenth century.

Cancionero General.

The earliest cancionero printed was at Saragossa, in 1492. It comprehended the works of Mena, Manrique, and six or seven other bards of less note.[22] A far more copious collection was made by Fernando del Castillo, and first published at Valencia, in 1511, under the title of " Cancionero General," since which period it has passed into repeated editions. This compilation is certainly more creditable to Castillo's industry, than to his discrimination or power of arrangement. Indeed, in this latter respect it is so defective, that it would almost seem to have been put together fortuitously, as the pieces came to hand. A large portion of the authors appear to have been persons of rank; a cir-

[22] The title of this work was " Coplas de Vita Christi, de la Cena con la Pasion, y de la Veronica con la Resurreccion de nuestro Redemtor. E las siete Angustias e siete Gozos de nuestra Señora, con otras obras mucho provechosas." It concludes with the following notice, " Fue la presente obra emprentada en la insigne Ciudad de Zaragoza de Aragon por industria e expensas de Paulo Hurus de Constancia aleman. A 27 dias de Noviembre, 1492." (Mendez, Typographia Española, pp. 134, 136.) It appears there were two or three other cancioneros compiled, none of which, however, were admitted to the honors of the press. (Bouterwek, Literatura Española, nota.) The learned Castro, some fifty years since, published an analysis with copious extracts from one of these made by Baena, the Jewish physician of John II., a copy of which existed in the royal library of the Escurial. Bibliotheca Española, tom. i. p. 265 et seq.

cumstance to which perhaps they were indebted,
more than to any poetic merit, for a place in the
miscellany, which might have been decidedly increased in value by being diminished in bulk.[23]

The *works of devotion* with which the collection
opens, are on the whole the feeblest portion of it.
We discern none of the inspiration and lyric glow,
which were to have been anticipated from the devout, enthusiastic Spaniard. We meet with ana-
grams on the Virgin, glosses on the creed and
pater noster, *canciones* on original sin and the like
unpromising topics, all discussed in the most bald,
prosaic manner, with abundance of Latin phrase,
scriptural allusion, and commonplace precept, un-
enlivened by a single spark of true poetic fire, and
presenting altogether a farrago of the most fantastic
pedantry.

The lighter, especially the amatory poems, are
much more successfully executed, and the primitive
forms of the old Castilian versification are developed
with considerable variety and beauty. Among the
most agreeable effusions in this way, may be noticed those of Diego Lopez de Haro, who, to borrow the encomium of a contemporary, was " the
mirror of gallantry for the young cavaliers of the
time." There are few verses in the collection

---

[23] Cancionero General, passim.
— Moratin has given a list of the
men of rank who contributed to this
miscellany; it contains the names
of the highest nobility of Spain.
(Orig. del Teatro Español, Obras,
om. i. pp. 85, 86.) Castillo's
Cancionero passed through several
editions, the latest of which appeared in 1573. See a catalogue,
not entirely complete, of the different Spanish Cancioneros in Bouterwek, Literatura Española, trad.,
p 217.

composed with more facility and grace.[24] Among the more elaborate pieces, Diego de San Pedro's " Desprecio de la Fortuna " may be distinguished, not so much for any poetic talent which it exhibits, as for its mercurial and somewhat sarcastic tone of sentiment.[25] The similarity of subject may suggest a parallel between it and the Italian poet Guidi's celebrated ode on Fortune ; and the different styles of execution may perhaps be taken, as indicating pretty fairly the distinctive peculiarities of the Tuscan and the old Spanish school of poetry. The Italian, introducing the fickle goddess, in person, on the scene, describes her triumphant march over the ruins of empires and dynasties, from the earliest time, in a flow of lofty dithyrambic eloquence, adorned with all the brilliant coloring of a stimulated fancy and a highly finished language. The Castilian, on the other hand, instead of this splendid personification, deepens his verse into a moral tone, and, dwelling on the vicissitudes and vanities of human life, points his reflections with some caustic warning, often conveyed with enchanting simplicity, but without the least approach to lyric exaltation, or indeed the affectation of it.

This proneness to moralize the song is in truth a characteristic of the old Spanish bard. He rarely abandons himself, without reserve, to the frolic

---

[24] Cancionero General, pp. 83–89. — Oviedo, Quincuagenas, MS.
[25] Cancionero General, pp. 158–161. — Some meagre information of this person is given by Nic. Antonio, whose biographical notices may be often charged with deficiency in chronological data ; a circumstance perhaps unavoidable from the obscurity of their subjects. Bibliotheca Vetus, tom. ii. lib. 10, cap 6.

puerilities so common with the sister Muse of Italy,

> " Scritta così come la penna getta,
>   Per fuggir l' ozio, e non per cercar gloria."

It is true, he is occasionally betrayed by verbal subtilties and other affectations of the age ;[26] but even his liveliest sallies are apt to be seasoned with a moral, or sharpened by a satiric sentiment. His defects, indeed, are of the kind most opposed to those of the Italian poet, showing themselves, especially in the more elaborate pieces, in a certain tumid stateliness and overstrained energy of diction.

On the whole, one cannot survey the " Cancionero General," without some disappointment at the little progress of the poetic art, since the reign of John the Second, at the beginning of the century. The best pieces in the collection are of that date, and no rival subsequently arose to compete with the masculine strength of Mena, or the delicacy and fascinating graces of Santillana. One cause of this tardy progress may have been, the direction to utility manifested in this active reign, which led such as had leisure for intellectual pursuits to cultivate science, rather than abandon themselves to the mere revels of the imagination.

Another cause may be found in the rudeness of

Low state of lyric poetry

---

[26] There are probably more direct puns in Petrarch's lyrics alone, than in all the Cancionero General. There is another kind of *niaiserie*, however, to which the Spanish poets were much addicted, being the transposition of the word in every variety of sense and combination; as, for example,

" Acordad vuestros olvidos
Y olvida vuestros acuerdos
Porque tales desacuerdos
Acuerden vuestros sentidos," &c.
    Cancionero General, fol. 226.
It was such subtilties as these, *entricadas razones*, as Cervantes calls them, that addled the brains of poor Don Quixote. Tom. i. cap. 1.

the language, whose delicate finish is so essentia
to the purposes of the poet, but which was so imperfect at this period, that Juan de la Encina, a
popular writer of the time, complained that he was
obliged, in his version of Virgil's Eclogues, to coin,
as it were, a new vocabulary, from the want of
terms corresponding with the original, in the old
one.[27]   It was not until the close of the present
reign, when the nation began to breathe awhile
from its tumultuous career, that the fruits of the
patient cultivation which it had been steadily,
though silently experiencing, began to manifest
themselves in the improved condition of the language, and its adaptation to the highest poetica
uses. The intercourse with Italy, moreover, by
naturalizing new and more finished forms of versification, afforded a scope for the nobler efforts of
the poet, to which the old Castilian measures, however well suited to the wild and artless movements
of the popular minstrelsy, were altogether inadequate.

Coplas of
Manrique

We must not dismiss the miscellaneous poetry of
this period, without some notice of the " Coplas "
of Don Jorge Manrique,[28] on the death of his father,
the count of Paredes, in 1474.[29] The elegy is of

---

[27] Velasquez, Poesía Castellana,
p. 122. — More than half a century later, the learned Ambrosio
Morales complained of the barren-
ness of the Castilian, which he
imputed to the too exclusive adoption of the Latin upon all subjects
of dignity and importance. Obras,
tom. xiv. pp. 147, 148.
[28] L. Marineo, speaking of this
accomplished nobleman, styles him

" virum satis illustrem. — Eum
enim poetam et philosophum natu-
ra formavit ac peperit." He unfortunately fell in a skirmish, five
years after his father's death, in
1479. Mariana, Hist. de España,
tom. ii. p. 531.
[29] An elaborate character of this
Quixotic old cavalier may be found
in Pulgar, Claros Varones. tit. 13.

considerable length, and is sustained throughout in a tone of the highest moral dignity, while the poet leads us up from the transitory objects of this lower world to the contemplation of that imperishable existence, which Christianity has opened beyond the grave. A tenderness pervades the piece, which may remind us of the best manner of Petrarch; while, with the exception of a slight taint of pedantry, it is exempt from the meretricious vices that belong to the poetry of the age. The effect of the sentiment is heightened by the simple turns and broken melody of the old Castilian verse, of which perhaps this may be accounted the most finished specimen; such would seem to be the judgment of his own countrymen,[30] whose glosses and commentaries on it have swelled into a separate volume.[31]

I shall close this survey with a brief notice of the drama, whose foundations may be said to have been laid during this reign. The sacred plays, or mysteries, so popular throughout Europe in the middle ages, may be traced in Spain to an ancient date. Their familiar performance in the churches, by the clergy, is recognised in the middle of the thirteenth century, by a law of Alfonso the Tenth, which, while it interdicted certain profane mum-

CHAPTER XX.

Rise of the Spanish drama

---

[30] "Don Jorge Manrique," says Lope de Vega, "cuyas coplas Castellanas admiren los ingenios estrangeros y merecen estar escritas con letras de oro." Obras Sueltas, tom. xii. Prólogo.

[31] Coplas de Don Jorge Manrique, ed. Madrid, 1779. — Dialogo de las Lenguas, apud Mayans y Siscar, Orig_nes, tom. ii. p. 149. —

Manrique's Coplas have also been the subject of a separate publication in the United States. Professor Longfellow's version, accompanying it, is well calculated to give the English reader a correct notion of the Castilian bard, and, of course, a very exaggerated one of the literary culture of the age.

meries that had come into vogue, prescribed the
legitimate topics for exhibition. [32]

The transition from these rude spectac es to
more regular dramatic efforts, was very slow and
gradual. In 1414, an allegorical comedy, composed by the celebrated Henry, marquis of Villena,
was performed at Saragossa, in the presence of the
court. [33] In 1469, a dramatic eclogue by an anon-
ymous author, was exhibited in the palace of the
count of Ureña, in the presence of Ferdinand, on
his coming into Castile to espouse the infanta Isabella. [34] These pieces may be regarded as the

[32] After proscribing certain profane mummeries, the law confines
the clergy to the representation of
such subjects as " the birth of our
Saviour, in which is shown how
the angels appeared, announcing
his nativity ; also his advent, and
the coming of the three Magi
kings to worship him ; and his re-
surrection, showing his crucifixion
and ascension on the third day ;
and other such things leading men
to do well and live constant in
the faith." (Siete Partidas, tit. 6,
ley 34.) It is worth noting, that
similar abuses continued common
among the ecclesiastics, down to
Isabella's reign, as may be inferred from a decree, very similar to
the law of the Partidas above
cited, published by the council
of Aranda, in 1473. (Apud Moratin,
Obras, tom. i. p. 87.) Moratin
considers it certain, that the representation of the mysteries existed in Spain, as far back as the
eleventh century. The principal
grounds for this conjecture appear
to be, the fact that such notorious
abuses had crept into practice by
the middle of the thirteenth century, as to require the intervention
of the law. (Ibid. pp. 11, 13.)

The circumstance would seem
compatible with a much more recent origin.

[33] Cervantes, Comedias y Entremeses, (Madrid, 1749,) tom. i.
prólogo de Nasarre. — Velazquez,
Poesía Castellana, p. 86. — The
fifth volume of the Memoirs of the
Spanish Royal Academy of History, contains a dissertation on the
" national diversions," by Don
Gaspar Melchor de Jovellanos,
replete with curious erudition, and
exhibiting the discriminating taste
to have been expected from its accomplished author. Among these
antiquarian researches, the writer
has included a brief view of the
first theatrical attempts in Spain.
See Mem. de la Acad. de Hist.,
tom. v. Mem. 6.

[34] Moratin, Obras tom. i. p.
115. — Nasarre (Cervantes, Comedias, pról.), Jovellanos (Mem.
de la Acad. de Hist., tom. v.
Memor. 6.), Pellicer (Orígen y
Progreso de la Comedia, (1804,)
tom. i. p. 12.), and others, refer
the authorship of this little piece,
without hesitation, to Juan de la
Encina, although the year of its
representation corresponds precisely with that of his birth. The

earliest theatrical attempts, after the religious dramas and popular pantomimes already noticed, but unfortunately they have not come down to us. The next production deserving attention is, a "Dialogue between Love and an Old Man," imputed to Rodrigo Cota, a poet of whose history nothing seems to be known, and little conjectured, but that he flourished during the reigns of John the Second, and Henry the Fourth. The dialogue is written with much vivacity and grace, and with as much dramatic movement as is compatible with only two interlocutors. [35]

A much more memorable production is referred to the same author, the tragicomedy of "Celestina," or "Calisto and Melibea," as it is frequently called. The first act, indeed, constituting nearly one third of the piece, is all that is ascribed to Cota. The remaining twenty, which however should rather be denominated scenes, were contin-

Tragicomedy of Celestina.

prevalence of so gross a blunder among the Spanish scholars, shows how little the antiquities of their theatre were studied before the time of Moratin.

[35] This little piece has been published at length by Moratin, in the first volume of his works. (See Orígenes del Teatro Español, Obras, tom. i. pp. 303 – 314.)

The celebrated marquis of Santillana's poetical dialogue, "Comedieta da Ponza," has no pretensions to rank as a dramatic composition, notwithstanding its title, which is indeed as little significant of its real character, as the term "Commedia" is of Dante's epic. It is a discourse on the vicissitudes of human life, suggested by a sea-fight near Ponza, in 1435. It is conducted without any attempt at dramatic action or character, or, indeed, dramatic developement of any sort. The same remarks may be made of the political satire, "Mingo Revulgo," which appeared in Henry IV.'s reign. Dialogue was selected by these authors as a more popular and spirited medium than direct narrative for conveying their sentiments. The "Comedieta da Ponza" has never appeared in print; the copy which I have used is a transcript from the one in the royal library at Madrid, and belongs to Mr. George Ticknor.

ued by another hand, some, though to judge from the internal evidence afforded by the style, not many years later. The second author was Fernando de Roxas, bachelor of law, as he informs us, who composed this work as a sort of intellectual relaxation, during one of his vacations. The time was certainly not misspent. The continuation, however, is not esteemed by the Castilian critics to have risen quite to the level of the original act. [36]

Criticism on it.

The story turns on a love intrigue. A Spanish youth of rank is enamoured of a lady, whose affections he gains with some difficulty, but whom he finally seduces, through the arts of an accomplished courtesan, whom the author has introduced under the romantic name of Celestina. The piece, although comic, or rather sentimental in its progress, terminates in the most tragical catastrophe, in which all the principal actors are involved.

[36] Tragicomedia de Calisto y Melibea, (Alcalá, 1586,) Introd. — Nothing is positively ascertained respecting the authorship of the first act of the Celestina. Some impute it to Juan de Mena; others with more probability to Rodrigo Cota el Tio, of Toledo, a person who, although literally nothing is known of him, has in some way or other obtained the credit of the authorship of some of the most popular effusions of the fifteenth century; such, for example, as the Dialogue above cited of " Love and an Old Man," the Coplas of " Mingo Revulgo," and this first act of the " Celestina." The principal foundation of these imputations would appear to be the bare assertion of an editor of the " Dialogue between Love and an Old Man," which appeared at Medina del Campo, in 1569, nearly a century, probably, after Cota's death; another example of the obscurity which involves the history of the early Spanish drama. Many of the Castilian critics detect a flavor of antiquity in the first act which should carry back its composition as far as John II.'s reign. Moratin does not discern this, however, and is inclined to refer its production to a date not much more distant, if any, than Isabella's time. To the unpractised eye of a foreigner, as far as style is concerned, the whole work might well seem the production of the same period. Moratin, Obras, tom. i. pp. 88, 115, 116. — Diálogo de las Lenguas, apud Mayans y Siscar, Orígenes, pp. 165 - 167. — Nic. Antonio, Bibliotheca Nova, tom. ii. p. 263.

The general texture of the plot is exceedingly clumsy, yet it affords many situations of deep and varied interest in its progress. The principal characters are delineated in the piece with considerable skill. The part of Celestina, in particular, in which a veil of plausible hypocrisy is thrown over the deepest profligacy of conduct, is managed with much address. The subordinate parts are brought into brisk comic action, with natural dialogue, though sufficiently obscene; and an interest of a graver complexion is raised by the passion of the lovers, the timid, confiding tenderness of the lady, and the sorrows of the broken-hearted parent. The execution of the play reminds us on the whole less of the Spanish, than of the old English theatre, in many of its defects, as well as beauties; in the contrasted strength and imbecility of various passages; its intermixture of broad farce and deep tragedy; the unseasonable introduction of frigid metaphor and pedantic allusion in the midst of the most passionate discourses; in the unveiled voluptuousness of its coloring, occasionally too gross for any public exhibition; but, above all, in the general strength and fidelity of its portraiture.

The tragicomedy, as it is styled, of Celestina, was obviously never intended for representation, to which, not merely the grossness of some of the details, but the length and arrangement of the piece, are unsuitable. But, notwithstanding this, and its approximation to the character of a romance, it must be admitted to contain within itself the essential elements of dramatic composition; and,

It opened the way to dramatic writing.

as such, is extolled by the Spanish critics, as opening the theatrical career of Europe. A similar
claim has been maintained for nearly contemporaneous productions in other countries, and especially
for Politian's "Orfeo," which, there is little doubt,
was publicly acted before 1483. Notwithstanding
its representation, however, the "Orfeo," presenting a combination of the eclogue and the ode,
without any proper theatrical movement, or attempt
at developement of character, cannot fairly come
within the limits of dramatic writing. A more ancient example than either, at least as far as the exterior forms are concerned, may be probably found
in the celebrated French farce of Pierre Pathelin,
printed as early as 1474, having been repeatedly
played during the preceding century, and which,
with the requisite modifications, still keeps possession of the stage. The pretensions of this piece,
however, as a work of art, are comparatively humble ; and it seems fair to admit, that in the higher
and more important elements of dramatic composition, and especially in the delicate, and at the same
time powerful delineation of character and passion,
the Spanish critics may be justified in regarding
the "Celestina" as having led the way in modern
Europe. [37]

[37] Such is the high encomium
of the Abate Andres, (Letteratura, tom. v. part. 2, lib. 1.) —
Cervantes does not hesitate to call
it "libro divino" ; and the acute
author of the "Diálogo de las
Lenguas" concludes a criticism
upon it with the remark, that

"there is no book in the Castilian
which surpasses it in the propriety
and elegance of its diction." (Don
Quixote, ed. de Pellicer, tom. i.
p. 239. — Mayans y Siscar, tom.
ii. p. 167.)
Its merits indeed seem in some
degree to have disarmed even the

Without deciding on its proper classification as a
work of art, however, its real merits are settled by
its wide popularity, both at home and abroad. It
has been translated into most of the European languages, and the preface to the last edition published in Madrid, so recently as 1822, enumerates
thirty editions of it in Spain alone, in the course of
the sixteenth century. Impressions were multiplied in Italy, and at the very time when it was
interdicted at home on the score of its immoral
tendency. A popularity thus extending through
distant ages and nations, shows how faithfully it is
built on the principles of human nature.[38]

*Numerous
editions of it*

The drama assumed the pastoral form, in its early
stages, in Spain, as in Italy. The oldest specimens
in this way, which have come down to us, are the
productions of Juan de la Encina, a contemporary
of Roxas. He was born in 1469, and, after completing his education at Salamanca, was received
into the family of the duke of Alva. He continued
there several years, employed in the composition of
various poetical works, among others, a version of
Virgil's Eclogues, which he so altered as to accommodate them to the principal events in the reign of
Ferdinand and Isabella. He visited Italy in the

*Juan de la
Encina.*

severity of foreign critics; and
Signorelli, after standing up stoutly in defence of the precedence of
the "Orfeo" as a dramatic composition, admits the "Celestina"
to be a "work, rich in various
beauties, and meriting undoubted
applause. In fact," he continues,
"the vivacity of the description of
character, and faithful portraiture

of manners, have made it immortal." Storia Critica de' Teatri An-
tichi e Moderni, (Napoli, 1813,)
tom. vi. pp. 146, 147.

[38] Bouterwek, Literatura Española, notas de traductores, p. 234.
— Andres, Letteratura, tom. v.
pp. 170, 171. — Lampillas, Letteratura Spagnuola, tom. vi. pp. 57 –
59.

beginning of the following century, and was attracted by the munificent patronage of Leo the
Tenth to fix his residence at the papal court.
While there, he continued his literary labors. He
embraced the ecclesiastical profession; and his skill
in music recommended him to the office of princ-
pal director of the pontifical chapel. He was subsequently presented with the priory of Leon, and
returned to Spain, where he died in 1534.[39]

His dramatic
eclogues.

Encina's works first appeared at Salamanca, in
1496, collected into one volume, folio.[40] Besides
other poetry, they comprehend a number of dramatic eclogues, sacred and profane; the former, suggested by topics drawn from Scripture, like the ancient mysteries; the latter, chiefly amatory. They
were performed in the palace of his patron, the
duke of Alva, in the presence of Prince John, the
duke of Infantado, and other eminent persons of
the court; and the poet himself occasionally assisted at the representation.[41]

[39] Rojas, Viage Entretenido,
(1614,) fol. 46. — Nic. Antonio,
Bibliotheca Nova, tom. i. p. 684.
— Moratin, Obras, tom. i. pp. 126,
127. — Pellicer, Orígen de la Comedia, tom. i. pp. 11, 12.

[40] They were published under
the title, "Cancionero de todas
las Obras de Juan de la Encina
con otras añadidas." (Mendez,
Typographia Española, p. 247.)
Subsequent impressions of his
works, more or less complete, appeared at Salamanca in 1509, and at
Saragossa in 1512 and 1516. — Moratin, Obras, tom. i. p. 127, nota.

[41] The comedian Rojas, who
flourished in the beginning of the
following century, and whose

"Viage Entretenido" is so essential to the knowledge of the early
histrionic art in Spain, identifies the
appearance of Encina's Eclogues
with the dawn of the Castilian
drama. His verses may be worth
quoting.

"Que es en nuestra madre España,
porque en la dichosa era,
que aquellos gloriosos Reyes
dignos de memoria eterna
Don Fernando e Ysabel
(que ya con los santos reynan)
de echar de España acabavan
todos los Moriscos, que eran
De aquel Reyno de Granada,
y entonces se dava en ella
principio a la Inquisicion,
se le dio a nuestra comedia.
Juan de la Encina el primero,
aquel insigne poeta,
que tanto bien empezo

Encina's eclogues are simple compositions, with little pretence to dramatic artifice. The story is too meagre to admit of much ingenuity or contrivance, or to excite any depth of interest. There are few interlocutors, seldom more than three or four, although on one occasion rising to as many as seven; of course there is little scope for theatrical action. The characters are of the humble class belonging to pastoral life, and the dialogue, which is extremely appropriate, is conducted with facility; but the rustic condition of the speakers precludes any thing like literary elegance or finish, in which respect they are doubtless surpassed by some of his more ambitious compositions. There is a comic air imparted to them, however, and a lively colloquial turn, which renders them very agreeable. Still, whatever be their merit as pastorals, they are entitled to little consideration as specimens of dramatic art; and, in the vital spirit of dramatic composition, must be regarded as far inferior to the "Celestina." The simplicity of these productions, and the facility of their exhibition, which required little theatrical decoration or costume, recommended them to popular imitation, which continued long after the regular forms of the drama were introduced into Spain.[42]

de quien tenemos tres eglogas
Que el mismo represento
al Almirante y Duquessa
de Castilla, y de Infantado
que estas fueron las primeras
Y para mas honra suya,
y de la comedia nuestra,
en los dias que Colon
descubrio la gran riqueza
De Indias y nuevo mundo,
y el gran Capitan empieza
a sugetar aquel Reyno
de Napoles, y su tierra.

A descubrirse empezo
el uso de la comedia
porque todos se animassen
a emprender cosas tan buenas."
fol. 46, 47.

[42] Signorelli, correcting what he denominates the "romance" of Lampillas, considers Encina to have composed only one pastoral drama, and that, on occasion of Ferdinand's entrance into Castile. The critic

The credit of this introduction belongs to Bartholomeo Torres de Naharro, often confounded by the Castilian writers themselves with a player of the same name, who flourished half a century later.[43] Few particulars have been ascertained of his personal history. He was born at Torre, in the province of Estremadura. In the early part of his life he fell into the hands of the Algerines, and was finally released from captivity by the exertions of certain benevolent Italians, who generously paid his ransom. He then established his residence in Italy, at the court of Leo the Tenth. Under the genial influence of that patronage, which quickened so many of the seeds of genius to production in every department, he composed his " Propaladia," a work embracing a variety of lyrical and dramatic poetry, first published at Rome, in 1517. Unfortunately, the caustic satire, levelled in some of the highei pieces of this collection at the license of the pontifical court, brought such obloquy on the head of the author as compelled him to take refuge in Naples, where he remained under the protection of the noble family of Colonna. No further particulars are recorded of him except that he embraced the

should have been more charitable, as he has made two blunders himself in correcting one. Storia Critica de' Teatri, tom. iv. pp. 192, 193.

[43] Andres, confounding Torres de Naharro the poet, with Naharro the comedian, who flourished about half a century later, is led into a ludicrous train of errors in controverting Cervantes, whose criticism on the actor is perpetually misapplied by Andres to the poet. Velasquez seems to have confounded them in like manner. Another evidence of the extremely superficia. acquaintance of the Spanish critics with their early drama. Comp. Cervantes, Comedias y Entremeses, tom. i. prólogo. — Andres, Letteratura, tom. v. p. 179. — Velazquez, Poesía Castellana, p. 88.

ecclesiastical profession; and the time and place of his death are alike uncertain. In person he is said to have been comely, with an amiable disposition, and sedate and dignified demeanor. [44]

His "Propaladia," first published at Rome, passed through several editions subsequently in Spain, where it was alternately prohibited, or permitted, according to the caprice of the Holy Office. It contains, among other things, eight comedies, written in the native *redondillas;* which continue to be regarded as the suitable measure for the drama. They afford the earliest example of the division into *jornadas,* or days, and of the *intróito,* or prologue, in which the author, after propitiating the audience by suitable compliment, and witticisms not over delicate, gives a view of the length and general scope of his play. [45]

His comedies

The scenes of Naharro's comedies, with a single exception, are laid in Spain and Italy; those in the latter country probably being selected with reference to the audiences before whom they were acted. The diction is easy and correct, without much affectation of refinement or rhetorical orna-

[44] Nic. Antonio, Bibliotheca Nova, tom. i. p. 202. — Cervantes, Comedias, tom. i. pról. de Nasarre. — Pellicer, Orígen de la Comedia. tom. ii. p. 17. — Moratin, Obras, tom. i. p. 48.

[45] Bartolomé Torres de Naharro, Propaladia, (Madrid, 1573.) — The deficiency of the earlier Spanish books, of which Bouterwek repeatedly complains, has led him into an error respecting the "Propaladia," which he had never seen. He states that Naharro was the first to distribute the play into three jornadas or acts, and takes Cervantes roundly to task for assuming the original merit of this distribution to himself. In fact, Naharro did introduce the division into *five* jornadas, and Cervantes assumes only the credit of having been the first to *reduce them to three.* Comp. Bouterwek, Geschichte der Poesie und Beredsamkeit, band iii. p. 285, — and Cervantes, Comedias, tom. i. pról.

ment. The dialogue, especially in the lower parts, is sustained with much comic vivacity; indeed Naharro seems to have had a nicer perception of character as it is found in lower life, than as it exists in the higher; and more than one of his plays are devoted exclusively to its illustration. On some occasions, however, the author assumes a more elevated tone, and his verse rises to a degree of poetic beauty, deepened by the moral reflection so characteristic of the Spaniards. At other times, his pieces are disfigured by such a Babel-like confusion of tongues, as makes it doubtful which may be the poet's vernacular. French, Spanish, Italian, with a variety of barbarous *patois*, and mongrel Latin, are all brought into play at the same time, and all comprehended, apparently with equal facility, by each one of the *dramatis personæ*. But it is difficult to conceive how such a jargon could have been comprehended, far more relished, by an Italian audience.[46]

Similar in spirit with the later dramas.

Naharro's comedies are not much to be commended for the intrigue, which generally excites but a languid interest, and shows little power or adroitness in the contrivance. With every defect, however, they must be allowed to have given the first forms to Spanish comedy, and to exhibit many of the features which continued to be characteristic of it in a state of more perfect developement under Lope de Vega and Calderon. Such, for instance,

---

[46] In the argument to the "Seraphina," he thus prepares the audience for this colloquial *olla podrida*.

"Mas haveis de estar alerta
  por sentir los personages

que hablan quatro lenguages,
hasta acabar su rehyerta
no salen de cuenta cierta
por Latin e Italiano
Castellano y Valenciano
que nirguno desconcierta."
      Propaladia, p. 50

's the amorous jealousy, and especially the point
of honor, so conspicuous on the Spanish theatre;
and such, too, the moral confusion too often produced by blending the foulest crimes with zeal for
religion.[47] These comedies, moreover, far from
blind conformity with the ancients, discovered much
of the spirit of independence, and deviated into
many of the eccentricities which distinguish the
national theatre in later times; and which the
criticism of our own day has so successfully explained and defended on philosophical principles.

Naharro's plays were represented, as appears
from his prologue, in Italy, probably not at Rome,
which he quitted soon after their publication, but
at Naples, which, then forming a part of the
Spanish dominions, might more easily furnish an
audience capable of comprehending them.[48]   It is

Not acted in Spain.

[47] The following is an example
of the precious reasoning with
which Floristan, in the play above
quoted, reconciles his conscience to
the murder of his wife Orfea, in
order to gratify the jealousy of his
mistress Seraphina. Floristan is
addressing himself to a priest.

" Y por mas daño escusar
no lo quiero hora hazer,
sino que es menester.
que yo mate luego a Orfea
do Serafina lo vea
porque lo pueda creer.
Que yo bien me mataria,
pues toda razon me inclina;
pero se de Serafina
que se desesperaria.
y Orfea, pues que haria?
quando mi muerte supiesse:
que creo que no pudiesse
sostener la vida un dia.
Pues hablando aca entre nos
a Orfea cabe la suerte;
porque con su sola muerte
se escusaran otras dos:
de modo que padre vos
si llamar me quereys,
a mi merced me hareys

y tambien servicio a Dios.
    *   *   *   *
porque si yo la matare
morira christianamente;
yo morire penitente,
quando mi suerte llegare."
            Propaladia, fol. 68.

[48] Signorelli waxes exceedingly
wroth with Don Blas Nasarre for
the assertion, that Naharro first
taught the Italians to write comedy,
taxing him with downright men-
dacity; and he stoutly denies the
probability of Naharro's comedies
ever having been performed on the
Italian boards. The critic seems
to be in the right, as far as regards
the influence of the Spanish dramatist; but he might have been spared
all doubts respecting their representation in the country, had he
consulted the prologue of Naharro
himself, where he asserts the fact
in the most explicit manner. Comp.
Propaladia, pról., and Signorelli,

remarkable, that notwithstanding their repeated editions in Spain, they do not appear to have ever been performed there. The cause of this, probably, was the low state of the histrionic art, and the total deficiency in theatrical costume and decoration, yet it was not easy to dispense with these in the representation of pieces, which brought more than a score of persons occasionally, and these crowned heads, at the same time, upon the stage. [49]

Low condition of the stage.

Some conception may be afforded of the lamentable poverty of the theatrical equipment, from the account given of its condition, half a century later, by Cervantes. " The whole wardrobe of a manager of the theatre, at that time," says he, " was contained in a single sack, and amounted only to four dresses of white fur trimmed with gilt leather, four beards, four wigs, and four crooks, more or less. There were no trapdoors, movable clouds, or machinery of any kind. The stage itself consisted only of four or six planks, placed across as many benches, arranged in the form of a square, and elevated but four palms from the ground. The only decoration of the theatre was an old coverlet, drawn from side to side by cords, behind which the musicians sang some ancient *romance*, without the guitar." [50] In fact, no further apparatus was employed than that demanded for the exhibition of

Storia Critica de' Teatri, tom. vi. pp. 171 – 179. — See also Moratin, Origenes, Obras, tom. i. pp. 149, 150.

[49] Propaladia ; see the comedies of " Trofea " and " Tinelaria."—

Jovellanos, Memoria sobre las Diversiones Públicas, apud Mem. de la Acad. de Hist., tom. v.

[50] Cervantes, Comedias tom. i pról.

mysteries, or the pastoral dialogues which succeeded them The Spaniards, notwithstanding their
precocity, compared with most of the nations of
Europe, in dramatic art, were unaccountably tardy
in all its histrionic accompaniments. The public
remained content with such poor mummeries, as
could be got up by strolling players and moun-
tebanks. There was no fixed theatre in Madrid
until the latter part of the sixteenth century; and
that consisted of a courtyard, with only a roof to
shelter it, while the spectators sat on benches
ranged around, or at the windows of the surrounding houses.[51]

A similar impulse with that experienced by comic
writing, was given to tragedy. The first that entered on this department were professed scholars,
who adopted the error of the Italian dramatists, in
fashioning their pieces servilely after the antique,
instead of seizing the expression of their own age.
The most conspicuous attempts in this way were
made by Fernan Perez de Oliva.[52] He was born

[51] Pellicer, Origen de la Comedia, tom. ii. pp. 58 – 62. — See
also American Quarterly Review,
no. viii. art. 3.

[52] Oliva, Obras, (Madrid, 1787.)
— Vasco Diaz Tanco, a native of
Estremadura, who flourished in the
first half of the sixteenth century,
mentions in one of his works three
tragedies composed by himself on
Scripture subjects. As there is no
evidence, however, of their having
been printed, or performed, or even
read in manuscript by any one,
they hardly deserve to be included
in the catalogue of dramatic compositions. (Moratin, Obras, tom.
i. pp. 150, 151. — Lampillas, Letteratura Spagnuola, tom. v. dis. 1,
sec. 5.) This patriotic *littérateur*
endeavours to establish the production of Oliva's tragedies in the year
1515, in the hope of antedating
that of Trissino's " Sophonisba,"
composed a year later, and thus securing to his nation the palm of
precedence, in time at least, though
it should be only for a few months,
on the tragic theatre of modern
Europe. Letteratura Spagnuola,
ubi supra.

at Cordova, in 1494, and, after many years passed
in the various schools of Spain, France, and Italy,
returned to his native land, and became a lecturer
in the university of Salamanca. He instructed in
moral philosophy and mathematics, and established
the highest reputation for his critical acquaintance
with the ancient languages and his own. He died
young, at the age of thirty-nine, deeply lamented
for his moral, no less than for his intellectual
worth. [53]

Oliva's clas-
sic imita-
tions.

His various works were published by the learned
Morales, his nephew, some fifty years after his
death. Among them are translations in prose of
the Electra of Sophocles, and the Hecuba of Euripides. They may with more propriety be termed
imitations, and those too of the freest kind. Although they conform, in the general arrangement
and progress of the story, to their originals, yet
characters, nay whole scenes and dialogues, are
occasionally omitted ; and in those retained, it is
not always easy to recognise the hand of the Gre-
cian artist, whose modest beauties are thrown into
shade by the ambitious ones of his imitator. [54] But
with all this, Oliva's tragedies must be admitted to
be executed, on the whole, with vigor ; and the
diction, notwithstanding the national tendency to

---

[53] Nic. Antonio, Bibliotheca Nova, tom. i. p. 386. — Oliva, Obras,
pref. de Morales.

[54] The following passage, for
example, in the " Venganza de
Agamemnon," imitated from the
Electra of Sophocles, will hardly
be charged on the Greek dramatist.

"Habed, yo os ruego, de mi
compassion, no querais atapar con
vuestros consejos los respiraderos
de las hornazas de fuego, que den-
tro me atormentan." See Oliva,
Obras, p. 185.

exaggeration above alluded to, may be generally commended for decorum and an imposing dignity, quite worthy of the tragic drama; indeed, they may be selected as affording probably the best specimen of the progress of prose composition during the present reign. [55]

Oliva's reputation led to a similar imitation of the antique. But the Spaniards were too national in all their tastes to sanction it. These classical compositions did not obtain possession of the stage, but were confined to the closet, serving only as a relaxation for the man of letters; while the voice of the people compelled all who courted it, to accommodate their inventions to those romantic forms, which were subsequently developed in such variety of beauty by the great Spanish dramatists. [56]

We have now surveyed the different kinds of poetic culture familiar to Spain under Ferdinand and Isabella. Their most conspicuous element is the national spirit which pervades them, and the exclusive attachment which they manifest to the primitive forms of versification peculiar to the Peninsula. The most remarkable portion of this body

Not popular

National spirit of the literature of this epoch

[55] Compare the diction of these tragedies with that of the "Centon Epistolario," for instance, esteemed one of the best literary compositions of John II.'s reign, and see the advance made, not only in orthography, but in the verbal arrangement generally, and the whole complexion of the style.

[56] Notwithstanding some Spanish critics, as Cueva, for example, have vindicated the romantic forms of the drama on scientific principles, it is apparent that the most successful writers in this department have been constrained to adopt them by public opinion, rather than their own, which would have suggested a nearer imitation of the classical models of antiquity, so generally followed by the Italians, and which naturally recommends itself to the scholar. See the canon's discourse in Cervantes, Don Quixote, ed. de Pellicer, tom. iii. pp. 207–220,— and, more explicitly, Lope de Vega, Obras Sueltas, tom. iv. p. 406.

of poetry may doubtless be considered the Spanish *romances,* or ballads; that popular minstrelsy, which, commemorating the picturesque and chivalrous incidents of the age, reflects most faithfully the romantic genius of the people, who gave it utterance. The lyric efforts of the period were less successful. There were few elaborate attempts in this field, indeed, by men of decided genius. But the great obstacle may be found in the imperfection of the language and the deficiency of the more exact and finished metrical forms, indispensable to high poetic execution.

The whole period, however, comprehending, as it does, the first decided approaches to a regular drama, may be regarded as very important in a literary aspect; since it exhibits the indigenous peculiarities of Castilian literature in all their freshness, and shows to what a degree of excellence it could attain, while untouched by any foreign influence. The present reign may be regarded as the epoch which divides the ancient from the modern school of Spanish poetry; in which the language was slowly but steadily undergoing the process of refinement, that " made the knowledge of it," to borrow the words of a contemporary critic, " pass for an elegant accomplishment, even with the cavaliers and dames of cultivated Italy;" [57] and which

[57] " Ya en Italia, assi entre Damas, como entre Caballeros, se tiene por gentileza y galania, saber hablar Castellano." Diálogo de las Lenguas, apud Mayans y Siscar, Orígenes, tom. ii. p. 4

I have had occasion to advert more than once in the course of this chapter, to the superficial acquaintance of the Spanish critics with the

finally gave full scope to the poetic talent, that raised the literature of the country to such brilliant heights in the sixteenth century.

early history of their own drama, authentic materials for which are so extremely rare and difficult of access, as to preclude the expectation of any thing like a satisfactory account of it out of the Peninsula. The nearest approach to this within my knowledge, is made in an article in the eighth number of the American Quarterly Review, ascribed to Mr. Ticknor, late Professor of Modern Literature in Harvard University. This gentleman, during a residence in the Peninsula, had every facility for replenishing his library with the most curious and valuable works, both printed and manuscript, in this department; and his essay embodies in a brief compass the results of a well-directed industry, which he has expanded in greater detail in his lectures on Spanish literature, delivered before the classes of the University. The subject is discussed with his usual elegance and perspicuity of style; and the foreign, and indeed Castilian scholar, may find much novel information there, in the views presented of the early progress of the dramatic and the histrionic art in the Peninsula.

Since the publication of this article, Moratin's treatise, so long and anxiously expected, "Orígenes del Teatro Español," has made its appearance under the auspices of the Royal Academy of History, which has enriched the national literature with so many admirable editions of its ancient authors. Moratin states in his Preface, that he was employed from his earliest youth in collecting notices, both at home and abroad, of whatever might illustrate the origin of the Spanish drama. The results have been two volumes, containing in the First Part an historical discussion, with ample explanatory notes, and a catalogue of dramatic pieces from the earliest epoch down to the time of Lope de Vega, chronologically arranged, and accompanied with critical analyses, and copious illustrative extracts from pieces of the greatest merit. The Second Part is devoted to the publication of entire pieces of various authors, which from their extreme rarity, or their existence only in manuscript, have had but little circulation. The selections throughout are made with that careful discrimination, which resulted from poetic talent combined with extensive and thorough erudition. The criticisms, although sometimes warped by the peculiar dramatic principles of the author, are conducted in general with great fairness; and ample, but not extravagant, commendation is bestowed on productions, whose merit, to be properly appreciated, must be weighed by one conversant with the character and intellectual culture of the period. The work unfortunately did not receive the last touches of its author, and undoubtedly something may be found wanting to the full completion of his design. On the whole, it must be considered as a rich repertory of old Castilian literature, much of it of the most rare and recondite nature, directed to the illustration of a department, that has hitherto been suffered to languish in the lowest obscurity, but which is now so arranged that it may be contemplated, as it were, under one aspect, and its real merits accurately determined.

Moratin's dramatic criticism.

It was not till some time after the publication of this History, that my attention was called to that portion of the writings of Don Martinez de la Rosa, in which he criticizes the various departments of the national literature. This criticism is embodied in the annotations and appendix to his elegant "Poetica" (Obras Literarias, (Paris, 1827,) tom. i. ii.) The former discuss the general laws, by which the various kinds of poetry are to be regulated; the latter presents a very searching and scientific analysis of the principal productions of the Spanish poets, down to the close of the last century. The critic exemplifies his own views by copious extracts from the subjects of his criticism, and throws much collateral light on the argument by illustrations borrowed from foreign literature In the examination of the Spanish drama, especially comedy, which he modestly qualifies as a "succinct notice, not very exact," he is very elaborate; and discovers the same taste and sagacity in estimating the merits of individual writers, which he had shown in discussing the general principles of the art. Had I read his work sooner, it would have greatly facilitated my own inquiries in the same obscure path; and I should have recognised, at least, one brilliant exception to my sweeping remark on the apathy manifested by the Castilian scholars to the antiquities of the national drama.

PART SECOND.

1493 — 1517.

THE PERIOD WHEN, THE INTERIOR ORGANIZATION OF THE MON-
ARCHY HAVING BEEN COMPLETED, THE SPANISH NATION
ENTERED ON ITS SCHEMES OF DISCOVERY AND CONQUEST;
OR THE PERIOD ILLUSTRATING MORE PARTICULARLY THE
FOREIGN POLICY OF FERDINAND AND ISABELLA.

PART SECOND.

CHAPTER I.

ITALIAN WARS. — GENERAL VIEW OF EUROPE. — INVASION OF ITALY BY CHARLES VIII., OF FRANCE.

1493 — 1495.

Europe at the Close of the Fifteenth Century. — More intimate Relations between States. — Italy the School of Politics. — Pretensions of Charles VIII. to Naples. — Treaty of Barcelona. — The French invade Naples. — Ferdinand's Dissatisfaction. — Tactics and Arms of the different Nations. — Preparations of Spain. — Mission to Charles VIII. — Bold Conduct of the Envoys. — The French enter Naples.

WE have now reached that memorable epoch, when the different nations of Europe, surmounting the barriers which had hitherto confined them within their respective limits, brought their forces, as if by a simultaneous impulse, against each other on a common theatre of action. In the preceding part of this work, we have seen in what manner Spain was prepared for the contest, by the concentration of her various states under one government, and by such internal reforms, as enabled the government to act with vigor. The genius of Ferdinand will appear as predominant in what concerns the foreign relations of the country, as did that of Isabella in its interior administration. So much so, indeed,

that the accurate and well-informed historian, who
has most copiously illustrated this portion of the
national annals, does not even mention, in his introductory notice, the name of Isabella, but refers
the agency in these events exclusively to her more
ambitious consort.[1] In this he is abundantly justified, both by the prevailing character of the policy
pursued, widely differing from that which distinguished the queen's measures, and by the circumstance that the foreign conquests, although achieved
by the united efforts of both crowns, were undertaken on behalf of Ferdinand's own dominions of
Aragon, to which in the end they exclusively appertained.

Europe at
close of the
fifteenth
century.

The close of the fifteenth century presents, on
the whole, the most striking point of view in modern history; one from which we may contemplate
the consummation of an important revolution in the
structure of political society, and the first application of several inventions destined to exercise the
widest influence on human civilization. The feudal
institutions, or rather the feudal principle, which
operated even where the institutions, strictly speaking, did not exist, after having wrought its appointed uses, had gradually fallen into decay; for it had
not the power of accommodating itself to the increased demands and improved condition of society.
However well suited to a barbarous age, it was
found that the distribution of power among the
members of an independent aristocracy, was unfa-

---

[1] Zurita, Historia del Rey Don   tom. v. vi., Zaragoza, 1580,) lib. 1.
Hernando el Cathólico, (Anales   introd.

vorable to that degree of personal security and tranquillity indispensable to great proficiency in the higher arts of civilization. It was equally repugnant to the principle of patriotism, so essential to national independence, but which must have operated feebly among a people, whose sympathies, instead of being concentrated on the state, were claimed by a hundred masters, as was the case in every feudal community. The conviction of this reconciled the nation to the transfer of authority into other hands; not those of the people, indeed, who were too ignorant, and too long accustomed to a subordinate, dependent situation, to admit of it, — but into the hands of the sovereign. It was not until three centuries more had elapsed, that the condition of the great mass of the people was to be so far improved, as to qualify them for asserting and maintaining the political consideration which of right belongs to them.

In whatever degree public opinion and the progress of events might favor the transition of power from the aristocracy to the monarch, it is obvious that much would depend on his personal character: since the advantages of his station alone made him by no means a match for the combined forces of his great nobility. The remarkable adaptation of the characters of the principal sovereigns of Europe to this exigency, in the latter half of the fifteenth century, would seem to have something providential in t. Henry the Seventh of England, Louis the Eleventh of France, Ferdinand of Naples, John the Second of Aragon and his son Ferdinand, and John

Character of reigning sovereigns.

PART
II.

the Second of Portugal, however differing in other
respects, were all distinguished by a sagacity, which
enabled them to devise the most subtile and comprehensive schemes of policy, and which was prolific in expedients for the circumvention of enemies
too potent to be encountered by open force.

Improved
political and
moral condi-
tion.

Their operations, all directed towards the same
point, were attended with similar success, resulting
in the exaltation of the royal prerogative at the expense of the aristocracy, with more or less deference
to the rights of the people, as the case might be ; in
France, for example, with almost total indifference
to them, while in Spain they were regarded, under
the parental administration of Isabella, which tempered the less scrupulous policy of her husband, with
tenderness and respect. In every country, however,
the nation at large gained greatly by the revolution,
which came on insensibly, at least without any violent shock to the fabric of society, and which, by
securing internal tranquillity and the ascendency of
law over brute force, gave ample scope for those
intellectual pursuits, that withdraw mankind from
sensual indulgence, and too exclusive devotion to
the animal wants of our nature.

More inti-
mate rela-
tions be-
tween
states.

No sooner was the internal organization of the
different nations of Europe placed on a secure
basis, than they found leisure to direct their views,
hitherto confined within their own limits, to a
bolder and more distant sphere of action. Their
international communication was greatly facilitated
by several useful inventions coincident with this
period, or then first extensively applied. Such was

the art of printing, diffusing knowledge with the CHAPTER I
speed and universality of light; the establishment
of posts, which, after its adoption by Louis the
Eleventh, came into frequent use in the beginning
of the sixteenth century; and lastly, the compass,
which, guiding the mariner unerringly through the
trackless wastes of the ocean, brought the remotest
regions into contact. With these increased facilities for intercommunication, the different European
states might be said to be brought into as intimate
relation with one another, as the different provinces of the same kingdom were before. They
now for the first time regarded each other as members of one great community, in whose action they
were all mutually concerned. A greater anxiety
was manifested to detect the springs of every
political movement of their neighbours. Missions
became frequent, and accredited agents were stationed, as a sort of honorable spies, at the different
courts. The science of diplomacy, on narrower
grounds, indeed, than it is now practised, began to
be studied.[2] Schemes of aggression and resistance,
leading to political combinations the most complex
and extended, were gradually formed. We are not
to imagine, however, the existence of any well-
defined ideas of a balance of power at this early

---

[2] The "Legazione," or official correspondence of Machiavelli, while stationed at the different
European courts, may be regarded
as the most complete manual of
diplomacy as it existed at the beginning of the sixteenth century.
It affords more copious and curious
information respecting the interior
workings of the governments with
whom he resided, than is to be
found in any regular history; and
it shows the variety and extent of
duties attached to the office of resident minister, from the first moment of its creation.

period. The object of these combinations was some positive act of aggression or resistance, for purposes of conquest or defence, not for the maintenance of any abstract theory of political equilibrium. This was the result of much deeper reflection, and of prolonged experience.

The management of the foreign relations of the nation, at the close of the fifteenth century, was resigned wholly to the sovereign. The people took no further part or interest in the matter, than if it had concerned only the disposition of his private property. His measures were, therefore, often characterized by a degree of temerity and precipitation, that could not have been permitted under the salutary checks afforded by popular interposition. A strange insensibility, indeed, was shown to the rights and interests of the nation. War was regarded as a game, in which the sovereign parties engaged, not on behalf of their subjects, but exclusively on their own. Like desperate gamblers, they contended for the spoils or the honors of victory, with so much the more recklessness as their own station was too elevated to be materially prejudiced by the results. They contended with all the animosity of personal feeling; every device, however paltry, was resorted to; and no advantage was deemed unwarrantable, which could tend to secure the victory. The most profligate maxims of state policy were openly avowed by men of reputed honor and integrity. In short, the diplomacy of that day is very generally characterized by a low cunning, subterfuge, and petty trickery, which would eave an indelible stain on the transactions of private individuals.

Italy was, doubtless, the great school where this political morality was taught. That country was broken up into a number of small states, too nearly equal to allow the absolute supremacy of any one; while, at the same time, it demanded the most restless vigilance on the part of each to maintain its independence against its neighbours. Hence such a complexity of intrigues and combinations as the world had never before witnessed. A subtile, refined policy was conformable to the genius of the Italians. It was partly the result, moreover, of their higher cultivation, which naturally led them to trust the settlement of their disputes to superior intellectual dexterity, rather than to brute force, like the *barbarians* beyond the Alps. [3] From these and other causes, maxims were gradually established, so monstrous in their nature as to give the work, which first embodied them in a regular system, the air of a satire rather than a serious performance, while the name of its author has been converted into a by-word of political knavery. [4]

[3] "Sed diu," says Sallust, noticing the similar consequence of increased refinement among the ancients, "magnum inter mortales certamen fuit, vine corporis an virtute animi res militaris magis procederet. * * * * * Tum demum periculo atque negotiis compertum est, in bello plurimum ingenium posse." Bellum Catilinarium, cap. 1, 2.

[4] Machiavelli's political treatises, his "Principe" and "Discorsi sopra Tito Livio," which appeared after his death, excited no scandal at the time of their publication. They came into the world, indeed, from the pontifical press, under the privilege of the reigning pope, Clement VII. It was not until thirty years later that they were placed on the Index; and this not from any exceptions taken at the immorality of their doctrines, as Ginguené has well proved, (Histoire Littéraire d'Italie, (Paris,

Her most
powerful
states.

At the period before us, the principal states of Italy were, the republics of Venice and Florence the duchy of Milan, the papal see, and the king dom of Naples. The others may be regarded mere ly as satellites, revolving round some one or other of these superior powers, by whom their respective movements were regulated and controlled. Venice may be considered as the most formidable of the great powers, taking into consideration her wealth, her powerful navy, her territory in the north, and princely colonial domain. There was no government in that age which attracted such general admiration, both from natives and foreigners; who seem to have looked upon it as affording the very best model of political wisdom. [5] Yet there was no country where the citizen enjoyed less positive freedom ; none whose foreign relations were conducted with more absolute selfishness, and with a more narrow, bargaining spirit, savouring rather of a company of traders than of a great and powerful state. But all this was compensated, in the eyes of her contemporaries, by the stability of her institutions, which still remained unshaken, amidst revolutions which had convulsed or overturned every other social fabric in Italy. [6]

1811 – 19,) tom. viii. pp. 32, 74,) but from the imputations they contained on the court of Rome.

[5] "Aquel Senado é Señoria de Venecianos," says Gonzalo de Oviedo, "donde me parece á mi que esta recogido todo el saber é prudencia de los hombres humanos ; porque és la gente del mundo que mejor se sabe gobernar ; é la republica, que mas tiempo há durado en el mundo por la buena forma de su regimiento, é donde con mejor manera hán los hombres vivido en comunidad sin tener Rey ;" &c. Quincuagenas, MS., bat. 1, quinc. 3, dial. 44.

[6] Of all the incense which poets and politicians have offered to the Queen of the Adriatic, none is

The government of Milan was at this time under the direction of Lodovico Sforza, or Lodovico the Moor, as he is commonly called ; an epithet suggested by his complexion, but which he willingly retained, as indicating the superior craftiness on which he valued himself.[7] He held the reins in the name of his nephew, then a minor, until a convenient season should arrive for assuming them in his own. His cool, perfidious character was stained with the worst vices of the most profligate class of Italian statesmen of that period.

The central parts of Italy were occupied by the republic of Florence, which had ever been the rallying point of the friends of freedom, too often of faction ; but which had now resigned itself to the dominion of the Medici, whose cultivated tastes and munificent patronage shed a splendid illusion over their administration, which has blinded the eyes of contemporaries, and even of posterity.

The papal chair was filled by Alexander the Sixth, a pontiff whose licentiousness, avarice, and unblushing effrontery have been the theme of unmingled reproach, with Catholic as well as Protestant writers. His preferment was effected by lavish bribery, and by his consummate address, as well as energy of character. Although a native Spaniard, his election was extremely unpalatable to Ferdi-

---

more exquisite than that conveyed in these few lines, where Sannazaro notices her position as the bulwark of Christendom.

' Una Italum regina, altæ pulcherrima
   Romæ
Æmula, quæ terris, quæ dominaris aquis!

Tu tibi vel reges cives tacis ; O decus! O lux
   Ausoniæ, per quam libera turba sumus ;
Per quam barbaries nobis non imperat,
   et Sol
Exoriens nostro clarius orbe micat ! "
     Opera Latina, lib. 3, el g. 1, 95.

7 Guicciardini. Istoria, tom. i lib. 3, p. 147.

nand and Isabella, who deprecated the scandal it must bring upon the church, and who had little to hope for themselves, in a political view, from the elevation of one of their own subjects even, whose mercenary spirit placed him at the control of the highest bidder. [8]

The Neapolitan sceptre was swayed by Ferdinand the First, whose father, Alfonso the Fifth, the uncle of Ferdinand of Aragon, had obtained the crown by the adoption of Joanna of Naples, or rather by his own good sword. Alfonso settled his conquest on his illegitimate son Ferdinand, to the prejudice of the rights of Aragon, by whose blood and treasure he had achieved it. Ferdinand's character, the very opposite of his noble father's, was dark, wily, and ferocious. His life was spent in conflict with his great feudal nobility, many of whom supported the pretensions of the Angevin family. But his superior craft enabled him to foil every attempt of his enemies. In effecting this, indeed, he shrunk from no deed of treachery or violence, however atrocious, and in the end had the satisfaction of establishing his authority, undisputed, on the fears of his subjects. He was about

---

[8] Peter Martyr, Opus Epist., epist. 119, 123.— Fleury, Histoire Ecclésiastique, contin. (Paris, 1722,) tom. xxiv. lib. 117, p. 545. —Peter Martyr, whose residence and rank at the Spanish court gave him access to the best sources of information as to the repute in which the new pontiff was held there, expresses himself in one of his letters to Cardinal Sforza, who had assisted at his election, in the following unequivocal language. " Sed hoc habeto, princeps illustrissime, non placuisse meis Regibus pontificatum ad Alexandrum, quamvis eorum ditionarium, pervenisse. Verentur namque ne illius cupiditas, ne ambitio, ne (quod gravius) mollities filialis Christiam religionem in præceps trahat ' Epist. 119.

seventy years of age at the period of which we are treating, 1493. The heir apparent, Alfonso, was equally sanguinary in his temper, though possessing less talent for dissimulation than his father.

Such was the character of the principal Italian courts at the close of the fifteenth century. The politics of the country were necessarily regulated by the temper and views of the leading powers. They were essentially selfish and personal. The ancient republican forms had been gradually effaced during this century, and more arbitrary ones introduced. The name of freedom, indeed, was still inscribed on their banners, but the spirit had disappeared. In almost every state, great or small, some military adventurer, or crafty statesman, had succeeded in raising his own authority on the liberties of his country; and his sole aim seemed to be to enlarge it still further, and to secure it against the conspiracies and revolutions, which the reminiscence of ancient independence naturally called forth. Such was the case with Tuscany, Milan, Naples, and the numerous subordinate states. In Rome, the pontiff proposed no higher object than the concentration of wealth and public honors in the hands of his own family. In short, the administration of every state seemed to be managed with exclusive reference to the personal interests of its chief. Venice was the only power of sufficient strength and stability to engage in more extended schemes of policy, and even these were conducted, as has been already noticed, in the narrow and calculating spirit of a trading corporation.

But, while no spark of generous patriotism seemed to warm the bosoms of the Italians; while no
sense of public good, or even menace of foreign invasion, could bring them to act in concert with one
another,[9] the internal condition of the country was
eminently prosperous. Italy had far outstripped the
rest of Europe in the various arts of civilized life;
and she everywhere afforded the evidence of facul-
ties developed by unceasing intellectual action.
The face of the country itself was like a garden;
" cultivated through all its plains to the very tops
of the mountains; teeming with population, with
riches, and an unlimited commerce; illustrated by
many munificent princes, by the splendor of many
noble and beautiful cities, and by the majesty of
religion; and adorned with all those rare and precious gifts, which render a name glorious among the
nations."[10] Such are the glowing strains in which
the Tuscan historian celebrates the prosperity of
his country, ere yet the storm of war had descended on her beautiful valleys.

This scene of domestic tranquillity was destined
to be changed, by that terrible invasion which the
ambition of Lodovico Sforza brought upon his country. He had already organized a coalition of the
northern powers of Italy, to defeat the interference
of the king of Naples in behalf of his grandson,

[9] A remarkable example of this
occurred in the middle of the fifteenth century, when the inundation of the Turks, which seemed
ready to burst upon them, after
overwhelming the Arabian and
Greek empires, had no power to
still the voice of faction, or to con
centrate the attention of the Italian
states, even for a moment.
[10] Guicciardini, Istoria, tom. i
lib. 1, p. 2.

the rightful duke of Milan, whom his uncle held in
subjection during a protracted minority, while he
exercised all the real functions of sovereignty in his
name. Not feeling sufficiently secure from his Italian confederacy, Sforza invited the king of France
to revive the hereditary claims of the house of Anjou to the crown of Naples, promising to aid him
in the enterprise with all his resources. In this
way, this wily politician proposed to divert the
storm from his own head, by giving Ferdinand sufficient occupation at home.

The throne of France was at that time filled by
Charles the Eighth, a monarch scarcely twenty-two
years of age. His father, Louis the Eleventh, had
given him an education unbecoming, not only a
great prince, but even a private gentleman. He
would allow him to learn no other Latin, says
Brantôme, than his favorite maxim, " Qui nescit
dissimulare, nescit regnare." [11] Charles made some
amends for this, though with little judgment, in later life, when left to his own disposal. His favorite
studies were the exploits of celebrated conquerors,
of Cæsar and Charlemagne particularly, which filled
his young mind with vague and visionary ideas of
glory. These dreams were still further nourished
by the tourneys and other chivalrous spectacles of
the age, in which he delighted, until he seems to
have imagined himself some doughty paladin of
romance, destined to the achievement of a grand
and perilous enterprise. It affords some proof of

[11] Brantôme, Vies des Hommes   is, 1822-3,) tom. ii. disc. 1, pp.
Illustres, Œuvres Complètes, (Par-   2, 20.

this exalted state of his imagination, that he gave his only son the name of Orlando, after the celebrated hero of Roncesvalles. [12]

With a mind thus excited by chimerical visions of military glory, he lent a willing ear to the artful propositions of Sforza. In the extravagance of vanity, fed by the adulation of interested parasites, he affected to regard the enterprise against Naples as only opening the way to a career of more splendid conquests, which were to terminate in the capture of Constantinople, and the recovery of the Holy Sepulchre. He even went so far as to purchase of Andrew Paleologus, the nephew and heir of Constantine, the last of the Cæsars, his title to the Greek empire. [13]

Nothing could be more unsound, according to the principles of the present day, than Charles's claims to the crown of Naples. Without discussing the original pretensions of the rival houses of Aragon and Anjou, it is sufficient to state, that, at the time of Charles the Eighth's invasion, the Neapolitan throne had been in the possession of the Aragonese family more than half a century, under three successive princes solemnly recognised by the people, sanctioned by repeated investitures of the papal suzerain, and admitted by all the states of Europe.

[12] Sismondi, Hist. des Français, tom. xv. p. 112. — Gaillard, Rivalité, tom. iv. pp. 2, 3.

[13] Daru, Histoire de la République de Venise, (Paris, 1821,) tom. iii. liv. 20. — See the deed of cession, in the memoir of M. de Foncemagne. (Mémoires de l'Académie des Inscriptions et Belles-Lettres, tom. xvii. pp. 539–579.) This document, as well as some others which appeared on the eve of Charles's expedition, breathes a tone of Quixotic and religious enthusiasm, that transports us back to the days of the crusades.

If all this did not give validity to their title, when was the nation to expect repose? Charles's claim, on the other hand, was derived originally from a testamentary bequest of René, count of Provence, operating to the exclusion of the son of his own daughter, the rightful heir of the house of Anjou; Naples being too notoriously a female fief to afford any pretext for the action of the Salic law. The pretensions of Ferdinand, of Spain, as representative of the legitimate branch of Aragon, were far more plausible.[14]

Independently of the defects in Charles's title, his position was such as to make the projected expedition every way impolitic. A misunderstanding had for some time subsisted between him and the Spanish sovereigns, and he was at open war with Germany and England; so that it was only by large concessions, that he could hope to secure their acquiescence in an enterprise most precarious in its character, and where even complete success could be of no permanent benefit to his kingdom. "He did not understand," says Voltaire, "that a dozen villages adjacent to one's territory, are of more value than a kingdom four hundred leagues distant."[15] By the treaties of Etaples and Senlis, he

---

[14] The conflicting claims of Anjou and Aragon are stated at length by Gaillard, with more candor and impartiality than were to be expected from a French writer. (Histoire de François I., (Paris, 1769,) tom. i. pp. 71–92.) They form the subject of a juvenile essay of Gibbon, in which we may discern the germs of many of the peculiarities which afterwards characterized

the historian of the Decline and Fall. Miscellaneous Works, (London, 1814,) vol. iii. pp. 206–222.
[15] Essai sur les Mœurs, chap 107. — His politic father, Louis XI., acted on this principle, for he made no attempt to maintain his pretensions to Naples; although Mably affects to doubt whether this were not the result of necessity rather than policy. "Il est

purchased a reconciliation with Henry the Seventh
of England, and with Maximilian, the emperor
elect; and finally, by that of Barcelona, effected an
amicable adjustment of his difficulties with Spain.[16]

This treaty, which involved the restoration of
Roussillon and Cerdagne, was of great importance
to the crown of Aragon. These provinces, it will
be remembered, had been originally mortgaged by
Ferdinand's father, King John the Second, to Louis
the Eleventh of France, for the sum of three hundred thousand crowns, in consideration of aid to be
afforded by the latter monarch against the Catalan
insurgents. Although the stipulated sum had never
been paid by Aragon, yet a plausible pretext for
requiring the restitution was afforded by Louis the
Eleventh's incomplete performance of his engagements, as well as by the ample reimbursement,
which the French government had already derived
from the revenues of these countries.[17] This treaty

douteux si cette modération fut
l'ouvrage d'une connoissance ap-
profondie de ses vrais intérêts, ou
seulement de cette défiance qu'il
avoit des grands de son royaume,
et qu'il n'osoit perdre de vue."
Observations sur l'Histoire de
France, Œuvres, (Paris, 1794 – 5,)
liv. 6, chap. 4.

[16] Flassan, Histoire de la Diplomatie Française, (Paris, 1809,)
tom. i. pp. 254 – 259. — Dumont,
Corps Universel Diplomatique du
Droit des Gens, (Amsterdam,
1726 – 31,) tom. iii. pp. 297 – 300.

[17] See the narrative of these
transactions in the Fifth and Sixth
Chapters of Part I. of this History.

Most historians seem to take it
for granted, that Louis XI. advanced a sum of money to the king
of Aragon; and some state, that
payment of the debt, for which the
provinces were mortgaged, was subsequently tendered to the French
king. (See, among others, Sismondi, Républiques Italiennes, tom.
xii. p. 93. — Roscoe, Life and Pon-
tificate of Leo X., (London, 1827,)
vol. i. p. 147.) The first of these
statements is a palpable error; and
I find no evidence of the last in any
Spanish authority, where, if true,
it would naturally have been noticed. I must, indeed, except Bernaldez, who says, that Ferdinand
having repaid the money, borrowed
by his father from Louis XI., to
Charles VIII., the latter monarch
returned it to Isabella, in consideration of the great expenses incurred by the Moorish war. It is

had long been a principal object of Ferdinand's policy. He had not, indeed, confined himself to negotiation, but had made active demonstrations more than once of occupying the contested territory by force. Negotiation, however, was more consonant to his habitual policy; and, after the termination of the Moorish war, he pressed it with the utmost vigor, repairing with the queen to Barcelona, in order to watch over the deliberations of the envoys of the two nations at Figueras.[18]

The French historians accuse Ferdinand of bribing two ecclesiastics, in high influence at their court, to make such a representation of the affair, as should alarm the conscience of the young monarch. These holy men insisted on the restoration of Roussillon as an act of justice; since the sums for which it had been mortgaged, though not repaid, had been spent in the common cause of Christendom, the Moorish war. The soul, they said, could never hope to escape from purgatory, until restitution was made of all property unlawfully held during life. His royal father, Louis the Eleventh, was clearly in this predicament, as he himself would hereafter be, unless the Spanish territories should be relinquished; a measure, moreover, the more obligatory on him, since it was well known to be the dying request of his parent. These

a pity that this romantic piece of gallantry does not rest on any better foundation than the Curate of Los Palacios, who shows a degree of ignorance in the first part of his statement, that entitles him to little credit in the last. Indeed, the worthy curate, although much to be relied on for what passed in his own province, may be found frequently tripping in the details of what passed out of it. Bernaldez, Reyes Católicos, MS., cap. 117.

[18] Zurita, Hist. del Rey Hernando, lib. 1, cap. 4, 7, 10.

arguments made a suitable impression on the young monarch, and a still deeper on his sister, the duchess of Beaujeu, who exercised great influence over him, and who believed her own soul in peril of eternal damnation by deferring the act of restoration any longer. The effect of this cogent reasoning was no doubt greatly enhanced by the reckless impatience of Charles, who calculated no cost in the prosecution of his chimerical enterprise. With these amicable dispositions an arrangement was at length concluded, and received the signatures of the respective monarchs on the same day, being signed by Charles at Tours, and by Ferdinand and Isabella at Barcelona, January 19th, 1493. [19]

Treaty of
Barcelona

The principal articles of the treaty provided, that the contracting parties should mutually aid each other against all enemies ; that they should reciprocally prefer this alliance to that with any other, *the vicar of Christ excepted* ; that the Spanish sovereigns should enter into no understanding with any power, *the vicar of Christ excepted*, prejudicial to the interests of France ; that their children should not be disposed of in marriage to the kings of England, or of the Romans, or to any enemy of France, with-

---

[19] Fleury, Histoire Ecclésiastique, contin., tom. xxiv. pp. 533 – 555. — Zurita, Hist. del Rey Hernando, lib. 1, cap. 14. — Daru, Hist. de Venise, tom. iii. pp. 51, 52. — Gaillard, Rivalité, tom. iv. p. 10. — Abarca, Reyes de Aragon, tom. ii. rey 30, cap. 6.

Comines, alluding to the affair of Roussillon, says that Ferdinand and Isabella, whether from motives of economy or hypocrisy, always employed priests in their negotiations. " Car toutes leurs œuvres ont fait mener et conduire par telles gens (religieux), ou par hypocrisie, ou afin de moins despendre." (Mémoires, p. 211.) The French king, however, made more use of the clergy in this very transaction than the Spanish. Zurita, Hist. del Rey Hernando, lib. 1, cap. 10.

out the French king's consent. It was finally stipulated that Roussillon and Cerdagne should be restored to Aragon ; but that, as doubts might be entertained to which power the possession of these countries rightfully appertained, arbitrators *named by Ferdinand and Isabella* should be appointed, if requested by the French monarch, with full power to decide the question, by whose judgment the contracting parties mutually promised to abide. This last provision, obviously too well guarded to jeopard the interests of the Spanish sovereigns, was introduced to allay in some measure the discontents of the French, who loudly inveighed against their cabinet, as sacrificing the interests of the nation ; accusing, indeed, the cardinal D'Albi, the principal agent in the negotiation, of being in the pay of Ferdinand.[20]

The treaty excited equal surprise and satisfaction in Spain, where Roussillon was regarded as of the last importance, not merely from the extent of its resources, but from its local position, which made it the key of Catalonia. The nation, says Zurita, looked on its recovery as scarcely less important

Its importance to Spain.

[20] Paolo Giovio, Historia sui Temporis, (Basiliæ, 1578,) lib. 1, p. 16. — The treaty of Barcelona is given at length by Dumont. (Corps Diplomatique, tom. iii. pp. 297 – 300.) It is reported with sufficient inaccuracy by many historians, who make no hesitation in saying, that Ferdinand expressly bound himself, by one of the articles, not to interfere with Charles's meditated attempt on Naples. (Gaillard, Rivalité, tom. iv. p. 11 — Voltaire, Essai sur les Mœurs, chap. 107. — Comines, Mémoires, liv. 8, chap. 23. — Giovio, Hist. sui Temporis, lib. 1, p. 16. — Varillas, Politique d'Espagne, ou du Roi Ferdinand, (Amsterdam, 1688,) pp. 11, 12. — Roscoe, Life of Leo X., tom. i. chap. 3.) So far from this, there is no allusion whatever to the proposed expedition in the treaty, nor is the name of Naples once mentioned in it.

than the conquest of Granada ; and they doubted some sinister motive, or deeper policy than appeared in the conduct of the French king. He was influenced, however, by no deeper policy than the cravings of a puerile ambition. [21]

Alarm at the French invasion, in Italy.

The preparations of Charles, in the mean while, excited general alarm throughout Italy. Ferdinand, the old king of Naples, who in vain endeavoured to arrest them by negotiation, had died in the beginning of 1494. He was succeeded by his son Alfonso, a prince of bolder but less politic character, and equally odious, from the cruelty of his disposition, with his father. He lost no time in putting his kingdom in a posture of defence ; but he wanted the best of all defences, the attachment of his subjects. His interests were supported by the Florentine republic and the pope, whose family had intermarried with the royal house of Naples. Venice stood aloof, secure in her remoteness, unwilling to compromise her interests by too precipitate a declaration in favor of either party.

In Europe, especially Spain.

The European powers regarded the expedition of Charles the Eighth with somewhat different feelings ; most of them were not unwilling to see so formidable a prince waste his resources in a remote and chimerical expedition ; Ferdinand, however, contemplated with more anxiety an event, which might terminate in the subversion of the Neapolitan branch of his house, and bring a powerful and active neighbour in contact with his own

[21] Zurita, Hist. del Rey Hernando, lib. 1, cap. 18. — Abarca, Reves de Aragon, ubi supra.

dominions in Sicily. He lost no time in fortifying
the faltering courage of the pope by assurances of
support. His ambassador, then resident at the papal court, was Garcilasso de la Vega, father of the
illustrious poet of that name, and familiar to the
reader by his exploits in the Granadine war. This
personage with rare political sagacity combined an
energy of purpose, which could not fail to infuse
courage into the hearts of others. He urged the
pope to rely on his master, the king of Aragon,
who, he assured him, would devote his whole resources, if necessary, to the protection of his person, honor, and estate. Alexander would gladly
have had this promise under the hand of Ferdinand; but the latter did not think it expedient,
considering his delicate relations with France, to
put himself so far in the power of the wily pontiff.[22]

In the mean time, Charles's preparations went
forward with the languor and vacillation resulting
from divided councils and multiplied embarrassments. "Nothing essential to the conduct of a
war was at hand," says Comines. The king was
very young, weak in person, headstrong in will,
surrounded by few discreet counsellors, and wholly
destitute of the requisite funds.[23] His own impatience, however, was stimulated by that of the
youthful chivalry of his court, who burned for an
opportunity of distinction; as well as by the repre-

---

[22] Zurita, Hist. del Rey Hernando, lib. 1, cap. 28. — Bembo, Istoria Viniziana, (Milano, 1809,) tom.
i. lib. 2, pp 118, 119. — Oviedo,
Quincuagenas, MS., bat. 1, quinc.
3, dial. 43.
[23] Comines, Mémoires, liv. 7,
introd.

sentations of the Neapolitan exiles, who hoped, under his protection, to reëstablish themselves in their own country. Several of these, weary with the delay already experienced, made overtures to King Ferdinand to undertake the enterprise on his own behalf, and to assert his legitimate pretensions to the crown of Naples, which, they assured him, a large party in the country was ready to sustain. The sagacious monarch, however, knew how little reliance was to be placed on the reports of exiles, whose imaginations readily exaggerated the amount of disaffection in their own country. But, although the season had not yet arrived for asserting his own paramount claims, he was determined to tolerate those of no other potentate.[24]

Charles entertained so little suspicion of this, that, in the month of June, he despatched an envoy to the Spanish court, requiring Ferdinand's fulfilment of the treaty of Barcelona, by aiding him with men and money, and by throwing open his ports in Sicily for the French navy. "This gracious proposition," says the Aragonese historian, "he accompanied with information of his proposed expedition against the Turks ; stating incidentally, as a thing of no consequence, his intention to take Naples by the way."[25]

[24] Zurita, Hist. del Rey Hernando, lib. 1, cap. 20. — Peter Martyr, Opus Epist., epist. 123. — Comines, Mémoires, liv. 7, chap. 3. — Mariana, Hist. de España, tom. ii. lib. 26, cap. 6. — Zurita concludes the arguments which decided Ferdinand against assuming the enterprise, with one which may be considered the gist of the whole matter. "El Rey entendia bien que no era tan facil la causa que se proponia." lib. 1, cap. 20.
[25] Zurita, Hist. del Rey Hernando, lib. 1, cap 31.

Ferdinand saw the time was arrived for coming to an explicit declaration with the French court. He appointed a special mission, in order to do this in the least offensive manner possible. The person selected for this delicate task was Alonso de Silva, brother of the count of Cifuentes, and *clavero* of Calatrava, a cavalier possessed of the coolness and address requisite for diplomatic success.[26]

CHAPTER I.

An envoy sent to the French court.

The ambassador, on arriving at the French court, found it at Vienne in all the bustle of preparation for immediate departure. After seeking in vain a private audience from King Charles, he explained to him the purport of his mission in the presence of his courtiers. He assured him of the satisfaction which the king of Aragon had experienced, at receiving intelligence of his projected expedition against the infidel. Nothing gave his master so great contentment, as to see his brother monarchs employing their arms, and expending their revenues, against the enemies of the Cross ; where even failure was greater gain than success in other wars. He offered Ferdinand's assistance in the prosecution of such wars, even though they should be directed against the Mahometans of Africa, over whom the papal sanction had given Spain exclusive rights of conquest. He besought the king not to employ the forces destined to so glorious a purpose against any one of the princes of Europe, but to

Announces Ferdinand's views

[26] Oviedo notices Silva as one of three brothers, all gentle cavaliers, of unblemished honor, remarkable for the plainness of their persons, the elegance and courtesy of their manners, and the magnificence of their style of living. This one, Alonso, he describes as a man of a singularly clear head. Quincuagenas, MS., bat. 1, quinc. 4.

reflect how great a scandal this must necessarily
bring on the Christian cause ; above all, he cautioned him against forming any designs on Naples,
since that kingdom was a fief of the church, in
whose favor an exception was expressly made by
the treaty of Barcelona, which recognised her alliance and protection as paramount to every other
obligation. Silva's discourse was responded to by
the president of the parliament of Paris in a formal
Latin oration, asserting generally Charles's right to
Naples, and his resolution to enforce it previously
to his crusade against the infidel. As soon as it
was concluded, the king rose and abruptly quitted
the apartment.[27]

Charles's dis-
satisfaction.

Some days after, he interrogated the Spanish
ambassador, whether his master would not, in
case of a war with Portugal, feel warranted by the
terms of the late treaty in requiring the coöperation
of France, and on what plea the latter power could
pretend to withhold it. To the first of these propositions the ambassador answered in the affirmative,
if it were a defensive war, but not, if an offensive
one, of his own seeking ; an explanation by no
means satisfactory to the French monarch. Indeed, he seems not to have been at all prepared for
this interpretation of the compact. He had relied
on this, as securing without any doubt the non-
interference of Ferdinand, if not his actual coöperation in his designs against Naples. The clause
touching the rights of the church was too frequent

[27] Zurita, Hist. del Rey Hernando, ubi supra.

in public treaties to excite any particular attention; and he was astounded at the broad ground, which it was now made to cover, and which defeated the sole object proposed by the cession of Roussillon. He could not disguise his chagrin and indignation at what he deemed the perfidy of the Spanish court. He refused all further intercourse with Silva, and even stationed a sentinel at his gate, to prevent his communication with his subjects; treating him as the envoy, not of an ally, but of an open enemy. [28]

The French cross the Alps.

The unexpected and menacing attitude, however, assumed by Ferdinand, failed to arrest the operations of the French monarch, who, having completed his preparations, left Vienne in the month of August, 1494, and crossed the Alps at the head of the most formidable host which had scaled that mountain barrier since the irruption of the northern barbarians. [29] It will be unnecessary to follow his movements in detail. It is sufficient

[28] Zurita, Hist. del Rey Hernando, lib. 1, cap. 31, 41.

[29] Villeneuve, Mémoires, apud Petitot, Collection des Mémoires, tom. xiv. pp. 255, 256.

The French army consisted of 3,600 gens d'armes, 20,000 French infantry, and 8,000 Swiss, without including the regular camp folloers. (Sismondi, Républiques Italiennes, tom. xii. p. 132.)

The splendor and novelty of their appearance excited a degree of admiration, which disarmed in some measure the terror of the Italians. Peter Martyr, whose distance from the theatre of action enabled him to contemplate more calmly the operation of events, be-held with a prophetic eye the magnitude of the calamities impending over his country. In one of his letters, he writes thus; " Scribitur exercitum visum fuisse nostrâ tempestate nullum unquam nitidiorem. Et qui futuri sunt calamitatis participes, Carolum aciesque illius ac peditum turmas laudibus extollunt; sed Italorum impensâ instructas." (Opus Epist., epist. 143.) He concludes another with this remarkable prediction; " Perimeris, Galle, ex majori parte, nec in patriam redibis. Jacebis insepultus; sed tua nor restituetur strages, Italia." Epist. 123.

to remark, that his conduct throughout was equally defective in principle and in sound policy. He
alienated his allies by the most signal acts of perfidy, seizing their fortresses for himself, and entering
their capitals with all the vaunt and insolent port
of a conqueror. On his approach to Rome, the
pope and the cardinals took refuge in the castle of
1494. St. Angelo, and on the 31st of December, Charles
defiled into the city at the head of his victorious
chivalry; if victorious they could be called, when,
as an Italian historian remarks, they had scarcely
broken a lance, or spread a tent, in the whole of
their progress. [30]

Italian
tactics
    The Italians were panic-struck at the aspect of
troops so different from their own, and so superior
to them in organization, science, and military
equipment; and still more in a remorseless ferocity
of temper, which had rarely been witnessed in
their own feuds. Warfare was conducted on peculiar principles in Italy, adapted to the character and
circumstances of the people. The business of
fighting, in her thriving communities, instead of
forming part of the regular profession of a gentleman, as in other countries at this period, was
intrusted to the hands of a few soldiers of fortune,
condottieri, as they were called, who hired themselves out, with the forces under their command,
consisting exclusively of heavy-armed cavalry, to

[30] Guicciardini, Istoria, tom. i.
lib. 1, p. 71. — Scipione Ammirato, Istorie Fiorentine, (Firenze,
1647,) p. 205. — Giannone, Istoria
di Napoli, tom. iii. lib. 29, introd.
— Comines, Mémoires, liv. 7, chap
17. — Oviedo, Quincuagenas, MS.
bat. 1, quinc. 3, dial. 43.

whatever state would pay them best. These forces constituted the capital, as it were, of the military chief, whose obvious interest it was to economize as far as possible all unnecessary expenditure of his resources. Hence, the science of defence was almost exclusively studied. The object seemed to be, not so much the annoyance of the enemy, as self-preservation. The common interests of the *condottieri* being paramount to every obligation towards the state which they served, they easily came to an understanding with one another to spare their troops as much as possible; until at length battles were fought with little more personal hazard than would be incurred in an ordinary tourney. The man-at-arms was riveted into plates of steel of sufficient thickness to turn a musket-ball. The ease of the soldier was so far consulted, that the artillery, in a siege, was not allowed to be fired on either side from sunset to sunrise, for fear of disturbing his repose. Prisoners were made for the sake of their ransom, and but little blood was spilled in an action. Machiavelli records two engagements, at Anghiari and Castracaro, among the most noted of the time for their important consequences. The one lasted four hours, and the other half a day. The reader is hurried along through all the bustle of a well-contested fight, in the course of which the field is won and lost several times; but, when he comes to the close, and looks for the list of killed and wounded, he finds to his surprise not a single man slain, in the first of these actions; and in the second, only one, who, having tumbled from his horse, and being unable to rise, from the weight of his armour, was suffocated in the mud! Thus war became disarmed of its terrors. Courage was no longer essential in a soldier; and the Italian, made effeminate, if not timid, was incapable of encountering the adventurous daring and severe discipline of the northern warrior. [31]

The Swiss
infantry.

The astonishing success of the French was still more imputable to the free use and admirable organization of their infantry, whose strength lay in the Swiss mercenaries. Machiavelli ascribes the misfortunes of his nation chiefly to its exclusive reliance on cavalry.[32] This service, during the whole of the middle ages, was considered among the European nations the most important; the horse being styled by way of eminence " the battle." The memorable conflict of Charles the Bold with the Swiss mountaineers, however, in which the latter broke in pieces the celebrated Burgundian *ordonnance*, constituting the finest body of chivalry of the age, demonstrated the capacity of infantry; and the Italian wars, in which we are now engaged, at length fully reëstablished its ancient superiority.

The Swiss were formed into battalions varying from three to eight thousand men each. They wore little defensive armour, and their principal weapon was the pike, eighteen feet long. Formed into these solid battalions, which, bristling with spears all around, received the technical appellation

[31] Du Bos, Histoire de la Ligue faite à Cambray, (Paris, 1728), tom. i. dissert. prélim. — Machiavelli, Istorie Fiorentine, lib. 5. — Denina, Rivoluzioni d' Italia, lib 18, cap. 3.
[32] Arte della Guerra, lib 2.

ot the *hedgehog*, they presented an invulnerable
front on every quarter. In the level field, with free
scope allowed for action, they bore down all opposition, and received unshaken the most desperate
charges of the steel-clad cavalry on their terrible
array of pikes. They were too unwieldy, however,
for rapid or complicated manœuvres ; they were
easily disconcerted by any unforeseen impediment,
or irregularity of the ground; and the event proved,
that the Spanish foot, armed with its short swords
and bucklers, by breaking in under the long pikes
of its enemy, could succeed in bringing him to close
action, where his formidable weapon was of no
avail. It was repeating the ancient lesson of the
Roman legion and the Macedonian phalanx.[33]

In artillery, the French were at this time in advance of the Italians, perhaps of every nation in
Europe. The Italians, indeed, were so exceedingly
defective in this department, that their best field-
pieces consisted of small copper tubes, covered with
wood and hides. They were mounted on unwieldy
carriages drawn by oxen, and followed by cars or
wagons loaded with stone balls. These guns were
worked so awkwardly, that the besieged, says Guicciardini, had time between the discharges to repair the mischief inflicted by them. From these

CHAPTER
I.

French art
ery

[33] Machiavelli, Arte deila Guerra, lib. 3. — Du Bos, Ligue de Cambray, tom. i. dis. prélim. — Giovio,
Hist. sui Temporis, lib. 2, p. 41.
  Polybius, in his minute account
of this celebrated military institution, has recapitu-
ated nearly all the advantages and
defects imputed to the Swiss *héris-
son*, by modern European writers.
(See lib. 17, sec. 25 et seq.) It is
singular, that these exploded arms
and tactics should be revived, after
the lapse of nearly seventeen centuries, to be foiled again in the
same manner as before

circumstances, artillery was held in so little repute
that some of the most competent Italian writers
thought it might be dispensed with altogether in
field engagements.[34]

The French, on the other hand, were provided
with a beautiful train of ordnance, consisting of
bronze cannon about eight feet in length, and
many smaller pieces.[35] They were lightly mounted,
drawn by horses, and easily kept pace with the
rapid movements of the army. They discharged
iron balls, and were served with admirable skill,
intimidating their enemies by the rapidity and accuracy of their fire, and easily demolishing their
fortifications, which, before this invasion, were constructed with little strength or science.[36]

The rapid successes of the French spread consternation among the Italian states, who now for
the first time seemed to feel the existence of a
common interest, and the necessity of efficient concert. Ferdinand was active in promoting these
dispositions, through his ministers, Garcilasso de la
Vega and Alonso de Silva. The latter had quitted
the French court on its entrance into Italy, and

Sforza jeal-
ous of the
French.

withdrawn to Genoa. From this point he opened
a correspondence with Lodovico Sforza, who now
began to understand, that he had brought a terrible
engine into play, the movements of which, however

---

[34] Guicciardini, Istoria, tom. i.
pp. 45, 46. — Machiavelli, Arte
della Guerra, lib. 3. — Du Bos,
Ligue de Cambray, ubi supra.
[35] Guicciardini speaks of the
name of " cannon," which the

French gave to their pieces, as a
novelty at that time in Italy. Istoria, pp. 45, 46.
[36] Giovio, Hist. sui Temporis
lib. 2, p. 42. — Machiavelli, Arte
della Guerra, lib. 7.

mischievous to himself, were beyond his strength to control. Silva endeavoured to inflame still further his jealousy of the French, who had already given him many serious causes of disgust; and, in order to detach him more effectually from Charles's interests, encouraged him with the hopes of forming a matrimonial alliance for his son with one of the infantas of Spain. At the same time, he used every effort to bring about a coöperation between the duke and the republic of Venice, thus opening the way to the celebrated league which was concluded in the following year.[37]

The Roman pontiff had lost no time, after the appearance of the French army in Italy, in pressing the Spanish court to fulfil its engagements. He endeavoured to propitiate the good-will of the sovereigns by several important concessions. He granted to them and their successors the *tercias*, or two ninths of the tithes, throughout the dominions of Castile; an impost still forming part of the regular revenue of the crown.[38] He caused bulls of crusade to be promulgated throughout Spain, granting at the same time a tenth of the ecclesiastical rents, with the understanding that the proceeds

---

[37] Zurita, Hist. del Rey Hernando, lib. 1, cap. 35. — Alonso de Silva acquitted himself to the entire satisfaction of the sovereigns, in his difficult mission. He was subsequently sent on various others to the different Italian courts, and uniformly sustained his reputation for ability and prudence. He did not live to be old. Oviedo, Quincuagenas, MS., bat. 1, quinc. 4.

[38] Mariana, Hist. de España, tom. ii. lib. 26, cap. 6. — Salazar de Mendoza, Monarquía, lib 3, cap. 14.
This branch of the revenue yields at the present day, according to Laborde, about 6,000,000 reals, or 1,500,000 francs. Itinéraire, tom. vi p. 51.

The pope
confers the
title of
Catholic.

should be devoted to the protection of the Holy See. Towards the close of this year, 1494, or the beginning of the following, he conferred the title of Catholic on the Spanish sovereigns, in consideration, as is stated, of their eminent virtues, their zeal in defence of the true faith and the apostolic see, their reformation of conventual discipline, their subjugation of the Moors of Granada, and the purification of their dominions from the Jewish heresy. This orthodox title, which still continues to be the jewel most prized in the Spanish crown, has been appropriated in a peculiar manner to Ferdinand and Isabella, who are universally recognised in history as *Los Reyes Católicos.*[39]

Naval prep
arations in
Spain.

Ferdinand was too sensible of the peril, to which the occupation of Naples by the French would expose his own interests, to require any stimulant to action from the Roman pontiff. Naval preparations

[39] Zurita, Abarca, and other Spanish historians, fix the date of Alexander's grant at the close of 1496. (Hist. del Rey Hernando, lib. 2, cap. 40. — Reyes de Aragon, rey 30, cap. 9.) Martyr notices it with great particularity as already conferred, in a letter of February, 1495. (Opus Epist., epist. 157.) The pope, according to Comines, designed to compliment Ferdinand and Isabella for their conquest of Granada, by transferring to them the title of Most Christian, hitherto enjoyed by the kings of France. He had even gone so far as to address them thus in more than one of his briefs. This produced a remonstrance from a number of the cardinals ; which led him to substitute the title of Most Catholic. The epithet of Catholic was not new in the royal house of Castile, nor indeed of Aragon ; having been given to the Asturian prince Alfonso I. about the middle of the eighth, and to Pedro II., of Aragon, at the beginning of the thirteenth century.

I will remark, in conclusion, that, although the phrase *Los Reyes Católicos*, as applied to a female equally with a male, would have a whimsical appearance literally translated into English, it is perfectly consonant to the Spanish idiom, which requires that all words, having reference to both a masculine and a feminine noun, should be expressed in the former gender. So also in the ancient languages ; Ημεν τυράννοι, says Queen Hecuba ; (Euripides, ΤΡΩΑΔ. v. 476.) But it is clearly incorrect to render *Los Reyes Católicos*, as usually done by

had been going forward during the summer, in the ports of Galicia and Guipuscoa. A considerable armament was made ready for sea by the latter part of December, at Alicant, and placed under the command of Galceran de Requesens, count of Trevento. The land forces were intrusted to Gonsalvo de Cordova, better known in history as the Great Captain. Instructions were at the same time sent to the viceroy of Sicily, to provide for the security of that island, and to hold himself in readiness to act in concert with the Spanish fleet. [40]

Ferdinand, however, determined to send one more embassy to Charles the Eighth, before coming to an open rupture with him. He selected for this mission Juan de Albion and Antonio de Fonseca, brother of the bishop of that name, whom we have already noticed as superintendent of the Indian department. The two envoys reached Rome, January 28th, 1495, the same day on which Charles set out on his march for Naples. They followed the army, and on arriving at Veletri, about twenty miles from the capital, were admitted to an audience by the monarch, who received them in the presence of his officers. The ambassadors freely enumerated the various causes of complaint entertained by their master against the French king; the insult offered to him in the person of his minister Alonso de Silva; the contumelious treatment of the pope, and forcible occupation of the fortresses and estates of

English writers by the corresponding term of " Catholic kings."

[40] Carbajal, Anales, MS., año 1495.

the church ; and finally the enterprise against Naples, the claims to which as a papal fief, could of
right be determined in no other way than by the
arbitration of the pontiff himself. Should King
Charles consent to accept this arbitration, they tendered the good offices of their master as mediator
between the parties ; should he decline it, however, the king of Spain stood absolved from all further obligations of amity with him, by the terms of
the treaty of Barcelona, which expressly recognised
his right to interfere in defence of the church. [41]

Charles, who could not dissemble his indignation
during this discourse, retorted with great acrimony,
when it was concluded, on the conduct of Ferdinand, which he stigmatized as perfidious, accusing
him, at the same time, of a deliberate design to
circumvent him, by introducing into their treaty
the clause respecting the pope. As to the expedition against Naples, he had now gone too far to
recede ; and it would be soon enough to canvass
the question of right, when he had got possession
of it. His courtiers, at the same time, with the
impetuosity of their nation, heightened by the insolence of success, told the envoys, that they knew
well enough how to defend their rights with their
arms, and that King Ferdinand would find the
French chivalry enemies of quite another sort from
the holiday tilters of Granada.

These taunts led to mutual recrimination, until

[41] Bernaldez, Reyes Católicos, 192 – 194. — Garibay, Compendio.
MS., cap. 138. — Sismondi, Ré- lib. 19, cap. 4.
publiques Italiennes, tom. xii. pp.

at length Fonseca, though naturally a sedate person, was so far transported with anger, that he exclaimed, " The issue then must be left to God, — arms must decide it ;" and, producing the original treaty, bearing the signatures of the two monarchs, he tore it in pieces before the eyes of Charles and his court. At the same time he commanded two Spanish knights who served in the French army to withdraw from it, under pain of incurring the penalties of treason. The French cavaliers were so much incensed by this audacious action, that they would have seized the envoys, and, in all probability, offered violence to their persons, but for Charles's interposition, who with more coolness caused them to be conducted from his presence, and sent back under a safe escort to Rome. Such are the circumstances reported by the French and Italian writers of this remarkable interview. They were not aware that the dramatic exhibition, as far as the ambassadors were concerned, was all previously concerted before their departure from Spain. [42]

Charles pressed forward on his march without further delay. Alfonso the Second, losing his con-

[42] Oviedo, Quincuagenas, MS., bat. 1, quinc. 3, dial. 43. — Zurita, Hist. del Rey Hernando, lib. 1, cap. 43. — Bernaldez, Reyes Católicos, MS., cap. 138. — Giovio, Hist. sui Temporis, lib. 2, p. 46. — Lanuza, Historias, tom. i. lib. 1, cap. 6.

This appears from a letter of Martyr's, dated three months before the interview ; in which he says, " Antonius Fonseca, vir equestris ordinis, et armis clarus, destinatus est orator, qui eum moneat, ne, priusquam de jure inter ipsum et Alfonsum regem Neapolitanum decernatur, ulterius procedat. Fert in mandatis Antonius Fonseca, ut Carolo capitulum id sonans ostendat, anteque ipsius oculos (si detrectaverit) pacti veteris chirographum laceret, atque indicat inimicitias." Opus Epist., epist. 144.

fidence and martial courage, the only virtues that he possessed, at the crisis when they were most demanded, had precipitately abandoned his kingdom while the French were at Rome, and taken refuge in Sicily, where he formally abdicated the crown in favor of his son, Ferdinand the Second. This prince, then twenty-five years of age, whose amiable manners were rendered still more attractive by contrast with the ferocious temper of his father, was possessed of talent and energy competent to the present emergency, had he been sustained by his subjects. But the latter, besides being struck with the same panic which had paralyzed the other people of Italy, had too little interest in the government to be willing to hazard much in its defence. A change of dynasty was only a change of masters, by which they had little either to gain or to lose. Though favorably inclined to Ferdinand, they refused to stand by him in his perilous extremity. They gave way in every direction, as the French advanced, rendering hopeless every attempt of their spirited young monarch to rally them, till at length no alternative was left, but to abandon his dominions to the enemy, without striking a blow in their defence. He withdrew to the neighbouring island of Ischia, whence he soon after passed into Sicily, and occupied himself there in collecting the fragments of his party, until the time should arrive for more decisive action. [43]

[43] Comines, Mémoires, liv. 7, chap. 16. — Villeneuve, Mémoires, apud Petitot, Collection des Mémoires, tom. xii. p. 260. — Ammirato, Istorie Fiorentine, tom. iii lib. 26. — Summonte, Hist. di Napoli, tom. iii. lib 6, cap. 1, 2.

Charles the Eighth made his entrance into Naples at the head of his legions, February 22d,
1495, having traversed this whole extent of hostile
territory in less time than would be occupied by a
fashionable tourist of the present day. The object
of his expedition was now achieved. He seemed
to have reached the consummation of his wishes ;
and, although he assumed the titles of King of Sicily and of Jerusalem, and affected the state and
authority of Emperor, he took no measures for
prosecuting his chimerical enterprise further. He
even neglected to provide for the security of his
present conquest ; and, without bestowing a thought
on the government of his new dominions, resigned
himself to the licentious and effeminate pleasures
so congenial with the soft voluptuousness of the
climate, and his own character. [44]

While Charles was thus wasting his time and
resources in frivolous amusements, a dark storm
was gathering in the north. There was not a state
through which he had passed, however friendly to
his cause, which had not complaints to make of his
insolence, his breach of faith, his infringement of
their rights, and his exorbitant exactions. His
impolitic treatment of Sforza had long since alienated that wily and restless politician, and raised
suspicions in his mind of Charles's designs against
his own duchy of Milan. The emperor elect,
Maximilian, whom the French king thought to

---

[44] Giovio, Hist. sui Temporis, André de la Vigne, Histoire de
lib. 2, p. 55. — Giannone, Istoria Charles VIII. (Paris, 1617,) p.
di Napoli, lib. 29, cap. 1, 2. — 201.

PART
II.

have bound to his interests by the treaty of Senlis, took umbrage at his assumption of the imperial title and dignity. The Spanish ambassadors, Garcilasso de la Vega, and his brother, Lorenzo Suarez, the latter of whom resided at Venice, were indefatigable in stimulating the spirit of discontent. Suarez, in particular, used every effort to secure the coöperation of Venice, representing to the government, in the most urgent terms, the necessity of general concert and instant action among the great powers of Italy, if they would preserve their own liberties.[45]

League of
Venice.

Venice, from its remote position, seemed to afford the best point for coolly contemplating the general interests of Italy. Envoys of the different European powers were assembled there, as if by common consent, with the view of concerting some scheme of operation for their mutual good. The conferences were conducted by night, and with such secrecy as to elude for some time the vigilant eye of Comines, the sagacious minister of Charles, then resident at the capital. The result was the celebrated league of Venice. It was signed the last day of March, 1495, on the part of Spain, Austria, Rome, Milan, and the Venetian republic. The ostensible object of the treaty, which was to last twenty-five years, was the preservation of the estates and rights of the confederates, especially of

[45] Giovio, Hist. sui Temporis, lib. 2, p. 56. — Guicciardini, Istoria, tom. i. pp. 86, 87. — Bembo, Istoria Viniziana, tom. i. lib. 2, p. 120. — Zurita, Hist. del Rey Hernando, lib. 2, chap. 3, 5. — Comines, Mémoires, liv. 7, chap. 19.

the Roman see. A large force, amounting in all to
thirty-four thousand horse and twenty thousand
foot, was to be assessed in stipulated proportions
on each of the contracting parties. The secret
articles of the treaty, however, went much further,
providing a formidable plan of offensive operations.
It was agreed in these, that King Ferdinand should
employ the Spanish armament, now arrived in Sicily, in reëstablishing his kinsman on the throne of
Naples ; that a Venetian fleet, of forty galleys,
should attack the French positions on the Neapolitan coasts ; that the duke of Milan should expel
the French from Asti, and blockade the passes of
the Alps, so as to intercept the passage of further
reinforcements ; and that the emperor and the king
of Spain should invade the French frontiers, and
their expenses be defrayed by subsidies from the
allies. [46] Such were the terms of this treaty, which
may be regarded as forming an era in modern political history, since it exhibits the first example
of those extensive combinations among European
princes, for mutual defence, which afterwards became so frequent. It shared the fate of many
other coalitions, where the name and authority of
the whole have been made subservient to the interests of some one of the parties, more powerful, or
more cunning, than the rest.

The intelligence of the new treaty diffused
general joy throughout Italy. In Venice, in par-

[46] Guicciardini, Istoria, tom. i. lib. 2, p. 88. — Comines, Mé-moires, liv. 7, chap. 20. — Bembo, Istoria Viniziana, tom. i. lib. 2, pp. 122, 123.— Daru, Hist. de Venise, tom., iii. pp. 255, 256. — Zurita, Hist. del Rey Hernando, lib. 2, cap. 5.

ticular, it was greeted with *fêtes*, illuminations, and the most emphatic public rejoicing, in the very eyes of the French minister, who was compelled to witness this unequivocal testimony of the detestation in which his countrymen were held.[47] The tidings fell heavily on the ears of the French in Naples. It dispelled the dream of idle dissipation in which they were dissolved. They felt little concern, indeed, on the score of their Italian enemies, whom their easy victories taught them to

---

[47] Comines, Mémoires, p. 96. — Comines takes great credit to himself for his perspicacity in detecting the secret negotiations carried on at Venice against his master. According to Bembo, however, the affair was managed with such profound caution, as to escape his notice until it was officially announced by the doge himself; when he was so much astounded by the intelligence, that he was obliged to ask the secretary of the senate, who accompanied him home, the particulars of what the doge had said, as his ideas were so confused at the time, that he had not perfectly comprehended it. Istoria Viniziana, lib. 2, pp. 128, 129.

Zurita's life and writings.

The principal light, by which we are to be guided through the remainder of this history, is the Aragonese annalist, Zurita, whose great work, although less known abroad, than those of some more recent Castilian writers, sustains a reputation at home, unsurpassed by any other, in the great, substantial qualities of an historian. The notice of his life and writings has been swelled into a bulky quarto by Dr. Diego Dormer, in a work entitled, " Progressos de la Historia en el Reyno de Aragon. Zaragoza, 1680;" from which I extract a few particulars.

Gerónimo Zurita, descended from an ancient and noble family, was born at Saragossa, December 4th, 1512. He was matriculated at an early age in the university of Alcalá. He there made extraordinary proficiency, under the immediate instruction of the learned Nuñez de Guzman, commonly called El Pinciano. He became familiar with the ancient, and a variety of modern tongues, and attracted particular attention by the purity and elegance of his Latinity. His personal merits, and his father's influence, recommended him, soon after quitting the university, to the notice of the emperor Charles V. He was consulted and employed in affairs of public importance, and subsequently raised to several posts of honor, attesting the entire confidence reposed in his integrity and abilities. His most honorable appointment, however, was that of national historiographer.

In 1547, an act passed the cortes general of Aragon, providing for the office of national chronicler,

egard with the same insolent contempt, that the paladins of romance are made to feel for the unknightly rabble, myriads of whom they could overturn with a single lance. But they felt serious alarm as they beheld the storm of war gathering from other quarters, — from Spain and Germany, in defiance of the treaties by which they had hoped to secure them. Charles saw the necessity of instant action. Two courses presented themselves ; either

with a fixed salary, whose duty it should be to compile, from authentic sources, a faithful history of the monarchy. The talents and eminent qualifications of Zurita recommended him to this post, and he was raised to it by the unanimous consent of the legislature, in the following year, 1548. From this time he conscientiously devoted himself to the execution of his great task. He visited every part of his own country, as well as Sicily and Italy, for the purpose of collecting materials. The public archives, and every accessible source of information, were freely thrown open to his inspection, by order of the government ; and he returned from his literary pilgrimage with a large accumulation of rare and original documents. The first portion of his annals was published at Saragossa, in two volumes folio, 1562. The work was not completed until nearly twenty years later, and the last two volumes were printed under his own eye at Saragossa, in 1580, a few months only before his death. This edition, being one of those used in the present history, is in large folio, fairly executed, with double columns on the page, in the fashion of most of the ancient Spanish historians. The whole work was again published, as before, at the expense of the state, in 1585, by his son, amended and somewhat enlarged, from the manuscripts left by his father. Bouterwek has fallen into the error of supposing, that no edition of Zurita's Annals appeared till after the reign of Philip II., who died in 1592. (Geschichte der Poesie und Beredsamkeit, band iii. p. 319.)

No incidents worthy of note seem to have broken the peaceful tenor of Zurita's life ; which he terminated at Saragossa, in the sixtyeighth year of his age, in the monastery of Santa Engracia, to which he had retired during a temporary residence in the city, to superintend the publication of his Annals. His rich collection of books and manuscripts was left to the Carthusian monastery of Aula Dei ; but, from accident or neglect, the greater part have long since perished. His remains were interred in the convent where he died, and a monument, bearing a modest inscription, was erected over them by his son.

The best monument of Zurita, however, is his Annals. They take up the history of Aragon from its first rise after the Arabic conquest, and continue it to the death of Ferdinand the Catholic. The reign of this prince, as possessing the largest interest and importance, is expanded into two volumes folio ; being one third of the whole work. The minuteness of Zurita's investigations has laid him open to the charge of prolixity, especially

to strengthen himself in his new conquests, and prepare to maintain them until he could receive fresh reinforcements from home, or to abandon them altogether and retreat across the Alps, before the allies could muster in sufficient strength to oppose him. With the indiscretion characteristic of his whole enterprise, he embraced a middle course, and lost the advantages which would have resulted from the exclusive adoption of either.

in the earlier and less important periods. It should be remembered, however, that his work was to be the great national repository of facts, interesting to his own countrymen, but which, from difficulty of access to authentic sources, could never before be fully exhibited to their inspection. But, whatever be thought of his redundancy, in this or the subsequent parts of his narrative, it must be admitted that he has uniformly and emphatically directed the attention of the reader to the topics most worthy of it; sparing no pains to illustrate the constitutional antiquities of the country, and to trace the gradual formation of her liberal polity, instead of wasting his strength on mere superficial gossip, like most of the chroniclers of the period.

There is no Spanish historian less swayed by party or religious prejudice, or by the feeling of nationality, which is so apt to overflow in the loyal effusions of the Castilian writers. This laudable temperance, indeed, has brought on him the rebuke of more than one of his patriotic countrymen. There is a sobriety and coolness in his estimate of historical evidence, equally removed from temerity on the one hand, and credulity on the other; in short, his whole manner is that of a man conversant with

public business, and free from the closet pedantry, which too often characterizes the monkish annalists. The greater part of his life was passed under the reign of Charles V., when the spirit of the nation was not yet broken by arbitrary power, nor debased by the melancholy superstition which settled on it under his successor; an age, in which the memory of ancient liberty had not wholly faded away, and when, if men did not dare express all they thought, they at least thought with a degree of independence, which gave a masculine character to their expression. In this, as well as in the liberality of his religious sentiments, he may be compared favorably with his celebrated countryman Mariana, who, educated in the cloister, and at a period when the nation was schooled to maxims of despotism, exhibits few glimpses of the sound criticism and reflection, which are to be found in the writings of his Aragonese rival. The seductions of style, however, the more fastidious selection of incidents, in short, the superior graces of narration, have given a wider fame to the former, whose works have passed into most of the cultivated languages of Europe, while those of Zurita remain, as far as I am aware, still undisturbed in the vernacular.

CHAPTER II.

ITALIAN WARS. — RETREAT OF CHARLES VIII. — CAMPAIGNS
OF GONSALVO DE CORDOVA. — FINAL EXPULSION OF THE
FRENCH

1495 — 1496.

Impolitic Conduct of Charles. — He plunders the Works of Art. — Gonsalvo de Cordova. — His Brilliant Qualities. — Raised to the Italian
Command. — Battle of Seminara. — Gonsalvo's Successes. — Decline
of the French. — He receives the Title of Great Captain. — Expulsion of the French from Italy.

CHARLES THE EIGHTH might have found abundant occupation, during his brief residence at Naples, in placing the kingdom in a proper posture of
defence, and in conciliating the good-will of the
inhabitants, without which he could scarcely hope
to maintain himself permanently in his conquest.
So far from this, however, he showed the utmost
aversion to business, wasting his hours, as has been
already noticed, in the most frivolous amusements.
He treated the great feudal aristocracy of the country with utter neglect; rendering himself difficult
of access, and lavishing all dignities and emoluments with partial prodigality on his French subjects. His followers disgusted the nation still
further by their insolence and unbridled licentiousness. The people naturally called to mind the

virtues of the exiled Ferdinand, whose temperate rule they contrasted with the rash and rapacious conduct of their new masters. The spirit of discontent spread more widely, as the French were too thinly scattered to enforce subordination. A correspondence was entered into with Ferdinand in Sicily, and in a short time several of the most considerable cities of the kingdom openly avowed their allegiance to the house of Aragon.[1]

Plunders the
works of art.

In the mean time, Charles and his nobles, satiated with a life of inactivity and pleasure, and feeling that they had accomplished the great object of the expedition, began to look with longing eyes towards their own country. Their impatience was converted into anxiety on receiving tidings of the coalition mustering in the north. Charles, however, took care to secure to himself some of the spoils of victory, in a manner which we have seen practised, on a much greater scale, by his countrymen in our day. He collected the various works of art with which Naples was adorned, precious antiques, sculptured marble and alabaster, gates of bronze curiously wrought, and such architectural ornaments as were capable of transportation, and caused them to be embarked on board his fleet for the south of France, " endeavouring," says the Curate of Los Palacios, " to build up his own renown on the ruins of the kings of Naples, of glorious memory." His vessels, however, did not reach

---

[1] Comines, Mémoires, liv. 7, chap. 17. — Summonte, Hist. di Napoli, tom. iii. lib. 6, cap. 2. — Giannone, Istoria di Napoli, lib. 29, cap. 2.

their place of destination, but were captured by a Biscayan and Genoese fleet off Pisa. [2]

Charles had entirely failed in his application to Pope Alexander the Sixth for a recognition of his right to Naples, by a formal act of investiture. [3] He determined, however, to go through the ceremony of a coronation ; and, on the 12th of May, he made his public entrance into the city, arrayed in splendid robes of scarlet and ermine, with the imperial diadem on his head, a sceptre in one hand, and a globe, the symbol of universal sovereignty, in the other ; while the adulatory populace saluted his royal ear with the august title of Emperor. After the conclusion of this farce, he made preparations for his instant departure from Naples. On the 20th of May he set out on his homeward march, at the head of one half of his army, amounting in all to not more than nine thousand fighting men. The other half was left for the defence of his new conquest. This arrangement was highly impolitic, since he neither took with him enough to cover his retreat, nor left enough to secure the preservation of Naples. [4]

It is not necessary to follow the French army in

Retreat of the French.

---

[2] Bernaldez, Reyes Católicos, MS., cap. 140 – 143.

[3] Summonte, Hist. di Napoli, tom. iii. lib. 6, cap. 2.

According to Giannone, (Istoria di Napoli, lib. 29, cap. 2,) he did obtain the investiture from the pope ; but this statement is contradicted by several, and confirmed by none, of the authorities I have consulted.

[4] Brantôme, Hommes Illustres,

Œuvres, tom. ii. pp. 3 – 5. — Comines, Mémoires, liv. 8, chap. 2.

The particulars of the coronation are recorded with punctilious precision by André de la Vigne, secretary of Queen Anne. (Hist. de Charles VIII., p. 201.) Daru has confounded this farce with Charles's original entry into Naples in February. Hist. de Venise, tom. iii. liv. 20, p. 247.

its retrograde movement through Italy. It is
enough to say, that this was not conducted with
sufficient despatch to anticipate the junction of
the allied forces, who assembled to dispute its passage on the banks of the Taro, near Fornovo. An
action was there fought, in which King Charles, at
the head of his loyal chivalry, achieved such deeds
of heroism, as shed a lustre over his ill-concerted
enterprise, and which, if they did not gain him an
undisputed victory, secured the fruits of it, by
enabling him to effect his retreat without further
molestation. At Turin he entered into negotiation
with the calculating duke of Milan, which terminated in the treaty of Vercelli, October 10th, 1495.
By this treaty Charles obtained no other advantage
than that of detaching his cunning adversary from
the coalition. The Venetians, although refusing to
accede to it, made no opposition to any arrangement, which would expedite the removal of their
formidable foe beyond the Alps. This was speedily accomplished; and Charles, yielding to his own
impatience and that of his nobles, recrossed that
mountain rampart which nature has so ineffectually
provided for the security of Italy, and reached
Grenoble with his army on the 27th of the month.
Once more restored to his own dominions, the
young monarch abandoned himself without reserve
to the licentious pleasures to which he was passionately addicted, forgetting alike his dreams of ambition, and the brave companions in arms whom he
had deserted in Italy. Thus ended this memorable
expedition, which, though crowned with complete

success, was attended with no other permanent result to its authors, than that of opening the way
to those disastrous wars, which wasted the resources of their country for a great part of the sixteenth century. [5]

Charles the Eighth had left as his viceroy in
Naples Gilbert de Bourbon, duke of Montpensier,
a prince of the blood, and a brave and loyal nobleman, but of slender military capacity, and so fond
of his bed, says Comines, that he seldom left it
before noon. The command of the forces in Calabria was intrusted to M. d'Aubigny, a Scottish
cavalier of the house of Stuart, raised by Charles
to the dignity of grand constable of France. He
was so much esteemed for his noble and chivalrous
qualities, that he was styled by the annalists of
that day, says Brantôme, " grand chevalier sans
reproche." He had large experience in military
matters, and was reputed one of the best officers
in the French service. Besides these principal
commanders, there were others of subordinate rank
stationed at the head of small detachments on
different points of the kingdom, and especially in
the fortified cities along the coasts. [6]

Scarcely had Charles the Eighth quitted Naples,
when his rival, Ferdinand, who had already completed his preparations in Sicily, made a descent on

[5] Villeneuve, Mémoires, apud
Petitot, Collection de Mémoires,
tom. xiv. pp. 262, 263. — Flassan,
Diplomatie Française, tom. i. pp.
267 – 269. — Comines, Mémoires,
liv. 8, chap. 10 — 12, 18

[6] Comines, Mémoires, liv. 8,
chap. 1. — Brantôme, Hommes Illustres, tom. ii. p. 59

the southern extremity of Calabria. He was supported in this by the Spanish levies under the
admiral Requesens, and Gonsalvo of Cordova, who
reached Sicily in the month of May. As the latter
of these commanders was destined to act a most
conspicuous part in the Italian wars, it may not be
amiss to give some account of his early life.

Gonsalvo
de Cordova.
Gonzalo Fernandez de Cordova, or Aguilar, as
he is sometimes styled from the territorial title
assumed by his branch of the family, was born at
Montilla, in 1453. His father died early, leaving
two sons, Alonso de Aguilar, whose name occurs in
some of the most brilliant passages of the war of
Granada, and Gonsalvo, three years younger than
his brother. During the troubled reigns of John
the Second and Henry the Fourth, the city of Cordova was divided by the feuds of the rival families
of Cabra and Aguilar; and it is reported that the
citizens of the latter faction, after the loss of their
natural leader, Gonsalvo's father, used to testify
their loyalty to his house by bearing the infant
children along with them in their rencontres; thus
Gonsalvo may be said to have been literally nursed
amid the din of battle.[7]

His early
life.
On the breaking out of the civil wars, the two
brothers attached themselves to the fortunes of
Alfonso and Isabella. At their court, the young
Gonsalvo soon attracted attention by the uncommon beauty of his person, his polished manners,

[7] Zurita, Hist. del Rey Hernan-   Magni Gonsalvi, lib. 1, pp. 204
do. lib. 2, cap. 7. — Giovio, Vita   205.

and proficiency in all knightly exercises. He indulged in a profuse magnificence in his apparel, equipage, and general style of living; a circumstance, which, accompanied with his brilliant qualities, gave him the title at the court of *el príncipe de los cavalleros,* the prince of cavaliers. This carelessness of expense, indeed, called forth more than once the affectionate remonstrance of his brother Alonso, who, as the elder son, had inherited the *mayorazgo,* or family estate, and who provided liberally for Gonsalvo's support. He served during the Portuguese war under Alonso de Cardenas, grand master of St. James, and was honored with the public commendations of his general for his signal display of valor at the battle of Albuera; where, it is remarked, the young hero incurred an unnecessary degree of personal hazard by the ostentatious splendor of his armour. Of this commander, and of the count of Tendilla, Gonsalvo always spoke with the greatest deference, acknowledging that he had learned the rudiments of war from them.[8]

The long war of Granada, however, was the great school in which his military discipline was perfected. He did not, it is true, occupy so eminent a position in these campaigns as some other chiefs of riper years and more enlarged experience; but on various occasions he displayed uncommon proofs both of address and valor. He particularly distinguished himself at the capture of Tajara, Illora,

His brilliant qualities

---

[8] Pulgar, Sumario de las Hazañas del Gran Capitan, (Madrid, 1834,) p. 145. — Giovio, Vita Magni Gonsalvi, lib. 1, pp. 205 et seq.

and Monte Frio. At the last place, he headed the scaling party, and was the first to mount the walls in the face of the enemy. He wellnigh closed his career in a midnight skirmish before Granada, which occurred a short time before the end of the war. In the heat of the struggle his horse was slain; and Gonsalvo, unable to extricate himself from the morass in which he was entangled, would have perished, but for a faithful servant of the family, who mounted him on his own horse, briefly commending to his master the care of his wife and children. Gonsalvo escaped, but his brave follower paid for his loyalty with his life. At the conclusion of the war, he was selected, together with Ferdinand's secretary Zafra, in consequence of his plausible address, and his familiarity with the Arabic, to conduct the negotiation with the Moorish government. He was secretly introduced for this purpose by night into Granada, and finally succeeded in arranging the terms of capitulation with the unfortunate Abdallah, as has been already stated. In consideration of his various services, the Spanish sovereigns granted him a pension, and a large landed estate in the conquered territory.[9]

After the war, Gonsalvo remained with the court,

---

[9] Peter Martyr, Opus Epist., epist. 90. — Giovio, Vita Magni Gonsalvi, lib. 1, pp. 211, 212. — Conde, Dominacion de los Arabes, tom. iii. cap. 42. — Quintana, Españoles Célebres, tom. i. pp. 207 -216. — Pulgar, Sumario, p. 193.

Florian has given circulation to a popular error by his romance of "Gonsalve de Cordoue," where the young warrior is made to play a part he is by no means entitled to, as hero of the Granadine war. Graver writers, who cannot lawfully plead the privilege of romancing, have committed the same error. See, among others, Varillas Politique de Ferdinand, p. 3.

and his high reputation and brilliant exterior made him one of the most distinguished ornaments of the royal circle. His manners displayed all the romantic gallantry characteristic of the age, of which the following, among other instances, is recorded. The queen accompanied her daughter Joanna on board the fleet which was to bear her to Flanders, the country of her destined husband. After bidding adieu to the infanta, Isabella returned in her boat to the shore; but the waters were so swollen, that it was found difficult to make good a footing for her on the beach. As the sailors were preparing to drag the bark higher up the strand, Gonsalvo, who was present, and dressed, as the Castilian historians are careful to inform us, in a rich suit of brocade and crimson velvet, unwilling that the person of his royal mistress should be profaned by the touch of such rude hands, waded into the water, and bore the queen in his arms to the shore, amid the shouts and plaudits of the spectators. The incident may form a counterpart to the well-known anecdote of Sir Walter Raleigh.[10]

Isabella's long and intimate acquaintance with Gonsalvo enabled her to form a correct estimate of his great talents. When the Italian expedition was

[10] Giovio, Vita Magni Gonsalvi, p. 214. — Chrónica del Gran Capitan Gonzalo Hernandez de Cordova y Aguilar, (Alcalá de Henares, 1584,) cap. 23.

Another example of his gallantry occurred during the Granadine war, when the fire of Santa Fe had onsumed the royal tent, with the greater part of the queen's apparel and other valuable effects. Gonsalvo, on learning the disaster, at his castle of Illora, supplied the queen so abundantly from the magnificent wardrobe of his wife Doña Maria Manrique, as led Isabella pleasantly to remark, that, "the fire had done more execution in his quarters, than in her own." Pulgar, Sumario, p. 187.

resolved on, she instantly fixed her eyes on him as the most suitable person to conduct it. She knew that he possessed the qualities essential to success in a new and difficult enterprise, — courage, constancy, singular prudence, dexterity in negotiation, and inexhaustible fertility of resource. She accordingly recommended him, without hesitation, to her husband, as the commander of the Italian army. He approved her choice, although it seems to have caused no little surprise at the court, which, notwithstanding the favor in which Gonsalvo was held by the sovereigns, was not prepared to see him advanced over the heads of veterans, of so much riper years and higher military renown than himself. The event proved the sagacity of Isabella.[11]

Arrives in Italy.

The part of the squadron destined to convey the new general to Sicily was made ready for sea in the spring of 1495. After a tempestuous voyage, he reached Messina on the 24th of May. He found, that Ferdinand, of Naples, had already begun operations in Calabria, where he had occupied Reggio with the assistance of the admiral Requesens, who reached Sicily with a part of the armament a short time previous to Gonsalvo's arrival. The whole effective force of the Spaniards did not exceed six hundred lances and fifteen hundred foot, besides those employed in the fleet, amounting to about three thousand and five hundred more. The

[11] Giovio, Vita Magni Gonsalvi, p 214. — Chrónica del Gran Capitan, cap. 23.

finances of Spain had been too freely drained in the late Moorish war to authorize any extraordinary expenditure ; and Ferdinand designed to assist his kinsman rather with his name, than with any great accession of numbers. Preparations, however, were going forward for raising additional levies, especially among the hardy peasantry of the Asturias and Galicia, on which the war of Granada had fallen less heavily than on the south.[12]

On the 26th of May, Gonsalvo de Cordova crossed over to Reggio in Calabria, where a plan of operation was concerted between him and the Neapolitan monarch. Before opening the campaign, several strong places in the province, which owed allegiance to the Aragonese family, were placed in the hands of the Spanish general, as security for the reimbursement of expenses incurred by his government in the war. As Gonsalvo placed little reliance on his Calabrian or Sicilian recruits, he was obliged to detach a considerable part of his Spanish forces to garrison these places.[13]

[12] Zurita, Hist. del Rey Hernando, lib. 2, cap. 7, 24. — Quintana, Españoles Célebres, tom. i. p. 222. — Chrónica del Gran Capitan, ubi supra.

Giovio, in his biography of Gonsalvo, estimates these forces at 5000 foot and 600 horse, which last in his History he raises to 700. I have followed Zurita, as presenting the more probable statement, and as generally more accurate in all that relates to his own nation. It is a hopeless task to attempt to reconcile the manifold inaccuracies, contradictions, and discrepancies, which perplex the narratives of the writers on both sides, in every thing relating to numerical estimates. The difficulty is greatly increased by the extremely vague application of the term *lance*, as we meet with it. including six, four, three, or even a less number of followers, as the case might be.

[13] Mariana, Hist. de España, tom. ii. lib. 26, cap. 10. — Zurita, Hist. del Rey Hernando, lib. 2, cap. 7.

The occupation of these places by Gonsalvo excited the pope's jealousy, as to the designs of the Spanish sovereigns. In consequence of his remonstrances, the

The presence of their monarch revived the dormant loyalty of his Calabrian subjects. They thronged to his standard, till at length he found himself at the head of six thousand men, chiefly composed of the raw militia of the country. He marched at once with Gonsalvo on St. Agatha, which opened its gates without resistance. He

then directed his course towards Seminara, a place of some strength about eight leagues from Reggio. On his way he cut in pieces a detachment of French on its march to reinforce the garrison there. Seminara imitated the example of St. Agatha, and, receiving the Neapolitan army without opposition, unfurled the standard of Aragon on its walls. While this was going forward, Antonio Grimani, the Venetian admiral, scoured the eastern coasts of the kingdom with a fleet of four and twenty galleys, and, attacking the strong town of Monopoli, in the possession of the French, put the greater part of the garrison to the sword.

D'Aubigny, who lay at this time with an inconsiderable body of French troops in the south of Calabria, saw the necessity of some vigorous movement to check the further progress of the enemy. He determined to concentrate his forces, scattered through the province, and march against Ferdinand,

---

Castilian envoy, Garcilasso de la Vega, was instructed to direct Gonsalvo, that, "in case any inferior places had been since put into his hands, he should restore them ; if they were of importance, however, he was first to confer with his own government." King Ferdinand, as Abarca assures his readers, "was unwilling to give cause of complaint to any one, *unless he were greatly a gainer by it.*" Reyes de Aragon, rey 30, cap. 8. — Zurita, Hist. del Rey Hernando, tom. v. lib. 2, cap. 8.

n the hope of bringing him to a decisive action. For this purpose, in addition to the garrisons dispersed among the principal towns, he summoned to his aid the forces, consisting principally of Swiss infantry, stationed in the Basilicate under Précy, a brave young cavalier, esteemed one of the best officers in the French service. After the arrival of this reinforcement, aided by the levies of the Angevin barons, D'Aubigny, whose effective strength now greatly surpassed that of his adversary, directed his march towards Seminara.[14]

Ferdinand, who had received no intimation of his adversary's junction with Précy, and who considered him much inferior to himself in numbers, no sooner heard of his approach, than he determined to march out at once before he could reach Seminara, and give him battle. Gonsalvo was of a different opinion. His own troops had too little experience in war with the French and Swiss veterans to make him willing to risk all on the chances of a single battle. The Spanish heavy-armed cavalry, indeed, were a match for any in Europe, and were even said to surpass every other in the beauty and excellence of their appointments, at a period, when arms were finished to luxury.[15] He had but a handful of these, however; by far the greatest part of his cavalry consisting of *ginetes*, or light-armed troops, of inestimable service in the wild

[14] Giovio, Vita Magni Gonsalvi, pp. 215–217. — Idem, Hist. sui Temporis, pp. 83–85. — Bembo, Istoria Viniziana, lib. 3, pp. 160, 185. — Zurita, Hist. del Rey Hernando, lib. 2, cap. 8. — Guicciardini, Istoria, lib. 2, pp. 88, 92. — Chrónica del Gran Capitan, cap. 25.

[15] Giovio, Vita Magni Gonsalvi, lib. 1. — Du Bos, Ligue de Cambray, introd., p. 58.

PART
II.

guerilla warfare to which they had been accus
tomed in Granada, but obviously incapable of coping
with the iron *gendarmerie* of France. He felt some
distrust, too, in bringing his little corps of infantry
without further preparation, armed, as they were,
only with short swords and bucklers, and much reduced, as has been already stated, in number, to
encounter the formidable phalanx of Swiss pikes.
As for the Calabrian levies, he did not place the
least reliance on them. At all events, he thought
it prudent, before coming to action, to obtain more
accurate information than they now possessed, of
the actual strength of the enemy.[16]

In all this, however, he was overruled by the
impatience of Ferdinand and his followers. The
principal Spanish cavaliers, indeed, as well as the
Italian, among whom may be found names which
afterwards rose to high distinction in these wars,
urged Gonsalvo to lay aside his scruples; representing the impolicy of showing any distrust of their
own strength at this crisis, and of balking the ardor
of their soldiers, now hot for action. The Spanish
chief, though far from being convinced, yielded to
these earnest remonstrances, and King Ferdinand
led out his little army without further delay against
the enemy.

Battle of
Seminara.

After traversing a chain of hills, stretching in an
easterly direction from Seminara, at the distance of
about three miles he arrived before a small stream,
on the plains beyond which he discerned the

---

[16] Zurita, Hist. del Rey Hernando, lib 2, ca   Giovio, Vita
Magni Gonsalvi, ubi supra.

French army in rapid advance against him.   He
resolved to wait its approach ; and, taking position
on the slope of the hills towards the river, he drew
up his horse on the right wing, and his infantry on
the left. [17]

The French generals, D'Aubigny and Précy, putting themselves at the head of their cavalry on the
left, consisting of about four hundred heavy-armed,
and twice as many light horse, dashed into the
water without hesitation.   Their right was occupied by the bristling phalanx of Swiss spearmen in
close array ; behind these were the militia of the
country.   The Spanish *ginetes* succeeded in throwing the French gendarmerie into some disorder, before it could form after crossing the stream ; but, no
sooner was this accomplished, than the Spaniards,
incapable of withstanding the charge of their enemy, suddenly wheeled about and precipitately retreated with the intention of again returning on
their assailants, after the fashion of the Moorish
tactics.   The Calabrian militia, not comprehending
this manœuvre, interpreted it into a defeat.   They
thought the battle lost, and, seized with a panic,
broke their ranks, and fled to a man, before the
Swiss infantry had time so much as to lower its
lances against them.

King Ferdinand in vain attempted to rally the
dastardly fugitives.   The French cavalry was soon
upon them, making frightful slaughter in their

---

[17] Giovio, Vita Magni Gonsalvi,   tana, Españoles Célebres, tom. i
lib 1, pp. 216, 217. — Chrónica   pp. 223-227.
del Gran Capitan, cap. 24. — Quin-

ranks. The young monarch, whose splendid arms
and towering plumes made him a conspicuous mark
in the field, was exposed to imminent peril. He
had broken his lance in the body of one of the
foremost of the French cavaliers, when his horse
fell under him, and as his feet were entangled in
the stirrups, he would inevitably have perished in
the *mêlée*, but for the prompt assistance of a young
nobleman named Juan de Altavilla, who mounted
his master on his own horse, and calmly awaited
the approach of the enemy, by whom he was immediately slain. Instances of this affecting loyalty
and self-devotion not unfrequently occur in these
wars, throwing a melancholy grace over the darker
and more ferocious features of the time.[18]

Gonsalvo was seen in the thickest of the fight,
long after the king's escape, charging the enemy
briskly at the head of his handful of Spaniards, not
in the hope of retrieving the day, but of covering
the flight of the panic-struck Neapolitans. At
length he was borne along by the rushing tide,
and succeeded in bringing off the greater part of
his cavalry safe to Seminara. Had the French followed up the blow, the greater part of the royal
army, with probably King Ferdinand and Gonsalvo
at its head, would have fallen into their hands, and
thus not only the fate of the campaign, but of Naples itself, would have been permanently decided by

[18] Giovio, Hist. sui Temporis,
lib. 3, pp. 83–85. — Chrónica del
Gran Capitan, cap. 24. — Summonte, Hist. di Napoli, tom. iii.
lib. 6, cap. 2. — Guicciardini, Istoria, lib. 2, p. 112. — Garibay
Compendio, tom. ii. lib. 19, p. 690

this battle. Fortunately the French did not understand so well how to use a victory, as to gain it. They made no attempt to pursue. This is imputed to the illness of their general, D'Aubigny, occasioned by the extreme unhealthiness of the climate. He was too feeble to sit long on his horse, and was removed into a litter as soon as the action was decided. Whatever was the cause, the victors by this inaction suffered the golden fruits of victory to escape them. Ferdinand made his escape on the same day on board a vessel, which conveyed him back to Sicily; and Gonsalvo, on the following morning before break of day, effected his retreat across the mountains to Reggio, at the head of four hundred Spanish lances. Thus terminated the first battle of importance in which Gonsalvo of Cordova held a distinguished command; the only one which he lost during his long and fortunate career. Its loss, however, attached no discredit to him, since it was entered into in manifest opposition to his judgment. On the contrary, his conduct throughout this affair tended greatly to establish his reputation by showing him to be no less prudent in council, than bold in action. [19]

King Ferdinand, far from being disheartened by this defeat, gained new confidence from his experience of the favorable dispositions existing towards him in Calabria. Relying on a similar feeling of loyalty in his capital, he determined to hazard a

Gonsalvo
retreats to
Reggio.

---

[19] Guicciardini, Istoria, lib. 1, p. 112. — Giovio, Hist. sui Tem-poris, lib. 3, p. 85. — Lanuza, His-torias, tom. i. lib. 1, cap. 7.

bold stroke for its recovery; and that, too, instantly, before his late discomfiture should have time to
operate on the spirits of his partisans. He accordingly embarked at Messina, with a handful of
troops only, on board the fleet of the Spanish admiral, Requesens. It amounted in all to eighty vessels, most of them of inconsiderable size. With
this armament, which, notwithstanding its formidable show, carried little effective force for land
operations, the adventurous young monarch appeared off the harbour of Naples before the end
of June.

Charles's viceroy, the duke of Montpensier, at
that time garrisoned Naples with six thousand
French troops. On the appearance of the Spanish
navy, he marched out to prevent Ferdinand's landing, leaving a few only of his soldiers to keep the
city in awe. But he had scarcely quitted it before
the inhabitants, who had waited with impatience
an opportunity for throwing off the yoke, sounded
the tocsin, and, rising to arms through every part
of the city, and massacring the feeble remains of
the garrison, shut the gates against him; while
Ferdinand, who had succeeded in drawing off the
French commander in another direction, no sooner
presented himself before the walls, than he was
received with transports of joy by the enthusiastic
people.[20]

[20] Summonte, Hist. di Napoli,   pp. 87, 88. — Villeneuve, Mé-
tom. vi. p. 519. — Guicciardini,   moires, apud Petitot, Collection
Istoria, lib. 2, pp. 113, 114. —   des Mémoires, tom. xiv. pp. 264,
Giovio, Hist. sui Temporis, lib. 3,   265.

The French, however, though excluded from the city, by making a circuit effected an entrance into the fortresses which commanded it. From these posts, Montpensier sorely annoyed the town, making frequent attacks on it, day and night, at the head of his gendarmerie, until they were at length checked in every direction by barricades which the citizens hastily constructed with wagons, casks of stones, bags of sand, and whatever came most readily to hand. At the same time, the windows, balconies, and house-tops were crowded with combatants, who poured down such a deadly shower of missiles on the heads of the French as finally compelled them to take shelter in their defences. Montpensier was now closely besieged, till at length, reduced by famine, he was compelled to capitulate. Before the term prescribed for his surrender had arrived, however, he effected his escape at night, by water, to Salerno, at the head of twenty-five hundred men. The remaining garrison, with the fortresses, submitted to the victorious Ferdinand, the beginning of the following year. And thus, by one of those sudden turns which belong to the game of war, the exiled prince, whose fortunes a few weeks before appeared perfectly desperate, was again established in the palace of his ancestors.[21]

Montpensier did not long remain in his new quarters. He saw the necessity of immediate ac-

[21] Giovio, Hist. sui Temporis, – 117. — Summonte, Hist. di Na
lib. 3, pp. 88 – 90, 114 – 119. —   poli, tom. vi. pp. 520, 521
Guicciardini, Istoria, lib. 2, pp. 114

tion, to counteract the alarming progress of the
enemy. He quitted Salerno before the end of
winter, strengthening his army by such reinforcements as he could collect from every quarter of the
country. With this body, he directed his course
towards Apulia, with the intention of bringing
Ferdinand, who had already established his head-
quarters there, to a decisive engagement. Ferdinand's force, however, was so far inferior to that of
his antagonist, as to compel him to act on the defensive, until he had been reinforced by a considerable body of troops from Venice. The two armies
were then so equally matched, that neither cared to
hazard all on the fate of a battle; and the campaign wasted away in languid operations, which
led to no important result.

Gonsalvo in
Calabria.

In the mean time, Gonsalvo de Cordova was
slowly fighting his way up through southern Calabria. The character of the country, rough and
mountainous, like the Alpuxarras, and thickly sprinkled with fortified places, enabled him to bring into
play the tactics which he had learned in the war
of Granada. He made little use of heavy-armed
troops, relying on his *ginetes*, and still more on his
foot; taking care, however, to avoid any direct encounter with the dreaded Swiss battalions. He
made amends for paucity of numbers and want
of real strength, by rapidity of movement and the
wily tactics of Moorish warfare; darting on the
enemy where least expected, surprising his strong-
holds at dead of night, entangling him in am-
buscades, and desolating the country with those

terrible forays, whose effects he had so often witnessed on the fair vegas of Granada. He adopted
the policy practised by his master Ferdinand the
Catholic in the Moorish war, lenient to the submissive foe, but wreaking terrible vengeance on
such as resisted.[22]

The French were sorely disconcerted by these
irregular operations, so unlike any thing to which
they were accustomed in European warfare. They
were further disheartened by the continued illness
of D'Aubigny, and by the growing disaffection of
the Calabrians, who in the southern provinces contiguous to Sicily were particularly well inclined to
Spain.

Gonsalvo, availing himself of these friendly dis- His suc-
positions, pushed forward his successes, carrying cesses
one strong-hold after another, until by the end of
the year he had overrun the whole of Lower Calabria. His progress would have been still more
rapid but for the serious embarrassments which he
experienced from want of supplies. He had received some reinforcements from Sicily, but very
few from Spain; while the boasted Galician levies,
instead of fifteen hundred, had dwindled to scarcely
three hundred men; who arrived in the most miserable plight, destitute of clothing and munitions
of every kind. He was compelled to weaken still
further his inadequate force by garrisoning the conquered places, most of which, however, he was

[22] Bembo, Istoria Viniziana, lib.
3, pp. 173, 174. — Chrónica del
Gran Capitan, cap. 26. — Giovio,
Vita Magni Gonsalvi, lib. 1, p. 218.
— Villeneuve, Mémoires, p. 313. —
Sismondi, Républiques Italiennes,
tom. xii. p. 386.

obliged to leave without any defence at all. In addition to this, he was so destitute of the necessary funds for the payment of his troops, that he was detained nearly two months at Nicastro, until February, 1496, when he received a remittance from Spain. After this, he resumed operations with such vigor, that by the end of the following spring he had reduced all Upper Calabria, with the exception of a small corner of the province, in which D'Aubigny still maintained himself. At this crisis, he was summoned from the scene of his conquests to the support of the king of Naples, who lay encamped before Atella, a town intrenched among the Apennines, on the western borders of the Basilicate.[23]

Decline of
the French.

The campaign of the preceding winter had terminated without any decisive results, the two armies of Montpensier and King Ferdinand having continued in sight of each other, without ever coming to action. These protracted operations were fatal to the French. Their few supplies were intercepted by the peasantry of the country; their Swiss and German mercenaries mutinied and deserted for want of pay; and the Neapolitans in their service went off in great numbers, disgusted with the insolent and overbearing manners of their new allies. Charles the Eighth, in the mean while, was wasting his hours and health in the usual round of profligate pleasures. From the moment

[23] Zurita, Hist. del Rey Hernando, lib. 2, cap. 11, 20. — Guicciardini, Istoria, lib. 2, p. 140. — Giovio, Vita Magni Gonsalvi, lib. 1, pp. 219, 220. — Chrónica del Gran Capitan, cap. 25, 26.

of recrossing the Alps he seemed to have shut out
Italy from his thoughts.   He was equally insensible
to the supplications of the few Italians at his court,
and the remonstrances of his French nobles, many
of whom, although opposed to the first expedition,
would willingly have undertaken a second to support their brave comrades, whom the heedless young
monarch now abandoned to their fate.[24]

At length Montpensier, finding no prospect of
relief from home, and straitened by the want of
provisions, determined to draw off from the neighbourhood of Benevento, where the two armies lay
encamped, and retreat to the fruitful province of
Apulia, whose principal places were still garrisoned
by the French.   He broke up his camp secretly at
dead of night, and gained a day's march on his
enemy, before the latter began his pursuit.   This
Ferdinand pushed with such vigor, however, that
he overtook the retreating army at the town of
Atella, and completely intercepted its further progress.   This town, which, as already noticed, is
situated on the western skirts of the Basilicate, lies
in a broad valley encompassed by a lofty amphi-
theatre of hills, through which flows a little river,

---

[24] Guicciardini, Istoria, lib. 3,
pp. 140, 157, 158. — Comines, Mémoires, liv. 8, chap. 23, 24. — Peter
Martyr, Opus Epist., epist. 183.
Du Bos discriminates between the
character of the German levies or
landsknechts and the Swiss, in the
following terms. " Les lansquenets
étoient même de beaucoup mieux
faits, généralement parlant, et de
bien meilleure mine sous les armes,
que les fantassins Suisses ; mais ils
étoient incapables de discipline. Au
contraire des Suisses, ils étoient
sans obéissance pour leur chefs, et
sans amitié pour leurs camarades."
(Ligue de Cambray, tom. i. dissert. prélim. p. 66.) Comines confirms the distinction with a high
tribute to the loyalty of the Swiss,
which has continued their honorable characteristic to the present
day. Mémoires, liv. 8, chap. 21.

tributary to the Ofanto, watering the town, and turn
ing several mills which supplied it with flour. At
a few miles' distance was the strong place of Ripa
Candida, garrisoned by the French, through which
Montpensier hoped to maintain his communications
with the fertile regions of the interior.

Ferdinand, desirous if possible to bring the war
to a close, by the capture of the whole French
army, prepared for a vigorous blockade. He disposed his forces so as to intercept supplies by commanding the avenues to the town in every direction.
He soon found, however, that his army, though
considerably stronger than his rival's, was incompetent to this without further aid. He accordingly
resolved to summon to his support Gonsalvo de
Cordova, the fame of whose exploits now resounded
through every part of the kingdom.[25]

The Spanish general received Ferdinand's summons while encamped with his army at Castrovil-
lari, in the north of Upper Calabria. If he complied with it, he saw himself in danger of losing
all the fruits of his long campaign of victories ; for
his active enemy would not fail to profit by his
absence to repair his losses. If he refused obedience, however, it might defeat the most favorable opportunity which had yet presented itself for
bringing the war to a close. He resolved, therefore, at once to quit the field of his triumphs, and
march to King Ferdinand's relief. But, before his

[25] Giovio, Vita Magni Gonsalvi,
lib. 1, pp. 218, 219. — Chrónica
del Gran Capitan, cap. 28. — Quintana, Españoles Célebres, tom. i. p.
226. — Bembo, Istoria Viniziana,
lib. 3, p. 184. — Guicciardini, Isto
ria, lib. 3, p. 158.

departure, he prepared to strike such a blow as
should, if possible, incapacitate his enemy for any
effectual movement during his absence.

He received intelligence that a considerable
number of Angevin lords, mostly of the powerful
house of San Severino, with their vassals and a reinforcement of French troops, were assembled at
the little town of Laino, on the northwestern borders of Upper Calabria; where they lay awaiting a
junction with D'Aubigny. Gonsalvo determined
to surprise this place, and capture the rich spoils
which it contained, before his departure. His road
lay through a wild and mountainous country. The
passes were occupied by the Calabrian peasantry in
the interest of the Angevin party. The Spanish
general, however, found no difficulty in forcing a
way through this undisciplined rabble, a large body
of whom he surrounded and cut to pieces, as they
lay in ambush for him in the valley of Murano.
Laino, whose base is washed by the waters of the
Lao, was defended by a strong castle built on the
opposite side of the river, and connected by a
bridge with the town. All approach to the place
by the high road was commanded by this fortress.
Gonsalvo obviated this difficulty, however, by a circuitous route across the mountains. He marched
all night, and fording the waters of the Lao about
two miles above the town, entered it with his little
army before break of day, having previously detached a small corps to take possession of the
bridge. The inhabitants, startled from their slum-
bers by the unexpected appearance of the enemy in

their streets, hastily seized their arms and made for
the castle on the other side of the river. The pass,
however, was occupied by the Spaniards; and the
Neapolitans and French, hemmed in on every side,
began a desperate resistance, which terminated with
the death of their chief, Americo San Severino, and
the capture of such of his followers as did not fall
in the *mêlée*. A rich booty fell into the hands of
the victors. The most glorious prize, however, was
the Angevin barons, twenty in number, whom Gonsalvo, after the action, sent prisoners to Naples.
This decisive blow, whose tidings spread like wild-
fire throughout the country, settled the fate of Calabria. It struck terror into the hearts of the French,
and crippled them so far as to leave Gonsalvo little
cause for anxiety during his proposed absence. [26]

Arrives be-
fore Atella.

The Spanish general lost no time in pressing forward on his march towards Atella. Before quitting
Calabria he had received a reinforcement of five
hundred soldiers from Spain, and his whole Spanish
forces, according to Giovio, amounted to one hundred men-at-arms, five hundred light cavalry, and
two thousand foot, picked men, and well schooled
in the hardy service of the late campaign.[27] Although a great part of his march lay through a hostile country, he encountered little opposition; for
the terror of his name, says the writer last quoted,
had everywhere gone before him. He arrived be-

[26] Giovio, Vita Magni Gonsalvi,
pp. 219, 220. — Chrónica del Gran
Capitan, cap. 27. — Zurita, Hist. del
Rey Hernando, tom. i. lib. 2, cap.
26. — Quintana, Españoles Célebres, tom. i. pp. 227, 228. — Guicciardini, Istoria, lib. 3, pp. 158,
159. — Mariana, Hist. de España,
tom. ii. lib. 26, cap. 12.
[27] Giovio, Hist. del Rey Hernando, lib. 4, p. 132.

fore Atella at the beginning of July. The king CHAPTER II.
of Naples was no sooner advised of his approach,
than he marched out of the camp, attended by the
Venetian general, the marquis of Mantua, and
the papal legate, Cæsar Borgia, to receive him.
All were eager to do honor to the man, who had
achieved such brilliant exploits ; who, in less than
a year, had made himself master of the larger part
of the kingdom of Naples, and that, with the most
limited resources, in defiance of the bravest and
best disciplined soldiery in Europe. It was then, Receives the title of Great Captain.
according to the Spanish writers, that he was by
general consent greeted with the title of the Great
Captain; by which he is much more familiarly
known in Spanish, and, it may be added, in most
histories of the period, than by his own name.[28]

[28] Quintana, Españoles Célebres, tom. i. p. 228. — Giovio, Vita Magni Gonsalvi, lib. 1, p. 220.

The Aragonese historians are much ruffled by the irreverent manner in which Guicciardini notices the origin of the cognomen of the Great Captain ; which even his subsequent panegyric cannot atone for. "Era capitano Consalvo Ernandes, di casa d'Aghilar, di patria Cordovese, uomo di molto valore, ed esercitato lungamente nelle guerre di Granata, il quale nel principio della venuta sua in Italia, cognominato *dalla jattanza Spagnuola* il Gran Capitano, per significare con questo titolo la suprema podestà sopra loro, meritò per le preclare vittorie che ebbe dipoi, che per consentimento universale gli fosse confermato e perpetuato questo sopranome, per significazione di virtù grande, e di grande eccellenza nella disciplina militare." (Istoria, tom. i. p. 112.) According

to Zurita, the title was not conferred till the Spanish general's appearance before Atella, and the first example of its formal recognition was in the instrument of capitulation at that place. (Hist. del Rey Hernando, lib. 2, cap. 27.) This seems to derive support from the fact that Gonsalvo's biographer and contemporary, Giovio, begins to distinguish him by that epithet from this period. Abarca assigns a higher antiquity to it, quoting the words of the royal grant of the duchy of Sessa, made to Gonsalvo, as authority. (Reyes de Aragon, rey 39, cap. 9.) In a former edition, I intimated my doubt of the historian's accuracy. A subsequent inspection of the instrument itself, in a work since come into my possession, shows this distrust to have been well founded ; for it is there simply said, that the title was conferred in Italy. Pulgar, Sumario, p. 138.

Gonsalvo found the French sorely distressed by the blockade, which was so strictly maintained as to allow few supplies from abroad to pass into the town. His quick eye discovered, at once, however, that in order to render it perfectly effectual, it would be necessary to destroy the mills in the vicinity, which supplied Atella with flour. He undertook this, on the day of his arrival, at the head of his own corps. Montpensier, aware of the importance of these mills, had stationed a strong guard for their defence, consisting of a body of Gascon archers, and the Swiss pikemen. Although the Spaniards had never been brought into direct collision with any large masses of this formidable infantry, yet occasional rencontres with small detachments, and increased familiarity with its tactics had stripped it of much of its terrors. Gonsalvo had even so far profited by the example of the Swiss, as to strengthen his infantry by mingling the long pikes with the short swords and bucklers of the Spaniards. [29]

He made two divisions of his cavalry, posting his handful of heavy-armed, with some of the light horse, so as to check any sally from the town, while he destined the remainder to support the infantry in the attack upon the enemy. Having made these arrangements, the Spanish chieftain led on his men confidently to the charge. The Gascon archery, however, seized with a panic, scarcely

[29] This was improving on the somewhat similar expedient ascribed by Polybius to King Pyrrhus, who mingled alternate cohorts, armed with short weapons after the Roman fashion, with those of his Macedonian spearmen. Lib. 17, sec. 24.

awaited his approach, but fled shamefully, before they had time to discharge a second volley of arrows, leaving the battle to the Swiss. These latter, exhausted by the sufferings of the siege, and dispirited by long reverses, and by the presence of a new and victorious foe, did not behave with their wonted intrepidity, but, after a feeble resistance, abandoned their position, and retreated towards the city. Gonsalvo, having gained his object, did not care to pursue the fugitives, but instantly set about demolishing the mills, every vestige of which, in a few hours, was swept from the ground Three days after, he supported the Neapolitan troops in an assault on Ripa Candida, and carried that important post, by means of which Atella maintained a communication with the interior.[30]

Thus cut off from all their resources, and no longer cheered by hopes of succour from their own country, the French, after suffering the severest privations, and being reduced to the most loathsome aliment for subsistence, made overtures for a capitulation. The terms were soon arranged with the king of Naples, who had no desire but to rid his country of the invaders. It was agreed, that, if the French commander did not receive assistance in thirty days, he should evacuate Atella, and cause every place holding under him in the kingdom of Naples, with all its artillery, to be sur-

Capitulation of Montpensier.

[30] Giovio, Hist. sui Temporis, lib. 4, p. 133.—Idem, Vita Magni Gonsalvi, pp. 220, 221.—Zurita, Hist. del Rey Hernando, lib. 2, cap. 27.—Chrónica del Gran Capitan, cap. 28.—Quintana, Españoles Célebres, tom. i. p. 229.—Abarca, Reyes de Aragon, rey 30, cap. 9.

rendered to King Ferdinand; and that, on these conditions, his soldiers should be furnished with vessels to transport them back to France; that the foreign mercenaries should be permitted to return to their own homes; and that a general amnesty should be extended to such Neapolitans as return- ed to their allegiance in fifteen days. [31]

Such were the articles of capitulation, signed on the 21st of July, 1496, which Comines, who re- ceived the tidings at the court of France, does not hesitate to denounce as " a most disgraceful treaty, without parallel, save in that made by the Roman consuls at the Caudine Forks, which was too dis- honorable to be sanctioned by their countrymen." The reproach is certainly unmerited; and comes with ill grace from a court, which was wasting in riotous indulgence the very resources indispen- sable to the brave and loyal subjects, who were endeavouring to maintain its honor in a foreign land. [32]

Miserable
state of the
French.

Unfortunately Montpensier was unable to enforce the full performance of his own treaty; as many of the French refused to deliver up the places in- trusted to them, under the pretence that their au- thority was derived, not from the viceroy, but from the king himself. During the discussion of this point, the French troops were removed to Baia and Pozzuolo, and the adjacent places on the coast. The unhealthiness of the situation, together with

[31] Villeneuve, Mémoires, p. 318.
— Comines, Mémoires, liv. 8, chap.
21. — Giovio, Hist. sui Temporis,
lib. 4, p. 136.

[32] Comines, Mémoires, liv. 8,
chap. 21.

that of the autumnal season, and an intemperate
indulgence in fruits and wine, soon brought on an epidemic among the soldiers, which swept them off in great numbers. The gallant Montpensier was one of the first victims. He refused the earnest solicitations of his brother-in-law, the marquis of Mantua, to quit his unfortunate companions, and retire to a place of safety in the interior. The shore was literally strewed with the bodies of the dying and the dead. Of the whole number of Frenchmen, amounting to not less than five thousand, who marched out of Atella, not more than five hundred ever reached their native country. The Swiss and other mercenaries were scarcely more fortunate. "They made their way back as they could through Italy," says a writer of the period, "in the most deplorable state of destitution and suffering, the gaze of all, and a sad example of the caprice of fortune." [33] Such was the miserable fate of that brilliant and formidable array, which scarcely two years before had poured down on the fair fields of Italy in all the insolence of expected conquest. Well would it be, if the name of every conqueror, whose successes, though built on human misery, are so dazzling to the imagination, could be made to point a moral for the instruction of his species, as effectually as that of Charles the Eighth.

The young king of Naples did not live long to enjoy his triumphs. On his return from Atella, he

Death of
Ferdinand
of Naples.

---

[33] Giovio, Hist. sui Temporis, p. 137. — Comines, Mémoires, liv. 3, chap. 21. — Giovio, Vita Magni Gonsalvi, lib. 1, p. 221. — Guicciar- dini, Istoria, lib. 3, p. 160. — Ville- neuve, Mémoires, apud Petitot, tom. xiv. p. 318.

contracted an inauspicious marriage with his aunt, a lady nearly of his own age, to whom he had been long attached. A careless and somewhat intemperate indulgence in pleasure, succeeding the hardy life which he had been lately leading, brought on a

flux which carried him off in the twenty-eighth year of his age, and second of his reign. He was the fifth monarch, who, in the brief compass of three years, had sat on the disastrous throne of Naples.

Ferdinand possessed many qualities suited to the turbulent times in which he lived. He was vigorous and prompt in action, and naturally of a high and generous spirit. Still, however, he exhibited glimpses, even in his last hours, of an obliquity, not to say ferocity of temper, which characterized many of his line, and which led to ominous conjectures as to what would have been his future policy.[34]

He was succeeded on the throne by his uncle Frederic, a prince of a gentle disposition, endeared to the Neapolitans by repeated acts of benevolence, and by a magnanimous regard for justice, of which the remarkable fluctuations of his fortune had elicited more than one example. His amiable virtues, however, required a kindlier soil and season for their expansion; and, as the event proved, made him no

[34] Giannone, Istoria di Napoli, lib. 29, cap. 2. — Summonte, Hist. di Napoli, lib. 6, cap. 2. — Peter Martyr, Opus Epist., epist. 188.

While stretched on his deathbed, Ferdinand, according to Bembo, caused the head of his prisoner, the Bishop of Teano, to be brought to him, and laid at the foot of his couch, that he might be assured with his own eyes of the execution of the sentence. Istoria Viniziana, lib. 3, p. 189.

match for the subtile and unscrupulous politicians of the age.

His first act was a general amnesty to the disaffected Neapolitans, who felt such confidence in his good faith, that they returned, with scarcely an exception, to their allegiance. His next measure was to request the aid of Gonsalvo de Cordova in suppressing the hostile movements made by the French during his absence from Calabria. At the name of the Great Captain, the Italians flocked from all quarters, to serve without pay under a banner, which was sure to lead them to victory. Tower and town, as he advanced, went down before him; and the French general, D'Aubigny, soon saw himself reduced to the necessity of making the best terms he could with his conqueror, and evacuating the province altogether. The submission of Calabria was speedily followed by that of the few remaining cities in other quarters, still garrisoned by the French; comprehending the last rood of territory possessed by Charles the Eighth in the kingdom of Naples.[35]

Total expulsion of the French.

---

[35] Giovio, Hist. sui Temporis, lib. 4, p. 139. — Zurita, Hist. del Rey Hernando, lib. 2, cap. 30, 33. — Guicciardini, Istoria, lib. 3, p. 160. — Giannone, Istoria di Napoli, tom. iii. lib. 29, cap. 3.

Our narrative now leads us on the beaten track of Italian history. I have endeavoured to make the reader acquainted with the peculiar character and pretensions of the principal Spanish authorities, on whom I have relied in the progress of the work. This would be superfluous in regard to the Italian who enjoy the rank of classics, not only in their own country, but throughout Europe, and have furnished the earliest models among the moderns of historic composition. Fortunately, two of the most eminent of them, Guicciardini and Paolo Giovio, lived at the period of our narrative, and have

Remarks on Guicciardini and Giovio.

embraced the whole extent of it in their histories. These two writers, besides the attractions of elegant scholarship, and talent, occupied a position which enabled them to take a clear view of all the principal political movements of their age; circumstances, which have made their accounts of infinite value in respect to foreign transactions, as well as domestic. Guicciardini was a conspicuous actor in the scenes he describes; and a long residence at the court of Ferdinand the Catholic opened to him the most authentic sources of information in regard to Spain. Giovio, from his intimate relations with the principal persons of his time, had also access to the best sources of knowledge, while in the notice of foreign transactions he was but

little exposed to those venal influences, which led him too often to employ the golden or iron pen of history as interest dictated. Unfortunately, a lamentable hiatus occurs in his greatest work, "Historiæ sui Temporis," embracing the whole period intervening between the end of Charles VIII.'s expedition and the accession of Leo X., in 1513. At the time of the memorable sack of Rome by the Duke of Bourbon, in 1527, Giovio deposited his manuscript, with a quantity of plate, in an iron chest, which he hid in an obscure corner of the church of Santa Maria sopra Minerva. The treasure, however, did not escape the searching eyes of two Spanish soldiers, who broke open the chest, and one of them seized on the plate, regarding the papers as of no value. The other, not being quite such a fool, says Giovio, preserved such of the manuscripts as were on vellum, and ornamented with rich bindings, but threw away what was written on paper. The part thus thrown away contained six books, relating to the period above mentioned, which were never afterwards recovered. The soldier brought the remainder to

their author, who bought them at the price of a vacant benefice, which he persuaded the pope to confer on the freebooter, in his native land of Cordova. It is not often that simony has found so good an apology. The deficiency, although never repaired by Giovio, was in some degree supplied by his biographies of eminent men, and, among others, by that of Gonsalvo de Cordova, in which he has collected with great industry all the events of any interest in the life of this great commander. The narrative is in general corroborated by the Spanish authorities, and contains some additional particulars, especially respecting his early life, which Giovio's personal intimacy with the principal characters of the period might easily have furnished.

This portion of our story is, moreover, illustrated by the labors of M. Sismondi, in his "Républiques Italiennes," which may undoubtedly claim to be ranked among the most remarkable historical achievements of our time; whether we consider the dexterous management of the narrative, or the admirable spirit of philosophy by which it is illumined. It must be admitted, that he has perfectly succeeded in unravelling the intricate web of Italian politics; and, notwithstanding the complicated, and, indeed, motley character of his subject, the historian has left a uniform and harmonious impression on the mind of the reader. This he has accomplished, by keeping constantly in view the principle which regulated all the various movements of the complex machinery; so that his narrative becomes, what he terms it in his English abridgment, a history of Italian liberty. By keeping this principle steadily before him, he has been able to solve much that hitherto was dark and problematical in his subject; and, if he has occasionally sacrificed something to theory, he has, on the whole, pursued the investigation in a truly philosophical manner, and arrived at results the most honorable and cheering to humanity.

Fortunately, his own mind was deeply penetrated with reverence for the free institutions, which he has analyzed. If it is too much to say, that the historian of republics should be himself a republican, it is at least true, that his soul should be penetrated to its very depths with the spirit which animates them. No one, who is not smitten with the love of freedom, can furnish the key to much that is enigmatical in her character, and reconcile his readers to the harsh and repulsive features, that she sometimes wears, by revealing the beauty and grandeur of the soul within.

That portion of our narrative which is incorporated with Italian story, is too small to occupy much space on Sismondi's plan. He has discussed it, moreover, in a manner not very favorable to the Spaniards, whom he seems to have regarded with somewhat of the aversion, with which an Italian of the sixteenth century viewed the ultramontane barbarians of Europe. Perhaps the reader may find some advantage in contemplating another side of the picture, and studying the less familiar details presented by the Spanish authorities.

CHAPTER III

ITALIAN WARS.—GONSALVO SUCCOURS THE POPE.—TREATY
WITH FRANCE.—ORGANIZATION OF THE SPANISH MILITIA.

1496 — 1498.

Gonsalvo Succours the Pope.—Storms Ostia.—Reception in Rome.
—Peace with France.—Ferdinand's Reputation advanced by his
Conduct in the War.—Organization of the Militia.

PART
II.
———
War on the
side of
Roussillon.

IT had been arranged by the treaty of Venice,
that, while the allies were carrying on the war in
Naples, the emperor elect and the king of Spain
should make a diversion in their favor, by invading
the French frontiers. Ferdinand had performed
his part of the engagement. Ever since the beginning of the war, he had maintained a large
force along the borders from Fontarabia to Perpi-
gnan. In 1496, the regular army kept in pay
amounted to ten thousand horse and fifteen thousand
foot; which, together with the Sicilian armament,
necessarily involved an expenditure exceedingly
heavy under the financial pressure occasioned by
the Moorish war. The command of the levies in
Roussillon was given to Don Enrique Enriquez de
Guzman, who, far from acting on the defensive,
carried his men repeatedly over the border, sweeping off fifteen or twenty thousand head of cattle in

a single foray, and ravaging the country as far as Carcassona and Narbonne.[1] The French, who had concentrated a considerable force in the south, retaliated by similar inroads, in one of which they succeeded in surprising the fortified town of Salsas. The works, however, were in so dilapidated a state that the place was scarcely tenable, and it was abandoned on the approach of the Spanish army. A truce soon followed, which put an end to further operations in that quarter.[2]

The submission of Calabria seemed to leave no further occupation for the arms of the Great Captain in Italy. Before quitting that country, however, he engaged in an adventure, which, as narrated by his biographers, forms a brilliant episode to his regular campaigns. Ostia, the seaport of Rome, was, among the places in the papal territory, forcibly occupied by Charles the Eighth, and on his retreat had been left to a French garrison under the command of a Biscayan adventurer named Menaldo Guerri. The place was so situated as entirely to command the mouth of the Tiber, enabling the piratical horde who garrisoned it almost wholly to destroy the commerce of Rome, and even to reduce the city to great distress for want of provis-

[1] Zurita, Hist. del Rey Hernando, lib. 2, cap. 12 – 14, 16, 24.
Giovio says, in allusion to King Ferdinand's show of preparation on the frontier, " Ferdinandus, maximè cautus et pecuniæ tenax, speciem ingentis coacti exercitûs ad deterrendos hostes præbere, quam bellum gerere mallet, quum id sine ingenti pecuniâ administrari non posse intelligeret." Hist. sui Temporis, p. 140.

[2] Zurita, Hist. del Rey Hernando, lib. 2, cap. 35, 36. — Abarca, Reyes de Aragon, rey 30, cap. 9. — Garibay, Compendio, tom. ii. lib. 19, cap. 5. — Comines, Mémoires, liv. 8, chap. 23. — Peter Martyr, Opus Epist., epist 169.

PART
II.

The pope
asks the aid
of Gonsalvo.

ions. The imbecile government, incapable of de-
fending itself, implored Gonsalvo's aid in dislodging
this nest of formidable freebooters. The Spanish
general, who was now at leisure, complied with the
pontiff's solicitations, and soon after presented himself before Ostia with his little corps of troops,
amounting in all to three hundred horse and fifteen
hundred foot.[3]

Storming
and capture
of Ostia.

Guerri, trusting to the strength of his defences,
refused to surrender. Gonsalvo, after coolly preparing his batteries, opened a heavy cannonade on
the place, which at the end of five days effected a
practicable breach in the walls. In the mean time,
Garcilasso de la Vega, the Castilian ambassador at
the papal court, who could not bear to remain inactive so near the field where laurels were to be won,
arrived to Gonsalvo's support, with a handful of his
own countrymen resident in Rome. This gallant
little band, scaling the walls on the opposite side to
that assailed by Gonsalvo, effected an entrance into
the town, while the garrison was occupied with
maintaining the breach against the main body of
the Spaniards. Thus surprised, and hemmed in
on both sides, Guerri and his associates made no
further resistance, but surrendered themselves prisoners of war ; and Gonsalvo, with more clemency
than was usually shown on such occasions, stopped
the carnage, and reserved his captives to grace his
entry into the capital.[4]

---

[3] Giovio, Vita Magni Gonsalvi,
lib. 1, p. 221. — Chrónica del Gran
Capitan, cap. 30. — Zurita, Hist.
del Rey Hernando, lib. 3, cap. 1.

— Villeneuve, Mémoires, p. 317
[4] Giovio, Vita Magni Gonsalvi
p. 222. — Quintana, Españoles Célebres, tom. i. p. 234.

This was made a few days after, with all the
pomp of a Roman triumph. The Spanish general
entered by the gate of Ostia, at the head of his
martial squadrons in battle array, with colors flying
and music playing, while the rear was brought up
by the captive chief and his confederates, so long
the terror, now the derision of the populace. The
balconies and windows were crowded with spectators, and the streets lined with multitudes, who
shouted forth the name of Gonsalvo de Cordova, the
" deliverer of Rome ! " The procession took its
way through the principal streets of the city towards the Vatican, where Alexander the Sixth
awaited its approach, seated under a canopy of
state in the chief saloon of the palace, surrounded
by his great ecclesiastics and nobility. On Gonsalvo's entrance, the cardinals rose to receive him.
The Spanish general knelt down to receive the
benediction of the pope ; but the latter, raising him
up, kissed him on the forehead, and complimented
him with the golden rose, which the Holy See was
accustomed to dispense as the reward of its most
devoted champions.

In the conversation which ensued, Gonsalvo obtained the pardon of Guerri and his associates, and
an exemption from taxes for the oppressed inhabitants of Ostia. In a subsequent part of the discourse, the pope taking occasion most inopportunely
to accuse the Spanish sovereigns of unfavorable dispositions towards himself, Gonsalvo replied with
much warmth, enumerating the various good offices
rendered by them to the church ; and, roundly

taxing the pope with ingratitude, somewhat bluntly
advised him to reform his life and conversation,
which brought scandal on all Christendom. His
Holiness testified no indignation at this unsavoury
rebuke of the Great Captain, though, as the historians with some simplicity inform us, he was greatly
surprised to find the latter so fluent in discourse,
and so well instructed in matters foreign to his
profession.[5]

Gonsalvo experienced the most honorable reception from King Frederic on his return to Naples.
During his continuance there, he was lodged and
sumptuously entertained in one of the royal fortresses ; and the grateful monarch requited his services
with the title of Duke of St. Angelo, and an estate,
in Abruzzo, containing three thousand vassals. He
had before pressed these honors on the victor, who
declined accepting them till he had obtained the
consent of his own sovereigns. Soon after, Gonsalvo, quitting Naples, revisited Sicily, where he
adjusted certain differences which had arisen betwixt the viceroy and the inhabitants respecting
the revenues of the island. Then embarking with
his whole force, he reached the shores of Spain in
the month of August, 1498. His return to his native land was greeted with a general enthusiasm far
more grateful to his patriotic heart, than any homage or honors conferred by foreign princes. Isabella welcomed him with pride and satisfaction, as

[5] Giovio, Vita Magni Gonsalvi,
p. 222. — Zurita, Hist. del Rey
Hernando, lib. 3, cap. 1. — Guicciardini, Istoria, lib. 3, p. 175. —
Chrónica del Gran Capitan, cap.
30.

having fully vindicated her preference of him to his
more experienced rivals for the difficult post of
Italy; and Ferdinand did not hesitate to declare,
that the Calabrian campaigns reflected more lustre
on his crown, than the conquest of Granada.[6]

The total expulsion of the French from Naples
brought hostilities between that nation and Spain
to a close. The latter had gained her point, and
the former had little heart to resume so disastrous
an enterprise. Before this event, indeed, overtures
had been made by the French court for a separate
treaty with Spain. The latter, however, was unwilling to enter into any compact, without the
participation of her allies. After the total aban
donment of the French enterprise, there seemed to
exist no further pretext for prolonging the war.
The Spanish government, moreover, had little
cause for satisfaction with its confederates. The
emperor had not coöperated in the descent on the
enemy's frontier, according to agreement ; nor had
the allies ever reimbursed Spain for the heavy
charges incurred in fulfilling her part of the engagements. The Venetians were taken up with
securing to themselves as much of the Neapolitan
territory as they could, by way of indemnification
for their own expenses.[7] The duke of Milan had
already made a separate treaty with King Charles.

---

[6] Giovio, Vita Magni Gonsalvi,
p. 223.—Chrónica del Gran Cap-
tan, cap. 31, 32.—Zurita, Hist.
del Rey Hernando, lib. 3, cap. 38.

[7] Comines says, with some *na-
iveté*, in reference to the places in
Naples which the Venetians had

got into their possession, "Je croy
que leur intention n'est point de
les rendre ; car ils ne l'ont point
de coustume quand elles leur sont
bienséantes comme sont cellescy,
qui sont du costé de leur goufre de
Venise." Mémoires, p. 194.

In short, every member of the league, after the first alarm subsided, had shown itself ready to sacrifice the common weal to its own private ends. With these causes of disgust, the Spanish government consented to a truce with France, to begin for itself on the 5th of March, and for the allies, if they chose to be included in it, seven weeks later, and to continue till the end of October, 1497. This truce was subsequently prolonged, and, after the death of Charles the Eighth, terminated in a definitive treaty of peace, signed at Marcoussi, August 5th, 1498. [8]

Ferdinand's views respecting Naples.

In the discussions to which these arrangements gave rise, the project is said to have been broached for the conquest and division of the kingdom of Naples by the combined powers of France and Spain, which was carried into effect some years later. According to Comines, the proposition originated with the Spanish court, although it saw fit, in a subsequent period of the negotiations, to disavow the fact. [9] The Spanish writers, on the other hand, impute the first suggestion of it to the French, who, they say, went so far as to specify the details of the partition subsequently adopted; according to which the two Calabrias were assigned to Spain. However this may be, there is little

[8] Guicciardini, Istoria, lib. 3, p. 178. — Zurita, Hist. del Rey Hernando, lib. 2, cap. 44 ; lib. 3, cap. 13, 19, 21, 26. — Comines, Mémoires, liv. 8, chap. 23.

[9] Comines gives some curious details respecting the French embassy, which he considers to have been completely outwitted by the superior management of the Spanish government; who intended nothing further at this time by the proposal of a division, than to amuse the French court until the fate of Naples should be decided. Mémoires liv. 8, chap. 23.

doubt that Ferdinand had long since entertained the idea of asserting his claim, at some time or other, to the crown of Naples. He, as well as his father, and indeed the whole nation, had beheld with dissatisfaction the transfer of what they deemed their rightful inheritance, purchased by the blood and treasure of Aragon, to an illegitimate branch of the family. The accession of Frederic, in particular, who came to the throne with the support of the Angevin party, the old enemies of Aragon, had given great umbrage to the Spanish monarch.

The Castilian envoy, Garcilasso de la Vega, agreeably to the instructions of his court, urged Alexander the Sixth to withhold the investiture of the kingdom from Frederic, but unavailingly, as the pope's interests were too closely connected, by marriage, with those of the royal family of Naples. Under these circumstances, it was somewhat doubtful what course Gonsalvo should be directed to pursue in the present exigency. That prudent commander, however, found the new monarch too strong in the affections of his people to be disturbed at present. All that now remained for Ferdinand, therefore, was to rest contented with the possession of the strong posts pledged for the reimbursement of his expenses in the war, and to make such use of the correspondence which the late campaigns had opened to him in Calabria, that, when the time arrived for action, he might act with effect. [10]

10 Zurita, Hist. del Rey Hernando, lib. 2, cap. 26, 33. — Mariana, Hist. de España, lib. 26, cap. 16. — Salazar de Mendoza, Monarquia, tom. i. lib. 3, cap. 10.

Ferdinand's conduct through the whole of the Italian war had greatly enhanced his reputation throughout Europe for sagacity and prudence. It afforded a most advantageous comparison with that of his rival, Charles the Eighth, whose very first act had been the surrender of so important a territory as Roussillon. The construction of the treaty relating to this, indeed, laid the Spanish monarch open to the imputation of artifice. But this, at least, did no violence to the political maxims of the age, and only made him regarded as the more shrewd and subtile diplomatist; while, on the other hand, he appeared before the world in the imposing attitude of the defender of the church, and of the rights of his injured kinsman. His influence had been clearly discernible in every operation of moment, whether civil or military. He had been most active, through his ambassadors at Genoa, Venice, and Rome, in stirring up the great Italian confederacy, which eventually broke the power of King Charles; and his representations had tended, as much as any other cause, to alarm the jealousy of Sforza, to fix the vacillating politics of Alexander, and to quicken the cautious and dilatory movements of Venice. He had shown equal vigor in action; and contributed mainly to the success of the war by his operations on the side of Roussillon, and still more in Calabria. On the latter, indeed, he had not lavished any extraordinary expenditure; a circumstance partly attributable to the state of his finances, severely taxed, as already noticed, by the Granadine war, as well as by the operations in

Roussillon, but in part, also, to his habitual frugal-
ity, which, with a very different spirit from that of
his illustrious consort, always stinted the measure
of his supplies to the bare exigency of the occasion.
Fortunately the genius of the Great Captain was
so fruitful in resources, as to supply every deficiency ; enabling him to accomplish such brilliant
results, as effectually concealed any poverty of
preparation on the part of his master.

CHAPTER
III.

Influence of
the war on
Spain

The Italian wars were of signal importance to
the Spanish nation. Until that time, they had
been cooped up within the narrow limits of the
Peninsula, uninstructed and taking little interest in
the concerns of the rest of Europe. A new world
was now opened to them. They were taught to
measure their own strength by collision with other
powers on a common scene of action ; and, success
inspiring them with greater confidence, seemed to
beckon them on towards the field, where they were
destined to achieve still more splendid triumphs.

This war afforded them also a most useful lesson
of tactics. The war of Granada had insensibly
trained up a hardy militia, patient and capable of
every privation and fatigue, and brought under
strict subordination. This was a great advance
beyond the independent and disorderly habits of
the feudal service. A most valuable corps of light
troops had been formed, schooled in all the wild,
irregular movements of guerrilla warfare. But the
nation was still defective in that steady, well-disci-
plined infantry, which, in the improved condition

PART
II.

of military science, seemed destined to decide the
fate of battles in Europe thenceforward.

The Calabrian campaigns, which were suited in
some degree to the display of their own tactics,
fortunately gave the Spaniards opportunity for
studying at leisure those of their adversaries. The
lesson was not lost. Before the end of the war
important innovations were made in the discipline
and arms of the Spanish soldier. The Swiss pike,
or lance, which, as has been already noticed, Gonsalvo de Cordova had mingled with the short sword
of his own legions, now became the regular weapon of one third of the infantry. The division of
the various corps in the cavalry and infantry services was arranged on more scientific principles,
and the whole, in short, completely reorganized. [11]

Organization
of the mili-
ia.

Before the end of the war, preparations were
made for embodying a national militia, which
should take the place of the ancient hermandad.
Laws were passed regulating the equipment of
every individual according to his property. A
man's arms were declared not liable for debt, even
to the crown; and smiths and other artificers were
restricted, under severe penalties, from working
them up into other articles. [12] In 1496, a census

11 Mem. de la Acad. de Hist.,
tom. vi. Ilust. 6.—Zurita, Hist.
del Rey Hernando, lib. 3, cap. 6.

The ancient Spaniards, who
were as noted as the modern, for
the temper and finish of their
blades, used short swords, in the
management of which they were
very adroit. "Hispano," says Livy,
"punctim magis, quam cæsim, ad-
sueto petere hostem, brevitate ha-

biles [gladii] et cum mucronibus."
(Hist., lib. 22, cap. 47.) Sandoval
notices the short sword, "cortas
espadas," as the peculiar weapon of the Spanish soldier in the
twelfth century. Historia de los
Reyes de Castilla y de Leon, (Madrid, 1792,) tom. ii. p. 240.

12 Pragmáticas del Reyno, fol.
83, 127, 129.

The former of these ordinances,

was taken of all persons capable of bearing arms ; and by an ordinance, dated at Valladolid, February 22d, in the same year, it was provided that one out of every twelve inhabitants, between twenty and forty-five years of age, should be enlisted in the service of the state, whether for foreign war, or the suppression of disorders at home. The remaining eleven were liable to be called on in case of urgent necessity. These recruits were to be paid during actual service, and excused from taxes ; the only legal exempts were the clergy, hidalgos, and paupers. A general review and inspection of

dated Taraçona, Sept. 18th, 1495, is extremely precise in specifying the appointments required for each individual.

Among other improvements, introduced somewhat earlier, may be mentioned that of organizing and thoroughly training a small corps of heavy-armed cavalry, amounting to twenty-five hundred. The number of men-at-arms had been greatly reduced in the kingdom of late years, in consequence of the exclusive demand for the *ginetes* in the Moorish war. Oviedo, Quincuagenas, MS.

Ordinances were also passed for encouraging the breed of horses, which had suffered greatly from the preference very generally given by the Spaniards to mules. This had been carried to such a length, that, while it was nearly impossible, according to Bernaldez, to mount ten or twelve thousand cavalry on horses, ten times that number could be provided with mules. (Reyes Católicos, MS., cap. 184.) " E porque si a esto se diesse lugar," says one of the *pragmáticas*, adverting to this evil, " muy prestamente se perderia en nuestros reynos la nobleza de la cauelleria que en ellos

suele auer, e se oluidaria el exercicio militar de que en los tiempos passados nuestra nacion de España ha alcançado gran fama e loor ; ' it was ordered that no person in the kingdom should be allowed to keep a mule, unless he owned a horse also ; and that none but ecclesiastics and women should be allowed the use of mules in the saddle. These edicts were enforced with the utmost rigor, the king himself setting the example of conformity to them. By these seasonable precautions, the breed of Spanish horses, so long noted throughout Europe, was restored to its ancient credit, and the mule consigned to the humble and appropriate offices of drudgery, or raised only for exportation. For these and similar provisions, see Pragmáticas del Reyno, fol. 127 – 132.

Matéo Aleman's whimsical *picaresco* novel, Guzman d' Alfarache, contains a comic adventure, showing the excessive rigor with which the edict against mules was enforced, as late as the close of Philip II.'s reign. The passage is extracted in Roscoe's elegant version of the Spanish Novelists, Vol. I. p. 132.

arms were to take place every year, in the months
of March and September, when prizes were to be
awarded to those best accoutred, and most expert
in the use of their weapons.   Such were the judicious regulations by which every citizen, without
being withdrawn from his regular occupation, was
gradually trained up for the national defence ; and
which, without the oppressive incumbrance of a
numerous standing army, placed the whole effective
force of the country, prompt and fit for action, at
the disposal of the government, whenever the public
good should call for it. [13]

[13] See a copy of the ordinance
taken from the Archives of Simancas; apud Mem. de la Acad. de
Hist., tom. vi. apend. 13.

When Francis I., who was destined to feel the effects of this careful military discipline, beheld, during his detention in Spain in the
beginning of the following century,
striplings with scarce down upon
the chin, all armed with swords at
their sides, he is said to have cried
out, " O bienaventurada España,
que pare y cria los hombres arma-
dos ! " (L. Marineo, Cosas Memorables, lib. 5.)   An exclamation
not unworthy of a Napoleon, — or
an Attila.

CHAPTER IV.

ALLIANCES OF THE ROYAL FAMILY. — DEATH OF PRINCE JOHN
AND PRINCESS ISABELLA.

Royal Family of Castile. — Matrimonial Alliances with Portugal. —
With Austria. — Marriage of John and Margaret. — Death of Prince
John. — The Queen's Resignation. — Independence of the Cortes of
Aragon. — Death of the Princess Isabella. — Recognition of her in-
fant Son Miguel.

THE credit and authority which the Castilian
sovereigns established by the success of their arms,
were greatly raised by the matrimonial connexions
which they formed for their children. This was
too important a spring of their policy to be passed
over in silence. Their family consisted of one son
and four daughters, whom they carefully educated
in a manner befitting their high rank; and who
repaid their solicitude by exemplary filial obedience,
and the early manifestation of virtues rare even in
a private station.[1] They seem to have inherited
many of the qualities which distinguished their

[1] The princess Doña Isabel, the eldest daughter, was born at Due-ñas, October 1st, 1470. Their second child and only son, Juan, prince of the Asturias, was not born until eight years later, June 30th, 1478, at Seville. Doña Juana, whom the queen used playfully to call her "mother-in-law," *suegra*, from her resemblance to King Ferdinand's mother, was born at Toledo, No-vember 6th, 1479. Doña Maria was born at Cordova, in 1482, and Doña Catalina, the fifth and last child, at Alcalá de Henares, December 5th, 1485. The daughters all lived to reign; but their brilliant destinies were clouded with domestic afflictions, from which royalty could afford no refuge. Carbajal, Anales, MS., loc. mult.

illustrious mother; great decorum and dignity of manners, combined with ardent sensibilities, and unaffected piety, which, at least in the eldest and favorite daughter, Isabella, was, unhappily, strongly tinctured with bigotry. They could not, indeed, pretend to their mother's comprehensive mind, and talent for business, although there seems to have been no deficiency in these respects; or, if any, it was most effectually supplied by their excellent education. [2]

Joanna
Beltraneja.

The marriage of the princess Isabella with Alonso, the heir of the Portuguese crown, in 1490, has been already noticed. This had been eagerly desired by her parents, not only for the possible contingency, which it afforded, of bringing the various monarchies of the Peninsula under one head, (a design of which they never wholly lost sight,) but from the wish to conciliate a formidable neighbour, who possessed various means of annoyance, which he had shown no reluctance to exert. The reigning monarch, John the Second, a bold and crafty prince, had never forgotten his ancient quarrel with the Spanish sovereigns in support of their rival Joanna Beltraneja, or Joanna the Nun, as she was generally called in the Castilian court after she had taken the veil. John, in open contempt of the treaty of Alcantara, and indeed of all monastic rule, had not only removed his relative from the convent of Santa Clara, but had permitted her to assume a royal

[2] The only exception to these remarks, was that afforded by the infanta Joanna, whose unfortunate eccentricities, developed in later life, must be imputed, indeed, to bodily infirmity.

state, and subscribe herself "I the Queen." This empty insult he accompanied with more serious efforts to form such a foreign alliance for the liberated princess as should secure her the support of some arm more powerful than his own, and enable her to renew the struggle for her inheritance with better chance of success.[3] These flagrant proceedings had provoked the admonitions of the Roman see, and had formed the topic, as may be believed, of repeated, though ineffectual remonstrance from the court of Castile.[4]

It seemed probable that the union of the princess of the Asturias with the heir of Portugal, as originally provided by the treaty of Alcantara, would so far identify the interests of the respective parties as to remove all further cause of disquietude. The new bride was received in Portugal in a spirit which gave cordial assurance of these friendly relations for the future ; and the court of Lisbon celebrated the auspicious nuptials with the gorgeous magnificence, for which, at this period of its successful enterprise, it was distinguished above every other court in Christendom.[5]

Marriage of the princess Isabella.

*1 4 9 0
Nov. 22*

---

[3] Nine different matches were proposed for Joanna in the course of her life ; but they all vanished into air, and "the excellent lady," as she was usually called by the Portuguese, died as she had lived, in single blessedness, at the ripe age of sixty-eight. In the Mem. de la Acad. de Hist., tom. vi., the 19th Ilustracion is devoted to this topic, in regard to which father Florez shows sufficient ignorance, or inaccuracy. Reynas Cathólicas, tom. ii. p. 780.

[4] Instructions relating to this matter, written with the queen's own hand, still exist in the archives of Simancas. Mem. de la Acad. de Hist., ubi supra.

[5] La Clède, Histoire de Portugal, tom. iv. p. 100.

The Portuguese historian, Faria y Sousa, expends half a dozen folio pages on these royal revelries, which cost six months' preparation, and taxed the wits of the most finished artists and artificers in France, England, Flanders, Cas-

Alonso's death, a few months after this event, however, blighted the fair hopes which had begun to open of a more friendly feeling between the two countries. His unfortunate widow, unable to endure the scenes of her short-lived happiness, soon withdrew into her own country to seek such consolation as she could find in the bosom of her family. There, abandoning herself to the melancholy regrets to which her serious and pensive temper naturally disposed her, she devoted her hours to works of piety and benevolence, resolved to enter no more into engagements, which had thrown so dark a cloud over the morning of her life.[6]

On King John's death, in 1495, the crown of Portugal devolved on Emanuel, that enlightened monarch, who had the glory in the very commencement of his reign of solving the grand problem, which had so long perplexed the world, of the existence of an undiscovered passage to the east. This prince had conceived a passion for the young and beautiful Isabella during her brief residence in Lisbon; and, soon after his accession to the throne, he despatched an embassy to the Spanish court inviting her to share it with him. But the princess, wedded to the memory of her early love, declined the proposals, notwithstanding they were strongly seconded by the wishes of her parents, who, how-

tile, and Portugal. (Europa Portuguesa, tom. ii. pp. 452 et seq.) We see, throughout, the same luxury of spectacle, the same elegant games of chivalry, as the tilt of reeds, the rings, and the like, which the Castilians adopted from the Spanish Arabs.

[6] Zurita, Hist. del Rey Hernando, tom. v. fol. 38. — Abarca Reyes de Aragon, tom. ii. fol. 312

ever, were unwilling to constrain their daughter's
inclinations on so delicate a point, trusting perhaps
to the effects of time, and the perseverance of her
royal suitor.[7]

In the mean while, the Catholic sovereigns were
occupied with negotiations for the settlement of the
other members of their family.   The ambitious
schemes of Charles the Eighth established a community of interests among the great European
states, such as had never before existed, or, at least,
been understood ; and the intimate relations thus
introduced naturally led to intermarriages between
the principal powers, who, until this period seem
to have been severed almost as far asunder as if
oceans had rolled between them.   The Spanish
monarchs, in particular, had rarely gone beyond the
limits of the Peninsula for their family alliances.
The new confederacy into which Spain had entered, now opened the way to more remote connexions, which were destined to exercise a permanent influence on the future politics of Europe.   It
was while Charles the Eighth was wasting his time
at Naples, that the marriages were arranged be-

[7] Zurita, Hist. del Rey Hernando, tom. v. fol. 78, 82. — La Clède,
Hist. de Portugal, tom. iv. p. 95.
—Peter Martyr, Opus Epist., epist.
146.

Martyr, in a letter written at the
close of 1496, thus speaks of the
princess Isabella's faithful attachment to her husband's memory ;
" Mira fuit hujus fœminæ in abji-
ciendis secundis nuptiis constantia.
Tanta est ejus modestia, tanta vi-

dualis castitas, ut nec mensâ post
mariti mortem comederit, nec lauti
quicquam degustaverit.   Jejuniis
sese vigiliisque ita maceravit, ut sic-
co stipite siccior sit effecta.   Suf-
fulta rubore perturbatur, quando-
cunque de jugali thalamo sermo
intexitur.   Parentum tamen aliquando precibus, veluti olfacimus,
inflectetur.   Viget fama, futuram
vestri regis Emmanuelis uxorem."
Epist. 171.

tween the royal houses of Spain and Austria, by
which the weight of these great powers was thrown
into the same scale, and the balance of Europe un-
settled for the greater part of the following century.[8]

The treaty provided, that Prince John, the heir
of the Spanish monarchies, then in his eighteenth
year, should be united with the princess Margaret,
daughter of the emperor Maximilian ; and that the
archduke Philip, his son and heir, and sovereign of
the Low Countries in his mother's right, should
marry Joanna, second daughter of Ferdinand and
Isabella.   No dowry was to be required with either
princess.[9]

In the course of the following year, arrangements were also concluded for the marriage of the
youngest daughter of the Castilian sovereigns with
a prince of the royal house of England, the first
example of the kind for more than a century.[10]
Ferdinand had cultivated the good-will of Henry
the Seventh, in the hope of drawing him into the
confederacy against the French monarch ; and in

[8] Zurita, Hist. del Rey Hernando, tom. v. fol. 63.

[9] Zurita, Hist. del Rey Hernando, tom. v. lib. 2, cap. 5. — Ferreras, Hist. d'Espagne, tom. viii.
p. 160.

[10] I believe there is no instance
of such a union, save that of John
of Gaunt, duke of Lancaster, with
Doña Constanza, daughter of Peter
the Cruel, in 1371, from whom
Queen Isabella was lineally descended on the father's side.

The title of *Prince of the Asturias*, appropriated to the heir apparent of Castile, was first created
for the infant Don Henry, afterwards Henry III., on occasion of
his marriage with John of Gaunt's
daughter, in 1388.   It was pro-
fessedly in imitation of the English
title of Prince of Wales ; and the
Asturias were selected as that portion of the ancient Gothic monarchy, which had never bowed beneath the Saracen yoke.   Florez,
Reynas Cathólicas, tom. ii. pp. 708
–715. — Mendoza, Dignidades, lib
3, cap. 23.

this had not wholly failed, although the wary king seems to have come into it rather as a silent partner, if we may so say, than with the intention of affording any open or very active coöperation.[11] The relations of amity between the two courts were still further strengthened by the treaty of marriage above alluded to, finally adjusted October 1st, 1496, and ratified the following year, between Arthur, prince of Wales, and the infanta Doña Catalina, conspicuous in English history, equally for her misfortunes and her virtues, as Catharine of Aragon.[12] The French viewed with no little jealousy the progress of these various negotiations, which they zealously endeavoured to thwart by all the artifices of diplomacy. But King Ferdinand had sufficient address to secure in his interests persons of the highest credit at the courts of Henry and Maximil-

[11] Zurita, Hist. del Rey Hernando, lib. 2, cap. 25. — Rymer, Fœdera, (London, 1727,) vol. xii. pp. 638 – 642.
Ferdinand used his good offices to mediate a peace between Henry VII. and the king of Scots; and it is a proof of the respect entertained for him by both these monarchs, that they agreed to refer their disputes to his arbitration. (Rymer, Fœdera, vol. xii. p. 671.) "And so," says the old chronicler Hall, of the English prince, "beying confederate and alied by treatie and league with al his neighbors, he gratefied with his moost heartie thanks kyng Ferdinand and the quene his wife, to which woman none other was comparable in her tyme, for that they were the mediators, organes, and instrumentes by the which the truce was concluded betwene the Scottish kynge and him, and rewarded his ambassa-

doure moost liberally and bountefully." Chronicle, p. 483.
[12] See the marriage treaty in Rymer. (Fœdera, vol. xii. pp. 658 – 666.) The marriage had been arranged between the Spanish and English courts as far back as March, 1489, when the elder of the parties had not yet reached the fifth year of her age. This was confirmed by another, more full and definite, in the following year, 1490. By this treaty, it was stipulated, that Catharine's portion should be 200,000 gold crowns, one half to be paid down at the date of her marriage, and the remainder in two equal payments in the course of the two years ensuing. The prince of Wales was to settle on her one third of the revenues of the principality of Wales, the dukedom of Cornwall, and earldom of Chester. Rymer, Fœdera, vol. xii. pp. 411 – 417.

PART
II.

Joanna em-
.uarks.

ian, who promptly acquainted him with the intrigues of the French government, and effectually aided in counteracting them.[13]

The English connexion was necessarily deferred for some years, on account of the youth of the parties, neither of whom exceeded eleven years of age. No such impediment occurred in regard to the German alliances, and measures were taken at once for providing a suitable conveyance for the infanta Joanna into Flanders, which should bring back the princess Margaret on its return. By the end of summer, in 1496, a fleet consisting of one hundred and thirty vessels, large and small, strongly manned and thoroughly equipped with all the means of defence against the French cruisers, was got ready for sea in the ports of Guipuscoa and Biscay.[14] The whole was placed under the direction of Don Fadrique Enriquez, admiral of Castile, who carried with him a splendid show of chivalry, chiefly drawn from the northern provinces of the kingdom. A more gallant and beautiful armada never before quitted the shores of Spain. The infanta Joanna, attended by a numerous suite, arrived

13 " Procuro," says Zurita, " que se effectuassen los matrimonios de sus hijos, no solo con promesas, pero con dadivas que se hizieron a los privados de aquéllos principes, que en ello entendian." Hist. del Rey Hernando, lib. 2, cap. 3.

14 Historians differ, as usual, as to the strength of this armament. Martyr makes it 110 vessels, and 10,000 soldiers, (Opus Epist., epist. 168;) while Bernaldez carries the number to 130 sail, and 25,000 soldiers, (Reyes Católicos, MS., cap. 153.) Ferreras adopts the latter estimate, (tom. viii. p. 173.) Martyr may have intended only the galleys and regular troops, while Bernaldez, more loosely, included vessels and seamen of every description. See also the royal ordinances, ap. Coleccion de Cédulas, (tom. i. nos. 79, 80, 82,) whose language implies a very large number, without specifying it.

on board the fleet towards the end of August, at the port of Laredo, on the eastern borders of the Asturias, where she took a last farewell of the queen her mother, who had postponed the hour of separation as long as possible, by accompanying her daughter to the place of embarkation.

The weather, soon after her departure, became extremely rough and tempestuous; and it was so long before any tidings of the squadron reached the queen, that her affectionate heart was filled with the most distressing apprehensions. She sent for the oldest and most experienced navigators in these boisterous northern seas, consulting them, says Martyr, day and night on the probable causes of delay, the prevalent courses of the winds at that season, and the various difficulties and dangers of the voyage; bitterly regretting that the troubles with France prevented any other means of communication, than the treacherous element to which she had trusted her daughter.[15] Her spirits were still further depressed at this juncture by the death of her own mother, the dowager Isabella, who, under the mental infirmity with which she had been visited for many years, had always experienced the most devoted attention from her daughter, who ministered to her necessities with her own hands, and watched over her declining years with the most tender solicitude.[16]

[15] Peter Martyr, Opus Epist., epist. 172. — Carbajal, Anales, MS., año 1496.—Mariana, Hist. de España, tom. ii. lib. 26, cap. 12.

[16] Carbajal, Anales, MS., año 1496. — Peter Martyr, Opus Epist., epist. 172.

At length, the long-desired intelligence came of the arrival of the Castilian fleet at its place of destination. It had been so grievously shattered, however, by tempests, as to require being refitted in the ports of England. Several of the vessels were lost, and many of Joanna's attendants perished from the inclemency of the weather, and the numerous hardships to which they were exposed. The infanta, however, happily reached Flanders in safety, and, not long after, her nuptials with the archduke Philip were celebrated in the city of Lisle with all suitable pomp and solemnity.

Margaret of
Austria.

The fleet was detained until the ensuing winter, to transport the destined bride of the young prince of the Asturias to Spain. This lady, who had been affianced in her cradle to Charles the Eighth of France, had received her education in the court of Paris. On her intended husband's marriage with the heiress of Brittany, she had been returned to her native land under circumstances of indignity never to be forgiven by the house of Austria. She was now in the seventeenth year of her age, and had already given ample promise of those uncommon powers of mind, which distinguished her in riper years, and of which she has left abundant evidence in various written compositions. [17]

[17] Peter Martyr, Opus Epist., epist. 174. — Garibay, Compendio, tom. ii. lib. 19, cap. 6. — Gaillard, Rivalité, tom. iii. pp. 416, 423. — Sandoval, Historia del Emperador Carlos V., (Amberes, 1681,) tom. 1. p. 2. These, comprehending her verses, public addresses, and discourse on her own life, have been collected into a single volume, under the title of "La Couronne Margaritique," Lyons, 1549, by the French writer Jean la Maire de Belges, her faithful follower, but whose greatest glory it is, to have been the instructer of Clement Marot.

On her passage to Spain, in mid winter, the
fleet encountered such tremendous gales, that part
of it was shipwrecked, and Margaret's vessel had
wellnigh foundered. She retained, however, sufficient composure amidst the perils of her situation,
to indite her own epitaph, in the form of a pleasant
distich, which Fontenelle has made the subject of
one of his amusing dialogues, where he affects to
consider the fortitude displayed by her at this awful
moment as surpassing that of the philosophic Adrian
in his dying hour, or the vaunted heroism of Cato
of Utica.[18] Fortunately, however, Margaret's epi
taph was not needed; she arrived in safety at the
port of Santander in the Asturias, early in March,
1497.

The young prince of the Asturias, accompanied
by the king his father, hastened towards the north
to receive his royal mistress, whom they met and
escorted to Burgos, where she was received with
the highest marks of satisfaction by the queen and
the whole court. Preparations were instantly made
for solemnizing the nuptials of the royal pair, after
the expiration of Lent, in a style of magnificence
such as had never before been witnessed under the
present reign. The marriage ceremony took place
on the 3d of April, and was performed by the archbishop of Toledo in the presence of the grandees

---

[18] Fontenelle, Œuvres, tom. i.
dial. 4.

' Ci gist Margot, la gentil' damoiselle
Qu'a deux maris, et encore est pucelle."

It must be allowed that Margaret's quiet *nonchalance* was much

more suited to Fontenelle's habitual
taste, than the imposing scene of
Cato's death. Indeed, the French
satirist was so averse to *scenes* of
all kinds, that he has contrived to
find a ridiculous side in this last act
of the patriot Roman.

and principal nobility of Castile, the foreign ambassadors, and the delegates from Aragon. Among these latter were the magistrates of the principal cities, clothed in their municipal insignia and crimson robes of office, who seem to have had quite as important parts assigned them by their democratic communities, in this and all similar pageants, as any of the nobility or gentry. The nuptials were followed by a brilliant succession of *fêtes*, tourneys, tilts of reeds, and other warlike spectacles, in which the matchless chivalry of Spain poured into the lists to display their magnificence and prowess in the presence of their future queen.[19] The chronicles of the day remark on the striking contrast, exhibited at these entertainments, between the gay and familiar manners of Margaret and her Flemish nobles, and the pomp and stately ceremonial of the Castilian court, to which, indeed, the Austrian princess, nurtured as she had been in a Parisian atmosphere, could never be wholly reconciled.[20]

---

[19] That these were not mere holiday sports, was proved by the melancholy death of Alonso de Cardenas, son of the comendador of Leon, who lost his life in a tourney. Oviedo, Quincuagenas, MS., bat. 1, quinc. 2, dial. 1.

[20] Carbajal, Anales, MS., año 1497. — Mariana, Hist. de España, tom. ii. lib. 26, cap. 16. — Lanuza, Historias, lib. 1, cap. 8. — Abarca, Reyes de Aragon, tom. ii. fol. 330. " Y aunque," says the last author, " a la princessa se le dexaron todos sus criados, estilos, y entretenimientos, se la advirtio, que en las ceremonias no havia de tratar a las personas Reales, y Grandes con la familiaridad y llaneza de las casas de Austria, Borgoña, y Francia, sino con la gravedad, y mesurada autoridad de los Reyes y naciones de España ! "

The sixth volume of the Spanish Academy of History contains an inventory, taken from the archives of Simancas, of the rich plate and jewels, presented to the princess Margaret on the day of her marriage. They are said to be " of such value and perfect workmanship, that the like was never before seen." (Ilust. 11, pp. 338 – 342.) Isabella had turned these baubles to good account in the war of Granada. She was too simple in her taste to attach much value to luxury of apparel.

The marriage of the heir apparent could not have been celebrated at a more auspicious period. It was in the midst of negotiations for a general peace, when the nation might reasonably hope to taste the sweets of repose, after so many uninterrupted years of war. Every bosom swelled with exultation in contemplating the glorious destinies of their country under the beneficent sway of a prince, the first heir of the hitherto divided monarchies of Spain. Alas! at the moment when Ferdinand and Isabella, blessed in the affections of their people, and surrounded by all the trophies of a glorious reign, seemed to have reached the very zenith of human felicity, they were doomed to receive one of those mournful lessons, which admonish us that all earthly prosperity is but a dream. [21]

Not long after Prince John's marriage, the sovereigns had the satisfaction to witness that of their daughter Isabella, who, notwithstanding her repugnance to a second union, had yielded at length to the urgent entreaties of her parents to receive the addresses of her Portuguese lover. She required as the price of this, however, that Emanuel should first banish the Jews from his dominions, where they had bribed a resting-place since their expulsion from Spain; a circumstance to which the su-

CHAPTER IV.

Second marriage of Princess Isabella

[21] It is precisely this period, or rather the whole period from 1493 to 1497, which Oviedo selects as that of the greatest splendor and festivity at the court of the Catholic sovereigns. " El año de 1493, y uno ó dos despues, y aun hasta el de 1497 años fué cuando la corte de los Reyes Católicos Don Fernando é Doña Isabel de gloriosa memoria, mas alegres tiempos é mas regozijados, vino en su corte, é mas encumbrada andubo la gala é las fiestas é servicios de galanes é damas." Quincuagenas, MS., bat. 1, quinc. 4, dial. 44.

perstitious princess imputed the misfortunes which
had fallen of late on the royal house of Portugal
Emanuel, whose own liberal mind revolted at this
unjust and impolitic measure, was weak enough to
allow his passion to get the better of his principles,
and passed sentence of exile on every Israelite in
his kingdom; furnishing, perhaps, the only example, in which love has been made one of the thousand motives for persecuting this unhappy race. [22]

Sudden ill-
ness of
Prince John.

The marriage, ushered in under such ill-omened
auspices, was celebrated at the frontier town of Valencia de Alcantara, in the presence of the Catholic
sovereigns, without pomp or parade of any kind
While they were detained there, an express arrived
from Salamanca, bringing tidings of the dangerous
illness of their son, the prince of the Asturias. He
had been seized with a fever in the midst of the public rejoicings to which his arrival with his youthful
bride in that city had given rise. The symptoms
speedily assumed an alarming character. The
prince's constitution, naturally delicate, though
strengthened by a life of habitual temperance, sunk
under the violence of the attack; and when his
father, who posted with all possible expedition to
Salamanca, arrived there, no hopes were entertained of his recovery. [23]

[22] Faria y Sousa, Europa Portuguesa, tom. ii. pp. 498, 499. —
La Clède, Hist. de Portugal, tom.
iv. p. 95. — Zurita, tom. v. lib. 3,
cap. 6. — Lanuza, Historias, ubi
supra.
[23] Carbajal, Anales, MS., año
1497. — Florez, Reynas Cathólicas,
tom. ii. pp. 846, 848. — Zurita,

Hist. del Rey Hernando, tom. v.
fol. 127, 128. — La Clède, Hist. de
Portugal, tom. iv. p. 101.
    The physicians recommended a
temporary separation of John from
his young bride; a remedy, however, which the queen opposed
from conscientious scruples somewhat singular. " Hortantur medici

Ferdinand, however, endeavoured to cheer his son with hopes which he did not feel himself; but the young prince told him that it was too late to be deceived; that he was prepared to part with a world, which in its best estate was filled with vanity and vexation; and that all he now desired was, that his parents might feel the same sincere resignation to the divine will, which he experienced himself. Ferdinand gathered new fortitude from the example of his heroic son, whose presages were unhappily too soon verified. He expired on the 4th of October, 1497, in the twentieth year of his age, in the same spirit of Christian philosophy which he had displayed during his whole illness. [24]

Ferdinand, apprehensive of the effect which the abrupt intelligence of this calamity might have on the queen, caused letters to be sent at brief intervals, containing accounts of the gradual decline of the prince's health, so as to prepare her for the inevitable stroke. Isabella, however, who through all her long career of prosperous fortune may be said to have kept her heart in constant training

Reginam, hortatur et Rex, ut a principis latere Margaritam aliquando semoveat, interpellet. Inducias precantur. Protestantur periculum ex frequenti copulâ ephebo imminere; qualiter eum suxerit, quamve subtristis incedat, consideret iterum atque iterum monent; medullas lædi, stomachum hebetari se sentire Reginæ renunciant. Intercidat, dum licet, obstetque principiis, instant. Nil proficiunt. Respondet Regina, homines non oportere, quos Deus jugali vinculo junxerit, separare." Peter Martyr, Opus Epist., epist. 176.

[24] Peter Martyr, Opus Epist., epist. 182. — L. Marineo, Cosas Memorables, fol. 182. — Carbajal, Anales, MS., año 1497. — Oviedo, Quincuagenas, MS., dial. de Deza.

Peter Martyr, in more of a classic than a Christian vein, refers Prince John's composure in his latter hours to his familiarity with the divine Aristotle. " Ætatem quæ ferebat superabat; nec mirum tamen. Perlegerat namque divini Aristotelis pleraque volumina," &c. Ubi supra.

fo· the dark hour of adversity, received the fata
tidings in a spirit of meek and humble acquiescence, testifying her resignation in the beautiful
language of Scripture, " The Lord hath given, and
the Lord hath taken away, blessed be his name! " [25]

His amiable
character.

" Thus," says Martyr, who had the melancholy
satisfaction of rendering the last sad offices to his
royal pupil, " was laid low the hope of all Spain."
" Never was there a death," says another chronicler, " which occasioned such deep and general
lamentation throughout the land." All the unavailing honors which affection could devise were
paid to his memory. His funeral obsequies were
celebrated with melancholy splendor, and his 1e-
mains deposited in the noble Dominican monastery
of St. Thomas at Avila, which had been erected
by his parents. The court put on a new and
deeper mourning than that hitherto used, as if tc
testify their unwonted grief. [26] All offices, public
and private, were closed for forty days ; and sable-
colored banners were suspended from the walls and
portals of the cities. Such extraordinary tokens of
public sorrow bear strong testimony to the interest
felt in the young prince, independently of his ex-

[25] Peter Martyr, Opus Epist.,
epist. 183.
 Martyr draws an affecting picture of the anguish of the bereaved
parents, which betrayed itself in
looks more eloquent than words.
" Reges tantam dissimulare ærum-
nam nituntur ; ast nos prostratum
in internis ipsorum animum cerni-
mus ; oculos alter in faciem alterius
crebro conjiciunt, in propatulo se-
dentes. Unde quid lateat proditur.

Nimirum tamen, desinerent huma-
nâ carne vestiti esse homines,
essentque adamante duriores, nisi
quid amiserint sentirent."
 [26] Blancas, Coronaciones de los
Serenissimos Reyes de Aragon,
(Zaragoza, 1641,) lib. 3, cap. 18. —
Garibay, Compendio, tom. ii. lib.
19, cap. 6. — Sackcloth was sub
stituted for the white serge, which
till this time had been used as the
mourning dress.

alted station ; similar, and perhaps more unequivocal
evidence of his worth, is afforded by abundance of
contemporary notices, not merely in works designed
for the public, but in private correspondence. The
learned Martyr, in particular, whose situation, as
prince John's preceptor, afforded him the best opportunities of observation, is unbounded in commendations of his royal pupil, whose extraordinary
promise of intellectual and moral excellence had
furnished him with the happiest, alas! delusive
auguries, for the future destiny of his country.[27]

By the death of John without heirs, the succession devolved on his eldest sister, the queen of Portugal.[28] Intelligence, however, was received soon
after that event, that the archduke Philip, with the
restless ambition which distinguished him in later

The king
and queen
of Portugal
visit Spain.

---

[27] Peter Martyr, Opus Epist.,
epist. 182. — Garibay, Compendio,
om. ii. lib. 19, cap. 6. — L. Marineo, Cosas Memorables, fol. 182. —
Blancas, Coronaciones, p. 248.

It must be allowed to furnish no
mean proof of the excellence of
Prince John's heart, that it was
not corrupted by the liberal doses
of flattery with which his worthy
tutor was in the habit of regaling
him, from time to time. Take the
beginning of one of Martyr's letters
to his pupil, in the following modest strain. " Mirande in pueritiâ
senex, salve. Quotquot tecum ver-
santur homines, sive genere pol-
leant, sive ad obsequium fortunæ
humiliores destinati ministri, te
laudant, extollunt, admirantur."
Opus Epist., epist. 98.

[28] Hopes were entertained of a
male heir at the time of John's
death, as his widow was left pregnant; but these were frustrated by
her being delivered of a still-born

infant at the end of a few months.
Margaret did not continue long in
Spain. She experienced the most
affectionate treatment from the king
and queen, who made her an extremely liberal provision. (Zurita,
Hist. del Rey Hernando, tom. v.
lib. 3, cap. 4.) But her Flemish
followers could not reconcile themselves to the reserve and burden-
some ceremonial of the Castilian
court, so different from the free and
jocund life to which they had been
accustomed at home ; and they prevailed on their mistress to return to
her native land in the course of the
year 1499. She was subsequently
married to the duke of Savoy, who
died without issue in less than
three years, and Margaret passed
the remainder of her life in widow-
hood, being appointed by her father, the emperor, to the government of the Netherlands, which
she administered with ability. She
died in 1530.

life, had assumed for himself and his wife Joanna the title of "princes of Castile." Ferdinand and Isabella, disgusted with this proceeding, sent to request the attendance of the king and queen of Portugal in Castile, in order to secure a recognition of their rights by the national legislature. The royal pair, accordingly, in obedience to the summons, quitted their capital of Lisbon, early in the spring of 1498. In their progress through the country, they were magnificently entertained at the castles of the great Castilian lords, and towards the close of April reached the ancient city of Toledo, where the cortes had been convened to receive them.[29]

After the usual oaths of recognition had been tendered, without opposition, by the different branches to the Portuguese princes, the court adjourned to Saragossa, where the legislature of Aragon was assembled for a similar purpose.

Some apprehensions were entertained, however, of the unfavorable disposition of that body, since the succession of females was not countenanced by

[29] Marina has transcribed from the archives of Toledo the writ of summons to that city on this occasion. Teoría, tom. ii. p. 16. — Zurita, Hist. del Rey Hernando, tom. v. lib. 3, cap. 18. — Bernaldez, Reyes Católicos, MS., cap. 154. — La Clède, Hist. de Portugal, tom. iv. p. 101. — Carbajal, Anales, MS., año 1498. — Faria y Sousa, Europa Portuguesa, tom. ii. pp. 500, 501.

The last writer expatiates with great satisfaction on the stately etiquette observed at the reception of the Portuguese monarchs and their suite by the Spanish sovereigns. "Queen Isabella," he says, "appeared leaning on the arm of her old favorite Gutierre de Cardenas, comendador of Leon, and of a Portuguese noble, Don Juan de Sousa. The latter took care to acquaint her with the rank and condition of each of his countrymen, as they were presented, in order that she might the better adjust the measure of condescension and courtesy due to each ; a perilous obligation," he continues, "with all nations, but with the Portuguese most perilous ! "

the ancient usage of the country; and the Aragonese, as Martyr remarks in one of his Epistles, "were well known to be a pertinacious race, who would leave no stone unturned, in the maintenance of their constitutional rights." [30]

These apprehensions were fully realized; for, no sooner was the object of the present meeting laid before cortes in a speech from the throne, with which parliamentary business in Aragon was always opened, than decided opposition was manifested to a proceeding, which it was declared had no precedent in their history. The succession of the crown, it was contended, had been limited by repeated testaments of their princes to male heirs, and practice and public sentiment had so far coincided with this, that the attempted violation of the rule by Peter the Fourth, in favor of his own daughters, had plunged the nation in a civil war. It was further urged that by the will of the very last monarch, John the Second, it was provided that the crown should descend to the male issue of his son Ferdinand, and in default of such to the male issue of Ferdinand's daughters, to the entire exclusion of the females. At all events, it was better to postpone the consideration of this matter until the result of the queen of Portugal's pregnancy, then far advanced, should be ascertained; since, should it prove to be a son, all doubts of constitutional validity would be removed.

[30] Peter Martyr, Opus Epist., epist. 194. — Abarca, Reyes de Aragon, tom. ii. fol. 334. — Mari- ana, Hist. de España, tom. ii. lib 27, cap. 3.

PART
II.

In answer to these objections, it was stated, that no express law existed in Aragon excluding females from the succession ; that an example had already occurred, as far back indeed as the twelfth century, of a queen who held the crown in her own right ; that the acknowledged power of females to transmit the right of succession necessarily inferred that right existing in themselves ; that the present monarch had doubtless as competent authority as his predecessors to regulate the law of inheritance, and that his act, supported by the supreme authority of cortes, might set aside any former disposition of the crown ; that this interference was called for by the present opportunity of maintaining the permanent union of Castile and Aragon ; without which they must otherwise return to their ancient divided state, and comparative insignificance. [31]

Isabella displeased.

These arguments, however cogent, were far from being conclusive with the opposite party ; and the debate was protracted to such length, that Isabella, impatient of an opposition to what the practice in her own dominions had taught her to regard as the inalienable right of her daughter, inconsiderately exclaimed, " It would be better to reduce the coun-

[31] Blancas, Commentarii, p. 273. — Idem, Coronaciones, lib. 1, cap. 18. — Mariana, Hist. de España, tom. ii. lib. 27, cap. 3. — Zurita, Hist. del Rey Hernando, tom. v. fol. 55, 56.

It is remarkable that the Aragonese should so readily have acquiesced in the right of females to convey a title to the crown which they could not enjoy themselves. This was precisely the principle on which Edward III. set up his claim to the throne of France, a principle too repugnant to the commonest rules of inheritance to obtain any countenance. The exclusion of females in Aragon could not pretend to be founded on any express law, as in France, but the practice, with the exception of a single example three centuries old was quite as uniform.

try by arms at once, than endure this insolence of the cortes." To which Antonio de Fonseca, the same cavalier who spoke his mind so fearlessly to King Charles the Eighth, on his march to Naples, had the independence to reply, " That the Aragonese had only acted as good and loyal subjects, who, as they were accustomed to mind their oaths, considered well before they took them; and that they must certainly stand excused if they moved with caution in an affair, which they found so difficult to justify by precedent in their history." [32] This blunt expostulation of the honest courtier, equally creditable to the sovereign who could endure, and the subject who could make it, was received in the frank spirit in which it was given, and probably opened Isabella's eyes to her own precipitancy, as we find no further allusion to coercive measures.

Before any thing was determined, the discussion was suddenly brought to a close by an unforeseen and most melancholy event, — the death of the queen of Portugal, the unfortunate subject of it. That princess had possessed a feeble constitution from her birth, with a strong tendency to pulmonary complaints. She had early felt a presentiment that she should not survive the birth of her child; this feeling strengthened as she approached the period

Her daughter's death.

---

[32] Blancas, Coronaciones, lib. 3, cap. 18. — Zurita, Hist. del Rey Hernando, tom. v. lib. 3, cap. 30.

It is a proof of the high esteem in which Isabella held this independent statesman, that we find his name mentioned in her testament among half a dozen others, whom she particularly recommended to her successors for their meritorious and loyal services. See the document in Dormer, Discursos Varios, p. 354.

of her delivery; and in less than one hour after that event, which took place on the 23d of August, 1498, she expired in the arms of her afflicted parents.[33]

This blow was almost too much for the unhappy mother, whose spirits had not yet had time to rally, since the death of her only son. She, indeed, exhibited the outward marks of composure, testifying the entire resignation of one who had learned to rest her hopes of happiness on a better world. She schooled herself so far, as to continue to take an interest in all her public duties, and to watch over the common weal with the same maternal solicitude as before; but her health gradually sunk under this accumulated load of sorrow, which threw a deep shade of melancholy over the evening of her life.

The infant, whose birth had cost so dear, proved a male, and received the name of Miguel, in honor of the saint on whose day he first saw the light. In order to dissipate, in some degree, the general gloom occasioned by the late catastrophe, it was thought best to exhibit the young prince before the eyes of his future subjects; and he was accordingly borne in the arms of his nurse, in a magnificent litter, through the streets of the city, escorted by the principal nobility. Measures were then taken for obtaining the sanction of his legitimate claims to the crown. Whatever doubts had been enter-

[33] Carbajal, Anales, MS., años 1470, 1498. — Florez, Reynas Cathólicas, tom. ii. pp. 846, 847. — Faria y Sousa, Europa Portug iesa, tom. ii. p. 504.

tained of the validity of the mother's title, there CHAPTER
could be none whatever of the child's; since those IV.
who denied the right of females to inherit for themselves, admitted their power of conveying such a
right to male issue. As a preliminary step to the
public recognition of the prince, it was necessary
to name a guardian, who should be empowered to
make the requisite engagements, and to act in his
behalf. The Justice of Aragon, in his official capacity, after due examination, appointed the grand-
parents, Ferdinand and Isabella, to the office of
guardians during his minority, which would expire
by law at the age of fourteen.[34]

On Saturday, the 22d of September, when the Prince Mi
queen had sufficiently recovered from a severe guel's recog
illness brought on by her late sufferings, the four nition
arms of the cortes of Aragon assembled in the
house of deputation at Saragossa; and Ferdinand
and Isabella made oath as guardians of the heir
apparent, before the Justice, not to exercise any
jurisdiction whatever in the name of the young
prince during his minority; engaging, moreover, as
far as in their power, that, on his coming of age, he
should swear to respect the laws and liberties of
the realm, before entering on any of the rights of
sovereignty himself. The four estates then took
the oath of fealty to Prince Miguel, as lawful heir
and successor to the crown of Aragon; with the

---

[34] Blancas, Commentarii, pp.
510. 511. — Idem, Coronaciones,
lib. 3, cap. 19. — Gerónimo Martel,
Forma de Celebrar Cortes en Aragon, (Zaragoza, 1641,) cap. 44. —

Alvaro Gomez, De Rebus Gestis
a Francisco Ximenio Cisnerio,
(Compluti, 1569,) fol. 28. — Lanuza, Historias, lib. 1, cap. 9

protestation, that it should not be construed into a
precedent for exacting such an oath hereafter during the minority of the heir apparent. With such
watchful attention to constitutional forms of pro-
cedure, did the people of Aragon endeavour to
secure their liberties ; forms, which continued to
be observed in later times, long after those liberties
had been swept away.[35]

In the month of January, of the ensuing year,
the young prince's succession was duly confirmed
by the cortes of Castile, and, in the following
March, by that of Portugal. Thus, for once, the
crowns of the three monarchies of Castile, Aragon,
and Portugal were suspended over one head. The
Portuguese, retaining the bitterness of ancient ri-
valry, looked with distrust at the prospect of a
union, fearing, with some reason, that the importance of the lesser state would be wholly merged
in that of the greater. But the untimely death of
the destined heir of these honors, which took place
before he had completed his second year, removed
the causes of jealousy, and defeated the only
chance, which had ever occurred, of bringing under
the same rule three independent nations, which,

---

[35] Blancas, Coronaciones, ubi
supra. — Idem, Commentarii, pp.
510, 511.

The reverence of the Aragonese
for their institutions is shown in
their observance of the most insignificant ceremonies. A remarkable
instance of this occurred in the
year 1481, at Saragossa, when the
queen having been constituted *lieu-
tenant general* of the kingdom, and
duly qualified to hold a cortes in
the absence of the king her husband, who, by the ancient laws of
the land, was required to preside
over it in person, it was deemed
necessary to obtain a formal act of
the legislature, for opening the
door for her admission. See Blancas, Modo de Proceder en Cortes
de Aragon, (Zaragoza, 1611,) fol
82, 83.

from their common origin, their geographical position, and, above all, their resemblance in manners,
sentiments, and language, would seem to have
originally been intended to form but one.[36]

[36] Faria y Sousa, Europa Por-
tuguesa, tom. ii. pp. 504, 507. —
Bernaldez, Reyes Católicos, MS.,
cap. 154.—Carbajal, Anales, MS.,
año 1499.— Zurita, Hist. del Rey
Hernando, tom. v. lib. 3, cap. 33.
—Sandoval, Hist. del Emp. Corlos
V., tom. i. p. 4.

CHAPTER V.

DEATH OF CARDINAL MENDOZA. — RISE OF XIMENES. — ECCLESIASTICAL REFORM.

Death of Mendoza. — His Early Life, and Character. — The Queen his Executor. — Origin of Ximenes. — He enters the Franciscan Order. — His Ascetic Life. — Confessor to the Queen. — Made Archbishop of Toledo. — Austerity of his Life. — Reform of the Monastic Orders. — Insults offered to the Queen. — She consents to the Reform

PART
II.
———
Death of
Mendoza.

In the beginning of 1495, the sovereigns lost their old and faithful minister, the grand cardinal of Spain, Don Pedro Gonzalez de Mendoza. He was the fourth son of the celebrated marquis of Santillana, and was placed by his talents at the head of a family, every member of which must be allowed to have exhibited a rare union of public and private virtue. The cardinal reached the age of sixty-six, when his days were terminated after a long and painful illness, on the 11th of January, at his palace of Guadalaxara.[1]

---

[1] Carbajal, Anales, MS., año 1495. — Salazar de Mendoza, Crón. del Gran Cardenal, lib. 2, cap. 45, 46. — Zurita, Anales, tom. v. fol. 61. — Pulgar, Claros Varones, tit. 4.

His disorder was an abscess on the kidneys, which confined him to the house nearly a year before his death. When this event happened, a white cross of extraordinary magnitude and splendor, shaped precisely like that on his arms, was seen in the heavens directly over his house, by a crowd of spectators, for more than two hours; a full account of which was duly transmitted to Rome by the Spanish court, and has obtained easy credit with the principal Spanish historians.

In the unhappy feuds between Henry the Fourth and his younger brother Alfonso, the cardinal had remained faithful to the former. But on the death of that monarch, he threw his whole weight, with that of his powerful family, into the scale of Isabella, whether influenced by a conviction of her superior claims, or her capacity for government. This was a most important acquisition to the royal cause ; and Mendoza's consummate talents for business, recommended by the most agreeable address, secured him the confidence of both Ferdinand and Isabella, who had long been disgusted with the rash and arrogant bearing of their old minister, Carillo.

On the death of that turbulent prelate, Mendoza succeeded to the archiepiscopal see of Toledo. His new situation naturally led to still more intimate relations with the sovereigns, who uniformly deferred to his experience, consulting him on all important matters, not merely of a public, but of a private nature. In short, he gained such ascendency in the cabinet, during a long ministry of more than twenty years, that he was pleasantly called by the courtiers the " third king of Spain." [2]

---

[2] Alvaro Gomez says of him, " Nam præter clarissimum tum natalium, tum fortunæ, tum dignitatis splendorem, quæ in illo ornamenta summa erant, incredibilem animi sublimitatem cum pari morum facilitate, elegantiâque conjunxerat ; ut merito locum in republicâ summo proximum ad supremum usque diem tenuerit." (De Rebus Gestis, fol. 9.) Mar tyr, noticing the cardinal's death, bestows the following brief but comprehensive panegyric on him. " Periit Gonsalus Mendotiæ, domûs splendor et lucida fax ; periit quem universa colebat Hispania, quem exteri etiam principes venerabantur, quem ordo cardineus collegam sibi esse gloriabatur." Opus Epist., epist. 158.

The minister did not abuse the confidence so
generously reposed in him. He called the attention of his royal mistress to objects most deserving
it. His views were naturally grand and lofty; and,
if he sometimes yielded to the fanatical impulse
of the age, he never failed to support her heartily in
every generous enterprise for the advancement of
her people. When raised to the rank of primate
of Spain, he indulged his natural inclination for
pomp and magnificence. He filled his palace with
pages, selected from the noblest families in the
kingdom, whom he carefully educated. He maintained a numerous body of armed retainers, which,
far from being a mere empty pageant, formed a
most effective corps for public service on all requisite occasions. He dispensed the immense revenues of his bishopric with the same munificent
hand which has so frequently distinguished the
Spanish prelacy, encouraging learned men, and en
dowing public institutions. The most remarkable
of these were the college of Santa Cruz at Valladolid, and the hospital of the same name for found-
lings at Toledo, the erection of which, completed
at his sole charge, consumed more than ten years
each.[3]

The cardinal, in his younger days, was occasionally seduced by those amorous propensities, in
which the Spanish clergy freely indulged, contaminated, perhaps, by the example of their Mahometan neighbours. He left several children by his

[3] Salazar de Mendoza, Crón. del Gran Cardenal, pp 265 273, 381
—410.

amours with two ladies of rank, from whom some
of the best houses in the kingdom are descended. [4]
A characteristic anecdote is recorded of him in
relation to this matter. An ecclesiastic, who one
day delivered a discourse in his presence, took occasion to advert to the laxity of the age, in general
terms, indeed, but bearing too pertinent an application to the cardinal to be mistaken. The attendants of the latter boiled with indignation at the
preacher's freedom, whom they determined to chastise for his presumption. They prudently, however, postponed this until they should see what effect
the discourse had on their master. The cardinal,
far from betraying any resentment, took no other
notice of the preacher than to send him a dish of
choice game, which had been served up at his own
table, where he was entertaining a party of friends
that day, accompanying it at the same time, by way
of sauce, with a substantial donative of gold doblas;
an act of Christian charity not at all to the taste of
his own servants. It wrought its effects on the
worthy divine, who at once saw the error of his
ways, and, the next time he mounted the pulpit,
took care to frame his discourse in such a manner
as to counteract the former unfavorable impressions,
to the entire satisfaction, if not edification of his
audience. " Now-a-days," says the honest biographer who reports the incident, himself a lineal
descendant of the cardinal, " the preacher would

---

[4] "Gran varon, y muy experi-
mentado y prudente en negocios,"
says Oviedo of the cardinal, " *pero
à vueltas de las negociaciones desta*
vida, tuvo trés hijos varones," &c.
Then follows a full notice of this
graceless progeny. Quincuagenas,
MS., bat. 1, quinc. 1, dial. 8

PART
II.

not have escaped so easily. And with good reason;
for the holy Gospel should be discreetly preached,
' cum grano salis,' that is to say, with the decorum
and deference due to majesty and men of high
estate. " [5]

The queen
his executor.

When cardinal Mendoza's illness assumed an
alarming aspect, the court removed to the neighbourhood of Guadalaxara, where he was confined.
The king and queen, especially the latter, with the
affectionate concern which she manifested for more
than one of her faithful subjects, used to visit him
in person, testifying her sympathy for his sufferings,
and benefiting by the lights of the sagacious mind,
which had so long helped to guide her. She still
further showed her regard for her old minister by
condescending to accept the office of his executor,
which she punctually discharged, superintending
the disposition of his effects according to his testament, [6] and particularly the erection of the stately
hospital of Santa Cruz, before mentioned, not a
stone of which was laid before his death. [7]

[5] Salazar de Mendoza, Crón. del
Gran Cardenal, lib. 2, cap. 66.
The doctor Pedro Salazar de
Mendoza's biography of his illustrious relative is a very fair specimen of the Spanish style of book-
making in ancient times. One event
seems to suggest another with
about as much cohesion as the
rhymes of " The House that Jack
built." There is scarcely a place
or personage of note, that the grand
cardinal was brought in contact
with in the course of his life, whose
history is not made the theme of
profuse dissertation. Nearly fifty chapters are taken up, for ex-

ample, with the distinguished men,
who graduated at the college of
Santa Cruz.

[6] " Non hoc," says Tacitus with
truth, " præcipuam amicorum mu-
nus est, prosequi defunctum ignavo
questu : sed quæ voluerit memi-
nisse, quæ mandaverit exsequi."
Annales, lib. 2, sect. 71.

[7] Peter Martyr, Opus Epist.,
epist. 143. — Carbajal, Anales,
MS., año 1494. — Salazar de Mendoza, Crón. del Gran Cardenal, lib.
2, cap. 45.
A foundling hospital does not
seem to have come amiss in Spain,
where, according to Salazar, the

In one of her interviews with the dying minister, the queen requested his advice respecting the nomination of his successor. The cardinal, in reply, earnestly cautioned her against raising any one of the principal nobility to this dignity, almost too exalted for any subject, and which, when combined with powerful family connexions, would enable a man of factious disposition to defy the royal authority itself, as they had once bitter experience in the case of Archbishop Carillo. On being pressed to name the individual, whom he thought best qualified, in every point of view, for the office, he is said to have recommended Fray Francisco Ximenez de Cisneros, a friar of the Franciscan order, and confessor of the queen. As this extraordinary personage exercised a more important control over the destinies of his country than any other subject, during the remainder of the present reign, it will be necessary to put the reader in possession of his history.[8]

Ximenez de Cisneros, or Ximenes, as he is usually called, was born at the little town of Tor-

Birth of
Ximenes.

---

wretched parents frequently destroyed their offspring by casting them into wells and pits, or exposing them in desert places to die of famine. " *The more compassionate*," he observes, " laid them at the doors of churches, where they were too often worried to death by dogs and other animals." The grand cardinal's nephew, who founded a similar institution, is said to have furnished an asylum in the course of his life to no less than 13,000 of these little victims ! Ibid., cap 61.

[8] Salazar de Mendoza, Crón. del Gran Cardenal, lib. 2, cap. 46.— Gomez, De Rebus Gestis, fol. 8.

The dying cardinal is said to have recommended, among other things, that the queen should repair any wrong done to Joanna Beltraneja, by marrying her with the young prince of the Asturias ; which suggestion was so little to Isabella's taste that she broke off the conversation, saying, " the good man wandered and talked nonsense."

delaguna, in the year 1436,[9] of an ancient but decayed family.[10] He was early destined by his parents for the church, and, after studying grammar at Alcalá, was removed at fourteen to the university of Salamanca. Here he went through the regular course of instruction then pursued, devoting himself assiduously to the civil and canon law, and at the end of six years received the degree of bachelor in each of them, a circumstance at that time of rare occurrence.[11]

Three years after quitting the university, the young bachelor removed by the advice of his parents to Rome, as affording a better field for ecclesiastical preferment than he could find at home. Here he seems to have attracted some notice by the diligence with which he devoted himself to his professional studies and employments. But still he was far from reaping the golden fruits presaged by his kindred; and at the expiration of six years he was suddenly recalled to his native country by the death of his father, who left his affairs in so embar-

[9] It is singular, that Fléchier should have blundered some twenty years, in the date of Ximenes's birth, which he makes 1457. (Hist. de Ximenés, liv. 1, p. 3.) It is not singular, that Marsollier should. Histoire du Ministère du Cardinal Ximenez, (Toulouse, 1694,) liv. 1, p. 3.

[10] The honorable extraction of Ximenes is intimated in Juan Vergara's verses at the end of the Complutensian Polyglot:

"Nomine Cisnerius clarà de stirpe parentum,
"Et meritis factus clarior ipse suis."

Fray Pedro de Quintanilla y

Mendoza makes a goodly genealogical tree for his hero, of which King Pelayo, King Pepin, Charlemagne, and other royal worthies are the respectable roots. (Procœmia Dedicatoria, pp. 5 – 35.) According to Gonzalo de Oviedo, his father was a poor hidalgo, who, having spent his little substance on the education of his children, was obliged to take up the profession of an advocate. Quincuagenas, MS.

[11] Quintanilla, Archetypo, p. 6. — Gomez, De Rebus Gestis, Ximen., fol. 2. — Idem, Miscellanear. MS., ex Bibliothecâ Regià Matritensi, tom. ii. fol. 139.

rassed a condition, as to require his immediate presence [12]

Before his return, Ximenes obtained a papal bull, or *expectative*, preferring him to the first benefice of a specified value, which should become vacant in the see of Toledo. Several years elapsed before such a vacancy offered itself by the death of the archpriest of Uzeda; and Ximenes took possession of that living by virtue of the apostolic grant.

This assumption of the papal court to dispose of the church livings at its own pleasure, had been long regarded by the Spaniards as a flagrant imposition; and Carillo, the archbishop of Toledo, in whose diocese the vacancy occurred, was not likely tamely to submit to it. He had, moreover, promised this very place to one of his own followers. He determined, accordingly, to compel Ximenes to surrender his pretensions in favor of the latter, and, finding argument ineffectual, resorted to force, confining him in the fortress of Uzeda, whence he was subsequently removed to the strong tower of Santorcaz, then used as a prison for contumacious ecclesiastics. But Carillo understood little of the temper of Ximenes, which was too inflexible to be broken by persecution. The archbishop in time became convinced of this, and was persuaded to release him, but not till after an imprisonment of more than six years. [13]

[12] Gomez, De Rebus Gestis, fol. 2. — Idem, Miscellanear., MS., ubi supra. — Eugenio de Robles, Compendio de la Vida y Hazañas del Cardenal Don Fray Francisco Ximenez de Cisneros, (Toledo, 1604,) cap. 11.

[13] Quintanilla, Archetypo, pp. 8, 10. — Gomez, De Rebus Gestis, fol. 2. — Fléchier, Hist. de Xime-

Ximenes, thus restored to freedom, and placed in undisturbed possession of his benefice, was desirous of withdrawing from the jurisdiction of his vindictive superior; and not long after effected an exchange for the chaplainship of Siguenza. In this new situation he devoted himself with renewed ardor to his theological studies, occupying himself diligently, moreover, with Hebrew and Chaldee, his knowledge of which proved of no little use in the concoction of his famous Polyglot.

Mendoza was at that time bishop of Siguenza. It was impossible that a man of his penetration should come in contact with a character like that of Ximenes, without discerning its extraordinary qualities. It was not long before he appointed him his vicar, with the administration of his diocese; in which situation he displayed such capacity for business, that the count of Cifuentes, on falling into the hands of the Moors, after the unfortunate affair of the Axarquia, confided to him the sole management of his vast estates during his captivity.[14]

But these secular concerns grew more and more distasteful to Ximenes, whose naturally austere and contemplative disposition had been deepened, probably, by the melancholy incidents of his life, into stern religious enthusiasm. He determined, there-

nés, pp. 8–10.—Suma de la Vida del R. S. Cardenal Don Fr. Francisco Ximenez de Cisneros, sacada de los Memoriales de Juan de Vallejo, Paje de Cámara, è de algunas Personas que en su Tiempo lo vieron: para la Ilustrisima Señora Doña Catalina de la Zerda, Condesa de Coruña, a quien Dios guarde, y de su Gracia, por un Criado de su Casa, MS.

[14] Suma de la Vida de Cisneros, MS.—Gomez, De Rebus Gestis, fol. 3.—Robles, Vida de Ximenez, cap. 11.—Oviedo, Quincuagenas. MS., dial. de Ximeni.

fore, to break at once from the shackles which
bound him to the world, and seek an asylum in
some religious establishment, where he might devote himself unreservedly to the service of Heaven.
He selected for this purpose the Observantines of
the Franciscan order, the most rigid of the monastic societies. He resigned his various employments
and benefices, with annual rents to the amount of
two thousand ducats, and, in defiance of the arguments and entreaties of his friends, entered on his
noviciate in the convent of San Juan de los Reyes,
at Toledo; a superb pile then erecting by the
Spanish sovereigns, in pursuance of a vow made
during the war of Granada.[15]

He distinguished his noviciate by practising   His severe
                                                penance.
every ingenious variety of mortification with which
superstition has contrived to swell the inevitable
catalogue of human sufferings. He slept on the
ground, or on the hard floor, with a billet of wood
for his pillow. He wore hair cloth next his skin,
and exercised himself with fasts, vigils, and stripes,
to a degree scarcely surpassed by the fanatical
founder of his order. At the end of the year, he
regularly professed, adopting then for the first time
the name of Francisco, in compliment to his patron

---

[15] Quintanilla, Archetypo, p. 11.
—Gomez, Miscellanear., MS., ubi
supra. — Idem, De Rebus Gestis,
fol. 4.
    This edifice, says Salazar de
Mendoza, in respect to its sacristy,
choir, cloisters, library, &c., was
the most sumptuous and noted of
its time. It was originally destined

by the Catholic sovereigns for their
place of sepulture; an honor afterwards reserved for Granada, on
its recovery from the infidels. The
great chapel was garnished with
the fetters taken from the dungeons
of Malaga, in which the Moors
confined their Christian captives.
Monarquía, tom. i. p. 410.

PART
II.

His ascetic
life.

saint, instead of that of Gonzalo, by which he had
been baptized.

No sooner had this taken place, than his reputation for sanctity, which his late course of life had
diffused far and wide, attracted multitudes of all
ages and conditions to his confessional; and he
soon found himself absorbed in the same vortex of
worldly passions and interests, from which he had
been so anxious to escape. At his solicitation,
therefore, he was permitted to transfer his abode to
the convent of our Lady of Castañar, so called
from a deep forest of chestnuts, in which it was
embosomed. In the midst of these dark mountain
solitudes, he built with his own hands a little hermitage or cabin, of dimensions barely sufficient to
admit his entrance. Here he passed his days and
nights in prayer, and in meditations on the sacred
volume, sustaining life, like the ancient anchorites,
on the green herbs and running waters. In this
state of self-mortification, with a frame wasted by
abstinence, and a mind exalted by spiritual contemplation, it is no wonder that he should have
indulged in ecstasies and visions, until he fancied
himself raised into communication with celestial
intelligences. It is more wonderful that his understanding was not permanently impaired by these
distempered fancies. This period of his life, however, seems to have been always regarded by him
with peculiar satisfaction; for long after, as his
biographer assures us, when reposing in lordly
palaces, and surrounded by all the appliances of
luxury, he looked back with fond regret on the

hours which glided so peacefully in the hermitage
of Castañar.[16]

Fortunately, his superiors choosing to change his
place of residence according to custom, transferred
him at the end of three years to the convent of
Salzeda. Here he practised, indeed, similar austerities, but it was not long before his high reputation raised him to the post of guardian of the
convent. This situation necessarily imposed on
him the management of the institution ; and thus
the powers of his mind, so long wasted in unprofitable reverie, were again called into exercise for
the benefit of others. An event which occurred
some years later, in 1492, opened to him a still
wider sphere of action.

By the elevation of Talavera to the metropolitan see of Granada, the office of queen's confessor
became vacant. Cardinal Mendoza, who was consulted on the choice of a successor, well knew the
importance of selecting a man of the highest integrity and talent ; since the queen's tenderness of
conscience led her to take counsel of her confessor,
not merely in regard to her own spiritual concerns,
but all the great measures of her administration.
He at once fixed his eye on Ximenes, of whom
he had never lost sight, indeed, since his first
acquaintance with him at Siguenza. He was far
from approving his adoption of the monastic life,
and had been heard to say, that " parts so extraor-

[16] Fléchier, Hist. de Ximenés,
p. 14. — Quintanilla, Archetypo,
pp. 13, 14. — Gomez, De Rebus
Gestis, fol. 4. — Suma de la Vida
de Cisneros, MS. — Oviedo, Quincuagenas, MS.

PART
II.

dinary would not long be buried in the shades of a convent." He is said, also, to have predicted that Ximenes would one day succeed him in the chair of Toledo. A prediction, which its author contributed more than any other to verify. [17]

Introduced
to the queen.

He recommended Ximenes in such emphatic terms to the queen, as raised a strong desire in her to see and converse with him herself. An invitation was accordingly sent him from the cardinal to repair to the court at Valladolid, without intimating the real purpose of it. Ximenes obeyed the summons, and, after a short interview with his early patron, was conducted, as if without any previous arrangement, to the queen's apartment. On finding himself so unexpectedly in the royal presence, he betrayed none of the agitation or embarrassment to have been expected from the secluded inmate of a cloister, but exhibited a natural dignity of manners, with such discretion and fervent piety, in his replies to Isabella's various interrogatories, as confirmed the favorable prepossessions she had derived from the cardinal.

Made her
confessor.

1492.

Not many days after, Ximenes was invited to take charge of the queen's conscience. Far from appearing elated by this mark of royal favor, and the prospects of advancement which it opened, he seemed to view it with disquietude, as likely to interrupt the peaceful tenor of his religious duties; and he accepted it only with the understanding,

[17] Salazar de Mendoza, Crón. del Gran Cardenal, lib. 2, cap. 63. — Gomez, De Rebus Gestis, fol. 4. — Suma de la Vida de Cisneros, MS. — Robles, Vida de Ximenez, cap. 12.

that he should be allowed to conform in every respect to the obligations of his order, and to remain in his own monastery when his official functions did not require attendance at court.[18]

Martyr, in more than one of his letters dated at this time, notices the impression made on the courtiers by the remarkable appearance of the new confessor, in whose wasted frame, and pallid, care-worn countenance, they seemed to behold one of the primitive anchorites from the deserts of Syria or Egypt.[19] The austerities and the blameless purity of Ximenes's life had given him a reputation for sanctity throughout Spain;[20] and Martyr indulges the regret, that a virtue, which had stood so many trials, should be exposed to the worst of all, in the seductive blandishments of a court. But Ximenes's heart had been steeled by too stern a discipline to be moved by the fascinations of pleasure, however it might be by those of ambition.

Two years after this event, he was elected provincial of his order in Castile, which placed him at

[18] Fléchier, Hist. de Ximenés, pp. 18, 19. — Peter Martyr, Opus Epist., epist. 108. — Robles, Vida de Ximenez, ubi supra. — Oviedo, Quincuagenas, MS.

[19] Peter Martyr, Opus Epist., epist. 108.

"Præterea," says Martyr, in a letter to Don Fernando Alvarez, one of the royal secretaries, "nonne tu sanctissimum quendam virum a solitudine abstrusisque silvis, macie ob abstinentiam confectum, relicti Granatensis loco fuisse suffectum, scriptitasti? In istius facie obductâ, nonne Hilarionis te imaginem aut primi Pauli vultum conspexisse

fateris?" Opus Epist, epist. 105.

[20] "Todos hablaban," says Oviedo, "de la sanctimonia é vida de este religioso." The same writer says, that he saw him at Medina del Campo, in 1494, in a solemn procession, on the day of Corpus Christi, his body much emaciated, and walking barefooted in his coarse friar's dress. In the same procession was the magnificent cardinal of Spain, little dreaming how soon his proud honors were to descend on the head of his more humble companion. Quincuagenas, MS

the head of its numerous religious establishments
In his frequent journeys for their inspection he
travelled on foot, supporting himself by begging
alms, conformably to the rules of his order. On his
return he made a very unfavorable report to the
queen of the condition of the various institutions,
most of which he represented to have grievously
relaxed in discipline and virtue. Contemporary
accounts corroborate this unfavorable picture, and
accuse the religious communities of both sexes
throughout Spain, at this period, of wasting their
hours, not merely in unprofitable sloth, but in luxury
and licentiousness. The Franciscans, in particular,
had so far swerved from the obligations of their in-
stitute, which interdicted the possession of property
of any description, that they owned large estates in
town and country, living in stately edifices, and in
a style of prodigal expense not surpassed by any of
the monastic orders. Those who indulged in this
latitude were called *conventuals*, while the comparatively small number who put the strictest construction on the rule of their founder were denominated *observantines*, or brethren of the observance
Ximenes, it will be remembered, was one of the
latter.[21]

Corruption
of the mon-
asteries.

The Spanish sovereigns had long witnessed with
deep regret the scandalous abuses which had crept

---

[21] Bernaldez, Reyes Católicos,
MS., cap. 201. — Suma de la Vida
de Cisneros, MS. — Mosheim, Ec-
clesiastical History, vol. iii. cent.
14, p. 2. — Peter Martyr, Opus
Epist., epist. 163. — L. Marineo,
Cosas Memorables, fol. 165. —
Oviedo, Epilogo Real, Imperial y
Pontifical, MS.; apud Mem. de la
Acad. de Hist., tom. vi. Ilust. 8. —
Zurita, Hist. del Rey Hernando. lib.
3, cap. 15.

.nto these ancient institutions, and had employed CHAPTER
commissioners for investigating and reforming them, V
but ineffectually. Isabella now gladly availed herself of the assistance of her confessor, in bringing
them into a better state of discipline. In the course
of the same year, 1494, she obtained a bull with
full authority for this purpose from Alexander the
Sixth, the execution of which she intrusted to Ximenes. The work of reform required all the energies
of his powerful mind, backed by the royal authority.
For, in addition to the obvious difficulty of per-
suading men to resign the good things of this world
for a life of penance and mortification, there were
other impediments, arising from the circumstance,
that the conventuals had been countenanced in
their lax interpretation of the rules of their order
bv many of their own superiors, and even the popes
tnemselves. They were besides sustained in their
opposition by many of the great lords, who were
apprehensive that the rich chapels and masses,
which they or their ancestors had founded in the
various monasteries, would be neglected by the observantines, whose scrupulous adherence to the vow
of poverty excluded them from what, in church as
well as state, is too often found the most cogent
incentive to the performance of duty.[22]

From these various causes, the work of reform Attempts a
went on slowly; but the untiring exertions of Xim- reform
enes gradually effected its adoption in many estab-

[22] Fléchier, Hist. de Ximenés, pp. 25, 26. — Quintanilla, Archety-po, pp 21, 22. — Gomez, De Re- bus Gestis, fol. 6, 7. — Robles, Vida de Ximenez, cap. 12.

lishments ; and, where fair means could not pre-
vail, he sometimes resorted to force. The monks
of one of the convents in Toledo, being ejected
from their dwelling, in consequence of their pertinacious resistance, marched out in solemn procession, with the crucifix before them, chanting, at the
same time, the psalm *De exitu Israël*, in token of
their persecution. Isabella resorted to milder meth-
ods. She visited many of the nunneries in person,
taking her needle or distaff with her, and endeavouring by her conversation and example to withdraw their inmates from the low and frivolous
pleasures to which they were addicted. [23]

While the reformation was thus silently going
forward, the vacancy in the archbishopric of Toledo
already noticed, occurred by the death of the grand
cardinal. Isabella deeply felt the responsibility of
providing a suitable person to this dignity, the most
considerable not merely in Spain, but probably in
Christendom, after the papacy ; and which, moreover, raised its possessor to eminent political rank,
as high chancellor of Castile. [24] The right of nomination to benefices was vested in the queen by the
original settlement of the crown. She had uni-

[23] Fléchier, Hist. de Ximenés,
p. 25. — Quintanilla, Archetypo,
lib. 1, cap. 11. — Mem. de la Acad.
de Hist., tom. vi. Ilust. 8. — Robles, Vida de Ximenez, ubi supra.

[24] Oviedo, Quincuagenas, MS.,
bat. 1, quinc. 2, dial. 1. — Ferdinand and Isabella annexed the dignity of high chancellor in perpetuity to that of archbishop of Toledo.
It seems, however, at least in later

times, to have been a mere honor-
ary title. (Mendoza, Dignidades,
lib. 2, cap. 8.) The revenues of
the archbishopric at the beginning
of the sixteenth century amounted
to 80,000 ducats, (Navagiero, Viaggio, fol. 9. — L. Marineo, Cosas
Memorab es, fol. 23.) equivalent
to about 702,200 dollars at the
present day. See Introd., Sect. 1,
Note 63, of this History.

formly discharged this trust with the most consci- CHAPTER
entious impartiality, conferring the honors of the ———
church on none but persons of approved piety and
learning. [25] In the present instance, she was
strongly solicited by Ferdinand, in favor of his natural son Alfonso, archbishop of Saragossa. But
this prelate, although not devoid of talent, had
neither the age nor experience, and still less the
exemplary morals, demanded for this important
station ; and the queen mildly, but unhesitatingly,
resisted all entreaty and expostulation of her husband on his behalf. [26]

The post had always been filled by men of high
family. The queen, loath to depart from this usage,
notwithstanding the dying admonition of Mendoza,
turned her eyes on various candidates before she
determined in favor of her own confessor, whose
character presented so rare a combination of talent

---

[25] "De mas desto," says Lucio
Marineo, "tenia por costumbre,
que quando avia de dar alguna dig-
nidad, o obispado, mas mirava en
virtud, honestidad, y sciencia de
las personas, que las riquezas, y
generosidad, aun que fuessen sus
deudos. Lo qual fue causa que
muchos de los que hablavan poco,
y tenian los cabellos mas cortos que
las cejas ; començaron a traer los
ojos baxos mirando la tierra, y an-
dar con mas gravedad, y hazer
mejor vida, *simulando por ventura
algunos mas la virtud, que exerci-
tando la.*" (Cosas Memorables,
fol. 182.) "L'hypocrisie est l'hom-
mage que le vice rend à la vertu."
The maxim is now somewhat stale,
like most others of its profound author.

[26] Quintanilla, Archetypo, lib. 1,
cap. 16. — Salazar de Mendoza,
Crón. del Gran Cardenal, lib. 2,
cap. 65.
This prelate was at this time only
twenty-four years of age. He had
been raised to the see of Saragossa when only six. This strange
abuse of preferring infants to the
highest dignities of the church
seems to have prevailed in Castile
as well as Aragon ; for the tombs
of five archdeacons might be seen
in the church of Madre de Dios at
Toledo, in Salazar's time, whose
united ages amounted only to thirty years. See Crón. del Gran Cardenal, ubi supra.

and virtue, as amply compensated any deficiency of birth.

As soon as the papal bull reached Castile, con-firming the royal nomination, Isabella summoned Ximenes to her presence, and, delivering to him the parcel, requested him to open it before her. The confessor, who had no suspicion of their real pur-port, took the letters and devoutly pressed them to his lips ; when his eye falling on the superscription, " To our venerable brother Francisco Ximenez de Cisneros, archbishop elect of Toledo," he changed color, and involuntarily dropped the packet from his hands, exclaiming, " There is some mistake in this, it cannot be intended for me ;" and abruptly quitted the apartment.

The queen, far from taking umbrage at this un-ceremonious proceeding, waited awhile, until the first emotions of surprise should have subsided. Finding that he did not return, however, she de-spatched two of the grandees, who she thought would have the most influence with him, to seek him out and persuade him to accept the office. The nobles instantly repaired to his convent in Madrid, in which city the queen then kept her court. They found, however, that he had already left the place. Having ascertained his route, they mounted their horses, and, following as fast as possible, succeeded in overtaking him at three leagues' distance from the city, as he was travelling on foot at a rapid rate, though in the noontide heat, on his way to the Franciscan monastery at Ocaña.

After a brief expostulation with Ximenes on his

abrupt departure, they prevailed on him to retrace
his steps to Madrid ; but, upon his arrival there,
neither the arguments nor entreaties of his friends,
backed as they were by the avowed wishes of his
sovereign, could overcome his scruples, or induce
him to accept an office, of which he professed
himself unworthy. " He had hoped," he said, " to
pass the remainder of his days in the quiet practice
of his monastic duties ; and it was too late now to
call him into public life, and impose a charge of
such heavy responsibility on him, for which he had
neither capacity nor inclination." In this resolution
he pertinaciously persisted for more than six months,
until a second bull was obtained from the pope,
commanding him no longer to decline an appointment, which the church had seen fit to sanction.
This left no further room for opposition, and Ximenes acquiesced, though with evident reluctance, in
his advancement to the first dignity in the kingdom. [27]

There seems to be no good ground for charging
Ximenes with hypocrisy in this singular display of
humility. The *nolo episcopari*, indeed, has passed
into a proverb ; but his refusal was too long and
sturdily maintained to be reconciled with affectation or insincerity. He was, moreover, at this
time, in the sixtieth year of his age, when ambition, though not extinguished, is usually chilled

[27] Garibay, Compendio, tom. ii. ib. 19, cap. 4. — Mariana, Hist. de España, tom. ii. lib. 26, cap. 7. — Suma de la Vida de Cisneros, MS. — Quintanilla, Archetypo, lib. 1, cap. 16. — Gomez, De Rebus Gestis, fol. 11. — Carbajal, Anales, MS., año 1495. — Robles, Vida de Xime-nez, cap. 13. — Oviedo, Quincua-genas, MS.

in the human heart. His habits had been long accommodated to the ascetic duties of the cloister, and his thoughts turned from the business of this world to that beyond the grave. However gratifying the distinguished honor conferred on him might be to his personal feelings, he might naturally hesitate to exchange the calm, sequestered way of life, to which he had voluntarily devoted himself, for the turmoil and vexations of the world.

But, although Ximenes showed no craving for power, it must be confessed he was by no means diffident in the use of it. One of the very first acts of his administration is too characteristic to be omitted. The government of Cazorla, the most considerable place in the gift of the archbishop of Toledo, had been intrusted by the grand cardinal to his younger brother, Don Pedro Hurtado de Mendoza. The friends of this nobleman applied to Ximenes to confirm the appointment, reminding him at the same time of his own obligations to the cardinal, and enforcing their petition by the recommendation which they had obtained from the queen. This was not the way to approach Ximenes, who was jealous of any improper influence over his own judgment, and, above all, of the too easy abuse of the royal favor. He was determined, in the outset, effectually to discourage all such applications; and he declared, that "the sovereigns might send him back to the cloister again, but that no personal considerations should ever operate with him in distributing the honors of the church." The applicants, nettled at this response, returned to the queen, complaining in the bitterest terms of the arrogance and ingratitude of the new primate Isabella, however, evinced no symptoms of disapprobation, not altogether displeased, perhaps, with the honest independence of her minister; at any rate she took no further notice of the affair. [28]

Some time after, the archbishop encountered Mendoza in one of the avenues of the palace, and, as the latter was turning off to avoid the meeting, he saluted him with the title of *adelantado* of Cazorla. Mendoza stared with astonishment at the prelate, who repeated the salutation, assuring him, " that, now he was at full liberty to consult his own judgment, without the suspicion of any sinister influence, he was happy to restore him to a station, for which he had shown himself well qualified." It is scarcely necessary to say, that Ximenes was not importuned after this with solicitations for office. Indeed, all personal application he affected to regard as of itself sufficient ground for a denial, since it indicated " the want either of merit or of humility in the applicant." [29]

After his elevation to the primacy, he retained the same simple and austere manners as before, dispensing his large revenues in public and private charities, but regulating his domestic expenditure with the severest economy, [30] until he was admon-

---

[28] Gomez, De Rebus Gestis, fol. 11.

[29] Ibid., ubi supra. — Robles, Vida de Ximenez, cap. 13, 14.

[30] " He kept five or six friars of his order," says Gonzalo de Oviedo, " in his palace with him, and as many asses in his stables; but the latter all grew sleek and fat, for the archbishop would not ride himself, nor allow his brethren to ride either." Quincuagenas, MS.

ished by the Holy See to adopt a state more consonant with the dignity of his office, if he would not
disparage it in popular estimation. In obedience
to this, he so far changed his habits, as to display
the usual magnificence of his predecessors, in all
that met the public eye, — his general style of
living, equipage, and the number and pomp of
his retainers ; but he relaxed nothing of his own
personal mortifications. He maintained the same
abstemious diet, amidst all the luxuries of his
table. Under his robes of silk or costly furs he
wore the coarse frock of St. Francis, which he
used to mend with his own hands. He used no
linen about his person or bed ; and he slept on a
miserable pallet like that used by the monks of his
fraternity, and so contrived as to be concealed from
observation under the luxurious couch in which he
affected to repose.[31]

Reform in
his diocese

As soon as Ximenes entered on the duties of his
office, he bent all the energies of his mind to the
consummation of the schemes of reform, which his
royal mistress, as well as himself, had so much at
heart. His attention was particularly directed to
the clergy of his diocese, who had widely departed
from the rule of St. Augustine, by which they

31 Suma de la Vida de Cisneros,
MS.— Quintanilla, Archetypo, lib.
2, cap. 8, 9. — Gomez, de Rebus
Gestis, fol. 12. — Oviedo, Quin-
cuagenas, MS. — Robles, Vida de
Ximenez, cap. 13.

He commonly slept in his Franciscan habit. Of course his toilet
took no long time. On one occasion, as he was travelling, and up

as usual long before dawn, he
urged his muleteer to dress himself quickly ; at which the latter
irreverently exclaimed, " Cuerpc
de Dios ! does your holiness think
I have nothing more to do, than to
shake myself like a wet spaniel,
and tighten my cord a little ! '
Quintanilla, Archetypo, ubi supra

were bound. His attempts at reform, however, excited such a lively dissatisfaction in this reverend body, that they determined to send one of their own number to Rome, to prefer their complaints against the archbishop at the papal court.[32]

The person selected for this delicate mission was a shrewd and intelligent canon by the name of Albornoz. It could not be conducted so privately as to escape the knowledge of Ximenes. He was no sooner acquainted with it, than he despatched an officer to the coast, with orders to arrest the emissary. In case he had already embarked, the officer was authorized to fit out a fast sailing vessel, so as to reach Italy, if possible, before him. He was at the same time fortified with despatches from the sovereigns, to the Spanish minister Garcilasso de la Vega, to be delivered immediately on his arrival.

The affair turned out as had been foreseen. On arriving at the port, the officer found the bird had flown. He followed, however, without delay, and had the good fortune to reach Ostia several days before him. He forwarded his instructions at once to the Spanish minister, who in pursuance of them caused Albornoz to be arrested the moment he set foot on shore, and sent him back as a prisoner of state to Spain; where a close confinement for two

---

[32] Gomez de Rebus Gestis, fol. 16.

The Venetian minister Navagiero, noticing the condition of the canons of Toledo, some few years later celebrates them, as "lording 't above all others in their own city, being especial favorites with the ladies, dwelling in stately mansions, passing, in short, the most agreeable lives in the world, without any one to trouble them." Viaggio, fol. 9.

PART
II.
and twenty months admonished the worthy canon of the inexpediency of thwarting the plans of Ximenes. [33]

Reform of
the monastic
orders.
His attempts at innovation among the regular clergy of his own order, were encountered with more serious opposition. The reform fell most heavily on the Franciscans, who were interdicted by their rules from holding property, whether as a community, or as individuals ; while the members of other fraternities found some compensation for the surrender of their private fortunes, in the consequent augmentation of those of their fraternity. There was no one of the religious orders, therefore, in which the archbishop experienced such a dogged resistance to his plans, as in his own. More than a thousand friars, according to some accounts, quitted the country and passed over to Barbary, preferring rather to live with the infidel, than conform to the strict letter of their founder's rules. [34]

Great excite-
ment caused
by it.
The difficulties of the reform were perhaps augmented by the mode in which it was conducted. Isabella, indeed, used all gentleness and persuasion ; [35] but Ximenes carried measures with a high

---

[33] Gomez, De Rebus Gestis, fol. 17.

[34] Quintanilla, Archetypo, pp. 22, 23. — Mem. de la Acad. de Hist., tom. vi. p. 201. — Zurita, Hist. del Rey Hernando, lib. 3, cap. 15.

One account represents the migration as being to Italy and other Christian countries, where the conventual order was protected ; which would seem the most probable, though not the best authenticated, statement of the two.

[35] "Trataba las monjas," says Riol, " con un agrado y amor tan cariñoso, que las robaba los corazones, y hecha dueña de ellas, las persuadia con suavidad y eficacia á que votasen clausura. Y es cosa admirable, que raro fue el convento donde entró esta celebre heroina, donde no lograse en el propio dia el efecto de su santo deseo.' Informe, apud Semanario Erudito, tom. iii. p. 110.

and inexorable hand. He was naturally of an austere and arbitrary temper, and the severe training which he had undergone, made him less charitable for the lapses of others; especially of those, who, like himself, had voluntarily incurred the obligations of monastic rule. He was conscious of the rectitude of his intentions; and, as he identified his own interests with those of the church, he regarded all opposition to himself as an offence against religion, warranting the most peremptory exertion of power.

The clamor raised against his proceedings became at length so alarming, that the general of the Franciscans, who resided at Rome, determined to anticipate the regular period of his visit to Castile for inspecting the affairs of the order. As he was himself a conventual, his prejudices were of course all enlisted against the measures of reform; and he came over fully resolved to compel Ximenes to abandon it altogether, or to undermine, if possible, his credit and influence at court. But this functionary had neither the talent nor temper requisite for so arduous an undertaking.

He had not been long in Castile before he was convinced that all his own power, as head of the order, would be incompetent to protect it against the bold innovations of his provincial, while supported by royal authority. He demanded, therefore, an audience of the queen, in which he declared his sentiments with very little reserve. He expressed his astonishment that she should have selected an individual for the highest dignity in the

church, who was destitute of nearly every qualifi-
cation, even that of birth; whose sanctity was a
mere cloak to cover his ambition; whose morose
and melancholy temper made him an enemy not
only of the elegances, but the common courtesies
of life; and whose rude manners were not compensated by any tincture of liberal learning. He de-
plored the magnitude of the evil, which his intemperate measures had brought on the church, but
which it was, perhaps, not yet too late to rectify;
and he concluded by admonishing her, that, if she
valued her own fame, or the interests of her soul,
she would compel this man of yesterday to abdicate
the office, for which he had proved himself so
incompetent, and return to his original obscurity!

The queen, who listened to this violent harangue
with an indignation, that prompted her more than
once to order the speaker from her presence, put a
restraint on her feelings, and patiently waited to
the end. When he had finished, she calmly asked
him, " If he was in his senses, and knew whom he
was thus addressing?" "Yes," replied the enraged friar, "I am in my senses, and know very
well whom I am speaking to; — the queen of Castile, a mere handful of dust, like myself!" With
these words, he rushed out of the apartment, shut-
ting the door after him with furious violence.[36]

Such impotent bursts of passion could, of course,
have no power to turn the queen from her purpose

[36] Fléchier, Hist. de Ximenés,   Rey Hernando, lib. 3, cap. 15 —
pp. 56, 58. — Gomez, De Rebus   Robles, Vida de Ximenez, cap. 13
Gestis, fol. 14. — Zurita, Hist. del

The general, however, on his return to Italy, had sufficient address to obtain authority from His Holiness to send a commission of conventuals to Castile, who should be associated with Ximenes in the management of the reform. These individuals soon found themselves mere ciphers ; and, highly offended at the little account which the archbishop made of their authority, they preferred such complaints of his proceedings to the pontifical court, that Alexander the Sixth was induced, with the advice of the college of cardinals, to issue a brief, November 9th, 1496, peremptorily inhibiting the sovereigns from proceeding further in the affair, until it had been regularly submitted for examination to the head of the church. [37]

Isabella, on receiving this unwelcome mandate, instantly sent it to Ximenes. The spirit of the latter, however, rose in proportion to the obstacles it had to encounter. He sought only to rally the queen's courage, beseeching her not to faint in the good work, now that it was so far advanced, and assuring her that it was already attended with such beneficent fruits, as could not fail to secure the protection of Heaven. Isabella, every act of whose administration may be said to have had reference, more or less remote, to the interests of religion, was as little likely as himself to falter in a matter, which proposed these interests as its direct and only object. She assured her minister that she would

CHAPTER
V.

The pope's
interference.

Consents to
the reform.

[37] Gomez De Rebus Gestis, fol. 23. — Quintanilla, Archetypo, lib. 1, cap. 11.

support him in all that was practicable; and she
lost no time in presenting the affair, through her
agents, in such a light to the court of Rome, as
might work a more favorable disposition in it. In
this she succeeded, though not till after multiplied
delays and embarrassments; and such ample powers were conceded to Ximenes, in conjunction with
the apostolic nuncio, as enabled him to consummate
his grand scheme of reform, in defiance of all the
efforts of his enemies. [38]

1497.

Its operation
and effects.

The reformation thus introduced extended to the
religious institutions of every order equally with his
own. It was most searching in its operation, reaching eventually to the moral conduct of the subjects
of it, no less than the mere points of monastic discipline. As regards the latter, it may be thought
of doubtful benefit to have enforced the rigid interpretation of a rule, founded on the melancholy principle, that the amount of happiness in the next
world is to be regulated by that of self-inflicted
suffering in this. But it should be remembered,
that, however objectionable such a rule may be in
itself, yet, where it is voluntarily assumed as an im-
perative moral obligation, it cannot be disregarded
without throwing down the barrier to unbounded
license; and that the reassertion of it, under these
circumstances, must be a necessary preliminary to
any effectual reform of morals.

[38] Quintanilla, Archetypo, lib. 1,
cap. 11 – 14. — Riol discusses the
various monastic reforms effected
by Ximenes, in his Memorial to
Philip V., apud Semanario Erudito
tom. iii. pp. 102 – 110.

The beneficial changes wrought in this latter CHAPTER V.
particular, which Isabella had far more at heart
than any exterior forms of discipline, are the theme
of unqualified panegyric with her contemporaries.[39]
The Spanish clergy, as I have before had occasion
to remark, were early noted for their dissolute way
of life, which, to a certain extent, seemed to be
countenanced by the law itself.[40] This laxity of
morals was carried to a most lamentable extent
under the last reign, when all orders of ecclesiastics, whether regular or secular, infected probably
by the corrupt example of the court, are represented (we may hope it is an exaggeration) as
wallowing in all the excesses of sloth and sensual-
ity. So deplorable a pollution of the very sanctu-
aries of religion could not fail to occasion sincere
regret to a pure and virtuous mind like Isabella's.
The stain had sunk too deep, however, to be readily purged away. Her personal example, indeed,
and the scrupulous integrity with which she reserved all ecclesiastical preferment for persons of
unblemished piety, contributed greatly to bring
about an amelioration in the morals of the secular
clergy. But the secluded inmates of the cloister

[39] L. Marineo, Cosas Memorables, fol. 165. — Bernaldez, Reyes
Católicos, MS., cap. 201. — et al.

[40] The practice of concubinage
by the clergy was fully recognised,
and the ancient *fueros* of Castile
permitted their issue to inherit the
estates of such parents as died
intestate. (See Marina, Ensayo
Histórico-Critico sobre la Antigua
Legislacion de Castilla, (Madrid,
1808,) p. 184.) The effrontery of
these legalized strumpets, *barraga-*

nas, as they were called, was at
length so intolerable as to call for
repeated laws, regulating their apparel, and prescribing a badge for
distinguishing them from honest
women. (Sempere, Hist. del Lu-
xo, tom. i. pp. 165–169.) Spain
is probably the only country in
Christendom, where concubinage
was ever sanctioned by law ; a circumstance doubtless imputable, in
some measure, to the influence of
the Mahometans.

were less open to these influences; and the work of reform could only be accomplished there, by bringing them back to a reverence for their own institutions, and by the slow operation of public opinion.

Notwithstanding the queen's most earnest wishes, it may be doubted whether this would have ever been achieved without the coöperation of a man like Ximenes, whose character combined in itself all the essential elements of a reformer. Happily, Isabella was permitted to see before her death, if not the completion, at least the commencement, of a decided amendment in the morals of the religious orders; an amendment, which, so far from being transitory in its character, calls forth the most emphatic eulogium from a Castilian writer far in the following century; who, while he laments their ancient laxity, boldly challenges comparison for the religious communities of his own country, with those of any other, in temperance, chastity, and exemplary purity of life and conversation. [41]

[41] Gomez, De Rebus Gestis, fol. 23.

Alvaro Gomez, and biographers of Ximenes.
The authority on whom the life of Cardinal Ximenes mainly rests, is Alvaro Gomez de Castro. He was born in the village of St. Eulalia, near Toledo, in 1515, and received his education at Alcalá, where he obtained great repute for his critical acquaintance with the ancient classics. He was afterwards made professor of the humanities in the university; a situation which he filled with credit, but subsequently exchanged for the rhetorical chair in a school recently founded at Toledo. While thus occupied, he was chosen by the university of Alcalá to pay the most distinguished honor, which could be rendered to the memory of its illustrious founder, by a faithful record of his extraordinary life. The most authentic sources of in-

formation were thrown open to him. He obtained an intimate acquaintance with the private life of the cardinal, from three of his principal domestics, who furnished abundance of reminiscences from personal observation, while the archives of the university supplied a mass of documents relating to the public services of its patron. From these and similar materials, Gomez prepared his biography, after many years of patient labor. The work fully answered public expectation ; and its merits are such as to lead the learned Nic. Antonio to express a doubt, whether any thing more excellent or perfect in its way could be achieved ; "quo opere in eo genere an præstantius quidquam aut perfectius, esse possit, non immerito sæpe dubitavi." (Bibliotheca Nova, tom. i. p. 59.) The encomium may be thought somewhat excessive ; but it cannot be denied, that the narrative is written in an easy and natural manner, with fidelity and accuracy, with commendable liberality of opinion, though with a judgment sometimes warped into an undue estimate of the qualities of his hero. It is distinguished, moreover, by such beauty and correctness of Latinity, as have made it a text-book in many of the schools and colleges of the Peninsula. The first edition, being that used in the present work, was published at Alcalá, in 1569. It has since been reprinted twice in Germany, and perhaps elsewhere. Gomez was busily occupied with other literary lucubrations during the remainder of his life, and published several works in Latin prose and verse, both of which he wrote with ease and elegance. He died of a catarrh, in 1580, in the sixty-sixth year of his age, leaving behind him a reputation for disinterestedness and virtue, which is sufficiently commemorated in two lines of his epitaph ;

" Nemini unquam sciens nocui,
Prodesse quam pluribus curavi "

The work of Gomez has furnished the basis for all those biographies of Ximenes which have since appeared in Spain. The most important of these, probably, is Quintanilla's ; which, with little merit of selection or arrangement, presents a copious mass of details, drawn from every quarter whence his patient industry could glean them. Its author was a Franciscan, and employed in procuring the beatification of Cardinal Ximenes by the court of Rome ; a circumstance which probably disposed him to easier faith in the marvellous of his story, than most of his readers will be ready to give. The work was published at Palermo in 1653.

In addition to these authorities I have availed myself of a curious old manuscript, presented to me by Mr. O. Rich, entitled " Suma de la Vida del R. S. Cardenal Don Fr. Francisco Ximenez de Cisneros." It was written within half a century after the cardinal's death, by " un criado de la casa de Coruña." The original, in " very ancient letter," was extant in the archives of that noble house in Quintanilla's time, and is often cited by him. (Archetypo, apeno. p. 77.) Its author evidently had access to those contemporary notices, some of which furnished the basis of Castro's narrative, from which, indeed, it exhibits no material discrepancy.

The extraordinary character of Ximenes has naturally attracted the attention of foreign writers, and especially the French, who have produced repeated biographies of him. The most eminent of these is by Fléchier, the eloquent bishop of Nismes. It is written with the simple elegance and perspicuity, which characterize his other compositions ; and in the general tone of its sentiments, on all matters both of church and state, is quite as orthodox as the most bigoted admirer of the cardinal could desire. Another life, by

Marsollier, has obtained a very undeserved repute. The author, not content with the extraordinary qualities really appertaining to his hero, makes him out a sort of universal genius, quite ridiculous, rivalling Molière's Dr. Pancrace himself. One may form some idea of the historian's accuracy from the fact, that he refers the commencement and conduct of the war of Granada chiefly to the counsels of Ximenes, who, as we have seen, was not even introduced at court till after the close of the war. Marsollier reckoned largely on the ignorance and *gullibility* of his readers. The event proved he was not mistaken.

Cardinal Ximenes de Cisneros
Regent of Castile.

CHAPTER VI.

XIMENES IN GRANADA. — PERSECUTION, INSURRECTION, AND CONVERSION OF THE MOORS.

1499 — 1500.

Tranquil State of Granada. — Mild Policy of Talavera. — Clergy Dissatisfied with it. — Violent Measures of Ximenes. — His Fanaticism. — Its mischievous Effects. — Insurrection in Granada. — Tranquillity restored. — Baptism of the Inhabitants.

MORAL energy, or constancy of purpose, seems to be less properly an independent power of the mind than a mode of action, by which its various powers operate with effect. But, however this may be, it enters more largely, perhaps, than mere talent, as commonly understood, into the formation of what is called character, and is often confounded by the vulgar with talent of the highest order. In the ordinary concerns of life, indeed, it is more serviceable than brilliant parts; while, in the more important, these latter are of little weight without it, evaporating only in brief and barren flashes, which may dazzle the eye by their splendor, but pass away and are forgotten

The importance of moral energy is felt not only, where it would be expected, in the concerns of active life, but in those more exclusively of an intellectual character, in deliberative assemblies, for example, where talent, as usually understood, might be supposed to assert an absolute supremacy, but where it is invariably made to bend to the controlling influence of this principle. No man destitute of it can be the leader of a party ; while there are few leaders, probably, who do not number in their ranks minds, from which they would be compelled to shrink in a contest for purely intellectual preëminence.

This energy of purpose presents itself in a yet more imposing form when stimulated by some intense passion, as ambition, or the nobler principle of patriotism or religion ; when the soul, spurning vulgar considerations of interest, is ready to do and to dare all for conscience' sake ; when, insensible alike to all that this world can give or take away, it loosens itself from the gross ties which bind it to earth, and, however humble its powers in every other point of view, attains a grandeur and elevation, which genius alone, however gifted, can never reach.

But it is when associated with exalted genius, and under the action of the potent principles above mentioned, that this moral energy conveys an image of power, which approaches, nearer than any thing else on earth, to that of a divine intelligence. It is, indeed, such agents that Providence selects for the accomplishment of those great revolutions, by which the world is shaken to its foundations, new and more beautiful systems created, and the human mind carried forward at a single stride, in the career of improvement, further than it had advanced CHAPTER VI. for centuries. It must, indeed, be confessed, that this powerful agency is sometimes for evil, as well as for good. It is this same impulse, which spurs guilty Ambition along his bloody track, and which arms the hand of the patriot sternly to resist him; which glows with holy fervor in the bosom of the martyr, and which lights up the fires of persecution, by which he is to win his crown of glory. The direction of the impulse, differing in the same individual under different circumstances, can alone determine whether he shall be the scourge or the benefactor of his species.

These reflections have been suggested by the Ximenes, his constancy of purpose. character of the extraordinary person brought forward in the preceding chapter, Ximenes de Cisneros, and the new and less advantageous aspect, in which he must now appear to the reader. Inflexible constancy of purpose formed, perhaps, the most prominent trait of his remarkable character. What direction it might have received under other circumstances it is impossible to say. It would be no great stretch of fancy to imagine, that the unyielding spirit, which in its early days could voluntarily endure years of imprisonment, rather than submit to an act of ecclesiastical oppression, might under similar influences have been aroused, like Luther's, to shake down the ancient pillars of Catholicism, instead of lending all its strength to uphold them. The latter position, however, would seem better assimilated to the constitution of his mind, whose sombre enthusiasm naturally prepared him for the vague and mysterious in the Romish faith, as his inflexible temper did for its bold and arrogant dogmas. At any rate, it was to this cause he devoted the whole strength of his talents and commanding energies.

We have seen in the preceding chapter, with what promptness he entered on the reform of religious discipline, as soon as he came into office, and with what pertinacity he pursued it, in contempt of all personal interest and popularity. We are now to see him with similar zeal devoting himself to the extirpation of heresy ; with contempt not merely of personal consequences, but also of the most obvious principles of good faith and national honor.

Tranquil
tate of
Granada.

1499.

Nearly eight years had elapsed since the conquest of Granada, and the subjugated kingdom continued to repose in peaceful security under the shadow of the treaty, which guarantied the unmolested enjoyment of its ancient laws and religion. This unbroken continuance of public tranquillity, especially difficult to be maintained among the jarring elements of the capital, whose motley population of Moors, renegades, and Christians, suggested perpetual points of collision, must be chiefly referred to the discreet and temperate conduct of the two individuals, whom Isabella had charged with the civil and ecclesiastical government. These were Mendoza, count of Tendilla, and Talavera, archbishop of Granada.

Tendilla.

The former, the brightest ornament of his illustrious house, has been before made known to the reader by his various important services, both military and diplomatic. Immediately after the conquest of Granada he was made alcayde and captain general of the kingdom, a post for which he was every way qualified by his prudence, firmness, enlightened views, and long experience.[1]

The latter personage, of more humble extraction,[2] was Fray Fernando de Talavera, a Hieronymite monk, who, having been twenty years prior of the monastery of Santa Maria del Prado, near Valladolid, was made confessor of Queen Isabella, and afterwards of the king. This situation necessarily gave him considerable influence in all public measures. If the keeping of the royal conscience could be safely intrusted to any one, it might certainly be to this estimable prelate, equally distinguished for his learning, amiable manners, and unblemished piety; and, if his character was somewhat tainted with bigotry, it was in so mild a form, so far tempered by the natural benevolence of his disposition, as to make a favorable contrast to the dominant spirit of the time.[3]

CHAPTER VI.

Talavera

[1] "Hombre," says his son, the historian, of him, "de prudencia en negocios graves, de animo firme, asegurado con luenga experiencia de rencuentros i battallas ganadas." (Guerra de Granada, lib. 1, p. 9.) Oviedo dwells with sufficient amplification on the personal history and merits of this distinguished individual, in his garrulous reminiscences. Quincuagenas, MS., bat. 1, quinc. 1, dial. 28.

[2] Oviedo, at least, can find no better pedigree for him, than that of Adam. "Quanto á su linage él fué del linage de todos los humanos ó de aquel barro y subce-

sion de Adan." (Quincuagenas, MS., dial. de Talavera.) It is a very hard case, when a Castilian cannot make out a better genealogy for his hero.

[3] Pedraza, Antiguedad de Granada, lib. 3, cap. 10. — Marmol, Rebelion de Moriscos, lib. 1, cap. 21.

Talavera's correspondence with the queen, published in various works, but most correctly, probably, in the sixth volume of the Mem. de la Acad. de Hist., (Ilust. 13.) is not calculated to raise his reputation. His letters are little else than homilies on the love of com-

After the conquest, he exchanged the bishopric of Avila for the archiepiscopal see of Granada Notwithstanding the wishes of the sovereigns, he refused to accept any increase of emolument in this new and more exalted station. His revenues, indeed, which amounted to two millions of maravedies annually, were somewhat less than he before enjoyed.[4] The greater part of this sum he liberally expended on public improvements and works of charity; objects, which, to their credit be it spoken, have rarely failed to engage a large share of the attention and resources of the higher Spanish clergy.[5]

The subject which pressed most seriously on the mind of the good archbishop, was the conversion of the Moors, whose spiritual blindness he regarded with feelings of tenderness and charity, very different from those entertained by most of his reverend brethren. He proposed to accomplish this by the most rational method possible. Though late in life, he set about learning Arabic, that he might communicate with the Moors in their own language, and commanded his clergy to do the same.[6] He

---

pany, dancing, and the like heinous offences. The whole savours more of the sharp twang of Puritanism than of the Roman Catholic school. But bigotry is neutral ground, on which the most opposite sects may meet.

[4] Pedraza, Antiguedad de Granada, lib. 3, cap. 10. — Marmol, lib. 1, cap. 21.
Equivalent to 56,000 dollars of the present day; a sum which Pedraza makes do quite as hard duty, according to its magnitude, as the 500 pounds of Pope's Man of Ross.

[5] Pedraza, ubi supr. — Oviedo, Quincuagenas, MS., dial. de Talavera.
The worthy archbishop's benefactions on some occasions were of rather an extraordinary character. "Pidiendole limosna," says Pedraza, "una muger que no tenia camisa, se entró en una casa, y se desnudó la suya y se la dio; diziendo con san Pedro, No tengc oro ni plata que darte, doyte lo que tengo." Antiguedad de Granada, lib. 3, cap. 10.
[6] Marmol, Rebelion de Moriscos

caused an Arabic vocabulary, grammar, and cate- CHAPTER
chism to be compiled ; and a version in the same VI.
tongue to be made of the liturgy, comprehending
the selections from the Gospels ; and proposed to
extend this at some future time to the whole
body of the Scriptures.[7] Thus unsealing the sacred
oracles which had been hitherto shut out from their
sight, he opened to them the only true sources
of Christian knowledge ; and, by endeavouring to
effect their conversion through the medium of their
understandings, instead of seducing their imaginations with a vain show of ostentatious ceremonies,
proposed the only method by which conversion
could be sincere and permanent.

These wise and benevolent measures of the good
prelate, recommended, as they were, by the most
exemplary purity of life, acquired him great authority among the Moors, who, estimating the value of
the doctrine by its fruits, were well inclined to listen to it, and numbers were daily added to the
church.[8]

The progress of proselytism, however, was neces-

---

lib. 1, cap. 21. — Pedraza, Antiguedad de Granada, ubi supra.

[7] Fléchier, Hist. de Ximenés,
p. 17. — Quintanilla, Archetypo,
lib. 2, cap. 2. — Gomez, De Rebus
Gestis, fol. 32. — Oviedo, Quincuagenas, MS.

These tracts were published at
Granada, in 1505, in the European
character, being the first books
ever printed in the Arabic language according to Dr. M'Crie,
(Reformation in Spain, p. 70,) who
cites Schnurrer, Bibl. Arabica, pp.
16 – 18.

[8] Bleda, Corónica, lib. 5, cap.
23. — Pedraza, Antiguedad de Granada, lib. 3, cap. 10. — Marmol,
Rebelion de Moriscos, lib. 1, cap.
21. — Gomez, De Rebus Gestis,
fol. 29. — " Hacia lo que predica-
ba, é predicó lo que hizo," says
Oviedo of the archbishop, briefly,
" é asi fué mucho provechoso é util
en aquella ciudad para la conversion de los Moros." Quincuagenas, MS.

sarily slow and painful among a people reared from the cradle, not merely in antipathy to, but abhorrence of, Christianity; who were severed from the Christian community by strong dissimilarity of language, habits, and institutions; and now indissolubly knit together by a common sense of national misfortune. Many of the more zealous clergy and religious persons, conceiving, indeed, this barrier altogether insurmountable, were desirous of seeing it swept away at once by the strong arm of power. They represented to the sovereigns, that it seemed like insensibility to the goodness of Providence, which had delivered the infidels into their hands, tc allow them any longer to usurp the fair inheritance of the Christians, and that the whole of the stiff-necked race of Mahomet might justly be required tc submit without exception to instant baptism, or to sell their estates and remove to Africa. This, they maintained, could be scarcely regarded as an infringement of the treaty, since the Moors would be so great gainers on the score of their eternal salvation; to say nothing of the indispensableness of such a measure to the permanent tranquillity and security of the kingdom![9]

But these considerations, " just and holy as they were," to borrow the words of a devout Spaniard,[10] failed to convince the sovereigns, who resolved to abide by their royal word, and to trust to the conciliatory measures now in progress, and a longer and more intimate intercourse with the Christians,

[9] Marmol, Rebelion de Moriscos, lib. 1, cap. 23. [10] Ibid., ubi supra

as the only legitimate means for accomplishing
their object. Accordingly, we find the various
public ordinances, as low down as 1499, recognising this principle, by the respect which they
show for the most trivial usages of the Moors, [11]
and by their sanctioning no other stimulant to conversion than the amelioration of their condition. [12]

Among those in favor of more active measures
was Ximenes, archbishop of Toledo. Having followed the court to Granada in the autumn of 1499,
he took the occasion to communicate his views to
Talavera, the archbishop, requesting leave at the
same time to participate with him in his labor of
love ; to which the latter, willing to strengthen
himself by so efficient an ally, modestly assented.
Ferdinand and Isabella soon after removed to
Seville ; but, before their departure, enjoined on
the prelates to observe the temperate policy hith
erto pursued, and to beware of giving any occasion
for discontent to the Moors. [13]

[11] In the *pragmática* dated Granada, October 30th, 1499, prohibiting silk apparel of any description,
an exception was made in favor of
the Moors, whose robes were usually of that material, among the
wealthier classes. Pragmáticas del
Reyno, fol. 120.

[12] Another law, October 31st,
1499, provided against the disin-
heritance of Moorish children who
had embraced Christianity, and
secured, moreover, to the female
converts a portion of the property
which had fallen to the state on the
conquest of Granada. (Pragmáticas del Reyno, fol. 5.) Llorente
has reported this pragmatic with

some inaccuracy. Hist. de l'Inquisition, tom. i. p. 334.

[13] Bleda, Corónica, lib. 5, cap.
23. — Gomez, De Rebus Gestis,
fol. 29. — Quintanilla, Archetypo,
lib. 2, p. 54. — Suma de la Vida de
Cisneros, MS.

Ferdinand and Isabella, according to Ferreras, took counsel of
sundry learned theologians and jurists, whether they could lawfully
compel the Mahometans to become
Christians, notwithstanding the
treaty, which guarantied to them
the exercise of their religion. After
repeated conferences of this erudite
body, "il fut décidé," says the
historian, " qu'on solliciteroit la

No sooner had the sovereigns left the city, than Ximenes invited some of the leading *alfaquies*, or Mussulman doctors, to a conference, in which he expounded, with all the eloquence at his command, the true foundations of the Christian faith, and the errors of their own ; and, that his teaching might be the more palatable, enforced it by liberal presents, consisting mostly of rich and costly articles of dress, of which the Moors were at all times exceedingly fond. This policy he pursued for some time, till the effect became visible. Whether the preaching or presents of the archbishop had most weight, does not appear.[14] It is probable, however, that the Moorish doctors found conversion a much more pleasant and profitable business than they had anticipated ; for they one after another declared their conviction of their errors, and their willingness to receive baptism. The example of these learned persons was soon followed by great numbers of their illiterate disciples, insomuch that no less than four thousand are said to have presented themselves in one day for baptism ; and Ximenes, unable to administer the rite to each individually, was obliged to adopt the expedient familiar to the Christian missionaries, of christening them *en masse* by aspersion ; scattering the con-

conversion des Mahométans de la Ville et du Royaume de Grenade, en ordonnant à ceux qui ne voudroient pas embrasser la religion Chrétienne, de vendre leurs biens et de sortir du royaume." (Hist. d'Espagne, tom. viii. p. 194.) Such was the idea of *solicitation* entertained by these reverend casuists ! The story, however, wants a better voucher than Ferreras.

[14] The honest Robles appears to be of the latter opinion. "Alfin," says he, with *naïveté*, "con halagos, dadivas, y caricias, los truxo a conocimiento del verdadero Dios" Vida de Ximenez, p. 100.

secrated drops from a mop, or hyssop, as it was called, which he twirled over the heads of the multitude. [15]

So far all went on prosperously; and the eloquence and largesses of the archbishop, which latter he lavished so freely as to encumber his rev enues for several years to come, brought crowds of proselytes to the Christian fold. [16] There were some, indeed, among the Mahometans, who regarded these proceedings as repugnant, if not to the letter, at least to the spirit of the original treaty of capitulation; which seemed intended to provide, not only against the employment of force, but of any undue incentive to conversion. [17] Several of the more sturdy, including some of the principal citizens, exerted their efforts to stay the tide of defection, which threatened soon to swallow up the whole population of the city. But Ximenes, whose zeal had mounted up to fever heat in the excitement of success, was not to be cooled by any opposition, however formidable; and, if he

---

[15] Robles, Vida de Ximenez, cap. 14. — Marmol, Rebelion de Moriscos, lib. 1, cap. 24. — Gomez, De Rebus Gestis, fol. 29. — Suma de la Vida de Cisneros, MS.

[16] Robles, Vida de Ximenez, cap. 14. — Quintanilla, Archetypo, fol. 55. — The sound of bells, so unusual to Mahometan ears, pealing day and night from the newly consecrated mosques, gained Ximenes the appellation of *alfaqui campanero* from the Granadines. Suma de la Vida de Cisneros, MS.

[17] Marmol, Rebelion de Moriscos, lib. 1, cap. 25.

Take for example the following provisions in the treaty. " Que si algun Moro tuviere alguna renegada por muger, no será apremiada á ser Christiana contra su voluntad, sino que será interrogada, en presencia de Christianos y de Moros, y se siguirá su voluntad; y lo mesmo se entenderá con los niños y niñas nacidos de Christiana y Moro. Que ningun Moro ni Mora serán apremiados á ser Christianos contra su voluntad; y que si alguna doncella, ó casada, ó viuda, por razon de algunos amores se quisiere tornar Christiana, tampoco será recebida, hasta ser interrogada." The whole treaty is given *in extenso* by Marmol, and by no other author that I have seen.

had hitherto respected the letter of the treaty, he now showed himself prepared to trample on letter and spirit indifferently, when they crossed his designs.

Among those most active in the opposition was a noble Moor named Zegri, well skilled in the learning of his countrymen, with whom he had great consideration. Ximenes, having exhausted all his usual artillery of arguments and presents on this obdurate infidel, had him taken into custody by one of his officers named Leon, "a lion," says a punning historian, " by nature as well as by name," [18] and commanded the latter to take such measures with his prisoner, as would clear the film from his eyes. This faithful functionary executed his orders so effectually, that, after a few days of fasting, fetters, and imprisonment, he was able to present his charge to his employer, penitent to all outward appearance, and with an humble mien strongly contrasting with his former proud and lofty bearing. After the most respectful obeisance to the archbishop, Zegri informed him, that " on the preceding night he had had a revelation from Allah, who had condescended to show him the error of his ways, and commanded him to receive instant baptism"; at the same time pointing to his gaoler, he "jocularly" remarked, " Your reverence has only to turn this *lion* of yours loose among the people, and my word for it, there will not be a Mussulman left many days within the walls of Granada." [19]

[18] Gomez, De Rebus Gestis, lib. 2, fol. 29.   [19] Robles, Rebelion de Moriscos, cap. 14.—Suma de la Vida de

" Thus," exclaims the devout Ferreras, " did Providence avail itself of the darkness of the dungeon to pour on the benighted minds of the infidel the light of the true faith! " [20]

The work of proselytism now went on apace; for terror was added to the other stimulants. The zealous propagandist, in the mean while, flushed with success, resolved not only to exterminate infidelity, but the very characters in which its teachings were recorded. He accordingly caused all the Arabic manuscripts which he could procure, to be heaped together in a common pile in one of the great squares of the city. The largest part were copies of the Koran, or works in some way or other connected with theology; with many others, however, on various scientific subjects. They were beautifully executed, for the most part, as to their chirography, and sumptuously bound and decorated; for, in all relating to the mechanical finishing, the Spanish Arabs excelled every people in Europe. But neither splendor of outward garniture, nor intrinsic merit of composition, could atone for the taint of heresy in the eye of the stern inquisitor; he reserved for his university of Alcalá three hundred works, indeed, relating to medical science, in which the Moors were as preëminent in that day as the Europeans were deficient; but all the rest,

Cisneros, MS. — Gomez, De Rebus Gestis, fol. 30. — Marmol, Rebelion de Moriscos, lib. 1, cap. 25.

Zegri assumed the baptismal name of the Great Captain, Gonzalo Hernandez whose prowess he had experienced in a personal rencontre in the vega of Granada. Marmol, Rebelion de Moriscos, ubi supra. — Suma de la Vida de Cisneros, MS.

[20] Hist. d'Espagne, tom. viii. p. 195.

amounting to many thousands,[21] he consigned to indiscriminate conflagration.[22]

This melancholy *auto da fe*, it will be recollected, was celebrated, not by an unlettered barbarian, but by a cultivated prelate, who was at that very time actively employing his large revenues in the publication of the most stupendous literary work of the age, and in the endowment of the most learned university in Spain.[23] It took place, not in the darkness of the middle ages, but in the dawn of the sixteenth century, and in the midst of an enlightened nation, deeply indebted for its own progress to these very stores of Arabian wisdom. It forms a counterpart to the imputed sacrilege of Omar,[24] eight centuries before, and shows that bigotry is the same in every faith, and every age.

[21] According to Robles, (Rebelion de Moriscos, p. 104.) and the Suma de la Vida de Cisneros, 1,005,000; to Conde, (El Nubiense, Descripcion d'España, p. 4, note,) 80,000; to Gomez and others 5,000. There are scarcely any data for arriving at probability in this monstrous discrepancy. The famous library of the Ommeyades at Cordova was said to contain 600,000 volumes. It had long since been dissipated; and no similar collection had been attempted in Granada, where learning was never in that palmy state which it reached under the Cordovan dynasty. Still, however, learned men were to be found there, and the Moorish metropolis would naturally be the depository of such literary treasures as had escaped the general shipwreck of time and accident. On the whole, the estimate of Gomez would appear much too small, and that of Robles as disproportionately exaggerated. Conde, better instructed in Arabic lore than any of his predecessors, may be found, perhaps, here, as elsewhere, the best authority.

[22] Gomez, De Rebus Gestis, lib. 2, fol. 30. — Marmol, Rebelion de Moriscos, lib. 1, cap. 25. — Robles, Vida de Ximenez, cap. 14. — Suma de la Vida de Cisneros, MS. — Quintanilla, Archetypo, p. 58.

[23] Yet the archbishop might find some countenance for his fanaticism, in the most polite capital of Europe. The faculty of Theology in Paris, some few years later, declared "que c'en était fait de la religion, si on permettait l'étude du Grec et de l'Hébreu!" Villers, Essai sur l'Esprit et l'Influence de la Reformation de Luther, (Paris, 1820,) p. 64, note.

[24] Gibbon's argument, if it does not shake the foundations of the whole story of the Alexandrian conflagration, may at least raise a

The mischief occasioned by this act, far from being limited to the immediate loss, continued to be felt still more severely in its consequences. Such as could, secreted the manuscripts in their possession till an opportunity occurred for convey ing them out of the country; and many thousands in this way were privately shipped over to Barbary.[25] Thus Arabian literature became rare in the libraries of the very country to which it was indigenous; and Arabic scholarship, once so flourishing in Spain, and that too in far less polished ages, gradually fell into decay from want of aliment to sustain it. Such were the melancholy results of this literary persecution; more mischievous, in one view, than even that directed against life; for the loss of an individual will scarcely be felt beyond his own generation, while the annihilation of a valuable work, or in other words, of mind itself embodied in a permanent form, is a loss to all future time.

The high hand with which Ximenes now carried measures, excited serious alarm in many of the more discreet and temperate Castilians in the city. They besought him to use greater forbearance, remonstrating against his obvious violations of the treaty, as well as against the expediency of forced conversions, which could not, in the nature of things, be lasting. But the pertinacious prelate

CHAPTER VI.

Mischievous effects.

natural skepticism as to the pretended amount and value of the works destroyed.

[25] The learned Granadine, Leo Africanus, who emigrated to Fez after the fall of the capital, notices a single collection of 3000 manuscripts belonging to an individual, which he saw in Algiers, whither they had been secretly brought by the Moriscoes from Spain. — Conde, Dominacion de los Arabes, prólogo. — Casiri, Bibliotheca Escurialensis, tom. i. p. 172.

only replied, that, "A tamer policy might, indeed, suit temporal matters, but not those in which the interests of the soul were at stake; that the unbeliever, if he could not be drawn, should be driven, into the way of salvation; and that it was no time to stay the hand, when the ruins of Mahometanism were tottering to their foundations." He accordingly went on with unflinching resolution.[26]

But the patience of the Moors themselves, which had held out so marvellously under this system of oppression, began now to be exhausted. Many signs of this might be discerned by much less acute optics than those of the archbishop; but his were blinded by the arrogance of success. At length, in this inflammable state of public feeling, an incident occurred which led to a general explosion.

Revolt of the
Albaycin.

Three of Ximenes's servants were sent on some business to the Albaycin, a quarter inhabited exclusively by Moors, and encompassed by walls, which separated it from the rest of the city.[27] These men had made themselves peculiarly odious to the people by their activity in their master's service. A dispute, having arisen between them and some inhabitants of the quarter, came at last to blows, when two of the servants were massacred on the spot, and their comrade escaped with difficulty from the infuriated mob.[28] The affair operated as the

[26] Gomez, De Rebus Gestis, fol. 30. — Abarca, Reyes de Aragon, rey 30, cap. 10.

[27] Casiri, Bibliotheca Escurialensis, tom. ii. p. 281. — Pedraza, Antiguedad de Granada, lib. 3, cap. 10.

[28] Gomez, De Rebus Gestis, fol. 31.

There are some discrepancies, not important however, between the narrative of Gomez and the other authorities. Gomez, considering his uncommon opportunities

signal for insurrection. The inhabitants of the district ran to arms, got possession of the gates, barricaded the streets, and in a few hours the whole Albaycin was in rebellion.[29]

In the course of the following night, a large number of the enraged populace made their way into the city to the quarters of Ximenes, with the purpose of taking summary vengeance on his head for all his persecutions. Fortunately, his palace was strong, and defended by numerous resolute and well-armed attendants. The latter, at the approach of the rioters, implored their master to make his escape, if possible, to the fortress of the Alhambra, where the count of Tendilla was established. But the intrepid prelate, who held life too cheap to be a coward, exclaimed, "God forbid I should think of my own safety, when so many of the faithful are perilling theirs! No, I will stand to my post and wait there, if Heaven wills it, the crown of martyrdom."[30] It must be confessed he well deserved it.

The building, however, proved too strong for the utmost efforts of the mob; and, at length, after some hours of awful suspense and agitation to the beleaguered inmates, the count of Tendilla arrived in person at the head of his guards, and succeeded in dispersing the insurgents, and driving them back to their own quarters. But no exertions could

CHAPTER VI.

Ximenes besieged in his palace.

---

of information, is worth them all.
[29] Suma de la Vida de Cisneros, MS. — Gomez, De Rebus Gestis, lib. 2, fol. 31. — Marmol, Rebelion de Moriscos, lib. 1, cap. 26.

[30] Robles, Vida de Ximenez, cap. 14. — Mariana, Hist. de España, tom. ii. lib. 27, cap. 5. — Quintanilla, Archetypo, p. 56. — Peter Martyr, Opus Epist., epist. 212.

restore order to the tumultuous populace, or indu e
them to listen to terms; and they even stoned the
messenger charged with pacific proposals from the
count of Tendilla. They organized themselves
under leaders, provided arms, and took every possible means for maintaining their defence. It
seemed as if, smitten with the recollections of ancient liberty, they were resolved to recover it again
at all hazards.[31]

At length, after this disorderly state of things
had lasted for several days, Talavera, the archbishop of Granada, resolved to try the effect of his
personal influence, hitherto so great with the
Moors, by visiting himself the disaffected quarter.
This noble purpose he put in execution, in spite of
the most earnest remonstrances of his friends. He
was attended only by his chaplain, bearing the crucifix before him, and a few of his domestics, on foot
and unarmed like himself. At the sight of their
venerable pastor, with his countenance beaming
with the same serene and benign expression, with
which they were familiar when listening to his
exhortations from the pulpit, the passions of the
multitude were stilled. Every one seemed willing
to abandon himself to the tender recollections of
the past; and the simple people crowded around
the good man, kneeling down and kissing the hem
of his robe, as if to implore his benediction. The
count of Tendilla no sooner learned the issue, than
he followed into the Albaycin, attended by a hand-

31 Mariana, Hist. de España, cap. 23. — Mendoza, Guerra de
ubi sup. — Bleda, Corónica, lib. 5, Granada, p. 11.

ful of soldiers. When he had reached the place where the mob was gathered, he threw his bonnet into the midst of them, in token of his pacific intentions. The action was received with acclamations, and the people, whose feelings had now taken another direction, recalled by his presence to the recollection of his uniformly mild and equitable rule, treated him with similar respect to that shown the archbishop of Granada.[32]

These two individuals took advantage of this favorable change of feeling to expostulate with the Moors on the folly and desperation of their conduct, which must involve them in a struggle with such overwhelming odds as that of the whole Spanish monarchy. They implored them to lay down their arms and return to their duty, in which event they pledged themselves, as far as in their power, to allow no further repetition of the grievances complained of, and to intercede for their pardon with the sovereigns. The count testified his sincerity, by leaving his wife and two children as hostages in the heart of the Albaycin; an act which must be admitted to imply unbounded confidence in the integrity of the Moors.[33] These various measures, backed, moreover, by the counsels and authority of some of the chief alfaquis,

[32] Marmol, Rebelion de Moriscos, lib. 1, cap. 26. — Peter Martyr, Opus Epist., epist. 212. — Quintanilla, Archetypo, p. 56. — Bleda, Corónica, ubi supra.

[33] Marmol, Rebelion de Moriscos, loc. cit. — Mendoza, Guerra de Granada, lib. 1, p. 11.
That such confidence was justified, may be inferred from a common saying of Archbishop Talavera, "That Moorish works and Spanish faith were all that were wanting to make a good Christian." A bitter sarcasm this on his own countrymen! Pedraza, Antiguedad de Granada, lib. 3, cap 10.

PART
II.

had the effect to restore tranquillity among the people, who, laying aside their hostile preparations,
returned once more to their regular employments. [34]

Displeasure
of the sove-
reigns.

The rumor of the insurrection, in the mean
while, with the usual exaggeration, reached Seville,
where the court was then residing. In one respect
rumor did justice, by imputing the whole blame of
the affair to the intemperate zeal of Ximenes.
That personage, with his usual promptness, had
sent early notice of the affair to the queen by a negro slave uncommonly fleet of foot. But the fel-
low had become intoxicated by the way, and the
court were several days without any more authentic
tidings than general report. The king, who always
regarded Ximenes's elevation to the primacy, to the
prejudice, as the reader may remember, of his own
son, with dissatisfaction, could not now restrain his
indignation, but was heard to exclaim tauntingly to
the queen, " So we are like to pay dear for your
archbishop, whose rashness has lost us in a few
hours, what we have been years in acquiring." [35]

Ximenes
hastens
court.

The queen, confounded at the tidings, and unable to comprehend the silence of Ximenes, instantly wrote to him in the severest terms, demanding
an explanation of the whole proceeding. The archbishop saw his error in committing affairs of moment to such hands as those of his sable messenger;
and the lesson stood him in good stead, according

[34] Peter Martyr, Opus Epist.,
epist. 212. — Bleda, Corónica, loc.
cit. — Marmol, Rebelion de Moriscos, ubi supra.

[35] Mariana, Hist. de España
tom. ii. lib. 27, cap. 5. — Robles
Vida de Ximenez, 14. — Suma de
la Vida de Cisneros, MS.

to his moralizing biographer, for the remainder of his life. [36] He hastened to repair his fault by proceeding to Seville in person, and presenting himself before the sovereigns. He detailed to them the history of all the past transactions; recapitulated his manifold services, the arguments and exhortations he had used, the large sums he had expended, and his various expedients, in short, for effecting conversion, before resorting to severity. He boldly assumed the responsibility of the whole proceeding, acknowledging that he had purposely avoided communicating his plans to the sovereigns for fear of opposition. If he had erred, he said, it could be imputed to no other motive, at worst, than too great zeal for the interests of religion; but he concluded with assuring them, that the present position of affairs was the best possible for their purposes, since the late conduct of the Moors involved them in the guilt, and consequently all the penalties of treason, and that it would be an act of clemency to offer pardon on the alternatives of conversion or exile! [37]

The archbishop's discourse, if we are to credit his enthusiastic biographer, not only dispelled the clouds of royal indignation, but drew forth the most emphatic expressions of approbation. [38] How far Ferdinand and Isabella were moved to this by his final recommendation, or what, in clerical language, may be called the "improvement of his discourse,"

CHAPTER
VI.

Conversion
of Granada

---

[36] Gomez, De Rebus Gestis, fol. 32. — Robles, Vida de Ximenez, cap. 14.

[37] Gomez De Rebus Gestis, ubi supra

[38] Gomez, De Rebus Gestis, fol. 33. — Suma de la Vida de Cisneros, MS.

does not appear. They did not at any rate adopt it in its literal extent. In due time, however, commissioners were sent to Granada, fully authorized to inquire into the late disturbances and punish their guilty authors. In the course of the investigation, many, including some of the principal citizens, were imprisoned on suspicion. The greater part made their peace by embracing Christianity. Many others sold their estates and migrated to Barbary; and the remainder of the population whether from fear of punishment, or contagion of example, abjured their ancient superstition and consented to receive baptism. The whole number of converts was estimated at about fifty thousand, whose future relapses promised an almost inexhaustible supply for the fiery labors of the Inquisition. From this period the name of Moors, which had gradually superseded the primitive one of Spanish Arabs, gave way to the title of Moriscoes, by which this unfortunate people continued to be known through the remainder of their protracted existence in the Peninsula.[39]

Applauded by the Spaniards.

The circumstances, under which this important revolution in religion was effected in the whole population of this great city, will excite only feelings of disgust at the present day, mingled, indeed,

---

[39] Bleda, Corónica, lib. 5, cap. 23. — Mariana, Hist. de España, tom. ii. lib. 27, cap. 5. — Peter Martyr, Opus Epist., epist. 215. — Marmol, Rebelion de Moriscos, lib. 1, cap. 27. — Gomez, De Rebus Gestis, lib. 2, fol. 32. — Lanuza, Historias, tom. i. lib. 1, cap. 11. — Carbajal, Anales, MS., año 1500. — Bernaldez, Reyes Catolicos, MS., cap. 159. — The last author carries the number of converts in Granada and its *environs* to 70,000

with compassion for the unhappy beings, who so heedlessly incurred the heavy liabilities attached to their new faith. Every Spaniard, doubtless, anticipated the political advantages likely to result from a measure, which divested the Moors of the peculiar immunities secured by the treaty of capitulation, and subjected them at once to the law of the land. It is equally certain, however, that they attached great value in a spiritual view to the mere show of conversion, placing implicit confidence in the purifying influence of the waters of baptism, to whomever and under whatever circumstances administered. Even the philosophic Martyr, as little tinctured with bigotry as any of the time, testifies his joy at the conversion, on the ground, that, although it might not penetrate beneath the crust of infidelity, which had formed over the mind of the older and of course inveterate Mussulman, yet it would have full effect on his posterity, subjected from the cradle to the searching operation of Christian discipline.[40]

With regard to Ximenes, the real author of the work, whatever doubts were entertained of his discretion, in the outset, they were completely dispelled by the results. All concurred in admiring

---

[40] " Tu vero inques," he says, in a letter to the cardinal of Santa Cruz, " hisdem in suum Mahometem vivent animis, atque id jure merito suspicandum est. Durum namque majorum instituta relinquere ; attamen ego existimo, consultum optime fuisse ipsorum admittere postulata : paulatim namque nova superveniente disciplinâ, juvenum saltem et infantum atque eo tutius nepotum, inanibus illis superstitionibus abrasis, novis imbuentur ritibus. De senescentibus, qui callosis animis induruerunt, haud ego quidem id futurum inficior." Opus Epist., epist. 215.— Also, Carta de Gonzalo, MS.

the invincible energy of the man, who, in the face
of such mighty obstacles, had so speedily effected
this momentous revolution in the faith of a people,
bred from childhood in the deadliest hostility to
Christianity; [41] and the good archbishop Talavera
was heard in the fulness of his heart to exclaim,
that "Ximenes had achieved greater triumphs than
even Ferdinand and Isabella; since they had conquered only the soil, while he had gained the souls
of Granada!" [42]

[41] "Magnæ deinceps," says Gomez, " apud omnes venerationi
Ximenius esse cœpit. — Porrò plus
mentis acie videre quàm solent
homines credebatur, quòd re anci-
piti, neque plane confirmatâ, bar-
barâ civitate adhuc suum Mahume-
tum spirante, tantâ animi conten-
tione, ut Christi doctrinam amplec-
terentur, laboraverat et effecerat."
(De Rebus Gestis, fol. 33.) The
panegyric of the Spaniard is en-
dorsed by Fléchier, (Histoire de
Ximenés, p. 119.) who, in the age
of Louis XIV., displays all the
bigotry of that of Ferdinand and
Isabella.

[42] Talavera, as I have already
noticed, had caused the offices,
catechisms, and other religious exercises to be translated into Arabic
for the use of the converts; proposing to ex*end the translation at
some future time to the great body
of the Scriptures. That time had
now arrived, but Ximenes vehemently remonstrated against the
measure. "It would be throwing
pearls before swine," said he, " to
open the Scriptures to persons in
their low state of ignorance, who
could not fail, as St. Paul says, to
wrest them to their own destruc-
tion. The word of God should be
wrapped in discreet mystery from
the vulgar, who feel little reverence for what is plain and obvious.
It was for this reason, that our
Saviour himself clothed his doctrines in parables, when he addressed the people. The Scriptures should be confined to the
three ancient languages, which
God with mystic import permitted
to be inscribed over the head of his
crucified Son; and the vernacular
should be reserved for such devotional and moral treatises, as holy
men indite, in order to quicken the
soul, and turn it from the pursuit
of worldly vanities to heavenly contemplation." De Rebus Gestis,
fol. 32, 33.

The narrowest opinion, as usual,
prevailed, and Talavera abandoned
his wise and benevolent purpose.
The sagacious arguments of the primate lead his biographer, Gomez,
to conclude, that he had a prophetic
knowledge of the coming heresy
of Luther, which owed so much of
its success to the vernacular versions of the Scriptures; in which
probable opinion he is faithfully
echoed, as usual, by the good
bishop of Nismes. Fléchier, Hist.
de Ximenés, pp. 117–119.

CHAPTER VII.

RISING IN THE ALPUXARRAS. — DEATH OF ALONSO DE
AGUILAR. — EDICT AGAINST THE MOORS.

1500 — 1502.

Rising in the Alpuxarras. — Expedition to the Sierra Vermeja. -
Alonso de Aguilar. — His noble Character, and Death. — Bloody
Rout of the Spaniards. — Final Submission to Ferdinand. — Cruel
Policy of the Victors. — Commemorative Ballads. — Edict against the
Moors. — Causes of Intolerance. — Last Notice of the Moors under
the present Reign.

WHILE affairs went forward so triumphantly in
the capital of Granada, they excited general discontent in other parts of that kingdom, especially
the wild regions of the Alpuxarras. This range of
maritime Alps, which stretches to the distance of
seventeen leagues in a southeasterly direction from
the Moorish capital, sending out its sierras like so
many broad arms towards the Mediterranean, was
thickly sprinkled with Moorish villages, cresting the
bald summits of the mountains, or chequering the
green slopes and valleys which lay between them.
Its simple inhabitants, locked up within the lonely
recesses of their hills, and accustomed to a life of
penury and toil, had escaped the corruptions, as
well as refinements, of civilization. In ancient
times they had afforded a hardy militia for the

princes of Granada; and they now exhibited an
unshaken attachment to their ancient institutions
and religion, which had been somewhat effaced in
the great cities by more intimate intercourse with
the Europeans.[1]

Rising of the
Moors

These warlike mountaineers beheld with gathering resentment the faithless conduct pursued
towards their countrymen, which, they had good
reason to fear, would soon be extended to themselves; and their fiery passions were inflamed tc
an ungovernable height by the public apostasy of
Granada. They at length resolved to anticipate
any similar attempt on themselves by a general
insurrection. They accordingly seized on the fortresses and strong passes throughout the country,
and began as usual with forays into the lands of
the Christians.

These bold acts excited much alarm in the
capital, and the count of Tendilla took vigorous
measures for quenching the rebellion in its birth.
Gonsalvo de Cordova, his early pupil, but who
might now well be his master in the art of war,
was at that time residing in Granada; and Ten
dilla availed himself of his assistance to enforce a
hasty muster of levies, and march at once against
the enemy.

[1] Alpuxarras,— an Arabic word,
signifying " land of warriors," according to Salazar de Mendoza.
(Monarquía, tom. ii. p. 138.) According to the more accurate and
learned Conde, it is derived from
an Arabic term for " pasturage."
(El Nubiense, Descripcion de España, p. 187.)

"La Alpuxarra, aquessa sierra
que al Sol la cérviz lavanta
y que poblada de Villas,
es Mar de peñas, y plantas,
adonde sus poblaciones
ondas navegan de plata."

Calderon, (Comedias, (Madrid
1760,) tom. i. p. 353,) whose gor
geous muse sheds a blaze of glory
over the rudest scenes.

His first movement was against Huejar, a fortified town situated in one of the eastern ranges of
the Alpuxarras, whose inhabitants had taken the
lead in the insurrection. The enterprise was attended with more difficulty than was expected.
"God's enemies," to borrow the charitable epithet of
the Castilian chroniclers, had ploughed up the lands
in the neighbourhood ; and, as the light cavalry
of the Spaniards was working its way through the
deep furrows, the Moors opened the canals which
intersected the fields, and in a moment the horses
were floundering up to their girths in the mire and
water. Thus embarrassed in their progress, the
Spaniards presented a fatal mark to the Moorish
missiles, which rained on them with pitiless fury ;
and it was not without great efforts and considerable loss, that they gained a firm landing on the
opposite side. Undismayed, however, they then
charged the enemy with such vivacity, as compelled him to give way and take refuge within the
defences of the town.

No impediment could now check the ardor of
the assailants. They threw themselves from their
horses, and bringing forward the scaling-ladders,
planted them against the walls. Gonsalvo was the
first to gain the summit ; and, as a powerful Moor
endeavoured to thrust him from the topmost round
of the ladder, he grasped the battlements firmly
with his left hand and dealt the infidel such a blow
with the sword in his right, as brought him head-
long to the ground. He then leapt into the place,
and was speedily followed by his troops. The

enemy made a brief and ineffectual resistance The greater part were put to the sword; the remainder, including the women and children, were made slaves, and the town was delivered up to pillage.[2]

The severity of this military execution had not the effect of intimidating the insurgents; and the revolt wore so serious an aspect, that King Ferdinand found it necessary to take the field in person, which he did at the head of as complete and beautiful a body of Castilian chivalry as ever graced the campaigns of Granada.[3] Quitting Alhendin, the place of rendezvous, in the latter end of February, 1500, he directed his march on Lanjaron, one of the towns most active in the revolt, and perched high among the inaccessible fastnesses of the sierra, southeast of Granada.

The inhabitants, trusting to the natural strength of a situation, which had once baffled the arms of the bold Moorish chief El Zagal, took no precautions to secure the passes. Ferdinand, relying on this, avoided the more direct avenue to the place, and, bringing his men by a circuitous route over dangerous ravines, and dark and dizzy precipices, where the foot of the hunter had seldom ventured, succeeded at length, after incredible toil and hazard,

---

[2] Marmol, Rebelion de Moriscos, tom. i. lib. 1, cap. 28. — Quintana, Españoles Célebres, tom. i. p. 239. — Bleda, Corónica, lib. 5, cap. 23. — Bernaldez, Reyes Católicos, MS., cap. 159. — Abarca, Reyes de Aragon, tom. ii. fol. 338. — Mendoza, Guerra de Granada, p. 12.

[3] If we are to believe Martyr, the royal force amounted to 80,000 foot and 15,000 horse; so large an army, so promptly brought into the field, would suggest high ideas of the resources of the nation; too high indeed to gain credit, ever from Martyr, without confirmation

in reaching an elevated point, which entirely commanded the Moorish fortress.

Great was the dismay of the insurgents at the
apparition of the Christian banners, streaming in
triumph in the upper air, from the very pinnacles of
the sierra. They stoutly persisted, however, in the
refusal to surrender. But their works were too
feeble to stand the assault of men, who had vanquished the more formidable obstacles of nature ;
and, after a short struggle, the place was carried by
storm, and its wretched inmates experienced the
same dreadful fate with those of Huejar. [4]

At nearly the same time, the count of Lerin took
several other fortified places in the Alpuxarras, in
one of which he blew up a mosque filled with wo
men and children. Hostilities were carried on with
all the ferocity of a civil, or rather servile war,
and the Spaniards, repudiating all the feelings of
courtesy and generosity, which they had once shown
to the same men, when dealing with them as honorable enemies, now regarded them only as rebel
lious vassals, or indeed slaves, whom the public
safety required to be not merely chastised, but
exterminated.

These severities, added to the conviction of their
own impotence, at length broke the spirit of the
Moors, who were reduced to the most humble concessions ; and the Catholic king, " unwilling out
of his great clemency," says Abarca, " to stain his

CHAPTER
VII.
_____

Carries Lan-
jaron

1500.
March 8.

Punishment
of the rebels

[4] Peter Martyr, Opus Epist.,   Anales, tom. v. lib. 3, cap. 45.—
epist. 215.—Abarca, Reyes de   Carbajal, Anales, MS., año 1500.
Aragon, tom. ii. fol. 338.—Zurita,

sword with the blood of all these wild beasts of the Alpuxarras," consented to terms, which may be deemed reasonable, at least in comparison with his previous policy. These were, the surrender of their arms and fortresses, and the payment of the round sum of fifty thousand ducats. [5]

As soon as tranquillity was reëstablished, measures were taken for securing it permanently, by introducing Christianity among the natives, without which they never could remain well affected to their present government. Holy men were therefore sent as missionaries, to admonish them, calmly and without violence, of their errors, and to instruct them in the great truths of revelation. [6] Various immunities were also proposed, as an additional incentive to conversion, including an entire exemption to the party from the payment of his share of the heavy mulct lately imposed. [7] The wisdom of these temperate measures became every day more visible in the conversion, not merely of the simple mountaineers, but of nearly all the population of the great cities of Baza, Guadix, and Almeria, who consented before the end of the year to abjure their ancient religion, and receive baptism. [8]

This defection, however, caused great scandal among the more sturdy of their countrymen, and a

[5] Marmol, Rebelion de Moriscos, lib. 1, cap. 28. — Abarca, Reyes de Aragon, tom. ii. fol. 338. — Bernaldez, Reyes Católicos, MS., cap. 159. — Bleda, Corónica, lib. 5, cap. 24.

[6] Bleda, Corónica, lib. 5, cap. 24. — Bernaldez, Reyes Católicos, MS., cap. 165.

[7] Privilegios á los Moros de Valdelecrin y las Alpuxarras que se convirtieren, á 30 de Julio de 1500. Archivo de Simancas, apud Mem. de la Acad. de Hist., tom. vi apend. 14.

[8] Carbajal, Anales, MS., año 1500. — Garibay, Compendio, tom ii. lib. 19, cap. 10.

new insurrection broke out on the eastern confines of the Alpuxarras, which was suppressed with similar circumstances of stern severity, and a similar exaction of a heavy sum of money; — money, whose doubtful efficacy may be discerned, sometimes in staying, but more frequently in stimulating, the arm of persecution.[9]

But while the murmurs of rebellion died away in the east, they were heard in thunders from the distant hills on the western borders of Granada. This district, comprehending the sierras Vermeja and Villa Luenga, in the neighbourhood of Ronda, was peopled by a warlike race, among whom was the African tribe of Gandules, whose blood boiled with the same tropical fervor as that which glowed in the veins of their ancestors. They had early shown symptoms of discontent at the late proceedings in the capital. The duchess of Arcos, widow of the great marquis duke of Cadiz, whose estates lay in that quarter, [10] used her personal exertions to appease them; and the government made the most earnest assurances of its intention to respect whatever had been guarantied by the treaty of capitulation. [11] But they had learned to place little trust in princes; and the rapidly extending apostasy of

9 Carbajal, Anales, MS., año 1501. — Zurita, Anales, tom. v. lib. 4, cap. 27, 31.

10 The great marquis of Cadiz was third count of Arcos, from which his descendants took their title on the resumption of Cadiz by the crown after his death. Mendoza, Dignidades, lib. 3, cap. 8, '7.

11 See two letters dated Seville, January and February, 1500, addressed by Ferdinand and Isabella to the inhabitants of the Serrania de Ronda, preserved in the archives of Simancas, apud Mem. de la Acad. de Hist., tom. vi. Ilust. 15.

PART
II.

their countrymen exasperated them to such a degree, that they at length broke out in the most
atrocious acts of violence; murdering the Christian
missionaries, and kidnapping, if report be true,
many Spaniards of both sexes, whom they sold as
slaves in Africa. They were accused, with far
more probability, of entering into a secret correspondence with their brethren on the opposite shore,
in order to secure their support in the meditated
revolt. [12]

Rendezvous
at Ronda.

The government displayed its usual promptness
and energy on this occasion. Orders were issued

---

[12] Bernaldez, Reyes Católicos, MS., cap. 165. — Bleda, Corónica, lib. 5, cap. 25. — Peter Martyr, Opus Epist., epist. 221.

The complaints of the Spanish and African Moors to the Sultan of Egypt, or of Babylon, as he was then usually styled, had drawn from that prince sharp remonstrances to the Catholic sovereigns against their persecutions of the Moslems, accompanied by menaces of strict retaliation on the Christians in his dominions. In order to avert such calamitous consequences, Peter Martyr was sent as ambassador to Egypt. He left Granada in August, 1501, proceeded to Venice, and embarked there for Alexandria, which place he reached in December. Though cautioned on his arrival, that his mission, in the present exasperated state of feeling at the court, might cost him his head, the dauntless envoy sailed up the Nile under a Mameluke guard to Grand Cairo. Far from experiencing any outrage, however, he was courteously received by the Sultan; although the ambassador declined compromising the dignity of the court he represented, by paying the usual humiliating mark of obeisance, in prostrating himself on the ground in the royal presence; an independent bearing highly satisfactory to the Castilian historians. (See Garibay, Compendio, tom. ii. lib. 19, cap. 12.) He had three audiences, in which he succeeded so completely in effacing the unfavorable impressions of the Moslem prince, that the latter not only dismissed him with liberal presents, but granted, at his request, several important privileges to the Christian residents, and the pilgrims to the Holy Land, which lay within his dominions. Martyr's account of this interesting visit, which gave him ample opportunity for studying the manners of a nation, and seeing the stupendous monuments of ancient art, then little familiar to Europeans, was published in Latin, under the title of "De Legatione Babylonicâ," in three books, appended to his more celebrated "Decades de Rebus Oceanicis et Novo Orbe." Mazzuchelli, (Scrittori d' Italia, voce Anghiera,) notices an edition which he had seen published separately, without date or name of the printer.

το the principal chiefs and cities of Andalusia, to muster their forces with all possible despatch, and concentrate them on Ronda.   The summons was obeyed with such alacrity, that, in the course of a very few weeks, the streets of that busy city were thronged with a shining array of warriors drawn from all the principal towns of Andalusia.   Seville sent three hundred horse and two thousand foot. The principal leaders of the expedition were the count of Cifuentes, who, as assistant of Seville, commanded the troops of that city; the count of Ureña, and Alonso de Aguilar, elder brother of the Great Captain, and distinguished like him for the highest qualities of mind and person.

It was determined by the chiefs to strike at once into the heart of the Sierra Vermeja, or Red Sierra, as it was called from the color of its rocks, rising to the east of Ronda, and the principal theatre of insurrection.   On the 18th of March, 1501, the little army encamped before Monarda, on the skirts of a mountain, where the Moors were understood to have assembled in considerable force.   They had not been long in these quarters before parties of the enemy were seen hovering along the slopes of the mountain, from which the Christian camp was divided by a narrow river, — the Rio Verde, probably, which has gained such mournful celebrity in Spanish song.[13]   Aguilar's troops, who occupied the van,

---

[13]   Rio Venle, Rio Verde,
    Tinto va en sangre viva ; " —
Percy, in his well-known version of one of these agreeable *romances*, adopts the tame epithet of " gentle river," from the awkwardness, he says, of the literal translation of " verdant river."   He was not aware, it appears, that the Spanish was a proper name. (See Reliques

were so much roused by the sight of the enemy
that a small party, seizing a banner, rushed across
the stream without orders, in pursuit of them.
The odds, however, were so great, that they would
have been severely handled, had not Aguilar, while
he bitterly condemned their temerity, advanced
promptly to their support with the remainder of his
corps. The count of Ureña followed with the central division, leaving the count of Cifuentes with
the troops of Seville to protect the camp.[14]

The Moors
retreat up
the moun-
tains.

The Moors fell back as the Christians advanced,
and, retreating nimbly from point to point, led them
up the rugged steeps far into the recesses of the
mountains. At length they reached an open level,
encompassed on all sides by a natural rampart of
rocks, where they had deposited their valuable
effects, together with their wives and children
The latter, at sight of the invaders, uttered dismal
cries, and fled into the remoter depths of the sierra.

The Christians were too much attracted by the
rich spoil before them to think of following, and
dispersed in every direction in quest of plunder,
with all the heedlessness and insubordination of

of Ancient English Poetry, (London, 1812,) vol. i. p. 357.) The
more faithful version of " green
river," however, would have nothing very unpoetical in it ; though
our gifted countryman, Bryant,
seems to intimate, by his omission,
somewhat of a similar difficulty, in
his agreeable stanzas on the beautiful stream of that name in New
England.

[14] Zuñiga, Annales de Sevilla.

año 1501. — Abarca, Reyes de
Aragon, tom. ii. p. 340. — Bleda,
Corónica, lib. 5, cap. 26. — Bernaldez, Reyes Católicos, MS., cap.
165.

" Fue muy gentil capitan," says
Oviedo, speaking of this latter
nobleman, " y valiente lanza ; y
muchas vezes dio testimonio grande
de su animoso esfuerzo." Quincuagenas, MS., bat. 1, quinc. 1
dial. 36

raw, inexperienced levies. It was in vain, that
Alonso de Aguilar reminded them, that their wily
enemy was still unconquered ; or that he endeavoured to force them into the ranks again, and
restore order. No one heeded his call, or thought
of any thing beyond the present moment, and of
securing as much booty to himself as he could
carry.

The Moors, in the mean while, finding themselves no longer pursued, were aware of the occupation of the Christians, whom they not improbably
had purposely decoyed into the snare. They
resolved to return to the scene of action, and surprise their incautious enemy. Stealthily advan
cing, therefore, under the shadows of night, now
falling thick around, they poured through the rocky
defiles of the inclosure upon the astonished Spaniards. An unlucky explosion, at this crisis, of a
cask of powder, into which a spark had accidentally fallen, threw a broad glare over the scene, and
revealed for a moment the situation of the hostile
parties ; — the Spaniards in the utmost disorder,
many of them without arms, and staggering under
the weight of their fatal booty ; while their enemies were seen gliding like so many demons of
darkness through every crevice and avenue of the
inclosure, in the act of springing on their devoted
victims. This appalling spectacle, vanishing almost
as soon as seen, and followed by the hideous yells
and war-cries of the assailants, struck a panic into
the hearts of the soldiers, who fled, scarcely offer-
ng any resistance. The darkness of the night

was as favorable to the Moors, familiar with all the intricacies of the ground, as it was fatal to the Christians, who, bewildered in the mazes of the sierra, and losing their footing at every step, fell under the swords of their pursuers, or went down the dark gulfs and precipices which yawned all around.[15]

Alonso de
Aguilar.

Amidst this dreadful confusion, the count of Ureña succeeded in gaining a lower level of the sierra, where he halted and endeavoured to rally his panic-struck followers. His noble comrade, Alonso de Aguilar, still maintained his position on the heights above, refusing all entreaties of his followers to attempt a retreat. " When," said he proudly, " was the banner of Aguilar ever known to fly from the field?" His eldest son, the heir of his house and honors, Don Pedro de Cordova, a youth of great promise, fought at his side. He had received a severe wound on the head from a stone, and a javelin had pierced quite through his leg. With one knee resting on the ground, however, he still made a brave defence with his sword. The sight was too much for the father, and he implored him to suffer himself to be removed from the field. " Let not the hopes of our house be crushed at a single blow," said he; " go, my son, live as becomes a Christian knight, — live, and cherish your desolate mother." All his entreaties

---

[15] Abarca, Reyes de Aragon, tom ii. fol. 340. — Zurita, Anales, tom. v. lib. 4, cap. 33. — Garibay, Compendio, tom. ii. lib. 19, cap. 10. — Bernaldez, Reyes Católicos MS., cap. 165. — Marmol, Rebelion de Moriscos, lib. 1. cap. 28.

were fruitless, however ; and the gallant boy refused to leave his father's side, till he was forcibly
borne away by the attendants, who fortunately
succeeded in bringing him in safety to the station
occupied by the count of Ureña.[16]

Meantime the brave little band of cavaliers, who
remained true to Aguilar, had fallen one after another ; and the chief, left almost alone, retreated to
a huge rock which rose in the middle of the plain,
and placing his back against it, still made fight,
though weakened by loss of blood, like a lion at
bay, against his enemies.[17] In this situation he
was pressed so hard by a Moor of uncommon size
and strength, that he was compelled to turn and
close with him in single combat. The strife was
long and desperate, till Don Alonso, whose corselet
had become unlaced in the previous struggle, having received a severe wound in the breast, followed
by another on the head, grappled closely with his
adversary, and they came rolling on the ground
together. The Moor remained uppermost ; but
the spirit of the Spanish cavalier had not sunk
with his strength, and he proudly exclaimed, as if
to intimidate his enemy, " I am Don Alonso de
Aguilar ; " to which the other rejoined, " And
I am the Feri de Ben Estepar," a well-known
name of terror to the Christians. The sound of

His gallantry and death.

[16] Mendoza, Guerra de Granada,
p. 13. — Abarca, Reyes de Aragon, tom. 2, fol. 340. — Marmol,
Rebelion de Moriscos, lib. 1, cap.
28. — Oviedo, Quincuagenas, MS.,
bat. 1, quinc. 1, dial. 36.
    The boy, who lived to man's es-
tate, was afterwards created marquis of Priego by the Catholic
sovereigns. Salazar de Mendoza,
Dignidades, lib. 2, cap. 13.
[17] It is the simile of the fine old
ballad ;
    " Solo queda Don Alonso
    Su campaña es acabada
    Pelea como un Leon
    Pero poco aprovechaba. "

PART ٦١.

1501.
March 18.

His noble character.

this detested name roused all the vengeance of the dying hero; and, grasping his foe in mortal agony, he rallied his strength for a final blow; but it was too late, — his hand failed, and he was soon despatched by the dagger of his more vigorous rival. [18]

Thus fell Alonso Hernandez de Cordova, or Alonso de Aguilar, as he is commonly called from the land where his family estates lay. [19] "He was of the greatest authority among the grandees of his time," says father Abarca, "for his lineage, personal character, large domains, and the high posts which he filled, both in peace and war. More than forty years of his life he served against the infidel, under the banner of his house in boyhood, and as leader of that same banner in later life, or as viceroy of Andalusia and commander of the royal armies. He was the fifth lord of his

---

[18] Bernaldez, Reyes Católicos, MS., ubi supra. — Abarca, Reyes de Aragon, tom. ii. ubi supra. — Garibay, Compendio, tom. ii. lib. 19, cap. 10. — Mendoza, Guerra de Granada, p. 13. — Sandoval, Hist. el Emp. Carlos V., tom. i. p. 5.

According to Hyta's prose, Aguilar had first despatched more than thirty Moors with his own hand. (Guerras de Granada, part. i. p. 568.) The ballad, with more discretion, does not vouch for any particular number.

"Don Alonso en este tiempo
Muy gran batalla hacia,
El cavallo le havian muerto,
Por muralla le tenia.
Y arrimado á un gran peñon
Con valor se defendia:
Muchos Moros tiene muertos,
Pero poco le valia.
Porque sobre el cargan muchos,
Y le dan grandes heridas,
Tantas que cayó alli muerto
Entre la gente enemiga."

The warrior's death is summed up with an artless brevity, that would be affectation in more studied composition.

"Muerto queda Don Alonso,
Y eterna fama ganada."

[19] Paolo Giovio finds an etymology for the name in the eagle (*aguila*), assumed as the device of the warlike ancestors of Don Alonso. St. Ferdinand of Castile, in consideration of the services of this illustrious house at the taking of Cordova, in 1236, allowed it to bear as a cognomen the name of that city. This branch, however, still continued to be distinguished by their territorial epithet of Aguilar; although Don Alonso's brother, the Great Captain, as we have seen, was more generally known by that of Cordova. Vita Magni Gonsalvi, fol. 204.

warlike and pious house, who had fallen fighting   CHAPTER
for their country and religion against the accursed   VII.
sect of Mahomet. And there is good reason to
believe," continues the same orthodox authority,
"that his soul has received the glorious reward of
the Christian soldier; since he was armed on that
very morning with the blessed sacraments of con-
fession and communion."[20]

The victorious Moors, all this time, were driving   Bloody rout
the unresisting Spaniards, like so many terrified   of the Spaniards.
deer, down the dark steeps of the sierra. The
count of Ureña, who had seen his son stretched
by his side, and received a severe wound himself,
made the most desperate efforts to rally the fugitives, but was at length swept away by the torrent.
Trusting himself to a faithful adalid, who knew
the passes, he succeeded with much difficulty in
reaching the foot of the mountain, with such a
small remnant of his followers as could keep in
his track.[21] Fortunately, he there found the count
of Cifuentes, who had crossed the river with the

[20] Reyes de Aragon, tom. ii. fol.
340, 341.

The hero's body, left on the field
of battle, was treated with decent
respect by the Moors, who restored
it to King Ferdinand; and the sovereigns caused it to be interred
with all suitable pomp in the church
of St. Hypolito at Cordova. Many
years afterwards the marchioness
of Priego, his descendant, had the
tomb opened; and, on examining
the mouldering remains, the iron
head of a lance, received in his last
mortal struggle, was found buried
in the bones. Bleda, Corónica,
lib 5, cap. 26.

[21] "Tambien el Conde de Ureña,
Mal herido en demasia,
Se sale de la batalla
Llevado por una guia.
  "Que sabia bien la senda
Que de la Sierra salia:
Muchos Moros dexaba muertos
Por su grande valentia.
  "Tambien algunos se escapan,
Que al buen Conde le seguian."

Oviedo, speaking of this retreat of
the good count and his followers,
says, "Volvieron las riendas a sus
caballos, y se retiraron a mas que
galope por la multitud de los Infieles." Quincuagenas, MS., bat.
1, quinc. 1, dial. 36.

rear-guard, and encamped on a rising ground in the neighbourhood. Under favor of this strong position, the latter commander and his brave Sevillians, all fresh for action, were enabled to cover the shattered remains of the Spaniards, and beat off the assaults of their enemies till the break of morn, when they vanished like so many foul birds of night into the recesses of the mountains.

The rising day, which dispersed their foes, now revealed to the Christians the dreadful extent of their own losses. Few were to be seen of all that proud array, which had marched up the heights so confidently under the banners of their ill-fated chiefs the preceding evening. The bloody roll of slaughter, besides the common file, was graced with the names of the best and bravest of the Christian knighthood. Among the number was Francisco Ramirez de Madrid, the distinguished engineer, who had contributed so essentially to the success of the Granadine war. [22]

Dismay of
he nation.

The sad tidings of the defeat soon spread throughout the country, occasioning a sensation such as had not been felt since the tragic affair of the Axarquia. Men could scarcely credit, that so much mischief could be inflicted by an outcast race, who, whatever terror they once inspired, had long since been regarded with indifference or contempt. Every Spaniard seemed to consider himself in some

[22] Zuñiga, Annales de Sevilla, año 1501. — Carbajal, Anales, MS. año 1501. — Bleda, Corónica, lib. 5, cap. 26. — Oviedo, Quincuage-nas, MS., bat. 1, quinc. 1, dial. 36.
For a more particular notice of Ramirez, see Part 1. Chapter 13 of this History.

way or other involved in the disgrace; and the most CHAPTER
VII. spirited exertions were made on all sides to retrieve it. By the beginning of April, King Ferdinand found himself at Ronda, at the head of a strong body of troops, which he determined to lead in person, notwithstanding the remonstrances of his courtiers, into the heart of the Sierra, and take bloody vengeance on the rebels.

These latter, however, far from being encourag- The rebels submit to Ferdinand. ed, were appalled by the extent of their own success; and, as the note of warlike preparation reached them in their fastnesses, they felt their temerity in thus bringing the whole weight of the Castilian monarchy on their heads. They accordingly abandoned all thoughts of further resistance, and lost no time in sending deputies to the king's camp, to deprecate his anger, and sue in the most submissive terms for pardon.

Ferdinand, though far from vindictive, was less Banishment or conversion. open to pity than the queen; and, in the present instance he indulged in a full measure of the indignation, with which sovereigns, naturally identifying themselves with the state, are wont to regard rebellion, by viewing it in the aggravated light of a personal offence. After some hesitation, however, his prudence got the better of his passions, as he reflected that he was in a situation to dictate the terms of victory, without paying the usual price for it. His past experience seems to have convinced him of the hopelessness of infusing sentiments of loyalty in a Mussulman towards a Christian prince, for, while he granted a general amnesty to those concerned in the insurrection, it was only on the alternative of baptism or exile, engaging at the same time to provide conveyance for such as chose to leave the country, on the payment of ten doblas of gold a head. [23]

These engagements were punctually fulfilled The Moorish emigrants were transported in public galleys from Estepona to the Barbary coast. The number, however, was probably small ; by far the greater part being obliged, however reluctantly, from want of funds, to remain and be baptized. " They would never have stayed," says Bleda, " if they could have mustered the ten doblas of gold ; a circumstance," continues that charitable writer, " which shows with what levity they received baptism, and for what paltry considerations they could be guilty of such sacrilegious hypocrisy ! " [24]

Commemorative ballads.
But, although every spark of insurrection was thus effectually extinguished, it was long, very long, before the Spanish nation could recover from the blow, or forget the sad story of its disaster in the Red Sierra. It became the theme, not only of chronicle, but of song ; the note of sorrow was prolonged in many a plaintive *romance*, and the names of Aguilar and his unfortunate companions were embalmed in that beautiful minstrelsy, scarcely less imperishable, and far more touching, than the state-

---

[23] Bleda, Corónica, lib. 5, cap. 26, 27. — Robles, Vida de Ximenez, cap. 16. — Bernaldez, Reyes Católicos, MS., cap. 165. — Mariana, Hist. de España, lib. 27, cap. 5. — Marmol, Rebelion de Moriscos, lib. 1, cap. 28.

[24] Corónica, lib. 5, cap. 27.
The Curate of Los Palacios disposes of the Moors rather summarily ; " The Christians stripped them, gave them a free passage and sent them to the devil ! " Reyes Católicos, cap. 165.

ly and elaborate records of history. [25] The popular CHAPTER VII.
feeling was displayed after another fashion in regard
to the count of Ureña and his followers, who were
accused of deserting their posts in the hour of peril;
and more than one ballad of the time reproachfully
demanded an account from him of the brave companions in arms whom he had left in the Sierra. [26]

The imputation on this gallant nobleman appears
wholly undeserved ; for certainly he was not called
on to throw away his own life and those of his
brave followers, in a cause perfectly desperate, for
a chimerical point of honor. And, so far from forfeiting the favor of his sovereigns by his conduct on
this occasion, he was maintained by them in the

---

[25] According to one of the *romances*, cited by Hyta, the expedition of Aguilar was a piece of romantic Quixotism, occasioned by King Ferdinand's challenging the bravest of his knights to plant his banner on the summits of the Alpuxarras.

"Qual de vosotros, amigos,
Ira à la Sierra mañana,
A poner mi Real pendon
Encima de la Alpuxarra ? "

All shrunk from the perilous emprise, till Alonso de Aguilar stepped forward and boldly assumed it or himself.

' A todos tiembla la barba,
Sino fuera don Alonso,
Que de Aguilar se llamaba.
Levantóse en pie ante el Rey
De esta manera le habla.
" Aquesa empresa, Señor,
Para mi estaba guardada,
Que mi señora la reyna
Ya me la tiene mandada.
" Alegróse mucho el Rey
Por la oferta que le daba,
Aun no era amanecido
Don Alonso ya cavalga."

These popular ditties, it cannot be denied, are slippery authorities for any important fact, unless supported by more direct historic testimony. When composed, however, by contemporaries, or those who lived near the time, they may very naturally record many true details, too insignificant in their consequences to attract the notice of history. The ballad translated with so much elaborate simplicity by Percy, is chiefly taken up, as the English reader may remember, with the exploits of a Sevillian hero named Saavedra. No such personage is noticed, as far as I am aware, by the Spanish chroniclers. The name of Saavedra, however, appears to have been a familiar one in Seville, and occurs two or three times in the muster-roll of nobles and cavaliers of that city, who joined King Ferdinand's army in the preceding year, 1500. Zuñiga, Annales de Sevilla, eodem anno.

[26] Mendoza notices these splenetic effusions (Guerra de Granada, p. 13) ; and Bleda (Corónica, p. 636,) cites the following couplet from one of them.

" Decid, conde de Ureña,
Don Alorso donde queda."

Melancholy
reminiscen-
ces.

same high stations, which he before held, and which he continued to fill with dignity to a good old age.[27]

It was about seventy years after this event, in 1570, that the duke of Arcos, descended from the great marquis of Cadiz, and from this same count of Ureña, led an expedition into the Sierra Vermeja, in order to suppress a similar insurrection of the Moriscoes. Among the party were many of the descendants and kinsmen of those who had fought under Aguilar. It was the first time since, that these rude passes had been trodden by Christian feet; but the traditions of early childhood had made every inch of ground familiar to the soldiers. Some way up the eminence, they recognised the point at which the count of Ureña had made his stand; and further still, the fatal plain, belted round with its dark rampart of rocks, where the strife had been hottest. Scattered fragments of arms and harness still lay rusting on the ground, which was covered with the bones of the warriors, that had lain for more than half a century unburied and bleaching in the sun.[28] Here was the spot on which the brave

[27] The Venetian ambassador, Navagiero, saw the count of Ureña at Ossuna, in 1526. He was enjoying a green old age, or, as the minister expresses it, " molto vecchio e gentil corteggiano però." " Diseases," said the veteran good-humoredly, " sometimes visit me, but seldom tarry long ; for my body is like a crazy old inn, where travellers find such poor fare, that they merely touch and go." Viaggio, fol. 17.

[28] Guerra de Granada, p. 301. — Compare the similar painting of Tacitus, in the scene where Germanicus pays the last sad offices to the remains of Varus and his legions. " Dein semiruto vallo, humili fossâ, accisæ jam reliquiæ consedisse intelligebantur : medio campi albentia ossa, ut fugerant, ut restiterant, disjecta vel aggerata ; adjacebant fragmina telorum, equorumque artus, simul truncis arborum antefixa ora." (Annales

son of Aguilar had fought so sturdily by his father's side; and there the huge rock, at whose foot the chieftain had fallen, throwing its dark shadow over the remains of the noble dead, who lay sleeping around. The strongly marked features of the ground called up all the circumstances, which the soldiers had gathered from tradition; their hearts beat high, as they recapitulated them one to another; and the tears, says the eloquent historian who tells the story, fell fast down their iron cheeks, as they gazed on the sad relics, and offered up a soldier's prayer for the heroic souls which once animated them.[29]

Tranquillity was now restored throughout the wide borders of Granada. The banner of the Cross floated triumphantly over the whole extent of its wild sierras, its broad valleys, and populous cities. Every Moor, in exterior at least, had become a Christian. Every mosque had been converted into a Christian church. Still the country was not entirely purified from the stain of Islamism, since many professing their ancient faith were scattered over different parts of the kingdom of Castile, where

lib. 1, sect. 61.) Mendoza falls nothing short of this celebrated description of the Roman historian;
" Pan etiam Arcadiâ dicat se judice victum."

[29] Mendoza, Guerra de Granada, pp. 300 – 302.

The Moorish insurrection of 1570 was attended with at least one good result, in calling forth this historic masterpiece, the work of the accomplished Diego Hurtado de Mendoza, accomplished alike as a statesman, warrior, and historian. His "Guerra de Granada," confined as it is to a barren fragment of Moorish history, displays such liberal sentiments, (too liberal, indeed, to permit its publication till long after its author's death,) profound reflection, and classic elegance of style, as well entitle him to the appellation of the Spanish Sallust.

they had been long resident before the surrender of their capital. The late events seemed to have no other effect than to harden them in error; and the Spanish government saw with alarm the pernicious influence of their example and persuasion, in shaking the infirm faith of the new converts.

Edict
against the
Moors of
Castile.

To obviate this, an ordinance was published, in the summer of 1501, prohibiting all intercourse between these Moors and the orthodox kingdom of Granada.[30]   At length, however, convinced that there was no other way to save the precious seed from being choked by the thorns of infidelity, than to eradicate them altogether, the sovereigns came to the extraordinary resolution of offering them the alternative of baptism or exile. They issued a *prágmatica* to that effect from Seville, February 12th, 1502. After a preamble, duly setting forth the obligations of gratitude on the Castilians to drive God's enemies from the land, which he in his good time had delivered into their hands, and the numerous backslidings occasioned among the new converts by their intercourse with their unbaptized brethren, the act goes on to state, in much the same terms with the famous ordinance against the Jews, that all the unbaptized Moors in the kingdoms of Castile and Leon, above fourteen years of age if males, and twelve if females, must leave the country by the end of April following; that they might sell their property in the mean time, and take the proceeds in any thing save gold and silver

[30] Pragmáticas del Reyno, fol. 6.

and merchandise regularly prohibited ; and, finally, that they might emigrate to any foreign country, except the dominions of the Grand Turk, and such parts of Africa as Spain was then at war with. Obedience to these severe provisions was enforced by the penalties of death and confiscation of property.[31]

This stern edict, so closely modelled on that against the Jews, must have been even more grievous in its application.[32] For the Jews may be said to have been denizens almost equally of every country ; while the Moors, excluded from a retreat among their countrymen on the African shore, were sent into the lands of enemies or strangers. The former, moreover, were far better qualified by their natural shrewdness and commercial habits for disposing of their property advantageously, than the simple, inexperienced Moors, skilled in little else than husbandry or rude mechanic arts. We have nowhere met with any estimate of the number who migrated on this occasion. The Castilian writers pass over the whole affair in a very few words ; not, indeed, as is too evident, from any feelings of disapprobation, but from its insignificance in a political view. Their silence implies a very inconsiderable amount of emigrants ; a circumstance not to be

[31] Pragmáticas del Reyno, fol. 7.

[32] Bleda anxiously claims the credit of the act of expulsion for Fray Thomas de Torquemada, of inquisitorial memory. (Corónica, p. 640.) That eminent personage had, indeed, been dead some years; but this edict was so obviously suggested by that against the Jews, that it may be considered as the result of his principles, if not directly taught by him. Thus it is, " the evil that men do lives after them "

wondered at, as there were very few, probably, who
would not sooner imitate their Granadine brethren,
in assuming the mask of Christianity, than encounter exile under all the aggravated miseries with
which it was accompanied. [33]

Castile might now boast, the first time for eight
centuries, that every outward stain, at least, of infidelity, was purified from her bosom. But how had
this been accomplished? By the most detestable
expedients which sophistry could devise, and oppression execute; and that, too, under an enlightened government, proposing to be guided solely by
a conscientious regard for duty. To comprehend
this more fully, it will be necessary to take a brief
view of public sentiment in matters of religion at
that time.

Christianity
and Mahom-
etanism.
It is a singular paradox, that Christianity, whose
doctrines inculcate unbounded charity, should have
been made so often an engine of persecution;
while Mahometanism, whose principles are those
of avowed intolerance, should have exhibited, at
least till later times, a truly philosophical spirit of
toleration. [34] Even the first victorious disciples
of the prophet, glowing with all the fiery zeal of

[33] The Castilian writers, especially the dramatic, have not been
insensible to the poetical situations
afforded by tne distresses of the
banished Moriscoes. Their sympathy for the exiles, however, is
whimsically enough contrasted by
an orthodox anxiety to justify the
conduct of their own government.
The reader may recollect a pertinent example in the story of San-

cho's Moorish friend, Ricote. Don
Quixote, part. 2, cap. 54.
[34] The *spirit of toleration* professed by the Moors, indeed, was
made a principal argument against
them in the archbishop of Valencia's memorial to Philip III.
The Mahometans would seem the
better Christians of the two See
Geddes, Miscellaneous Tracts
(London, 1702–6,) vol. i. p. 94

CHAPTER
VII.

proselytism, were content with the exaction of tribute from the vanquished ; at least, more vindictive feelings were reserved only for idolaters, who did not, like the Jews and Christians, acknowledge with themselves the unity of God. With these latter denominations they had obvious sympathy, since it was their creed which formed the basis of their own.[35] In Spain, where the fiery temperament of the Arab was gradually softened under the influence of a temperate climate and higher mental culture, the toleration of the Jews and Christians, as we have already had occasion to notice, was so remarkable, that, within a few years after the conquest, we find them not only protected in the enjoyment of civil and religious freedom, but mingling on terms almost of equality with their conquerors.

It is not necessary to inquire here, how far the different policy of the Christians was owing to the peculiar constitution of their hierarchy, which, composed of a spiritual militia drawn from every country in Europe, was cut off by its position from all human sympathies, and attached to no interests but its own; which availed itself of the superior

Causes of intolerance.

---

[35] Heeren seems willing to countenance the learned Pluquet in regarding Islamism, in its ancient form, as one of the modifications of Christianity ; placing the principal difference between that and Socinianism, for example, in the mere rites of circumcision and baptism. (Essai sur l'Influence des Croisades, traduit par Villers, (Paris, 1808,) p. 175, not.) "The Mussulmans," says Sir William Jones, ' are a sort of heterodox Christians, if Locke reasons justly, because they firmly believe the immaculate conception, divine character, and miracles of the Messiah ; heterodox in denying vehemently his character of Son, and his equality, as God, with the Father, of whose unity and attributes they entertain and express the most awful ideas." See his Dissertation on the Gods of Greece, Italy, and India ; Works, (London, 1799,) vol. i. p. 279.

science and reputed sanctity, that were supposed
to have given it the key to the dread mysteries of
a future life, not to enlighten but to enslave the
minds of a credulous world ; and which, making
its own tenets the only standard of faith, its own
rites and ceremonial the only evidence of virtue,
obliterated the great laws of morality, written by
the divine hand on every heart, and gradually built
up a system of exclusiveness and intolerance most
repugnant to the mild and charitable religion of
Jesus Christ.

Aggravated
in the
fifteenth
century.
Before the close of the fifteenth century, several circumstances operated to sharpen the edge of
intolerance, especially against the Arabs. The
Turks, whose political consideration of late years
had made them the peculiar representatives and
champions of Mahometanism, had shown a ferocity
and cruelty in their treatment of the Christians,
which brought general odium on all the professors
of their faith, and on the Moors, of course, though
most undeservedly, in common with the rest. The
bold, heterodox doctrines, also, which had occasionally broken forth in different parts of Europe
in the fifteenth century, like so many faint streaks
of light ushering in the glorious morn of the
Reformation, had roused the alarm of the champions of the church, and kindled on more than one
occasion the fires of persecution ; and, before the
close of the period, the Inquisition was introduced
into Spain.

From that disastrous hour, religion wore a new
aspect in this unhappy country. The Spirit of in-

tolerance, no longer hooded in the darkness of the
cloister, now stalked abroad in all his terrors. Zeal
was exalted into fanaticism, and a rational spirit of
proselytism, into one of fiendish persecution. It
was not enough now, as formerly, to conform pas-
sively to the doctrines of the church, but it was
enjoined to make war on all who refused them.
The natural feelings of compunction in the discharge of this sad duty was a crime ; and the tear
of sympathy, wrung out by the sight of mortal
agonies, was an offence to be expiated by humili
ating penance. The most frightful maxims were
deliberately engrafted into the code of morals.
Any one, it was said, might conscientiously kill an
apostate wherever he could meet him. There was
some doubt whether a man might slay his own
father, if a heretic or infidel, but none whatever as
to his right, in that event, to take away the life of
his son or of his brother.[36] These maxims were
not a dead letter, but of most active operation, as
the sad records of the dread tribunal too well
prove. The character of the nation underwent a
melancholy change. The milk of charity, nay of
human feeling, was soured in every bosom. The
liberality of the old Spanish cavalier gave way to
the fiery fanaticism of the monk. The taste for
blood, once gratified, begat a cannibal appetite in

---

[36] See the bishop of Orihuela's
treatise, " De Bello Sacro," etc.,
cited by the industrious Clemencin.
(Mem. de la Acad. de Hist., tom.
vi. Ilust. 15.) The Moors and
Jews, of course, stood no chance in
this code ; the reverend father expresses an opinion, with which
Bleda heartily coincides, that the
government would be perfectly justified in taking away the life of
every Moor in the kingdom, for
their shameless infidelity. Ubi supra. ;—and Bleda, Corónica, p. 995.

the people, who, cheered on by the frantic clergy, seemed to vie with one another in the eagerness, with which they ran down the miserable game of the Inquisition.

Defects of the treaty of Granada.

It was at this very time, when the infernal monster, gorged but not sated with human sacrifice, was crying aloud for fresh victims, that Granada surrendered to the Spaniards, under the solemn guaranty of the full enjoyment of civil and religious liberty. The treaty of capitulation granted too much, or too little, — too little for an independent state, too much for one, whose existence was now merged in that of a greater; for it secured to the Moors privileges in some respects superior to those of the Castilians, and to the prejudice of the latter. Such, for example, was the permission to trade with the Barbary coast, and with the various places in Castile and Andalusia, without paying the duties imposed on the Spaniards themselves; [37] and that article, again, by which runaway Moorish slaves from other parts of the kingdom were made free and incapable of being reclaimed by their masters, if they could reach Granada. [38] The former of these provisions struck at the commercial profits of the Spaniards, the latter directly at their property.

Evasion of it by the Christians.

It is not too much to say, that such a treaty, depending for its observance on the good faith and forbearance of the stronger party, would not hold together a year in any country of Christendom,

---

[37] The articles of the treaty are detailed at length by Marmol, Re- belion de Moriscos, lib. 1, cap. 19
[38] Idem, ubi supra.

even at the present day, before some flaw or pretext would be devised to evade it. How much greater was the probability of this in the present case, where the weaker party was viewed with all the accumulated odium of long hereditary hostility and religious rancor?

The work of conversion, on which the Christians, no doubt, much relied, was attended with greater difficulties than had been anticipated by the conquerors. It was now found, that, while the Moors retained their present faith, they would be much better affected towards their countrymen in Africa, than to the nation with which they were incorporated. In short, Spain still had enemies in her bosom; and reports were rife in every quarter, of their secret intelligence with the Barbary states, and of Christians kidnapped to be sold as slaves to Algerine corsairs. Such tales, greedily circulated and swallowed, soon begat general alarm; and men are not apt to be over-scrupulous as to measures. which they deem essential to their personal safety.

The zealous attempt to bring about conversion by preaching and expostulation was fair and commendable. The intervention of bribes and promises, if it violated the spirit, did not, at least, the letter of the treaty. The application of force to a few of the most refractory, who by their blind obstinacy were excluding a whole nation from the benefits of redemption, was to be defended on other grounds; and these were not wanting to cunning theologians, who considered, that the sanctity of the end justified extraordinary means, and that,

PART
II.

where the eternal interests of the soul were at
stake, the force of promises and the faith of treaties were equally nugatory.[39]

Priestly
casuistry

But the *chef-d'œuvre* of monkish casuistry was
the argument imputed to Ximenes for depriving the
Moors of the benefits of the treaty, as a legitimate
consequence of the rebellion, into which they had
been driven by his own malpractices. This proposition, however, far from outraging the feelings of
the nation, well drilled by this time in the meta-
physics of the cloister, fell short of them, if we are
to judge from recommendations of a still more
questionable import, urged, though ineffectually, on
the sovereigns at this very time, from the highest
quarter.[40]

Such are the frightful results to which the fairest

[39] See the arguments of Ximenes, or of his enthusiastic biographer Fléchier, for it is not always
easy to discriminate between them.
Hist. de Ximenés, pp. 108, 109.

[40] The duke of Medina Sidonia
proposed to Ferdinand and Isabella
to be avenged on the Moors, in
some way not explained, after their
disembarkation in Africa, on the
ground that, the term of the royal
safe-conduct having elapsed, they
might lawfully be treated as enemies. To this proposal, which
would have done honor to a college
of Jesuits in the sixteenth century,
the sovereigns made a reply too
creditable not to be transcribed.
"El Rei é la Réina. Fernando de
Zafra, nuestro secretário. Vimos
vuestra letra, en que nos fecistes
saber lo que el duque de Medinasi-
dónia tenia pensado que se podia
facer contra los Moros de Villa-
luenga después de desembarcados

allende. Decidle que le agrade
cemos y tenemos en servicio el
buen deseo que tiene de nos servir ·
*pero porqué nuestra palabra y seguro
real así se debe guardar á los infieles
como á los Cristianos*, y faciéndose
lo que él dice parecería cautela y
engaño armado sobre nuestro seguro para no le guardar, que en ninguna manera se haga eso, ni otra
cosa de que pueda parecer que
se quebranta nuestro seguro. De
Granada véinte y nueve de mayo
de quiniéntos y un años. — Yo el
Rei. — Yo la Réina — Por manda-
do del Rei é del Réina, Miguel Perez Almazan." Would that the
suggestions of Isabella's own heart,
instead of the clergy, had always
been the guide of her conduct in
these matters! Mem. de la Acad.
de Hist., tom. vi. Ilust. 15, from
the original in the archives of the
family of Medina Sidonia.

mind may be led, when it introduces the refinements of logic into the discussions of duty ; when,
proposing to achieve some great good, whether in
politics or religion, it conceives that the importance
of the object authorizes a departure from the plain
principles of morality, which regulate the ordinary
affairs of life ; and when, blending these higher interests with those of a personal nature, it becomes
incapable of discriminating between them, and is
led insensibly to act from selfish motives, while it
fondly imagines itself obeying only the conscientious dictates of duty.[41]

With these events may be said to terminate the
history of the Moors, or the Moriscoes, as henceforth called, under the present reign. Eight centuries had elapsed since their first occupation of the
country ; during which period they had exhibited
all the various phases of civilization, from its dawn
to its decline. Ten years had sufficed to overturn
the splendid remains of this powerful empire ; and

Last notice
of the Moors
in the pres-
ent reign.

[41] A memorial of the archbishop
of Valencia to Philip III. affords
an example of this moral obliquity,
that may make one laugh, or weep,
according to the temper of his philosophy. In this precious document
he says, " Your Majesty may,
without any scruple of conscience,
make slaves of all the Moriscoes,
and may put them into your own
galleys or mines, or sell them to
strangers. And as to their children, they may be all sold at good
rates here in Spain; which will be
so far from being a punishment,
that it will be a mercy to them;
since by that means they will all
become Christians ; which they
would never have been, had they
continued with their parents. By
the holy execution of which piece
of justice, *a great sum of money
will flow into your Majesty's treasury.*" (Geddes, Miscellaneous
Tracts, vol. i. p. 71.) " Il n'est
point d'hostilité excellente comme
la Chrestienne," says old Mon-
taigne ; " nostre zele faict mer-
veilles, quand il va secondant nostre
pente vers la haine, la cruauté, l'ambition, l'avarice, la detraction, la
rebellion. Nostre religion est faicte
pour extirper les vices ; elle les
couvre, les nourrit, les incite." Es-
sais, liv. 2, chap. 12.

ten more, for its nominal conversion to Christianity. A long century of persecution, of unmitigated and unmerited suffering, was to follow, before the whole was to be consummated by the expulsion of this unhappy race from the Peninsula. Their story, in this latter period, furnishes one of the most memorable examples in history, of the impotence of persecution, even in support of a good cause against a bad one. It is a lesson that cannot be too deeply pondered through every succeeding age. The fires of the Inquisition are, indeed, extinguished, probably to be lighted no more. But where is the land, which can boast, that the spirit of intolerance, which forms the very breath of persecution, is altogether extinct in its bosom?

CHAPTER VIII.

COLUMBUS. — PROSECUTION OF DISCOVERY. — HIS
TREATMENT BY THE COURT.

1494 — 1503.

Progress of Discovery. — Reaction of Public Feeling. — The Queen's
Confidence in Columbus. — He discovers Terra Firma. — Isabella
sends back the Indian Slaves. — Complaints against Columbus. —
Superseded in the Government. — Vindication of the Sovereigns.
— His fourth and last Voyage.

THE reader will turn with satisfaction from the
melancholy and mortifying details of superstition,
to the generous efforts, which the Spanish government was making to enlarge the limits of science
and dominion in the west. " Amidst the storms
and troubles of Italy, Spain was every day stretching her wings over a wider sweep of empire, and
extending the glory of her name to the far Antipodes." Such is the swell of exultation with
which the enthusiastic Italian, Martyr, notices the
brilliant progress of discovery under his illustrious
countryman Columbus.[1] The Spanish sovereigns
had never lost sight of the new domain, so unexpectedly opened to them, as it were, from the

[1] "Inter has Italiæ procellas
magis indies ac magis alas proten-
dit Hispania, imperium auget, glo-
riam nomenque suum ad Antipodes
porriget." Peter Martyr, Opus
Epist., epist. 146.

depths of the ocean. The first accounts transmitted by the great navigator and his companions, on
his second voyage, while their imaginations were
warm with the beauty and novelty of the scenes
which met their eyes in the New World, served to
keep alive the tone of excitement, which their
unexpected successes had kindled in the nation.[2]
The various specimens sent home in the return
ships, of the products of these unknown regions,
confirmed the agreeable belief that they formed
part of the great Asiatic continent, which had so
long excited the cupidity of Europeans. The
Spanish court, sharing in the general enthusiasm,
endeavoured to promote the spirit of discovery and
colonization, by forwarding the requisite supplies,
and complying promptly with the most minute
suggestions of Columbus. But, in less than two
years from the commencement of his second
voyage, the face of things experienced a melancholy change. Accounts were received at home
of the most alarming discontent and disaffection in
the colony; while the actual returns from these
vaunted regions were so scanty, as to bear no
proportion to the expenses of the expedition.

[2] See, among others, a letter of
Dr. Chanca, who accompanied
Columbus on his second voyage.
It is addressed to the authorities of
Seville. After noticing the evidences of gold in Hispaniola, he
says; "Ansi que de cierto los
Reyes nuestros Señores desde agora se pueden tener por los mas
prosperos e mas ricos Principes del
mundo, porque tal cosa hasta agora
no se ha visto ni leido de ninguno
en el mundo, porque verdadera-
mente a otro camino que los navios
vuelvan puedan llevar tanta canti-
dad de oro que se pueden maravi-
llar cualesquiera que lo supieren."
In another part of the letter, the
Doctor is equally sanguine in regard to the fruitfulness of the soil
and climate. Letra de Dr. Chanca,
apud Navarrete, Coleccion de Viages, tom. i. pp. 198–224.

This unfortunate result was in a great measure imputable to the misconduct of the colonists themselves. Most of them were adventurers, who had embarked with no other expectation than that of getting together a fortune as speedily as possible in the golden Indies. They were without subordination, patience, industry, or any of the regular habits demanded for success in such an enterprise. As soon as they had launched from their native shore, they seemed to feel themselves released from the constraints of all law. They harboured jealousy and distrust of the admiral as a foreigner. The cavaliers and hidalgos, of whom there were too many in the expedition, contemned him as an upstart, whom it was derogatory to obey. From the first moment of their landing in Hispaniola, they indulged the most wanton license in regard to the unoffending natives, who, in the simplicity of their hearts, had received the white men as messengers from Heaven. Their outrages, however, soon provoked a general resistance, which led to such a war of extermination, that, in less than four years after the Spaniards had set foot on the island, one third of its population, amounting, probably, to several hundred thousands, were sacrificed! Such were the melancholy auspices, under which the intercourse was opened between the civilized white man and the simple natives of the western world.[3]

[3] Fernando Colon, Hist. del Almirante, cap. 60, 62. — Muñoz, Hist. del Nuevo-Mundo, lib. 5, sec. 25. — Herrera, Indias Occidentales, dec. 1, lib. 2, cap. 9. — Benzoni Novi Orbis Hist., lib. 1, cap. 9.

These excesses, and a total neglect of agriculture, — for none would condescend to turn up the
earth for any other object than the gold they could
find in it, — at length occasioned an alarming
scarcity of provisions; while the poor Indians neglected their usual husbandry, being willing to
starve themselves, so that they could starve out
their oppressors.[4] In order to avoid the famine
which menaced his little colony, Columbus was
obliged to resort to coercive measures, shortening
the allowance of food, and compelling all to work,
without distinction of rank. These unpalatable
regulations soon bred general discontent. The
high-mettled hidalgos, especially, complained loudly
of the indignity of such mechanical drudgery, while
Father Boil and his brethren were equally outraged
by the diminution of their regular rations.[5]

The Spanish sovereigns were now daily assailed
with complaints of the mal-administration of Columbus, and of his impolitic and unjust severities to
both Spaniards and natives. They lent, however,
an unwilling ear to these vague accusations; they
fully appreciated the difficulties of his situation;
and, although they sent out an agent to inquire into

the nature of the troubles which threatened the
existence of the colony, they were careful to select
an individual who they thought would be most

---

[4] The Indians had some grounds
for relying on the efficacy of starva-
tion, if, as Las Casas gravely asserts, " one Spaniard consumed in
a single day as much as would suffice three families!" Llorente,
Œuvres de Don Barthélemi de las

Casas, précédées de sa Vie, (Paris.
1822,) tom. i. p. 11.
[5] Martyr, De Rebus Oceanicis
dec. 1, lib. 4. — Gomara, Hist de
las Indias, cap. 20, tom. ii. — Her
rera, Indias Occidentales, dec. 1
lib. 2, cap. 12.

grateful to the admiral ; and when the latter in the CHAPTER
VIII.
following year, 1496, returned to Spain, they received him with the most ample acknowledgments 1496.
July 12
of regard. " Come to us," they said, in a kind
letter of congratulation, addressed to him soon
after his arrival, " when you can do it without
inconvenience to yourself, for you have endured
too many vexations already." [6]

The admiral brought with him, as before, such His second
return.
samples of the productions of the western hemisphere, as would strike the public eye, and keep
alive the feeling of curiosity. On his journey
through Andalusia, he passed some days under the
hospitable roof of the good curate, Bernaldez, who
dwells with much satisfaction on the remarkable
appearance of the Indian chiefs, following in the
admiral's train, gorgeously decorated with golden
collars and coronets, and various barbaric ornaments. Among these he particularly notices certain " belts and masks of cotton and of wood, with
figures of the Devil embroidered and carved thereon, sometimes in his own proper likeness, and at
others in *that of a cat or an owl.* There is much
reason," he infers, " to believe that he appears to
the islanders in this guise, and that they are all
idolaters, having Satan for their lord ! " [7]

But neither the attractions of the spectacle, nor

[6] Navarrete, Coleccion de Viages, tom. ii. Doc. Dipl., no. 101.
— Fernando Colon, Hist. del Almirante, cap. 64. — Muñoz, Hist.
del Nuevo-Mundo, lib. 5, sec. 31.

[7] Bernaldez, Reyes Católicos,
MS., cap 131. — Herrera express

es the same charitable opinion.
" Muy claramente se conocio que
el demonio estava apoderado de
aquella gente, y la traia ciega y
engañada, hablandoles, y mostran-
doles en diversas figuras." Indias
Occidentales, lib. 3, cap. 4.

PART
II.

the glowing representations of Columbus, who fancied he had discovered in the mines of Hispaniola the golden quarries of Ophir, from which King Solomon had enriched the temple of Jerusalem, could rekindle the dormant enthusiasm of the nation The novelty of the thing had passed. They heard a different tale, moreover, from the other voyagers, whose wan and sallow visages provoked the bitter jest, that they had returned with more gold in their faces than in their pockets. In short, the skepti cism of the public seemed now quite in proportion to its former overweening confidence ; and the returns were so meagre, says Bernaldez, " that it was very generally believed there was little or no gold in the island." [8]

The queen's
confidence
in him un-
shaken.

Isabella was far from participating in this unreasonable distrust. She had espoused the theory of Columbus, when others looked coldly or contemptuously on it. [9] She firmly relied on his repeated assurances, that the track of discovery would lead to other and more important regions. She formed a higher estimate, moreover, of the value of the new acquisitions than any founded on the actual proceeds in gold and silver ; keeping ever in view, as her letters and instructions abundantly show, the

---

[8] Bernaldez, Reyes Católicos, MS., cap. 131. — Muñoz, Hist. del Nuevo-Mundo, lib. 6, sec. 1.

[9] Columbus, in his letter to Prince John's nurse, dated 1500, makes the following ample acknowledgment of the queen's early protection of him. " En todos hobo incredulidad, y a la Reina mi Señora dio Nuestro Señor el espiritu de inteligencia y esfuerzo grande, y la hizo de todo heredera como a cara y muy amada hija." " Su Alteza lo aprobaba al contrario, y lo sostuvo fasta que pudo.' Navarrete, Coleccion de Viages, tom. i. p. 266.

glorious purpose of introducing the blessings of
Christian civilization among the heathen.[10] She
entertained a deep sense of the merits of Columbus,
to whose serious and elevated character her own
bore much resemblance; although the enthusiasm,
which distinguished each, was naturally tempered
in hers with somewhat more of benignity and discretion.

But although the queen was willing to give the
most effectual support to his great enterprise, the
situation of the country was such as made delay in
its immediate prosecution unavoidable. Large expense was necessarily incurred for the actual maintenance of the colony;[11] the exchequer was liberally drained, moreover, by the Italian war, as well as
by the profuse magnificence with which the nuptials
of the royal family were now celebrating. It was,
indeed, in the midst of the courtly revelries attending the marriage of Prince John, that the admiral
presented himself before the sovereigns at Burgos,
after his second voyage. Such was the low condition of the treasury from these causes, that Isabella
was obliged to defray the cost of an outfit to the
colony, at this time, from funds originally destined
for the marriage of her daughter Isabella with the
king of Portugal.[12]

[10] See the letters to Columbus, dated May 14th, 1493, August, 1494, apud Navarrete, Coleccion de Viages, tom. ii. pp. 66, 154, et mult. al.

[11] The salaries alone, annually disbursed by the crown to persons resident in the colony, amounted to six million maravedies. Muñoz, Hist. del Nuevo-Mundo, lib. 5, sec. 33.

[12] Idem, lib. 6, sec. 2.—Fernando Colon, Hist. del Almirante, cap. 64.—Herrera, Indias Occidentales, lib. 3, cap. 1.

This unwelcome delay, however, was softened
to Columbus by the distinguished marks which he
daily received of the royal favor; and various ordinances were passed, confirming and enlarging his
great powers and privileges in the most ample manner, to a greater extent, indeed, than his modesty,
or his prudence, would allow him to accept.[13] The
language in which these princely gratuities were
conferred, rendered them doubly grateful to his
noble heart, containing, as they did, the most emphatic acknowledgments of his " many, good, loyal,
distinguished, and continual services," and thus
testifying the unabated confidence of his sovereigns
in his integrity and prudence.[14]

Among the impediments to the immediate completion of the arrangements for the admiral's departure on his third voyage, may be also noticed
the hostility of Bishop Fonseca, who, at this period,
had the control of the Indian department; a man
of an irritable, and, as it would seem, most unfor-
giving temper, who, from some causes of disgust
which he had conceived with Columbus previous to
his second voyage, lost no opportunity of annoying

[13] Such, for example, was the
grant of an immense tract of land
in Hispaniola, with the title of
count or duke, as the admiral might
prefer. Muñoz, Hist. del Nuevo-
Mundo, lib. 6, sec. 17.

[14] The instrument establishing
the *mayorazgo*, or perpetual entail
of Columbus's estates, contains an
injunction, that "his heirs shall
never use any other signature than

that of ' the Admiral,' *el Almirante*,
whatever other titles and honors
may belong to them." That title indicated his peculiar achievements, and it was an honest pride
which led him by this simple expedient to perpetuate the remem-
brance of them in his posterity
See the original document, apud
Navarrete, Coleccion de Viages
tom. ii. pp. 221 – 235.

and thwarting him, for which his official station unfortunately afforded him too many facilities.[15]

From these various circumstances the admiral's
fleet was not ready before the beginning of 1498.
Even then further embarrassment occurred in man
ning it, as few were found willing to embark in a
service which had fallen into such general discredit.
This led to the ruinous expedient of substituting
convicts, whose regular punishments were commuted into transportation, for a limited period, to the Indies. No measure could possibly have been devised
more effectual for the ruin of the infant settlement.
The seeds of corruption, which had been so long festering in the old world, soon shot up into a plentiful
harvest in the new, and Columbus, who suggested
the measure, was the first to reap the fruits of it.

At length, all being in readiness, the admiral embarked on board his little squadron, consisting of
six vessels, whose complement of men, notwithstanding every exertion, was still deficient, and took
his departure from the port of St. Lucar, May 30th,
1498. He steered in a more southerly direction
than on his preceding voyages, and on the first of
August succeeded in reaching *terra firma;* thus en-

titling himself to the glory of being the first to set
foot on the great southern continent, to which he
had before opened the way.[16]

It is not necessary to pursue the track of the

---

[15] Muñoz, Hist. del Nuevo-Mun-
lo, lib. 6, sec. 20. — Fernando
Colon, Hist. del Almirante, cap.
64. — Zuñiga, Annales de Sevilla,
año 1496.

[16] Peter Martyr, De Rebus Oceanicis, dec. 1, lib. 6. — Navarrete, Coleccion de Viages, tom. ii. Doc.
Dipl., nos. 116, 120. — Tercer Viage
de Colon, apud Navarrete, tom. i

illustrious voyager, whose career, forming the most
brilliant episode to the history of the present reign,
has been so recently traced by a hand which few
will care to follow. It will suffice briefly to notice
his personal relations with the Spanish government,
and the principles on which the colonial administration was conducted.

Mutiny in
the colony.
On his arrival at Hispaniola, Columbus found the
affairs of the colony in the most deplorable confusion. An insurrection had been raised by the arts
of a few factious individuals against his brother
Bartholomew, to whom he had intrusted the government during his absence. In this desperate rebellion, all the interests of the community were
neglected. The mines, which were just beginning
to yield a golden harvest, remained unwrought.
The unfortunate natives were subjected to the most
inhuman oppression. There was no law but that
of the strongest. Columbus, on his arrival, in vain
endeavoured to restore order. The very crews
he brought with him, who had been unfortunately
reprieved from the gibbet in their own country,
served to swell the mass of mutiny. The admiral
exhausted art, negotiation, entreaty, force, and succeeded at length in patching up a specious reconciliation by such concessions as essentially impaired
his own authority. Among these was the grant of
large tracts of land to the rebels, with permission to
the proprietor to employ an allotted number of the

p. 245. — Benzoni, Novi Orbis
Hist., lib. 1, cap. 10, 11. — Herrera, Indias Occidentales, dec. 1 lib.
3, cap. 10, 11. — Muñoz, Hist. del
Nuevo-Mundo, lib. 6, sec. 19

natives in its cultivation. This was the origin of the celebrated system of *repartimientos*, which subsequently led to the foulest abuses that ever disgraced humanity.[17]

Nearly a year elapsed after the admiral's return to Hispaniola, before he succeeded in allaying these intestine feuds. In the mean while, rumors were every day reaching Spain of the distractions of the colony, accompanied with most injurious imputations on the conduct of Columbus and his brother, who were loudly accused of oppressing both Spaniards and Indians, and of sacrificing the public interests, in the most unscrupulous manner, to their own. These complaints were rung in the very ears of the sovereigns by numbers of the disaffected colonists, who had returned to Spain, and who surrounded the king, as he rode out on horseback, clamoring loudly for the discharge of the arrears, of which they said the admiral had defrauded them.[18]

There were not wanting, even, persons of high consideration at the court, to give credence and circulation to these calumnies. The recent discovery of the pearl fisheries of Paria, as well as of more prolific veins of the precious metals in Hispaniola, and the prospect of an indefinite extent of unexplored country, opened by the late voyage of Co-

---

[17] Gomara, Hist. de las Indias, cap. 20. — Benzoni, Novi Orbis Hist., lib. 1, cap. 10, 11. — Garibay, Compendio, tom. ii. lib. 19, cap. 7. — Fernando Colon, Hist. del Almirante, cap. 73 – 82. — Peter Martyr, De Rebus Oceanicis, dec. 1, lib. 5. — Herrera, Indias Occidentales dec. 1, lib. 3, cap. 16 — Muñoz, Hist. del Nuevo-Mundo, lib. 6, sec. 40 – 42.

[18] Garibay, Compendio, tom. ii. lib. 19, cap. 7. — Peter Martyr, De Rebus Oceanicis, dec. 1, lib. 7. — Gomara, Hist. de las Indias. cap. 23. — Benzoni, Novi Orbis Hist., cap. 11.
Ferdinand Columbus mentions

lumbus, made the viceroyalty of the New World a
tempting bait for the avarice and ambition of the
most potent grandee. They artfully endeavoured,
therefore, to undermine the admiral's credit with
the sovereigns, by raising in their minds suspicions
of his integrity, founded not merely on vague reports, but on letters received from the colony,
charging him with disloyalty, with appropriating to
his own use the revenues of the island, and with
the design of erecting an independent government
for himself.[19]

Whatever weight these absurd charges may have
had with Ferdinand, they had no power to shake
the queen's confidence in Columbus, or lead her to
suspect his loyalty for a moment. But the long-
continued distractions of the colony made her feel
a natural distrust of his capacity to govern it,
whether from the jealousy entertained of him as a
foreigner, or from some inherent deficiency in his
own character. These doubts were mingled, it is
true, with sterner feelings towards the admiral, on
the arrival, at this juncture, of several of the rebels

that he and his brother, who were
then pages to the queen, could not
stir out into the courtyard of the
Alhambra, without being followed
by fifty of these vagabonds, who
insulted them in the grossest manner, " as the sons of the adventurer, who had led so many brave
Spanish hidalgos to seek their
graves in the land of vanity and
delusion which he had found out."
Hist. del Almirante, cap. 85.

[19] Benzoni, Novi Orbis Hist., lib.
1, cap. 12. — National feeling operated, no doubt, as well as avarice
to sharpen the tooth of slander
against the admiral. " Ægre mul-
ti patiuntur," says Columbus'
countryman, with honest warmth,
" peregrinum hominem, et quidem
e nostrâ Italiâ ortum, tantum hon-
oris ac gloriæ consequutum, ut non
tantum Hispanicæ gentis, sed et
cujusvis alterius homines superave-
rit." Benzoni, lib. 1, cap. 5.

with the Indian slaves assigned to them by his orders.[20]

It was the received opinion among good Catholics of that period, that heathen and barbarous nations were placed by the circumstance of their infidelity without the pale both of spiritual and civil rights. Their souls were doomed to eternal perdition. Their bodies were the property of the Christian nation who should occupy their soil.[21] Such, in brief, were the profession and the practice of the most enlightened Europeans of the fifteenth century; and such the deplorable maxims which regulated the intercourse of the Spanish and Portuguese navigators with the uncivilized natives of the western world.[22] Columbus, agreeably to these views,

[20] Herrera, Indias Occidentales, lib. 4, cap. 7, 10, and more especially lib. 6, cap. 13. — Las Casas, Œuvres, ed. de Llorente, tom i. p. 306.

[21] " La qualité de Catholique Romain," says the philosophic Villers, " avait tout-à-fait remplacé celle d'homme, et même de Chrétien. Qui n'était pas Catholique Romain, n'était pas homme, était moins qu'homme ; et eût-il été un souverain, c'était une bonne action que de lui ôter la vie." (Essai sur la Réformation, p. 56. ed. 1820.) Las Casas rests the title of the Spanish crown to its American possessions on the original papal grant, made on condition of converting the natives to Christianity. The pope, as vicar of Jesus Christ, possesses plenary authority over all men for the safety of their souls. He might, therefore, in furtherance of this, confer on the Spanish sovereigns *imperial supremacy* over all lands discovered by them, — not, however, to the prejudice of authorities already existing there, and over such nations only as voluntarily embraced Christianity. Such is the sum of his thirty propositions, submitted to the council of the Indies for the inspection of Charles V. (Œuvres, ed. de Llorente, tom. i. pp. 286 – 311.) One may see in these arbitrary and whimsical limitations, the good bishop's desire to reconcile what reason told him were the natural rights of man, with what faith prescribed as the legitimate prerogative of the pope. Few Roman Catholics at the present day will be found sturdy enough to maintain this lofty prerogative, however carefully limited. Still fewer in the sixteenth century would have challenged it. Indeed, it is but just to Las Casas, to admit, that the general scope of his arguments, here and elsewhere, is very far in advance of his age.

[22] A Spanish casuist founds the

had, very soon after the occupation of Hispaniola recommended a regular exchange of slaves for the commodities required for the support of the colony ; representing, moreover, that in this way their conversion would be more surely effected, — an object, it must be admitted, which he seems to have ever had most earnestly at heart.

More liberal
sentiments
of Isabella.
Isabella, however, entertained views on this matter far more liberal than those of her age. She had been deeply interested by the accounts she had received from the admiral himself of the gentle, unoffending character of the islanders ; and she revolted at the idea of consigning them to the horrors of slavery, without even an effort for their conversion. She hesitated, therefore, to sanction his proposal ; and when a number of Indian captives were advertised to be sold in the markets of Andalusia, she commanded the sale to be suspended, till the opinion of a counsel of theologians and doctors, learned in such matters, could be obtained, as to its conscientious lawfulness. She yielded still further to the benevolent impulses of her nature, causing holy men to be instructed as far as possible in the Indian languages, and sent out as missionaries for the conversion of the natives.[23] Some of them, as Father Boil and his brethren, seem, indeed, to have been

right of his nation to enslave the Indians, among other things, on their smoking tobacco, and not trimming their beards à l'Espagnole. At least, this is Montesquieu's interpretation of it. (Esprit des Loix, lib. 15, chap. 3.) The doctors of the Inquisition could hardly have found a better reason.

[23] Muñoz, Hist. del Nuevo-Mundo, lib. 5, sec. 34. — Navarrete Coleccion de Viages, tom. ii. Doc Dipl., no. 92. — Herrera, Indias Occidentales, lib. 3, cap. 4.

more concerned for the welfare of their own bodies, than for the souls of their benighted flock. But others, imbued with a better spirit, wrought in the good work with disinterested zeal, and, if we may credit their accounts, with some efficacy. [24]

In the same beneficent spirit, the royal letters and ordinances urged over and over again the paramount obligation of the religious instruction of the natives, and of observing the utmost gentleness and humanity in all dealings with them. When, therefore, the queen learned the arrival of two vessels from the Indies, with three hundred slaves on board, which the admiral had granted to the mutineers, she could not repress her indignation, but impatiently asked, " By what authority does Columbus venture thus to dispose of my subjects? " She instantly caused proclamation to be made in the southern provinces, that all who had Indian slaves in their possession, granted by the admiral, should forthwith provide for their return to their own country; while the few, still held by the crown, were to be restored to freedom in like manner. [25]

After a long and visible reluctance, the queen acquiesced in sending out a commissioner to inves-

---

[24] " Among other things that the holy fathers carried out," says Robles, " was a little organ and several bells, which greatly delighted the simple people, so that from one to two thousand persons were baptized every day." (Vida de Ximenez, p. 120.)

Ferdinand Columbus remarks with some *naïveté*, that " the Indians were so obedient from their fear of the admiral, and at the same time so desirous to oblige him, that they *voluntarily* became Christians! " Hist. del Almirante, cap. 84.

[25] Herrera, Indias Occidentales, lib. 4, cap. 7. — Navarrete, Coleccion de Viages, tom. ii. Doc. Dipl., no. 134.

Las Casas observes, that " so great was the queen's indignation

tigate the affairs of the colony. The person ap
pointed to this delicate trust, was Don Francisco de
Bobadilla, a poor knight of Calatrava. He was invested with supreme powers of civil and criminal
jurisdiction. He was to bring to trial and pass
sentence on all such as had conspired against the
authority of Columbus. He was authorized to take
possession of the fortresses, vessels, public stores,
and property of every description, to dispose of all
offices, and to command whatever persons he might
deem expedient for the tranquillity of the island,
without distinction of rank, to return to Spain, and
present themselves before the sovereigns. Such,
in brief, was the sum of the extraordinary powers
intrusted to Bobadilla.[26]

Outrage of
Columbus.

It is impossible now to determine what motives
could have led to the selection of so incompetent an
agent, for an office of such high responsibility. He
seems to have been a weak and arrogant man,
swelled up with unmeasurable insolence by the
brief authority thus undeservedly bestowed on him.
From the very first, he regarded Columbus in the
light of a convicted criminal, on whom it was his
business to execute the sentence of the law. Accordingly, on his arrival at the island, after an

at the admiral's misconduct in this
particular, that nothing but the
consideration of his great public
services saved him from immediate disgrace." Œuvres, ed. de
Llorente, tom. i. p. 306.

[26] Navarrete, Coleccion de Viages, tom. ii. Doc. Dipl. nos. 127 –
130. The original commission to

Bobadilla was dated March 21st,
and May 21st, 1499; the execution
of it, however, was delayed until
July, 1500, in the hope, doubtless,
of obtaining such tidings from Hispaniola as should obviate the necessity of a measure so prejudicial to
the admiral.

ostentatious parade of his credentials, he commanded the admiral to appear before him, and, without
affecting the forms of a legal inquiry, at once caused
him to be manacled, and thrown into prison. Columbus submitted without the least show of resistance, displaying in this sad reverse that magnanimity of soul, which would have touched the heart
of a generous adversary. Bobadilla, however, discovered no such sensibility; and, after raking together all the foul or frivolous calumnies, which
hatred or the hope of favor could extort, he caused
the whole loathsome mass of accusation to be sent
back to Spain with the admiral, whom he commanded to be kept strictly in irons during the passage; "afraid," says Ferdinand Columbus bitterly,
"lest he might by any chance swim back again to
the island." [27]

This excess of malice served, as usual, however,
to defeat itself. So enormous an outrage shocked
the minds of those most prejudiced against Columbus. All seemed to feel it as a national dishonor,
that such indignities should be heaped on the man,
who, whatever might be his indiscretions, had done
so much for Spain, and for the whole civilized
world; a man, who, in the honest language of an
old writer, "had he lived in the days of ancient
Greece or Rome, would have had statues raised,

[27] Fernando Colon, Hist. del Almirante, cap. 86. — Garibay, Compendio, tom. ii. lib. 19, cap. 7. —
Peter Martyr, De Rebus Oceanicis,
dec. 1, lib. 7. — Gomara, Hist. de
las Indias, cap. 23. — Herrera, Indias Occidentales, lib. 4, cap. 10. —
Benzoni, Novi Orbis Hist., lib. 1,
cap. 12.

and temples and divine honors dedicated to him, as to a divinity !" [28]

Deep regret
of the
sovereigns.

None partook of the general indignation more strongly than Ferdinand and Isabella, who, in addition to their personal feelings of disgust at so gross an act, readily comprehended the whole weight of obloquy, which its perpetration must necessarily attach to them. They sent to Cadiz without an instant's delay, and commanded the admiral to be released from his ignominious fetters. They wrote to him in the most benignant terms, expressing their sincere regret for the unworthy usage which he had experienced, and requesting him to appear before them as speedily as possible, at Granada, where the court was then staying. At the same time, they furnished him a thousand ducats for his expenses, and a handsome retinue to escort him on his journey.

Reception of
Columbus.

Columbus, revived by these assurances of the kind dispositions of his sovereigns, proceeded without delay to Granada, which he reached on the 17th of December. Immediately on his arrival he obtained an audience. The queen could not repress her tears at the sight of the man, whose illustrious services had met with such ungenerous requital, as it were, at her own hands. She endeavoured to cheer his wounded spirit with the most earnest

1500.

[28] Benzoni, Novi Orbis Hist., lib. 1, cap. 12. — Herrera, Indias Occidentales, lib. 6, cap. 15.

Ferdinand Columbus tells us, that his father kept the fetters in which he was brought home, hanging up in an apartment of his house, as a perpetual memorial of national ingratitude, and, when he died ordered them to be buried in the same grave with himself. Hist. del Almirante, cap. 86.

assurances of her sympathy and sorrow for his misfortunes. Columbus, from the first moment of his disgrace, had relied on the good faith and kindness of Isabella ; for, as an ancient Castilian writer remarks, " she had ever favored him beyond the king her husband, protecting his interests, and showing him especial kindness and good-will." When he beheld the emotion of his royal mistress, and listened to her consolatory language, it was too much for his loyal and generous heart ; and, throwing himself on his knees, he gave vent to his feelings, and sobbed aloud. The sovereigns endeavoured to soothe and tranquillize his mind, and, after testifying their deep sense of his injuries, promised him, that impartial justice should be done his enemies, and that he should be reinstated in his emoluments and honors.[29]

Much censure has attached to the Spanish government for its share in this unfortunate transaction ; both in the appointment of so unsuitable an agent as Bobadilla, and the delegation of such broad and indefinite powers. With regard to the first, it is now too late, as has already been remarked, to ascertain on what grounds such a selection could have been made. There is no evidence of his being indebted for his promotion to intrigue or any undue influence. Indeed, according to the testimony of one of his contemporaries, he was

[29] Garibay, Compendio, tom. ii. lib. 19, cap. 7. — Peter Martyr, De Rebus Oceanicis, dec. 1, lib. 7. — Fernando Colon, Hist. del Almirante, cap. 86, 87. — Herrera, Indias Occidentales, dec. 1, lib. 4, cap. 8 - 10. — Benzoni, Novi Orbis Hist., lib. 1, cap. 12

reputed "an extremely honest and religious man",
and the good bishop Las Casas expressly declares,
that "no imputation of dishonesty or avarice had
ever rested on his character." [30]   It was an error of
judgment; a grave one, indeed, and must pass for
as much as it is worth.

But in regard to the second charge, of delegat-
ing unwarrantable powers, it should be remembered, that the grievances of the colony were represented as of a most pressing nature, demanding
a prompt and peremptory remedy; that a more
limited and partial authority, dependent for its
exercise on instructions from the government at
home, might be attended with ruinous delays; that
this authority must necessarily be paramount to
that of Columbus, who was a party implicated,
and that, although unlimited jurisdiction was given
over all offences committed against him, yet neither
he nor his friends were to be molested in any other
way than by temporary suspension from office, and
a return to their own country, where the merits of
their case might be submitted to the sovereigns
themselves.

This view of the matter, indeed, is perfectly
conformable to that of Ferdinand Columbus, whose
solicitude, so apparent in every page, for his
father's reputation, must have effectually counterbalanced any repugnance he may have felt at
mpugning the conduct of his sovereigns. " The
only ground of complaint," he remarks, in sum-

---

[30] Oviedo, Hist. Gen. de las   sas, lib. 2, cap. 6, apud Navarrete
Ind., P. 1, lib. 3, cap. 6. — Las Ca-   tom. i., introd., p. 99.

ming up his narrative of the transaction, " which CHAPTER VIII. I can bring against their Catholic Highnesses is, the unfitness of the agent whom they employed, equally malicious and ignorant. Had they sent out a suitable person, the admiral would have been highly gratified; since he had more than once requested the appointment of some one with full powers of jurisdiction in an affair, where he felt some natural delicacy in moving, in consequence of his own brother having been originally involved in it." And, as to the vast magnitude of the powers intrusted to Bobadilla, he adds, " It can scarcely be wondered at, considering the manifold complaints against the admiral made to their Highnesses." [31]

Although the king and queen determined without hesitation on the complete restoration of the admiral's honors, they thought it better to defer his reappointment to the government of the colony, until the present disturbances should be settled, and he might return there with personal safety and advantage. In the mean time, they resolved to send out a competent individual, and to support him with such a force as should overawe faction, and enable him to place the tranquillity of the island on a permanent basis.

The person selected was Don Nicolas de Ovan- Commission to Ovando. do, comendador of Lares, of the military order of Alcantara. He was a man of acknowledged prudence and sagacity, temperate in his habits, and

[31] Fernando Colon, Hist. del Almirante, cap. 86

PART
II.

plausible and politic in his address. It is sufficient evidence of his standing at court, that he had been one of the ten youths selected to be educated in the palace as companions for the prince of the Asturias. He was furnished with a fleet of two and thirty sail, carrying twenty-five hundred persons, many of them of the best families in the kingdom, with every variety of article for the nourishment and permanent prosperity of the colony; and the general equipment was in a style of expense and magnificence, such as had never before been lavished on any armada destined for the western waters.[32]

1501.
Sept.

The new governor was instructed immediately on his arrival to send Bobadilla home for trial. Under his lax administration, abuses of every kind had multiplied to an alarming extent, and the poor natives, in particular, were rapidly wasting away under the new and most inhuman arrangement of the *repartimientos*, which he established. Isabella now declared the Indians free; and emphatically enjoined on the authorities of Hispaniola to respect them as true and faithful vassals of the crown. Ovando was especially to ascertain the amount of losses sustained by Columbus and his brothers, to provide for their full indemnification, and to secure the unmolested enjoyment in future of all their lawful rights and pecuniary perquisites.[33]

[32] Herrera, Indias Occidentales, dec. 1, lib. 4, cap. 11. — Fernando Colon, Hist. del Almirante, cap. 87. — Benzoni, Novi Orbis Hist., lib. 1, cap. 12. — Mem. de la Acad. de Hist., tom. vi. p. 385.

[33] Herrera, Indias Occidentales, lib. 4, cap. 11 – 13. — Navarrete, Coleccion de Viages, tom. ii., Doc. Dipl., nos. 138, 144. — Fernando Colon, Hist. del Almirante, cap 87.

Fortified with the most ample instructions in
regard to these and other details of his administration, the governor embarked on board his magnificent flotilla, and crossed the bar of St. Lucar,
February 15th, 1502. A furious tempest dispersed
the fleet, before it had been out a week, and a
report reached Spain that it had entirely perished.
The sovereigns, overwhelmed with sorrow at this
fresh disaster, which consigned so many of their best
and bravest to a watery grave, shut themselves up
in their palace for several days. Fortunately, the
report proved ill-founded. The fleet rode out the
storm in safety, one vessel only having perished,
and the remainder reached in due time its place of
destination.[34]

The Spanish government has been roundly taxed
with injustice and ingratitude for its delay in restoring Columbus to the full possession of his colonial authority; and that too by writers generally
distinguished for candor and impartiality. No such
animadversion, however, as far as I am aware, is
countenanced by contemporary historians ; and it
appears to be wholly undeserved. Independent of
the obvious inexpediency of returning him immediately to the theatre of disaffection, before the em-
bers of ancient animosity had had time to cool,
there were several features in his character, which
make it doubtful whether he were the most competent person, in any event, for an emergency demanding at once the greatest coolness, consummate

[34] Herrera, Indias Occidentales, lib. 5, cap. 1.

address, and acknowledged personal authority. His sublime enthusiasm, which carried him victorious over every obstacle, involved him also in numerous embarrassments, which men of more phlegmatic temperament would have escaped. It led him to count too readily on a similar spirit in others,—and to be disappointed. It gave an exaggerated coloring to his views and descriptions, that inevitably led to a reaction in the minds of such as embarked their all on the splendid dreams of a fairy land, which they were never to realize.[35] Hence a fruitful source of discontent and disaffection in his followers. It led him, in his eagerness for the achievement of his great enterprises, to be less scrupulous and politic as to the means, than a less ardent spirit would have been. His pertinacious adherence to the scheme of Indian slavery, and his impolitic regulation compelling the labor of the hidalgos, are pertinent examples of this.[36] He was, moreover,

---

[35] The high devotional feeling of Columbus, led him to trace out allusions in Scripture to the various circumstances and scenes of his adventurous life. Thus he believed his great discovery announced in the Apocalypse, and in Isaiah; he identified, as I have before stated, the mines of Hispaniola with those which furnished Solomon with materials for his temple; he fancied that he had determined the actual locality of the garden of Eden in the newly discovered region of Paria. But his greatest extravagance was his project of a crusade for the recovery of the Holy Sepulchre. This he cherished from the first hour of his discovery, pressing it in the most urgent manner on the sovereigns, and making

actual provision for it in his testament. This was a flight, however, beyond the spirit even of this romantic age, and probably received as little serious attention from the queen, as from her more cool and calculating husband. Peter Martyr, De Rebus Oceanicis, dec. 1, lib. 6.—Tercer Viage de Colon, apud Navarrete, Coleccion de Viages, tom. i. p. 259.—tom. ii., Doc. Dipl., no. 140.—Herrera, Indias Occidentales, lib. 6, cap. 15.

[36] Another example was the injudicious punishment of delinquents by diminishing their regular allowance of food, a measure so obnoxious as to call for the interference of the sovereigns, who prohibited it altogether. (Navarrete, Coleccion de Viages, tom. ii., Doc. Dipl.,

CHAPTER
VIII

a foreigner, without rank, fortune, or powerful friends; and his high and sudden elevation naturally raised him up a thousand enemies among a proud, punctilious, and intensely national people. Under these multiplied embarrassments, resulting from peculiarities of character and situation, the sovereigns might well be excused for not intrusting Columbus, at this delicate crisis, with disentangling the meshes of intrigue and faction, in which the affairs of the colony were so unhappily involved.

I trust these remarks will not be construed into an insensibility to the merits and exalted services of Columbus. "A world," to borrow the words, though not the application of the Greek historian, "is his monument." His virtues shine with too bright a lustre to be dimmed by a few natural blemishes; but it becomes necessary to notice these, to vindicate the Spanish government from the imputation of perfidy and ingratitude, where it has been most freely urged, and apparently with the least foundation.

It is more difficult to excuse the paltry equipment with which the admiral was suffered to undertake his fourth and last voyage. The object proposed by this expedition was the discovery of a passage to the great Indian Ocean, which, he inferred sagaciously enough from his premises,

97.) Herrera, who must be admitted to have been in no degree insensible to the merits of Columbus, closes his account of the various accusations urged against him and his brothers, with the remark, that, "with every allowance for calumny, they must be confessed not to have governed the Castilians with the moderation that they ought to have done." Indias Occidentales, lib. 4, cap. 9.

PART
II

though, as it turned out, to the great inconven
ience of the commercial world, most erroneously,
must open somewhere between Cuba and the coast
of Paria. Four caravels, only, were furnished for
the expedition, the largest of which did not exceed
seventy tons' burden ; a force forming a striking
contrast to the magnificent armada lately intrusted
to Ovando, and altogether too insignificant to be
vindicated on the ground of the different objects
proposed by the two expeditions.[37]

The admi
ral's despon-
dency.

Columbus, oppressed with growing infirmities
and a consciousness, perhaps, of the decline of
popular favor, manifested unusual despondency previously to his embarkation. He talked, even, of
resigning the task of further discovery to his brother Bartholomew. " I have established," said he,
" all that I proposed, — the existence of land in
the west. I have opened the gate, and others may
enter at their pleasure ; as indeed they do, arrogat-
ing to themselves the title of discoverers, to which
they can have little claim, following as they do in
my track." He little thought the ingratitude of
mankind would sanction the claims of these adventurers so far as to confer the name of one of them
on that world, which his genius had revealed.[38]

[37] Garibay, Compendio, tom. ii.
lib. 19, cap. 14. — Fernando Colon, Hist. del Almirante, cap. 88.
— Herrera, Indias Occidentales,
lib. 5, cap. 1. — Benzoni, Novi
Orbis Hist., cap. 14.

[38] It would be going out of our
way to investigate the pretensions
of Amerigo Vespucci to the hon-
or of first discovering the South

American continent. The reader
will find them displayed with perspicuity and candor by Mr. Irving, in his " Life of Columbus."
(Appendix, No. 9.) Few will be
disposed to contest the author's
conclusion respecting their fallacy,
though all may not have the same
charity as he, in tracing its possible origin to an editorial blunder

The great inclination, however, which the admiral had to serve the Catholic sovereigns, and especially the most serene queen, says Ferdinand Columbus, induced him to lay aside his scruples, and encounter the perils and fatigues of another voyage. A few weeks before his departure, he received a gracious letter from Ferdinand and Isabella, the last ever addressed to him by his royal mistress, assuring him of their purpose to maintain inviolate all their engagements with him, and to perpetuate the inheritance of his honors in his family.[39] Comforted and cheered by these assurances,

instead of wilful fabrication on the part of Vespucci; in which light, indeed, it seems to have been regarded by the two most ancient and honest historians of the event, Las Casas and Herrera.

Mr. Irving's conclusions, however, have since been confirmed, in the fullest manner, by M. de Humboldt, in the fifth volume of his "Géographie du Nouveau Continent," published in 1839, a year after the preceding portion of this note was first printed; in which he has assembled a mass of testimony, suggesting the most favorable impressions of Vespucci's innocence of the various charges brought against him.

Since the appearance of Mr. Irving's work, Señor Navarrete has published the third volume of his "Coleccion de Viages y Descubrimientos," &c., containing, among other things, the original letters recording Vespucci's American voyages, illustrated by all the authorities and facts, that could come within the scope of his indefatigable researches. The whole weight of evidence leads irresistibly to the

conviction, that Columbus is entitled to the glory of being the original discoverer of the southern continent, as well as islands, of the western hemisphere. (Coleccion de Viages, tom. iii. pp. 183–334.)

In addition to the preceding writers, the American reader will find the claims of Vespucci discussed, with much ingenuity and careful examination of authorities, by Mr. Cushing, in his "Reminiscences of Spain," Vol. ii. pp. 210 et seq.

[39] Fernando Colon, Hist. del Almirante, cap. 87.—Herrera notices this letter, written, he says, "con tanta humanidad, que parecia extraordinaria de lo que usavan con otros, y no sin razon, pues jamas nadie les hizo tal servicio." Indias Occidentales, lib. 5, cap. 1.

Among other instances of the queen's personal regard for Columbus, may be noticed her receiving his two sons, Diego and Fernando, as her own pages, on the death of Prince John, in whose service they had formerly been. (Navarrete, Coleccion de Viages, tom. ii., Doc. Dipl., 125.)

the veteran navigator, quitting the port of Cadiz, on the 9th of March, 1502, once more spread his sails for those golden regions, which he had approached so near, but was destined never to reach.

Remarkable fate of his enemies.

It will not be necessary to pursue his course further than to notice a single occurrence of most extraordinary nature. The admiral had received instructions not to touch at Hispaniola on his outward voyage. The leaky condition of one of his ships, however, and the signs of an approaching storm, induced him to seek a temporary refuge there; at the same time, he counselled Ovando to delay for a few days the departure of the fleet, then riding in the harbour, which was destined to carry Bobadilla and the rebels with their ill-gotten treasures back to Spain. The churlish governor, however, not only refused Columbus admittance, but gave orders for the instant departure of the vessels. The apprehensions of the experienced mariner were fully justified by the event. Scarcely had the Spanish fleet quitted its moorings, before one of those tremendous hurricanes came on, which so often desolate these tropical regions, sweeping down every thing before it, and fell with such violence on the little navy, that out of eighteen ships, of which it was composed, not more than three or four escaped. The rest all foundered, including those which contained Bobadilla, and the late enemies of Columbus. Two hundred thousand *castella*

By an ordinance of 1503, we find Diego Colon made *contino* of the royal household, with an annual salary of 50,000 maravedies. Ibid Doc. Dipl., no. 150.

nos of gold, half of which belonged to the government, went to the bottom with them. The only one of the fleet which made its way back to Spain was a crazy, weather-beaten bark, which contained the admiral's property, amounting to four thousand ounces of gold. To complete these curious coincidences, Columbus with his little squadron rode out the storm in safety under the lee of the island, where he had prudently taken shelter, on being so rudely repulsed from the port. This evenhanded retribution of justice, so uncommon in human affairs, led many to discern the immediate interposition of Providence. Others, in a less Christian temper, referred it all to the necromancy of the admiral.[40]

[40] Peter Martyr, De Rebus Oceanicis, dec. 1, lib. 10. — Garibay, Compendio, tom. ii. lib. 19, cap. 14. — Fernando Colon, Hist. del Almirante, cap. 88. — Benzoni Novi Orbis Hist., cap. 12. — Herrera, Indias Occidentales, lib. 5 cap. 2.

CHAPTER IX

SPANISH COLONIAL POLICY

Careful Provision for the Colonies. — License for Private Voyages. — Important Papal Concessions. — The Queen's Zeal for Conversion. — Immediate Profits from the Discoveries.—Their moral Consequences. —Their geographical Extent.

PART II.

A CONSIDERATION of the colonial policy pursued during Isabella's lifetime has been hitherto deferred to avoid breaking the narrative of Columbus's personal adventures. I shall now endeavour to present the reader with a brief outline of it, as far as can be collected from imperfect and scanty materials ; for, however incomplete in itself, it becomes important as containing the germ of the gigantic system developed in later ages.

Careful provision for the colonies.

Ferdinand and Isabella manifested from the first an eager and enlightened curiosity in reference to their new acquisitions, constantly interrogating the admiral minutely as to their soil and climate, their various vegetable and mineral products, and especially the character of the uncivilized races who inhabited them. They paid the greatest deference to his suggestions, as before remarked, and liberally supplied the infant settlement with whatever could contribute to its nourishment and permanent prosperity.[1]

Through their provident attention, in a very few years after its discovery, the island of Hispaniola was in possession of the most important domestic animals, as well as fruits and vegetables of the old world, some of which have since continued to furnish the staple of a far more lucrative commerce than was ever anticipated from its gold mines.[2]

Emigration to the new countries was encouraged by the liberal tenor of the royal ordinances passed from time to time. The settlers in Hispaniola were to have their passage free ; to be excused from taxes ; to have the absolute property of such plantations on the island as they should engage to cultivate for four years ; and they were furnished with a gratuitous supply of grain and stock for their farms. All exports and imports were exempted from duty ; a striking contrast to the narrow policy of later ages. Five hundred persons, including scientific men and artisans of every description, were sent out and maintained at the expense of government. To provide for the greater security and quiet of the island, Ovando was authorized to

[1] See, in particular, a letter to Columbus, dated August, 1494 ; (apud Navarrete, Coleccion de Viages, tom. ii., Doc. Dipl., no. 79.) also an elaborate memorial presented by the admiral in the same year, setting forth the various necessities of the colony, every item of which is particularly answered by the sovereigns, in a manner showing how attentively they considered his suggestions. — Ibid., tom. i. pp. 226 – 241.

[2] Abundant evidence of this is furnished by the long enumeration of articles subjected to tithes, contained in an ordinance dated October 5th, 1501, showing with what indiscriminate severity this heavy burden was imposed from the first on the most important products of human industry. Recopilacion de Leyes de los Reynos de las Indias, (Madrid, 1774,) tom. i. lib. 1, tit. 16, ley 2

PART
II.

gather the residents into towns, which were endow
ed with the privileges appertaining to similar corporations in the mother country ; and a number of
married men, with their families were encouraged to
establish themselves in them, with the view of giving
greater solidity and permanence to the settlement.[3]

With these wise provisions were mingled others
savouring too strongly of the illiberal spirit of the
age. Such were those prohibiting Jews, Moors, or
indeed any but Castilians, for whom the discovery
was considered exclusively to have been made, from
inhabiting, or even visiting, the New World. The
government kept a most jealous eye upon what it
regarded as its own peculiar perquisites, reserving
to itself the exclusive possession of all minerals,
dyewoods, and precious stones, that should be discovered; and, although private persons were allowed
to search for gold, they were subjected to the exorbitant tax of two thirds, subsequently reduced to
one fifth, of all they should obtain, for the crown.[4]

License for
private
voyages.

The measure which contributed more effectually
than any other, at this period, to the progress of
discovery and colonization, was the license granted,
under certain regulations, in 1495, for voyages undertaken by private individuals. No use was made
of this permission until some years later, in 1499.

---

[3] Navarrete, Coleccion de Viages,
tom. ii., Doc. Dipl., no. 86, April
10th, 1495. — Nos. 103, 105–108,
April 23d, 1497. — No. 110, May
6th, 1497. — No. 121, July 22d,
1497. — Herrera, Indias Occidentales, dec. 1, lib. 4, cap. 12.

[4] Navarrete, Coleccion de Viages,
tom. ii., Doc. Dipl., nos. 86, 121. —

Herrera, Indias Occidentales, lib.
3, cap. 2. — Muñoz, Hist. del
Nuevo-Mundo, lib. 5, sec. 34.

The exclusion of foreigners, at
least all but " Catholic Christians,"
is particularly recommended by Columbus in his first communication
to the crown. Primer Viage de
Colon.

The spirit of enterprise had flagged, and the nation had experienced something like disappointment on contrasting the meagre results of their own discoveries with the dazzling successes of the Portuguese, who had struck at once into the very heart of the jewelled east. The reports of the admiral's third voyage, however, and the beautiful specimens of pearls which he sent home from the coast of Paria, revived the cupidity of the nation. Private adventurers now proposed to avail themselves of the license already granted, and to follow up the track of discovery on their own account. The government, drained by its late heavy expenditures, and jealous of the spirit of maritime adventure beginning to show itself in the other nations of Europe,[5] willingly acquiesced in a measure, which, while it opened a wide field of enterprise for its subjects, secured to itself all the substantial benefits of discovery, without any of the burdens.

The ships fitted out under the general license were required to reserve one tenth of their tonnage for the crown, as well as two thirds of all the gold, and ten per cent. of all other commodities which they should procure. The government promoted these expeditions by a bounty on all vessels of six hundred tons and upwards, engaged in them.[6]

[5] Among the foreign adventurers were the two Cabots, who sailed in the service of the English monarch, Henry VII., in 1497, and ran down the whole coast of North America, from Newfoundland to within a few degrees of Florida thus encroaching, as it were, on the very field of discovery preoccupied by the Spaniards.

[6] Muñoz, Hist. del Nuevo-Mundo, lib. 5, sect. 32. — Navarrete, Coleccior de Viages, Doc. Dipl., no. 86.

Their suc-
cess.

With this encouragement the more wealthy merchants of Seville, Cadiz, and Palos, the old theatre
of nautical enterprise, freighted and sent out little
squadrons of three or four vessels each, which they
intrusted to the experienced mariners, who had
accompanied Columbus in his first voyage, or since
followed in his footsteps. They held in general
the same course pursued by the admiral on his last
expedition, exploring the coasts of the great southern continent. Some of the adventurers returned
with such rich freights of gold, pearls, and other
precious commodities, as well compensated the
fatigues and perils of the voyage. But the greater
number were obliged to content themselves with
the more enduring, but barren honors of discovery.[7]

Indian de-
partment.

The active spirit of enterprise now awakened,
and the more enlarged commercial relations with
the new colonies, required a more perfect organiza-

---

[7] Columbus seems to have taken
exceptions at the license for private voyages, as an infringement
of his own prerogatives. It is difficult, however, to understand in
what way. There is nothing in
his original capitulations with the
government having reference to the
matter, (see Navarrete, Coleccion
de Viages, Doc. Dipl., no. 5;) while,
in the letters patent made out previously to his second voyage, the
right of granting licenses is expressly reserved to the crown, and
to the superintendent, Fonseca,
equally with the admiral. (Doc.
Dipl., no. 35.) The only legal
claim which he could make in all
such expeditions as were not conducted under him, was to one
eighth of the tonnage, and this
was regularly provided for in the
general license. (Doc. Dipl., no.

86.) The sovereigns, indeed, in
consequence of his remonstrances,
published an ordinance, June 2d,
1497, in which, after expressing
their unabated respect for all the
rights and privileges of the admiral,
they declare, that whatever shall be
found in their previous license repugnant to these shall be null and
void. (Doc. Dipl., 113.) The hy-
pothetical form in which this is
stated shows, that the sovereigns,
with an honest desire of keeping
their engagements with Columbus,
had not a very clear perception in
what manner they had been violated.

Peter Martyr, De Rebus Oceanicis, Dec. 1, lib. 9. — Herrera, Indias Occidentales, lib. 4, cap. 11.
— Benzoni, Novi Orbis Hist., cap
13.

tion of the department for Indian affairs, the earliest vestiges of which have been already noticed in a preceding chapter.[8] By an ordinance dated at Alcalá, January 20th, 1503, it was provided that a board should be established, consisting of three functionaries, with the titles of treasurer, factor, and comptroller. Their permanent residence was assigned in the old alcazar of Seville, where they were to meet every day for the despatch of business. The board was expected to make itself thoroughly acquainted with whatever concerned the colonies, and to afford the government all information, that could be obtained, affecting their interests and commercial prosperity. It was empowered to grant licenses under the regular conditions, to provide for the equipment of fleets, to determine their destination, and furnish them instructions, on sailing. All merchandise for exportation was to be deposited in the alcazar, where the return cargoes were to be received, and contracts made for their sale. Similar authority was given to it over the trade with the Barbary coast and the Canary Islands. Its supervision was to extend in like manner over all vessels which might take their departure from the port of Cadiz, as well as from Seville. With these powers were combined others of a purely judicial character, authorizing them to take cognizance of questions arising out of particular voyages, and of the colonial trade in general. In this latter capacity they were to be assisted by the

8 Part I. Chap. 18, of this History.

PART
II.

advice of two jurists, maintained by a regular salary from the government.[9]

Casa de
Contra
tacion.

Such were the extensive powers intrusted to the famous *Casa de Contratacion,* or House of Trade on this its first definite organization; and, although its authority was subsequently somewhat circumscribed by the appellate jurisdiction of the Council of the Indies, it has always continued the great organ by which the commercial transactions with the colonies have been conducted and controlled.

important
papal con-
cessions.

The Spanish government, while thus securing to itself the more easy and exclusive management of the colonial trade, by confining it within one narrow channel, discovered the most admirable foresight in providing for its absolute supremacy in ecclesiastical affairs, where alone it could be contested. By a bull of Alexander the Sixth, dated November 16th, 1501, the sovereigns were empowered to receive all the tithes in the colonial dominions.[10] Another bull, of Pope Julius the Second, July 28th, 1508, granted them the right of collating to all benefices, of whatever description, in the colonies, subject only to the approbation of the Holy See. By these two concessions, the Spanish crown was placed at once at the head of the church in its transatlantic dominions,

[9] Navarrete, Coleccion de Viages, tom. ii., Doc. Dipl., no. 148.—Solorzano y Pereyra, Politica Indiana, (Madrid, 1776,) lib. 6, cap. 17.—Linage de Veitia, Norte de la Contratacion de las Indias Occidentales, (Sevilla, 1672,) lib. 1, cap. 1.—Zuñiga, Annales de Sevilla, año 1503.—Herrera, Indias Occidentales, lib. 5, cap. 12.—Navagiero, Viaggio, fol. 15.

[10] See the original bull, apud Navarrete, Coleccion de Viages, tom. ii. apend. 14, and a Spanish version of it, in Solorzano, Politica Indiana, lib. 4, cap. 1, sec. 7.

with the absolute disposal of all its dignities and emoluments.[11]

It has excited the admiration of more than one historian, that Ferdinand and Isabella, with their reverence for the Catholic church, should have had the courage to assume an attitude of such entire independence of its spiritual chief.[12] But whoever has studied their reign, will regard this measure as perfectly conformable to their habitual policy, which never suffered a zeal for religion, or a blind deference to the church, to compromise in any degree the independence of the crown. It is much more astonishing, that pontiffs could be found content to divest themselves of such important prerogatives. It was deviating widely from the subtle and tenacious spirit of their predecessors; and, as the consequences came to be more fully disclosed, furnished ample subject of regret to those who succeeded them.

Such is a brief summary of the principal regulations adopted by Ferdinand and Isabella for the administration of the colonies. Many of their peculiarities, including most of their defects, are to be referred to the peculiar circumstances under which the discovery of the New World was effected. Unlike the settlements on the comparatively sterile shores of North America, which were permitted to devise laws accommodated to their

Spirit of the colonial legislation.

[11] Solorzano, Política Indiana, tom. ii. lib. 4, cap. 2, sec. 9.— Riol, Informe, apud Semanario Erudito, tom. iii. pp. 160, 161.
[12] Among others see Raynal, History of the East and West Indies, translated by Justamond, (London, 1788,) vol. iv. p. 277. — Robertson, History of America, (London, 1796,) vol. iii. p. 283.

necessities, and to gather strength in the habitua
exercise of political functions, the Spanish colonies
were from the very first checked and controlled by
the over-legislation of the parent country. The
original project of discovery had been entered into
with indefinite expectations of gain. The verifica-
tion of Columbus's theory of the existence of land
in the west gave popular credit to his conjecture,
that that land was the far-famed Indies. The
specimens of gold and other precious commodities
found there, served to maintain the delusion. The
Spanish government regarded the expedition as its
own private adventure, to whose benefits it had
exclusive pretensions. Hence those jealous regulations for securing to itself a monopoly of the
most obvious sources of profit, the dyewoods and
the precious metals.

These impolitic provisions were relieved by
others better suited to the permanent interests of
the colony. Such was the bounty offered in various ways on the occupation and culture of land ;
the erection of municipalities ; the right of inter-
colonial traffic, and of exporting and importing
merchandise of every description free of duty.[13]
These and similar laws show, that the government
far from regarding the colonies merely as a foreign
acquisition to be sacrificed to the interests of the
mother country, as at a later period, was disposed

[13] Muñoz, Hist. del Nuevo-
Mundo, lib. 5, sec. 32, 33. — Herrera, Indias Occidentales, lib. 4,
cap. 11, 12. — Navarrete, Coleccion de Viages, tom. ii., Doc. Dipl.,
no. 86.

to legislate for them on more generous principles, as an integral portion of the monarchy.

Some of the measures, even, of a less liberal tenor, may be excused, as sufficiently accommodated to existing circumstances. No regulation, for example, was found eventually more mischievous in its operation than that which confined the colonial trade to the single port of Seville, instead of permitting it to find a free vent in the thousand avenues naturally opened in every part of the king dom; to say nothing of the grievous monopolies and exactions, for which this concentration of a mighty traffic on so small a point was found, in later times, to afford unbounded facility. But the colonial trade was too limited in its extent, under Ferdinand and Isabella, to involve such consequences. It was chiefly confined to a few wealthy seaports of Andalusia, from the vicinity of which the first adventurers had sallied forth on their career of discovery. It was no inconvenience to them to have a common port of entry, so central and accessible as Seville, which, moreover, by this arrangement became a great mart for European trade, thus affording a convenient market to the country for effecting its commercial exchanges with every quarter of Christendom.[14] It was only when laws, adapted to the incipient stages of commerce, were perpetuated to a period when that commerce had swelled

[14] The historian of Seville mentions, that it was the resort especial-y cf the merchants of Flanders, with whom a more intimate intercourse had been opened by the intermarriages of the royal family with the house of Burgundy. See Zuñiga, Annales de Sevilla, p. 415.

to such gigantic dimensions as to embrace every
quarter of the empire, that their gross impolicy
became manifest.

The queen's
zeal for con-
verting the
natives.

It would not be giving a fair view of the great
objects proposed by the Spanish sovereigns in their
schemes of discovery, to omit one which was paramount to all the rest, with the queen at least, —
the propagation of Christianity among the heathen
The conversion and civilization of this simple people form, as has been already said, the burden of
most of her official communications from the earliest
period.[15] She neglected no means for the furtherance of this good work, through the agency of missionaries exclusively devoted to it, who were to
establish their residence among the natives, and win
them to the true faith by their instructions, and the
edifying example of their own lives It was with
the design of ameliorating the condition of the

natives, that she sanctioned the introduction into
the colonies of negro slaves born in Spain. This
she did on the representation, that the physical
constitution of the African was much better fitted
than that of the Indian, to endure severe toil
under a tropical climate. To this false principle
of economizing human suffering, we are indebted
for that foul stain on the New World, which has
grown deeper and darker with the lapse of years.[16]

[15] Navarrete, Coleccion de Viages, tom. ii., Doc. Dipl., no. 45, et
loc. al. — Las Casas, amidst his
unsparing condemnation of the
guilty, does ample justice to the
pure and generous, though alas!
unavailing efforts of the queen. See

Œuvres, ed. de Llorente, tom. i.
pp. 21, 307, 395, et alibi.
[16] Herrera, Indias Occidentales,
lib. 4, cap. 12. — A good account
of the introduction of negro slavery into the New World, comprehending the material facts, and

Isabella, however, was destined to have her benevolent designs, in regard to the natives, defeated by her own subjects. The popular doctrine of the absolute rights of the Christian over the heathen seemed to warrant the exaction of labor from these unhappy beings to any degree, which avarice on the one hand could demand, or human endurance concede on the other. The device of the *repartimientos* systematized and completed the whole scheme of oppression. The queen, it is true, abolished them under Ovando's administration, and declared the Indians " as free as her own subjects."[17] But his representation, that the Indians, when no longer compelled to work, withdrew from all intercourse with the Christians, thus annihilating at once all hopes of their conversion, subsequently induced her to consent, that they should be required to labor moderately and for a reasonable compensation.[18] This was construed with their usual latitude by the Spaniards. They soon revived the old system

CHAPTER
IX.
——
Unhappily
defeated.

some little known, may be found in the fifth chapter of Bancroft's "History of the United States "; a work in which the author has shown singular address in creating a unity of interest out of a subject which, in its early stages, would seem to want every other unity. It is the deficiency of this, probably, which has prevented Mr. Grahame's valuable History from attaining the popularity, to which its solid merits justly entitle it. Should the remaining volumes of Mr. Bancroft's work be conducted with the same spirit, scholarship, and impartiality as the volume before us, it cannot fail to take a permanent rank in American literature.

[17] Herrera, Indias Occidentales, lib. 4, cap. 11.

[18] Dec. 20th, 1503.—Ibid. lib. 5, cap. 11. — See the instructions to Ovando in Navarrete, (Coleccion de Viages, tom. ii., Doc. Dipl., no. 153.) " Pay them regular wages," says the ordinance, " for their labor," " como personas libres como lo son, y no como siervos." Las Casas, who analyzes these instructions, which Llorente, by the by, has misdated, exposes the atrocious manner in which they were violated, in every particular, by Ovando and his successors. Œuvres, ed. de Llorente, tom. i. p. 309. et seq.

of distribution on so terrific a scale, that a letter of
Columbus, written shortly after Isabella's death,
represents more than six sevenths of the whole
population of Hispaniola to have melted away under it![19] The queen was too far removed to enforce
the execution of her own beneficent measures; nor
is it probable, that she ever imagined the extent of
their violation, for there was no intrepid philanthro-
pist, in that day, like Las Casas, to proclaim to the
world the wrongs and sorrows of the Indian.[20] A
conviction, however, of the unworthy treatment of
the natives seems to have pressed heavily on her
heart; for in a codicil to her testament, dated a
few days only before her death, she invokes the
kind offices of her successor in their behalf in such
strong and affectionate language, as plainly indi
cates how intently her thoughts were occupied with
their condition down to the last hour of her existence.[21]

*Immediate
profits from
the discov-
eries*

The moral grandeur of the maritime discoveries
under this reign must not so far dazzle us, as to
lead to a very high estimate of their immediate results in an economical view. Most of those articles

[19] Ibid. ubi supra. — Las Casas,
Hist. Ind., lib. 2, cap. 36, MS.,
apud Irving, vol. iii. p. 412. — The
venerable bishop confirms this
frightful picture of desolation, in its
full extent, in his various memorials prepared for the council of the
Indies. Œuvres, ed. de Llorente,
tom. i. passim.

[20] Las Casas made his first
voyage to the Indies, it is true, in
1498, or at latest 1502; but there is
no trace of his taking an active
part in denouncing the oppressions
of the Spaniards earlier than 1510,
when he combined his efforts with
those of the Dominican missionaries lately arrived in St. Domingo,
in the same good work. It was
not until some years later, 1515,
that he returned to Spain and plead
ed the cause of the injured natives before the throne. Llorente,
Œuvres de Las Casas, tom. i. pp.
1–23. — Nic. Antonio, Bibliotheca
Nova, tom. i. pp. 191, 192.

[21] See the will, apud Dormer,
Discursos Varios, p. 381.

which have since formed the great staples of South American commerce, as cocoa, indigo, cochineal, tobacco, &c., were either not known in Isabella's time, or not cultivated for exportation. Smal quantities of cotton had been brought to Spain, but it was doubted whether the profit would compensate the expense of raising it. The sugar-cane had been transplanted into Hispaniola, and thrived luxuriantly in its genial soil. But it required time to grow it to any considerable amount as an article of commerce; and this was still further delayed by the distractions, as well as avarice of the colony, which grasped at nothing less substantial than gold itself. The only vegetable product extensively used in trade was the brazil-wood, whose beautiful dye and application to various ornamental purposes made it, from the first, one of the most important monopolies of the crown.

The accounts are too vague to afford any probable estimate of the precious metals obtained from the new territories previous to Ovando's mission. Before the discovery of the mines of Hayna it was certainly very inconsiderable. The size of some of the specimens of ore found there would suggest magnificent ideas of their opulence. One piece of gold is reported by the contemporary historians to have weighed three thousand two hundred castellanos, and to have been so large, that the Spaniards served up a roasted pig on it, boasting that no potentate in Europe could dine off so costly a dish.[22]

CHAPTER IX.

_____

[22] Herrera, Indias Occidentales, Hist. del Almirante, cap. 84. — lib. 5, cap. 1. — Fernando Colon, Oviedo, Relacion Sumaria de la

The admiral's own statement, that the miners ob
tained from six gold castellanos to one hundred o.
even two hundred and fifty in a day, allows a latitude too great to lead to any definite conclusion. [23]
More tangible evidence of the riches of the island
is afforded by the fact, that two hundred thousand
castellanos of gold went down in the ships with
Bobadilla. But this, it must be remembered, was
the fruit of gigantic efforts, continued, under a system of unexampled oppression, for more than two
years. To this testimony might be added that of
the well-informed historian of Seville, who infers
from several royal ordinances, that the influx of the
precious metals had been such, before the close of
the fifteenth century, as to affect the value of the
currency, and the regular prices of commodities. [24]
These large estimates, however, are scarcely reconci-
cilable with the popular discontent at the meagre-
ness of the returns obtained from the New World,
or with the assertion of Bernaldez, of the same date
with Zuñiga's reference, that "so little gold had
been brought home as to raise a general belief, that
there was scarcely any in the island." [25] This is

Historia Natural de las Indias,
cap. 84, apud Barcia, Historiadores
Primitivos, tom. i.

[23] Tercer Viage de Colon, apud
Navarrete, Coleccion de Viages,
tom. i. p. 274.

[24] Zuñiga, Annales de Sevilla,
p. 415.

The alteration was in the gold
currency; which continued to rise
in value till 1497, when it gradually sunk, in consequence of the
importation from the mines of Hispaniola. Clemencin has given its

relative value as compared with
silver, for several different years;
and the year he assigns for the
commencement of its depreciation,
is precisely the same with that indicated by Zuñiga. (Mem. de la
Acad. de Hist., tom. vi. Ilust. 20.)
The value of silver was not materially affected till the discovery of
the great mines of Potosí and Zaca-
tecas.

[25] Bernaldez, Reyes Católicos.
MS., cap. 131.

still further confirmed by the frequent representations of contemporary writers, that the expenses of the colonies considerably exceeded the profits ; and may account for the very limited scale on which the Spanish government, at no time blind to its own interests, pursued its schemes of discovery, as compared with its Portuguese neighbours, who followed up theirs with a magnificent apparatus of fleets and armies, that could have been supported only by the teeming treasures of the Indies.[26]

Origin of the venereal disease.

While the colonial commerce failed to produce immediately the splendid returns which were expected, it was generally believed to have introduced a physical evil into Europe, which, in the language of an eminent writer, " more than counterbalanced all the benefits that resulted from the discovery of the New World." I allude to the loathsome disease, which Heaven has sent as the severest scourge of licentious intercourse between the sexes; and

---

[26] The estimates in the text, it will be noticed, apply only to the period antecedent to Ovando's administration, in 1502. The operations under him were conducted on a far more extensive and efficient plan. The system of *repartimientos* being revived, the whole physical force of the island, aided by the best mechanical apparatus, was employed in extorting from the soil all its hidden stores of wealth. The success was such that in 1506, within two years after Isabella's death, the four founderies established in the island yielded an annual amount, according to Herrera, of 450,000 ounces of gold. It must be remarked, however, that one fifth only of the gross sum obtained from the mines was at that time paid to the crown. It is a proof how far these returns exceeded the expectations at the time of Ovando's appointment, that the person then sent out, as marker of the gold, was to receive, as a reasonable compensation, one per cent. of all the gold assayed. The perquisite, however, was found to be so excessive, that the functionary was recalled, and a new arrangement made with his successor. (See Herrera, Indias Occidentales, dec. 1, lib. 6, cap. 18.) When Navagiero visited Seville, in 1520, the royal fifth of the gold, which passed through the mints, amounted to about 100,000 ducats annually Viaggio, fol. 15.

which broke out with all the virulence of an epi demic in almost every quarter of Europe, in a very short time after the discovery of America. The coincidence of these two events led to the populai belief of their connexion with each other, though it derived little support from any other circumstance. The expedition of Charles the Eighth, against Naples, which brought the Spaniards, soon after, in immediate contact with the various nations of Christendom, suggested a plausible medium for the rapid communication of the disorder; and this theory of its origin and transmission, gaining credit with time, which made it more difficult to be refuted, has passed with little examination from the mouth of one historian to another to the present day.

The extremely brief interval which elapsed, between the return of Columbus and the simultaneous appearance of the disorder at the most distant points of Europe, long since suggested a reasonable distrust of the correctness of the hypothesis; and an American, naturally desirous of relieving his own country from so melancholy a reproach, may feel satisfaction that the more searching and judicious criticism of our own day has at length established beyond a doubt that the disease, far from originating in the New World, was never known there till introduced by Europeans. [27]

[27] The curious reader is particularly referred to a late work, entitled *Lettere sulla Storia de' Mali Venerei, di Domenico Thiene, Venezia*, 1823; for the knowledge and loan of which I am indebted to my

Whatever be the amount of physical good or evil, immediately resulting to Spain from her new discoveries, their moral consequences were inestimable. The ancient limits of human thought and action were overleaped ; the veil which had covered the secrets of the deep for so many centuries was removed ; another hemisphere was thrown open ; and a boundless expansion promised to science, from the infinite varieties in which nature was exhibited in these unexplored regions. The success

CHAPTER IX.

Moral consequences of the discoveries.

friend, Dr. Walter Channing. In this work, the author has assembled all the early notices of the disease of any authority, and discussed their import with great integrity and judgment. The following positions may be considered as established by his researches. 1. That neither Columbus nor his son, in their copious narratives and correspondence, allude in any way to the existence of such a disease in the New World. I must add, that an examination of the original documents published by Navarrete since the date of Dr. Thiene's work, fully confirms this statement. 2. That among the frequent notices of the disease, during the twenty-five years immediately following the discovery of America, there is not a single intimation of its having been brought from that country ; but, on the contrary, a uniform derivation of it from some other source, generally France. 3. That the disorder was known and circumstantially described previous to the expedition of Charles VIII., and of course could not have been introduced by the Spaniards in that way, as vulgarly supposed. 4. That various contemporary authors trace its existence in a variety of countries, as far back as 1493, and the

beginning of 1494, showing a rapidity and extent of diffusion perfectly irreconcilable with its importation by Columbus in 1493. 5. Lastly, that it was not till after the close of Ferdinand and Isabella's reigns, that the first work appeared affecting to trace the origin of the disease to America ; and this, published 1517, was the production not of a Spaniard, but a foreigner

A letter of Peter Martyr to the learned Portuguese Arias Barbosa, professor of Greek at Salamanca, noticing the symptoms of the disease in the most unequivocal manner, will settle at once this much vexed question, if we can rely on the genuineness of the date, the 5th of April, 1488, about five years before the return of Columbus. Dr. Thiene, however, rejects the date as apocryphal, on the ground, 1. That the name of " morbus Gallicus," given to the disease by Martyr, was not in use till after the French invasion, in 1494. 2. That the superscription of Greek professor at Salamanca was premature, as no such professorship existed there till 1508.

As to the first of these objections, it may be remarked, that there is but one author prior to the French invasion, who notices the disease at

of the Spaniards kindled a generous emulation in their Portuguese rivals, who soon after accomplished their long-sought passage into the Indian seas, and thus completed the great circle of maritime discovery.[28]   It would seem as if Providence had postponed this grand event, until the possession of America, with its stores of precious metals, might supply such materials for a commerce with the east, as should bind together the most distant quarters of the globe.   The impression made on

all. He derives it from Gaul, though not giving it the technical appellation of *morbus Gallicus;* and Martyr, it may be observed, far from confining himself to this, alludes to one or two other names, showing that its title was then quite undetermined.   In regard to the second objection, Dr. Thiene does not cite his authority for limiting the introduction of Greek at Salamanca to 1508.   He may have found a plausible one in the account of that university compiled by one of its officers, Pedro Chacon, in 1569, inserted in the eighteenth volume of the Semanario Erudito, (Madrid, 1789.) The accuracy of the writer's chronology, however, may well be doubted from a gross anachronism on the same page with the date referred to, where he speaks of Queen Joanna, as inheriting the crown in 1512. (Hist. de la Universidad de Salamanca, p. 55.) Waving this, however, the fact of Barbosa being Greek professor at Salamanca in 1488 is directly intimated by his pupil the celebrated Andrew Resendi. "Arias Lusitanus," says he, " quadraginta, et eo plus annos Salmanticæ tum Latinas litteras, tum Græcas, magnâ cum laude professus est." (Responsio ad Quevedum, apud Bar-

bosa, Bibliotheca Lusitana, tom. 1. p. 77.) Now as Barbosa, by general consent, passed several years in his native country, Portugal, before his death in 1530, this assertion of Resendi necessarily places him at Salamanca in the situation of Greek instructer some time before the date of Martyr's letter. It may be added, indeed, that Nic. Antonio, than whom a more competent critic could not be found, so far from suspecting the date of the letter, cites it as settling the period when Barbosa filled the Greek chair at Salamanca. (See Bibliotheca, Nova, tom. i. p. 170.)

Martyr's epistle, if we admit the genuineness of the date, must dispose at once of the whole question of the American origin of the venereal disease. But as this question is determined quite as conclusively, though not so summarily, by the accumulated evidence from other sources, the reader will probably think the matter not worth so much discussion.

[28] This event occurred in 1497, Vasco de Gama doubling the Cape of Good Hope, November 20th, in that year, and reaching Calicut in the following May, 1498. La Clède, Hist. de Portugal tom. iii pp. 104 – 109.

the enlightened minds of that day is evinced by CHAPTER
the tone of gratitude and exultation, in which they IX
indulge, at being permitted to witness the consummation of these glorious events, which their fathers
had so long, but in vain, desired to see.[29]

The discoveries of Columbus occurred most op- Their geo-
portunely for the Spanish nation, at the moment graphical
when it was released from the tumultuous struggle extent.
in which it had been engaged for so many years
with the Moslems. The severe schooling of these
wars had prepared it for entering on a bolder theatre of action, whose stirring and romantic perils
raised still higher the chivalrous spirit of the people. The operation of this spirit was shown, in
the alacrity with which private adventurers embarked in expeditions to the New World, under
cover of the general license, during the last two
years of this century. Their efforts, combined with
those of Columbus, extended the range of discovery from its original limits, twenty-four degrees of
north latitude, to probably more than fifteen south,
comprehending some of the most important territories in the western hemisphere. Before the end
of 1500, the principal groups of the West Indian
islands had been visited, and the whole extent of
the southern continent coasted, from the Bay of
Honduras to Cape St. Augustine. One adventurous mariner, indeed, named Lepe, penetrated
several degrees south of this, to a point not reached

[29] See, among others, Peter Martyr, Opus Epist., epist. 181.

by any other voyager for ten or twelve years
after   A great part of the kingdom of Brazil
was embraced in this extent, and two successive
Castilian navigators landed and took formal pos
session of it for the crown of Castile, previous to
its reputed discovery by the Portuguese Cabral; [30]
although the claims to it were subsequently relinquished by the Spanish Government, conformably
to the famous line of demarkation established by
the treaty of Tordesillas.[31]

[30] Navarrete, Coleccion de Viages, tom. iii. pp. 18–26. — Cabral's pretensions to the discovery
of Brazil appear not to have been
doubted until recently. They are
sanctioned both by Robertson and
Raynal.

[31] The Portuguese court formed,
probably, no very accurate idea of
the geographical position of Brazil. King Emanuel, in a letter to
the Spanish sovereigns acquainting
them with Cabral's voyage, speaks
of the newly discovered region as
not only convenient, but *necessary*,
for the navigation to India. (See
the letter, apud Navarrete, Coleccion de Viages, tom. iii. no. 13.)
The oldest maps of this country,
whether from ignorance or design,
bring it twenty-two degrees east of
its proper longitude, so that the
whole of the vast tract now comprehended under the name of Brazil, would fall on the Portuguese
side of the partition line agreed on
by the two governments, which, it
will be remembered, was removed
to 370 leagues west of the Cape de
Verd Islands. The Spanish court

made some show at first of resist-
ing the pretensions of the Portuguese, by preparations for establishing a colony on the northern
extremity of the Brazilian territory.
(Navarrete, Coleccion de Viages,
tom. iii. p. 39.) It is not easy to
understand how it came finally to
admit these pretensions. Any correct admeasurement with the Castilian league would only have included the fringe, as it were, of the
northeastern promontory of Brazil.
The Portuguese league, allowing
seventeen to a degree, may have
been adopted, which would embrace nearly the whole territory
which passed under the name of
Brazil, in the best ancient maps,
extending from Para on the north
to the great river of San Pedro
on the south. (See Malte Brun,
Universal Geography, (Boston
1824–9,) book 91. Mariana seems
willing to help the Portuguese, by
running the partition line one hundred leagues farther west than
they claimed themselves. Hist. de
España, tom. ii. p. 607.

The discovery of the New World
was fortunately reserved for a period when the human race was sufficiently enlightened to form some

While the colonial empire of Spain was thus every day enlarging, the man to whom it was all due was never permitted to know the extent, or the value of it. He died in the conviction in which he lived, that the land he had reached was the long-sought Indies. But it was a country far richer than the Indies ; and, had he on quitting Cuba struck

conception of its importance. Public attention was promptly and eagerly directed to this momentous event, so that few facts worthy of note, during the whole progress of discovery from its earliest epoch, escaped contemporary record. Many of these notices have, indeed, perished through neglect, in the various repositories in which they were scattered. The researches of Navarrete have rescued many, and will, it is to be hoped, many more from their progress to oblivion. The first two volumes of his compilation, containing the journals and letters of Columbus, the correspondence of the sovereigns with him, and a vast quantity of public and private documents, form, as I have elsewhere remarked, the most authentic basis for a history of that great man. Next to these in importance is the "History of the Admiral," by his son Ferdinand, whose own experience and opportunities, combined with uncommon literary attainments, eminently qualified him for recording his father's extraordinary life. It must be allowed, that he has done this with a candor and good faith seldom warped by any overweening, though natural, partiality for his subject. His work met with a whimsical fate. The original was early lost, but happily not before it had been translated into the Italian, from which a Spanish version was afterwards made : and from this latter,

thus reproduced in the same tongue in which it originally appeared, are derived the various translations of it into the other languages of Europe. The Spanish version, which is incorporated into Barcia's collection, is executed in a slovenly manner, and is replete with chronological inaccuracies ; a circumstance not very wonderful, considering the curious transmigration it has undergone.

Another contemporary author of great value is Peter Martyr, who took so deep an interest in the nautical enterprise of his day, as to make it, independently of the abundant notices scattered through his correspondence, the subject of a separate work. His history, " De Rebus Oceanicis et Novo Orbe," has all the value which extensive learning, a reflecting, philosophical mind, and intimate familiarity with the principal actors in the scenes he describes, can give. Indeed, that no source of information might be wanting to him, the sovereigns authorized him to be present at the council of the Indies, whenever any communication was made to that body, respecting the progress of discovery. The principal defects of his work arise from the precipitate manner in which the greater part of it was put together, and the consequently imperfect and occasionally contradictory statements which appear in it. But the honest intentions of the author, who

Peter Martyr.

into a westerly, instead of southerly direction, it would have carried him into the very depths of the golden regions, whose existence he had so long and vainly predicted. As it was, he "only opened the gates," to use his own language, for others more fortunate than himself; and, before he quitted Hispaniola for the last time, the young adventurer

seems to have been fully sensible of his own imperfections, and his liberal spirit, are so apparent, as to disarm criticism in respect to comparatively venial errors.

Herrera and Muñoz.

But the writer who has furnished the greatest supply of materials for the modern historian is Antonio de Herrera. He did not flourish, indeed, until near a century after the discovery of America; but the post which he occupied of historiographer of the Indies gave him free access to the most authentic and reserved sources of information. He has availed himself of these with great freedom; transferring whole chapters from the unpublished narratives of his predecessors, especially of the good bishop Las Casas, whose great work, "Crónica de las Indias Occidentales," contained too much that was offensive to national feeling to be allowed the honors of the press. The Apostle of the Indians, however, lives in the pages of Herrera, who, while he has omitted the tumid and overheated declamation of the original, is allowed by the Castilian critics to have retained whatever is of most value, and exhibited it in a dress far superior to that of his predecessor. It must not be omitted, however, that he is also accused of occasional inadvertence in stating as fact, what Las Casas only adduced as tradition or conjecture. His "Historia General de las Indias Occidentales," bringing down the

narrative to 1554, was published in four volumes, at Madrid, in 1601. Herrera left several other histories of the different states of Europe, and closed his learned labors in 1625, at the age of sixty.

No Spanish historian had since arisen to contest the palm with Herrera on his own ground, until at the close of the last century, Don Juan Bautista Muñoz was commissioned by the government to prepare a history of the New World. The talents and liberal acquisitions of this scholar, the free admission opened to him in every place of public and private deposit, and the immense mass of materials collected by his indefatigable researches, authorized the most favorable auguries of his success. These were justified by the character of the first volume, which brought the narrative of early discovery to the period of Bobadilla's mission, written in a perspicuous and agreeable style, with such a discriminating selection of incident and skilful arrangement, as convey the most distinct impression to the mind of the reader. Unfortunately, the untimely death of the author crushed his labors in the bud. Their fruits were not wholly lost, however. Señor Navarrete availing himself of them, in connexion with those derived from his own extensive investigations, is pursuing in part the plan of Muñoz, by the publication of original documents; and Mr

arrived there, who was destined, by the conquest of Mexico, to realize all the magnificent visions, which had been derided as only visions, in the lifetime of Columbus.

Irving has completed this design in regard to the early history of Spanish discovery, by the use which he has made of these materials in constructing out of them the noblest monument to the memory of Columbus.

END OF VOL. II.

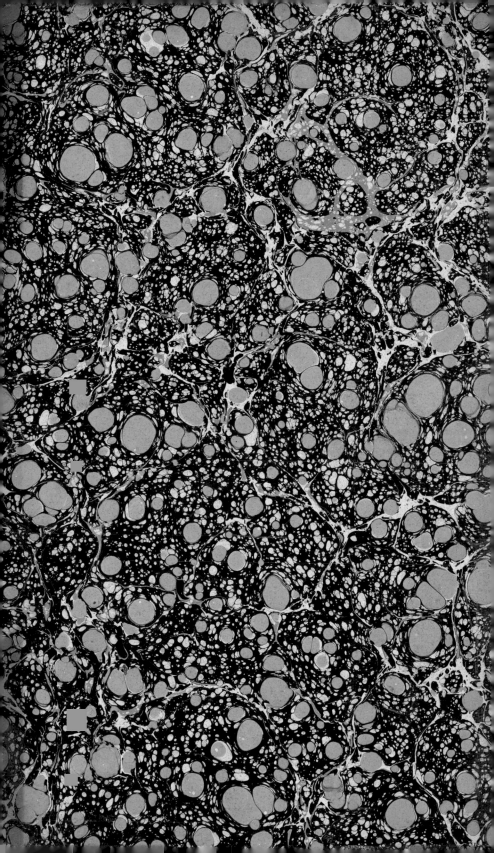